The Worm in the Wheat

The Worm in the Wheat

Rosalie Evans and

Agrarian Struggle in the Puebla-Tlaxcala

Valley of Mexico, 1906–1927

TIMOTHY J. HENDERSON

DUKE UNIVERSITY PRESS   DURHAM AND LONDON

© 1998 Duke University Press
All rights reserved
Printed in the United States of America on acid-free paper
Designed by Mary Mendell
Typeset in Carter and Cone Galliard by Keystone Typesetting, Inc.
Library of Congress Cataloging-in-Publication Data appear
on the last printed page of this book.

Contents

Acknowledgments

MOST STUDENTS of Mexican history have at one time or another had the frustrating yet exhilarating sense that the more they learn about their subject, the less they really understand it. Of course, the task is exhilarating precisely *because* it is so frustrating. After all, a topic that yields its secrets easily is hardly worth the effort. I realized early on in my career that the effort to understand Mexico's past and present is easily worth a lifetime. I would like to thank all those who helped bring me to this realization: Richard Sinkin, David Baird, Jurgen Buchenau, Doug Murphy, Alejandra García Quintanilla, Moisés Zamora Peregrina, Robert Bell, Marcela Escobedo, Josué César Romero, Roberto Sánchez Nieto, José Luis González Girón, as well as Moisés Cerdán Minor and Sr. Juventina Abarca Vargas and their family. María Alba Pastor kindly granted me permission to photocopy her invaluable interviews with villagers of the Texmelucan region. Jesús Contreras Hernández, *archivista* and *cronista oficial* of San Martín Texmelucan, gave me the run of the municipal archive of his city and made me feel very much at home, and the staff of the Judicial Archive in Puebla allowed me free access.

Others helped in very specific ways. Alan Knight read the entire dissertation manuscript and was extremely generous with his insights. Linda Hall also read the manuscript and offered many kind and valuable comments. The readers on my dissertation committee at the University of North Carolina — Sarah Chambers, John Chasteen, Michael Hunt, and Harry Watson — gave my work their serious attention and offered much appreciated advice. Ken Wissoker of Duke University Press was encouraging and endlessly patient with the numerous delays in delivering the finished product. And Ross Parmenter, a meticulous researcher and a true gentleman, gave me complete access to the rich materials he collected on Rosalie Evans during his investigation of the life of her friend, Zelia Nuttall. Mr. Parmenter met or corresponded with many of the protagonists of this story and kindly shared his memories, documents, and photographs with me. I hope that none of the material I have used here will take anything away from Mr. Parmenter's own magnificent work on Ms. Nuttall. I offer him my profound thanks.

I also owe a debt to all those who helped financially to make this project possible: the University of North Carolina's Office of International Programs, the Foreign Languages and Area Studies section of the U.S. Department of Education, and the Doris G. Quinn Foundation.

My greatest debt is to my advisor, mentor, and friend Gilbert Joseph. My project was fairly unorthodox by academia's current standards, yet Gil did not flinch when I proposed it, and he never tried to talk me out of it. He instead offered brilliant criticism, unstinting encouragement, and solid support. Thanks to him, the frustrations were bearable and the exhilarations that much more exhilarating. I doubt that I will ever be able to repay his kindness, but in the meantime it is a great pleasure to acknowledge it.

Finally, I offer thanks to my family for their constant support and to Liz Pauk for everything.

The breakup of fortunes has diminished the distance between rich and poor, but while bringing them closer, it seems to have provided them with new reasons for hating each other, so that with mutual fear and envy they rebuff each other's claims to power. Neither has any conception of rights, and for both force is the only argument in the present or guarantee for the future. —Alexis de Tocqueville, DEMOCRACY IN AMERICA

I honour the man who has a distinct idea of his intentions, whose progress towards their attainment is unwearied, and who knows how to seize and to use the proper means for securing his end. It is a matter of minor importance how far that end is noble or contemptible, or how far it is deserving of praise or censure. — Goethe, WILHELM MEISTER'S APPRENTICESHIP

If my land has cried out in reproach at me, and its furrows have joined in weeping, if I have eaten its produce without payment and have disappointed my creditors, may thistles spring up instead of wheat, and weeds instead of barley. — Job 31:38–40

The Worm in the Wheat

Introduction

HIS BOOK tells the story of Rosalie Evans, a woman who willfully gave up her life to keep the property she loved, roughly two thousand acres of fertile farmland in the Puebla-Tlaxcala Valley on Mexico's central plateau, as well as the stories of those who struggled to take that property from her. The most determined contenders claimed that absolute justice was on their side, each citing unimpeachable truths. On the one hand, Rosalie Evans and her fellow landowners acquired their titles legally, at a time when the law was on their side. On the other hand, the villagers who lived nearby and worked on her hacienda were, in the main, poor, exploited, and deserving of a better life. In such elemental struggles, force and violence are practically inevitable.

This book, then, offers a detailed case study of agrarian reform, a conflict so fundamental that it seldom occurs without violence and brutality, at least in its initial stages and especially when it occurs — as this struggle did — as an addendum to war. At its simplest — a simplicity that has little to do with reality — agrarian reform is a feud between the "haves" and the "have nots." Yet, if students of agrarian reform agree on anything, it is that an agrarian reform where rich and poor fight each other *mano a mano* is probably no reform at all, but more probably a spontaneous jacquerie of little lasting consequence. Surely, both participants and observers long for a happy outcome and listen for the flourish of trumpets proclaiming the triumph of justice. But in truth, although notions of justice may undergird the agrarian reform process and provide inspiration for revolutionary poets and propagandists, it is not justice that ultimately matters most in the process. Nor are economic calculations usually paramount. Agrarian reform is nothing if not political. As a leading student of the topic has observed, "the timing and extent of the reform are determined more by political pressure than by the genuine social and economic needs of the rural population." Agrarian reform is a tool traditionally wielded by elites "to win the support of specific groups, to create or restore political stability, to legitimize their own political positions, or to create what they consider to be democracy."[1]

Mexico's violent agrarian reform of the 1920s was no Manichaean clash between light and darkness. It is enlightening, however, to consider the stories the protagonists told in order to place themselves on the side of the angels. Rosalie Evans herself had many admirable qualities: she was brave, intelligent, determined, and even compassionate, in her own way, and she made sacrifices that few are willing to make. At the same time, however, she was obstinate, bigoted, selfish, self-righteous, and prepared to bend the facts to suit her purposes. Among her most remarkable traits was her tendency to cast her struggle in epic terms — to see herself as the heroine of noble drama, the defender of civilization and all it entails. To her, the land was not merely a piece of real estate, its value fixed by assessors and duly recorded in some dusty records office. It was a symbol of all that was good and worthwhile in life, a monument to dead loved ones. By virtue of her knowledge, breeding, and commitment, she believed that she deserved to keep the land, which in the hands of feckless "Indian" peasants would become an unforgiving desert. By imbuing the land with such spiritual significance — in her view, less a factor of production than a sacred trust — Mrs. Evans succeeded in making it the one thing she could never afford to lose. Even life itself became less important.

On the other side, the Mexican revolution, which generated the demand for agrarian reform, was waged in large measure by the rural poor, yet few would claim that Mexico's rural warriors attained a high degree of "peasant consciousness." Solidarity and class consciousness were often in short supply, attenuating all efforts of the rural poor to force their will onto the political agenda. Many of the self-styled spokesmen for the rural poor were lawyers, military men, schoolteachers, shopkeepers, factory workers, and others who were less than intimately acquainted with the land.[2] "Land and liberty" — the sloganeers' version of agrarian reform — was the battle cry, although those who raised the cry did so with a variety of objectives. There were, of course, many true idealists among both the leadership and the rank and file, yet even the noblest ideals were often leavened with practical motives. The regime in Mexico City probably hoped to shore up its rural support by satisfying the ardent demands of the peasants and, in the bargain, to pacify the country and create a reliable rural clientele who would never be allowed to forget all they owed to the regime's largess. At the state level, governments came and went, differing dramatically in their commitment both to agrarian reform and to the national government. Conservative local elites in the state of Puebla stayed active and were usually capable of turning up the heat on state governors whom they judged overly zealous. At the local level, agrarian *caciques* — political bosses who staked their reputations on their ability to deliver land to their followers — hoped to build political careers on the ruins of the great haciendas, but found that their support from above was often mercurial and that the villagers were divided along complex axes of wealth, status, occupation, and kinship. Those who resisted the agrarian reform did so for a variety of reasons: some had a jaundiced attitude toward all government; some hated the local agrarian leaders; some were reluctant to forgo a steady, if niggardly, wage; some did not work the land and had little interest in acquiring it; and some were already small landowners. Even some of those villagers who *did* demand land give evidence that landownership was, for them, no panacea: ultimately, they might have preferred better homes, more schools, higher wages, and steadier work.[3]

Everything points to a desperate murkiness in the objectives of the Mexican revolutionaries. At a time when idealism is on the ropes, when people everywhere — and perhaps in Mexico even more than in most places — long for simplicity, nobility, and heroism, it may seem heretical to suggest that historians have done their bit to overromanticize Mexico's agrarian struggles. The distance between historians and their subjects is far greater than the distance — so masterfully portrayed by Mariano Azuela in his novel *Los de abajo* — between the opportunistic urban intellectual Luis Cervantes and the earthy peasant leader Demetrio Macías. Whereas the former spouts high-minded slogans, the latter revels in the anarchic freedom of war and wonders innocently, "What *are* we fighting for? That's what I'd like to know."[4]

Prologue

You, spirit of the earth, seem close to mine:
I look and feel my powers growing,
As if I'd drunk new wine I'm glowing,
I feel sudden courage, and should dare
To plunge into the world, to bear
All earthly grief, all earthly joy — compare
With gales my strength, face shipwreck without care.
— Goethe, *Faust,* part 1 [1]

ONE NIGHT in the warm spring of 1917, Rosalie Evans fell asleep on the porch of her San Antonio home and had a dream unlike any she had known. She saw herself lying still and chatting idly with her husband Harry, "saying things I would say." Toward dawn, she awoke to find the moon shining bright and full upon her, the spot on the bed where Harry had been vacant but still warm. "Something left it as I waked," she wrote excitedly to her sister. "A palpable form moved slowly off. I knew I could have held it but did not. I was too surprised." The spirit faded into the moonlight. [2]

The dream was extraordinary, for at that time Harry Evans was some 800 miles away, in the heart of war-torn Mexico. His objective was simple yet perilous: to snatch valuable farmland — a hacienda known as San Pedro Coxtocán — from the jaws of revolution.

The revolution had erupted in 1910 with an ugly political upheaval that had escalated and deepened steadily, plunging the Mexican countryside into prolonged and desperate violence. The Evanses had been forced to abandon their hacienda that year and spent the next several years in the relative safety of the large cities or in exile in Europe and the United States. Their hacienda, along with the neighboring haciendas, had been invaded and parceled out by local villagers led by a one-armed peasant general named Domingo Arenas.

By the start of 1917, however, there were some encouraging signs. Mexico at last had a government to reckon with, one that had written a new constitution and appeared well on its way to dominating all rival factions. Landowners of the Evanses' region — the Puebla-Tlaxcala Valley of central Mexico — had begun paying tentative visits to lawyers and bureaucrats or sending out trusted scouts and intrepid administrators to see what, if anything, might be done.

Harry Evans's objective was risky, perhaps, but he saw few options. The couple's situation was turning urgent. During their years of exile, they had lived off of their savings and the dividends from a few mining and railroad investments. Now, the savings were nearly depleted, and the dividends were dwindling.

Harry Evans was forty-eight years old that spring. His hair was white and thinning, but he showed no sign of distress as he stood for his passport photo, wearing an easy and untroubled expression that seemed to say that he planned to leave the worrying to his wife.

And worry she would. Still, the dream she had of him that spring night in San Antonio calmed her fears for a while. She was elated to receive a letter from Harry describing an identical experience, which, he claimed, was simply too real to have been a dream: "If I were certain no one would read this, I would repeat part of your conversation." He asked jokingly if perhaps she had projected her astral body, but she was certain that this was precisely what had happened, for the dates of the two dreams coincided. It seemed that neither the miles nor an international border and the pervasive horror of a nation at war could impede the mystical union she felt with her husband. At least she could take some comfort in that.

Later that year, however, the magic of an astral body exchange had come to seem less comforting than ominous. Harry's letters grew gloomier and took on an uncharacteristic fatalism. Rosalie moved to Santa Barbara, California to be near her sister, Daisy. Harry visited them briefly in September, then returned to Mexico to carry on his struggle, although he also asked the attorneys of his former employer, the Bank of London and Mexico, to notarize his will. He was, he wrote, leaving everything to Rosalie, "so you will have absolute liberty to follow your own sweet fancy."

Rosalie grew sick with worry. She read Henry James, nursed headaches, slept little, lost weight. She pleaded: "I think you have done all you can with *this* government, and might as well return before things get worse. . . . [I]t all looks very dark."

Few bright spots appeared that fall, and Harry only slid deeper into frustration and despair. It seemed all he could do was sit at the Jockey Club staring helplessly at the perfectly legal title to his hacienda—a title that, for the moment, impressed no one. He wrote his wife lugubrious letters in which he spoke of dying in poverty. His father had come to Mexico when it was a wild and unwelcoming frontier, finding a niche and making a fortune, only now to have his son lose everything in that same mercurial country.

Rosalie continued her pleading: if he was unwilling to come home, then she would join him in Mexico. Despair was quite unlike him, and it made her frantic. She scolded him for his gloomy meanderings, "for in talking one can give shades of meaning, and in black and white such sentences have a terrible power. . . . What I count on is if we lose one way we may make it up in another. If that country only settles, and that will have to be, for the Mexicans themselves are tired of it. . . . [I]f you don't get sick and I stay well we will yet talk over hard times in our prosperous ease."[3]

But no prosperous ease was in the offing. On Friday, November 23, Rosalie received a telegram telling her to come to Mexico at once because Harry was gravely ill. On Monday, while riding on a southbound train, she thought she felt invisible lips kissing her hair and was reminded of that strange night in spring and her vivid dream of Harry. When she arrived at San Antonio the next Wednesday, she received another telegram telling her that her husband had died two days before — perhaps at the precise moment she had felt a spirit kiss her hair — and was already buried in the English cemetery in Mexico City.

She went to South Carolina to stay with her sister. From her waterfront room in Daisy's high-ceilinged home, she continued to write to Harry, not quite sure if her writing was merely therapeutic or if it might achieve some result, "like our glorious dream." These days she dreamed only of ghosts — not benign ones but hordes of evil spirits. "I became afraid," she wrote to her late husband, "and instead of the serene calm and perfect confidence you were near, you became dead and I felt each minute I must open my eyes, or just your body would be there. No spirit to sustain me, no light, no translucent shape as I saw before." She fretted that perhaps Harry would break the bond between them: "If you will but sustain me as you have done this week," she pleaded, "I will accept it simply and unquestioningly and pursue my work as it seems right to me, feeling we are both under a higher power who will help me if I will stop struggling and let it. I will no longer try to lift the veil and see you as I knew you and as you now are." She tried to forestall that moment when he would slip out of her life forever and leave her to "grope only in blackest darkness pursued by disordered imaginings and cruelest, self-inflicted tortures."

She wrote volumes as the days passed. She read and reread the telegram that told her of Harry's illness as if hoping to divine something new. She spoke of contacting a medium who might help her bridge the gap to the other world and left her pencil lying on blank sheets of paper in the hope that Harry's ghost might take it up and write something there. She flipped through Milton in search of some metaphysical comfort, supplementing that with the recent book by the famed physicist, Sir Oliver Lodge, who had lost a son in the Great War and, he claimed, contacted him in the beyond.[4]

Gradually her mood of terror and desperation gave way to a new determination. The key to conquering her grief, she saw, was to focus her energies: "I don't want to die of anguish or live a cheerful human existence again, but one with an object. You often said I need one to rouse me, surely it is now or never. This is my last chance on Earth. Do not let me slacken or despond."

Three weeks after Harry's death, she applied for a passport — "with the secret hope," she confessed to her dead husband, "that, like yours, it be for another world."[5]

One

DESPITE THE sober pleadings of friends and family, Rosalie Evans went to Mexico City in mid-January 1918, resolved to take up the fight where Harry had left it. Among her first stops was the hospital where Harry had died three weeks earlier. On a pulpit in the hospital's chapel she found a Bible opened to St. Paul's first letter to the Corinthians. Eager for any tender mercies, she approached the Bible, her eye drawn to one passage in particular: "And that which thou sowest, thou sowest not that body that shall be, but bare grain, it may chance of wheat or of some other grain. But God giveth it a body as it hath pleased him, and to every seed his own body."

She was quick to grasp this comforting assurance, surely of divine providence, that her husband's spirit had survived the loss of his corporeal self, but the passage was eerily appropriate even in its central metaphor. Wheat was the crop of the Puebla-Tlaxcala Valley — the product of the hacienda that Harry had died trying to regain, the object of his sacrifice.

It would be no mean feat to reclaim the farm from the clutches of revolutionaries and a rural population fired by the promise of land. At some level, she knew, the fierce civil war ravaging the valley and much of Mexico was all about abstractions such as *justice* and *dignity,* but it also had to do with the substance of life, with the land, its fruits, and their claimants.

Her mind drifted back to an image of the utopia that had been Mexico before the war: she and Harry standing in the fields of their hacienda, admiring the young wheat that "seemed to stretch a great plain of green to the mountains," Harry holding a bit of grain proudly in his palm and, imagining a bright future.

Few places in the world, it had seemed, produced such splendid grain as their own newly irrigated fields.[1]

HARRY AND ROSALIE BUY A FARM

Mexican agriculture was not a popular pursuit among British and American entrepreneurs, who apparently viewed the countryside as anachronistic and ill suited to their special skills. To be sure, Harry and Rosalie Evans had never intended to become farmers. They both hailed from families that had built comfortable fortunes in commerce or engineering. Harry was born in Mexico, the son of a longtime employee of the British-owned Mexican Railway, Mexico's first important rail line.[2] Except for a brief apprenticeship with a cotton-importing firm in Bristol, he had spent his entire twenty-seven years in Mexico, grooming himself for a career in banking.[3] When he met Rosalie Caden in 1896, he was a branch manager of the Bank of London and Mexico.

Rosalie Caden was born in Galveston, Texas, probably on January 6, 1875, one of four daughters of Thomas Caden, an Irish immigrant, and Charlotte Brooks, a New Orleans belle.[4] The Galveston of Rosalie's youth was a teeming, cosmopolitan city, one said to be as rich as any city its size anywhere in the world.[5] Immigrants, mostly from Germany and the United Kingdom, had swelled the city's population to more than twenty thousand by 1880. By then it had an opera house modeled on Europe's finest, graced by the likes of Oscar Wilde, Sarah Bernhardt, John Philip Sousa, and Lily Langtry. Along its main street, known as the Strand, fashionable shops stayed open late selling French perfume, Cuban cigars, and apparel made of English wool. It was a modern city with electric lights, streetcars, telephones, and direct steamship service to New York. Rich Britons could celebrate at the posh Agiola Club, while Germans bowled, drank, and played tennis at the fashionable and exclusive Garten Verein, where the flags of all nations were flown.

Galveston — which Rosalie would resurrect in her memory as a place of "pink seashells, childhood dreams and drives on the beach"[6] — was not without its contradictions, however. For all of the city's fabled civility, the wild frontier was alive and well only a few blocks from the opera house and the Strand in the notorious neighborhood of Fat Alley, where the less seemly elements of Gulf Coast society gathered to gamble and drink and fight. Mornings often found the victims of murder or drugs lying in the streets beside open sewers. Wild pigs ran through the streets, devouring the detritus of the city.[7]

In a word, Galveston was a boomtown, and young Rosalie Caden responded to its occasional savagery by turning inward: learning foreign languages, imbibing the classics of world literature, writing poetry, imagining herself in illustrious roles (in a drawing in a child's notebook, she appears with eyes flashing and hair flying wildly above the caption: "Rosalie Caden as Lady Macbeth"). She saw herself living amid rather small-minded folk and was determined to find something nobler within herself. Her own infrequent efforts at verse extolled an idealized world of sanitized nature, where rivers fall in love with trees and the moon worships the sun, but where people seldom appear:[8] "[T]owards people I feel very cold," she would confess.[9]

But if her ideal was of something timeless, noble, and untainted, the world around her went on its brutish way. Her home town owed its prosperity to the commerce unleashed by the completion in 1881 of the International and Great Northern Railroad linking the United States directly to Mexico via Texas. Empresarios of the day were drunk with the possibilities: "No country in the world," said General John Frisbie, who reportedly favored annexing the whole of Mexico, "offers such inducements to American enterprise and capital as does Mexico at this moment." There were mines to be worked, railroads to be built, crops to be harvested and imported. Likewise, Mexico afforded a great potential market for U.S. manufactures. General Ulysses S. Grant, a tireless promoter of Mexico's potential, preached that the Veracruz–Mexico City railway had already spurred a boom in coffee, sugar, and tobacco and was fast creating "a conservative, well-to-do population." Better yet, he noted (apparently blind to any contradiction), Mexico could supply workers who were "industrious, frugal, and willing to work for even a pittance, if afforded an opportunity."[10]

Thomas Caden, Rosalie's father, was among the Americans who heeded the call. Working alone or in a series of partnerships, he sought his fortune as an importer of hides and wool, a booming commerce in those years. Leather, goatskins, deerhides—even the skins of otter, beaver, rabbit, and bear—were shipped through Matamoros en route to the factories and markets of New York and Philadelphia.[11]

Business was good, but it kept Mr. Caden on the road much of the time and his family scattered. Rosalie, a slight and sickly child, spent most of her youth in Galveston and Laredo, but she would later recall as her happiest years those she spent living with her aunt and attending St. Catherine's School in New York City. It was owing to her frequent separations from her sisters, especially her younger sister Florence, that she began to cultivate her epistolary skills.

Florence, even more than Rosalie, suffered from a delicate constitution and a melodramatically morose disposition. "I am as dead to men and life as a statue," she once confessed laconically to Rosalie; "[t]hat is my most alarming symptom."[12] Although "the utter nothingness of existence" preoccupied the sisters, they also discussed love and jealousy and family matters with a profound intimacy. Rosalie was always more fortunate in matters of the heart, a fact that provoked some jealousy in Florence. When the sisters toured Scotland in 1893, Florence wrote of Rosalie's charms to her mother in Laredo: "[T]here was hardly one day that she did not have a caller. And yet she is disposed to grumble and does not seem a bit proud."[13] Two years later, when she was back East and Rosalie in Laredo, she chastized her sister for allowing a man named Varrios — a man Florence herself claimed to be in love with — to do "some passionate love-making." She was convinced her sister's relationship with Varrios could never work. "I am sorry Varrios is a Mexican," she wrote. "I think he has very attractive qualities and you could be happy with him. But when you think of what marrying is, the responsibility is too great a risk. That Mexican blood is there and I believe it is impossible to change them [sic]. . . . Marrying and living in a civilized state with a man who was differently formed and incapable of entering into your soul would be awful."[14]

As it turned out, neither sister married Varrios, although marriage prospects remained a major preoccupation. The eldest sister, Daisy, had married "quite well," to Jerdone Pettus, an assistant surgeon general of the Navy, a man who traced his American ancestry back to 1646. The sisters stayed with them for a time on the *Jamestown,* a battleship dating from the War of 1812, which had been fitted up as a quarantine hospital anchored in the Chesapeake Bay. A visitor to that ship was charmed by Dr. Pettus and his beautiful wife, who had fitted out the quarantine ship as if it were a luxury yacht, with "white enamel paint, yellow China silk curtains, book shelves and divans." The visitor recalled that Mrs. Pettus's younger sisters were pretty, although they looked too much like Mexican women for his taste. Even so, he had to confess that they were highly intelligent, chatting in several languages as they "reclined on steamer chairs beneath the great awnings, sucking in the cool breeze from the sea." No doubt the sisters' happiness at being together after so many extended separations was infectious. He spoke of the family's "delightful manner of life for the summer quarantine season" as though that season should highlight anyone's social calendar.[15]

The idyll was short-lived. In late 1896, Thomas Caden moved permanently to the city of Puebla, capital of the state of the same name and an important commercial center on Mexico's central plateau about sixty miles southeast of the national capital, taking along Florence and her sixty-seven-year-old aunt, Rosalie and her mother joining them a month later. The highland climate and the thinness of the air quickly took its toll: within four months, the girls' aunt fell ill and died.

It was in Puebla that Rosalie met Harry Evans and before long the two were engaged to be married. From the start theirs was clearly a felicitous match, even though their correspondence suggests that they were quite different personalities. Harry was a sober fellow, somewhat given to clichés. His fastidious and precisely penned letters invariably filled the four sides of a single folded sheet, as though the paper itself would determine their content. Rosalie's letters, by

Rosalie Caden. *Credit: The Rosalie Evans Letters from Mexico* (Indianapolis: Bobbs-Merrill, 1926). Harry Evans. *Credit:* Rosalie Evans Papers (#2895), Special Collections Department, University of Virginia Library.

contrast, lunged forward in a breathless, sprawling hand, oblivious to lines and margins, as though the paper were too small and mundane to contain her thoughts. Often, her letters ended in increasingly cramped words dribbled down the top of her first page — "Love, Rosalie" appearing in a narrow space just above "Dearest Harry."

Yet, though their personalities and nationalities were different, they shared an outlook that highlighted the contradictions between themselves and their surroundings. Harry Evans was a proper British gentlemen who had been brought up in what he regarded as a semisavage country. Rosalie Caden grew up on the Texas-Mexico border at a time when Indian and bandit raids were not so distant memories. She had always been acutely aware of the country to the south and appears to have regarded its inhabitants as exotic, mysterious, often childlike, and not altogether human. She and Harry came to see themselves as inevitable allies in a world where they did not entirely belong.

They were married at the Chamberlain Hotel in Fortress Monroe, Virginia, on October 6, 1898, six months after Harry had received a promotion to head the Puebla branch of his bank. Florence served as a bridesmaid, together with Daisy's young daughter Charlotte.[16]

The new couple settled in Puebla, where they found solitary diversions.

Rosalie wrote poems and stories and became an expert horsewoman. Harry became an amateur archaeologist who in fact was credited with finding a set of mammoth tusks of some use in dating the region geologically.[17] Together, they would ride horses and climb the treacherous volcanoes. Although Rosalie was always eager to shine in that mysterious and exclusive realm known as "society," she was concerned more with image than amusement. Her thirst for admiration was tempered by a profound misanthropy. Even while visiting Germany, which she considered something of a spiritual homeland, she found the human stock unimpressive: "These people interest me for their foreign ways and their language, even as I would go to a zoo," she confessed to her diary, "but in my heart I prefer my own dogs."[18] She considered the English to be "dull and unbearable unless one drinks" (which she did not). The Mexicans who entered her social circles were witty and fun, but when she looked deeper, she could see that they were essentially "vicious and shallow." Among the couple's acquaintances of the prerevolutionary years, only Lady Carden, wife of the British ambassador, stood out, for although she was bombastic at times, she at least had opinions. "The worst evil I can think of," Rosalie Evans wrote in 1917, "is being bored."[19]

Apart from Harry, Rosalie's closest relationship continued to be with her sister Florence, who felt bereft by the marriage of her elder sister. To Florence, it seemed a betrayal of the symbiosis that had sustained them both, and she gave full vent to her already lugubrious disposition, at times refusing even to speak Harry's name. Florence's own marriage prospects remained dim. A certain "Henri," the son of a French banker, was, like many others who knew Florence, put off by her frailty and wondered why she seemed haunted by her childhood in Galveston and Laredo, why "that time of your life was at the same time so full, so empty, so full of regrets?" At some point, though, Henri returned to France, from whence he dismissed Florence with a philosophical flourish: "We are both free to marry not whom we like, but whom we have a chance to, since circumstances play such a powerful role in human action."[20]

Circumstances gave Florence her chance in the person of Bernardo de Olivares, whom she met in Celaya, Guanajuato, and to whom she was soon engaged. Olivares appears only as a shadowy figure in the family's correspondence, perhaps because most family members seem to have found him distasteful. He would join the Evans party on their occasional trips up the sides of the volcanoes, an activity that envigorated Rosalie but was poorly suited to Florence's delicate constitution. On one such trip, at an altitude of twelve thousand feet, Florence became violently ill. She gasped for air, her pulse raced, she took a bad chill. The Indian guides made her a tea from a lichen that adhered to the high mountain pines, which restored her breathing almost to normal, and they set her to rest beneath a lean-to hut that had once been used for smelting sulphur before European competition had ruined the business.[21]

Florence and Bernardo de Olivares were married in Chevy Chase, Maryland, in the fall of 1903. One evening, while awaiting her fiancee's arrival in Maryland just before the wedding, Florence leapt up from the dinner table without warning and ran off sobbing, inconsolable for much of the night. "I have been expecting a breakdown," Rosalie confessed to Harry.[22]

There is no way of knowing what sort of life the couple had together or what sort of life they might have had. Almost exactly one year after the wedding, on October 27, 1904, Florence died suddenly of typhoid fever, a victim of the crowded and unsanitary conditions that prevailed in Puebla during that year of depression. The family was hardly prepared for so sudden an end to her short, unhappy life. Her father—who had already lost his wife and sister to Puebla—suffered a breakdown, and sister Daisy wrote despondently to Bernardo de Olivares that she had practically lost the will to live.[23] Rosalie took it hardest of all. Recent months had been difficult for her in any event, as she had had problems with her eyes, suffering a series of operations and treatments with cocaine and belladonna. She tried to contact her sister's spirit, as she would later try to reach her dead husband, but without result. Much later, anticipating a reunion with Florence in the beyond, she scribbled at the foot of one Florence's old letters her thoughts of the "years of sorrow pulling you away, far, far away."[24]

Florence's death increased Rosalie's sense of isolation. "Now I realize," she wrote to Harry, "that you are the only person left in the world who understands me and our unworldly point of view."[25] In fact, however, if Harry's point of view was at all unworldly, it is not evident from his correspondence. He advised his wife to "get well and strong and do not let the loss of Florence make you view life either sadly or hopelessly. . . . You know I only live for you and if you are unhappy, so shall I be."[26] Harry was as determinedly practical as he was optimistic, punctuating his letters with upbeat clichés: "[O]ne has to get out and hustle. Ripe plums do not fall into one's mouth. We were both born to be rich but unfortunately have not the ready cash."[27]

Gradually, Rosalie came to accept some of his optimism, but she insisted that the time had come for a major change in their lives. Harry had casually mentioned making a move, and now Rosalie endorsed the idea enthusiastically. They would leave Puebla for some other Mexican city. She briefly considered Querétaro, Veracruz, and Mazatlán, but rejected them all for their "impossible climate." Monterrey she thought too much like Laredo. Eventually she narrowed their choices down to Morelia in Michoacán or Guadalajara in Jalisco. At the time, Rosalie was still in the United States undergoing treatments for her eyes. So intent was she on never returning to Puebla that she authorized Harry to make the decision as well as the move without her, suggesting he speak immediately to his superior at the bank "while he is still sorry for us," but barely

San Pedro Coxtocán. *Credit:* Rosalie Evans Papers (#2895),
Special Collections Department, University of Virginia Library.

acknowledging that Harry might not share her enthusiasm: "Perhaps you were
not thinking when you spoke and Guadalajara would be out of the question —
but it might be worth trying for Puebla will be so hard."[28]

In fact, Harry did not share her enthusiasm. Years earlier, just before their
wedding, he had confessed to Rosalie that he was not very happy away from
Puebla. So they compromised. Harry abandoned the banking profession and
the city of Puebla, and the couple purchased the hacienda San Pedro Coxtocán,
some fifteen miles northwest of the city. They would be farmers on an estate
with a history dating back to the sixteenth century and a permanent labor force
of forty-one. They paid three hundred thousand pesos in cash and mortgages —
an excellent price at the time — and another two hundred thousand for a 1,500-
meter filtration gallery running under Coxtocán Hill, which doubled the farm's
water supply.[29] For Rosalie, the time there would be idyllic, spent riding horses
and climbing volcanoes. At the same time, however, it would be no dalliance:
the farm was to be a modern capitalist concern, for its size the most productive
wheat farm in the region.

As she stood beside her husband surveying the promising crop of green
wheat sprouting in the shadow of the great volcanoes, Rosalie Evans had every
reason to think that they would grow old in this rustic life, enjoying a relatively
modest but reasonably secure income. Administrators would run the day-to-
day operations of the farm, but Harry would manage the business end, often
dictating his correspondence to his wife. It would be a comfortable life, livened
now and then with dabblings in the high society of Mexico City and Puebla. To

the new "master and mistress," the peasants who worked the land, although perhaps not everything they might wish for, seemed generally docile and perfectly respectful, never failing to greet them with a small bow of the head, a curt wave of the hand, and a muttered "Ave Maria." In the tradition of hacienda wives, Mrs. Evans fancied herself an "active source of good among them," dispensing charity to the most wretched, bandaging the wounded, and treating the infirm.[30]

There were disquieting rumors, of course, and the Evanses cannot help but have heard them: speculation that Mexico could not survive without its venerable dictator, Porfirio Díaz, the man who had brought peace and progress to a country that had known little but war and suffering for the first five decades of its independent life. Self-styled experts found such talk easy to dismiss. Díaz was mortal, but clever enough to have "institutionalized" his reforms, and they would surely outlast him. Moreover, argued one observer, the majority of the Mexican people were perfectly content and quite indifferent to politics, "and so long as [the peons] are earning sufficient to fill their stomachs with tortillas and frijoles . . . they are perfectly willing to abstain from risings and revolts."[31]

What was more, those who talked of the "bugbear of revolution" doubted the evidence of peace seen by their own eyes. A typical Sunday in Puebla City was anything but unsettling. The well-to-do, their skin whitened and made delicate by expensive European potions, would strut in sparkling jewels and silks, high collars and ivory-colored blouses, bright scarves and Parisian frock coats, or would circle the main square in carriages bedecked by bouquets of flowers and drawn by fine Andalusian horses. The poor, who lingered on the side of the square unshaded by awnings, would doff their hats humbly, appearing sullenly resigned to their fate.[32] Revolution seemed the stuff of distant history, not at all likely in this opulent, orderly modern world.

THE STORM IN THE OFFING

Appearances and wishful thinking notwithstanding, Mexico's peace and prosperity rested on shaky foundations. The regime that had ruled it since 1876 was now old and only feebly coping with the complex and troubling trends it had set in motion. By 1910, Porfirio Díaz was eighty years old, a portly man with a walrus mustache and an irascible bearing, his dark skin lightened by powders and potions. The chief justice of his Supreme Court was eighty-three, and the Congress, according to one acerbic voice, "housed a collection of senile mummies in a state of lingering stupor."[33]

In Puebla, Díaz crony Mucio P. Martínez, an old military man with a pinched face and a white goatee, was celebrating his eighteenth year in the governor's chair, with no apparent intention of leaving it. Martínez had an unenviable reputation. Few disputed that his longevity in office owed nearly everything to the president's favor, yet even Díaz had been known to scold him for his excesses. Far from controlling the abuses of the *hacendados* (the landowners), Martínez was himself a prominent perpetrator: his sugar plantations in the district of Tehuacán had expanded at the expense of peasant landowners, and Indians from the surrounding hills were drafted at gunpoint to fill plantation labor quotas.[34] The governor also earned the wrath of the urban middle classes by running gambling dens, taking kickbacks on public works projects, and holding monopolies on the distribution of meat and *pulque* (the fermented juice of the century plant, which was the beverage of choice for Mexico's rural poor). Critics of his regime might find themselves conscripted into the army, exiled, or imprisoned; others simply disappeared without a trace. A British observer noted that the governor's crimes "were sufficently numerous and grave to merit any punishment."[35]

Resentment against President Díaz and the increasingly shaky system he presided over was so great that when the dictator announced in 1908 that he planned to retire and to permit free elections in 1910, his words were met with widespread jubilation. The announcement gave hope to a disparate array of dissidents, ranging from middle-class folk bitter at their exclusion from the calcified political process to radical ideologues out to reform society from the ground up. The most prominent of the professional dissidents — the Flores Magón brothers, anarchosyndicalists whose influence had been felt in factories and workplaces throughout the republic — had already visited San Martín Texmelucan in central Puebla, a city only two-and-a-half miles from the Evans estate. From the kiosk in the main plaza, they spoke of freedom, the Constitution, and workers' rights until Martínez's troops arrived,[36] but by then the Díaz regime had more to fear than noisy fringe elements. The scion of a wealthy hacendado family from the northern state of Coahuila, Francisco I. Madero — a diminutive, soft-spoken, and altogether unlikely firebrand — soon emerged as the most prominent contender for the presidency, and for a time his campaign was permitted to gather steam unimpeded.

Poblanos (as the residents of Puebla are known) from all walks of life were ready to receive him. The state's first Maderista "club" was founded in June of 1909 among the textile workers of a new, ultramodern textile factory called Metepec, in the district of Atlixco. By September of that year, more than two thousand people belonged to Maderista clubs throughout the state. The most important was the Club Luz y Progreso ("Light and Progress") of Puebla City, a shoemaker named Aquiles Serdán serving as its distinguished leader.

Aquiles Serdán hated the Díaz regime with a consuming passion. With some justification, he blamed the regime for taking his father, a liberal lawyer who in 1879 had joined a dissident military man named Alberto Santa Fé in fomenting a rebellion among the rural poor of western Puebla and southern Tlaxcala — the very region where the Evanses would later buy their hacienda. The rebellion aimed to force Díaz to redeem promises of land for the poor who had joined him in his own successful rebellion three years earlier, promises he had disregarded upon attaining power. When the rebellion was ruthlessly crushed and Colonel Santa Fé sent to prison, the elder Serdán disappeared without a trace. Many reckoned he was executed or sent to the deadly work camps in southern Mexico. In Puebla, "gone looking for Guanes" — a phrase used to remark any unaccountable absence or tardiness — became a matter of folklore.[37]

Serdán's shoeshop became a meeting place for Madero's supporters, and it was largely owing to his tireless efforts that some thirty thousand people turned out to greet Madero on May 14, 1910, with cheers, fireworks, factory whistles, and the music of brass bands. It began to look as if this candidate had a fair chance of winning the election slated for June 26.

President Díaz, alarmed at Madero's success and the groundswell of opposition, forswore his promise to allow free elections and prepared to have himself voted into office for yet another term. His local minions, such as Mucio P. Martínez, fearing that Díaz's demise would foreshadow their own, opted for stepped-up repression. No sooner had Madero left the state than Martínez's troops began to arrest, expel, and otherwise harrass Madero's supporters. The Puebla police raided homes and offices in search of propaganda and weapons, and were so zealous that they even arrested a parrot who had been taught by its mistress to cry "Viva Madero!" For good measure, they also arrested the parrot's owner — the wife of a professor at the normal school — as the "intellectual author" of the crime of sedition.[38]

Madero himself was arrested in Monterrey shortly before the election, so Díaz and his vice president Ramón Corral were "elected" by an overwhelming margin. Later out on bail, Madero fled the country disguised as a railroad mechanic, while in Mexico his supporters prepared to pursue their politics by other means. From his exile in San Antonio, Texas, he issued his "Plan of San Luis Potosí," which called for a national revolution to break out on November 20.

Impromptu militia units began preparing for battle.

Two

Where grows? — Where grows it not? If vain our toil
We ought to blame the culture, not the soil.
— Alexander Pope, *Essay on Man*

---

*T*HE TURMOIL surrounding the national presidential elections of 1910 touched Mexican society at every level. Among its many causes was one that was as little appreciated by the leadership of the antireelectionist movement as it was by Rosalie and Harry Evans: the misery that pervaded the Mexican countryside. An uneasy alliance lay at the heart of Francisco I. Madero's movement. Once Madero and his followers had determined that violence was needed to dislodge the old dictator, they had few qualms about raising ragged armies among the rural poor. That should be safe enough, they reasoned: once the revolution triumphed, they would reward their peasant supporters by appointing a commission or two to study land issues. In the meantime, the country folk could take comfort in the knowledge that they were now free to elect good men who would see to their interests. Few realized quite how impatient those country folk would be once the promise of meaningful change was dangled before their eyes.

THE INDIANS

To be sure, Mexico's landowners had some inkling of what a powder keg rural discontent could become — a realization evident in the speed with which they closed ranks in the face of any hint of unrest and in the utter ruthlessness of the repression they would mete out to contain it.

A few landowners even acknowledged that the abysmal conditions of rural workers might be an economic liability. At a 1906 agricultural convention in Mexico City, one speaker surprised his fellow farmers when he rose to address an issue that most took to be a simple fact of Mexican rural life: the appallingly low productivity of the Mexican farm laborer, the famous *peón*. The speaker challenged his fellow farmers with a troubling contradiction: the amount paid out in wages was not an accurate measure of the cost of labor because higher wages often meant higher productivity. From this general principle, he drew the blunt and bitter lesson, "I am sad to confess that in Mexico we pay the world's highest wages."[1]

The recipients of those wages were — according to a monotonous parade of travelers, experts, and employers — poor workers and all-around sad specimens. In this respect, Harry and Rosalie Evans showed little originality. In 1898, Harry wrote irritably to his fiancee about the workers fixing up their residence in Puebla, who customarily celebrated an unauthorized holiday colloquially known as "San Lunes" (Holy Monday), during which they slept off the alcoholic excesses of their only authorized day of rest. Even when they showed up for work, Harry complained, they displayed an inordinate love of leisure, which apparently became a favorite topic of conversation among Harry and his cronies: "We enjoyed the evening very much and then remained talking about the worthlessness of the Indian race."[2]

Rosalie, for her part, hit upon a similar and well-worn theme in a rare attempt at fiction. In her story, she finds herself leaning against the wall of the Fortress of Guadalupe overlooking Puebla City, fairly hypnotized by the methodical thud of pickaxes from a nearby stone quarry as she watches a desultory parade of unpromising human specimens. "These under-sized people," she wrote, "with their dark and degraded countenances, swollen by pulque and uncleanliness, the dregs of a nation, these Indians of modern Mexico. A faintness came over me, a weariness of life, mingled with a distrust of man, a lack of faith in the innate nobility of the soul claimed, with so much confidence, by the human race. Could there ever have dwelt among them, in times long past, men and women of loftier form and nobler feature? — though bronzed by the tropical Sun and Steeped in eastern superstitions."[3]

This same question was often raised by the racial determinists of the day: how could this human flotsam, the mere sight of whom could cause one to despair of humankind, ever have built up a civilization that awed the worldly Spanish conquerors? To be sure, said writer after writer, the Indians had their virtues, but even these tended to bode ill for their advancement. They generally received high marks for humility, docility, and obsequiousness — characteristics that one writer summed up as "the apparently instinctive appreciation of the superiority of the white man."[4] Moreover, as many a traveler noted, their material wants were few and easily supplied, so they were able to live lives of primeval innocence and savage simplicity that made them the envy of those who, every now and then, wearied of the hectic pace of modern times.

Still, the Indians' defects, according to many observers, were legion. A fine compendium of stereotypes can be found in a fairly typical travel book written in 1909 by one W. E. Carson.[5] Indians, said Carson, are nearly all "agricultural," and yet "as a farmer the Indian is a rank failure." He eschewed modern innovations in favor of the primitive implements his ancestors had used for centuries, his sole ambition to while away his days in blissful indolence — tending his pig and his small plot of ground, eating tortillas and beans, and shirking any activity that threatened to improve his condition.

Apart from their ignorance and sloth, noted Carson, Indians were much given to vice and lax in matters of morality — "polygamy being quite general, marriages seldom taking place and kinship being disregarded." Inordinately fond of pulque and mescal, they could and would get insanely drunk for little expense, whereupon they would become murderous, machete-wielding fiends. Any savings they had would be gambled away or squandered on lavish and wasteful fiestas that celebrated a naive religion consisting of "the grossest superstition, [which] amounts to sheer idolatry." They vigorously practiced "weird and horrible" customs — such as self-flagellation, elaborate displays of penitence, and fasting — and indiscriminately massed ancient idols with a variety of other objects that they imagined to have supernatural powers, even the power to make life less onerous. There was little sense among them that life might be made better by anything short of supernatural intervention. The notion that hard work and frugality might advance their prospects seemed far more preposterous than the belief that the whole world might one day turn turtle, with the rich laid low and the poor raised up beyond their wildest imaginings.

In fairness, Carson, like many other writers, acknowledged the reality of oppression on rural estates. The peon was often obligated to remain on the hacienda by debts owed to the landlord or to the company store; he was always watched by overseers and driven to carry out his labors by constant cajolery, threats, insults, and corporal punishments. In the most extreme cases, Indians were lured from their home villages by bogus promises and forced to work on tropical plantations where they were overseen by armed guards. Few survived the experience. Carson and his contemporaries seemed to have little sense, however, that repression might in fact be the cause of the symptoms they observed. In fact, they held the opposite to be the case: harsh methods were needed; otherwise, the Indian would simply succumb to his natural indolence and while away his life to no purpose. Harry and Rosalie Evans had no trouble endorsing this point of view.

Although more recent writers have observed many of the same traits noted by the old travelers, they have offered more reasonable explanations for the existence of such traits among the indigenous peoples of Mexico. Long-term endurance of oppression, for instance, would be enough to persuade any sensible person of the futility of hard work: a bleak past and a bleak present hardly inspire optimism about the future. Divine intervention and magic seem more likely routes to happiness. Guardedness, suspicion, hostility, and exaggerated deference toward social superiors are better explained as adaptations to oppression — a matter of surviving and holding discomfort to a tolerable minimum — than racial character traits. By the same token, the low rate of matrimony could be ascribed to the shortage of priests rather than to any supposed genetic predisposition toward sin.[6]

In any case, Harry and Rosalie Evans, in buying into Mexican agriculture, surely did not see themselves as participants in any dark heritage of oppression: their role was to bring the light of modernity and progress to the Mexican countryside, or at least to that portion of it delimited as the Texmelucan Valley of Puebla. To them, the available farmhands were childlike, inept, at times endearing, and their less-than-satisfactory work habits merely an inevitable frustration of their new profession. The apparent respect and deference accorded to the Evanses by the villagers reassured them of their own benevolence. There was nothing sinister in the 200,000 pesos spent on an ultramodern irrigation system, the contacts with bankers and buyers throughout the republic, or the reapers and threshers brought in for the harvest. Yet, as Karl Marx put it, people do not make history under circumstances of their own choosing: "the tradition of all the dead generations weighs like a nightmare on the brain of the living."[7]

To understand that nightmare, we must at least briefly review nearly four centuries of Mexico's history.

THE BIRTH OF THE HACIENDA

A key fact of life among the rural poor of central Mexico was that although they lived from agriculture, few had much land of their own. Also, from the second half of the nineteenth century onward, many of those who had land were losing it to the expanding commercial haciendas. In the Puebla-Tlaxcala Valley, the growth of the hacienda was far less notorious than in certain other regions. Sugarcane became suddenly profitable in the state of Morelos to the southwest, for instance, creating a voracious demand among planters for more land and more laborers. Forcing peasants off of their traditional lands nicely served this dual purpose. It was not surprising that during the revolution Morelos became the epicenter of a whirlwind of agrarian rage.

There was no shortage of discontent among the rural poor of the Puebla-Tlaxcala Valley, but the most notorious usurpation of village lands in this region was not a recent occurrence. It had, in fact, taken place three centuries earlier.[8]

An accident of geography had placed the Puebla-Tlaxcala Valley squarely in the path of the shortest route between Mexico's traditional center of gravity —

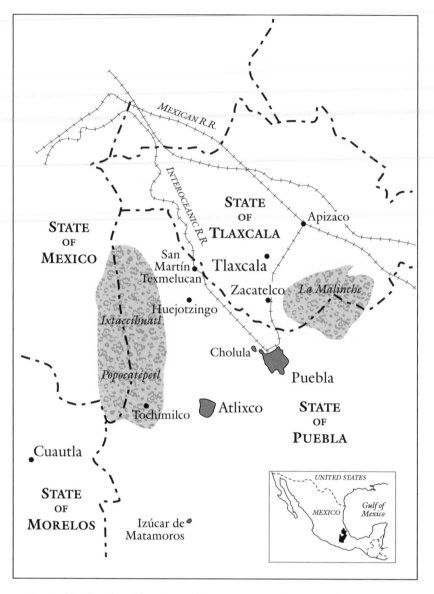

1. The Puebla-Tlaxcala Valley. *Source of Inset Map: Everyday Forms of State Formation: Revolution and the Negotiation of Rule in Modern Mexico,* ed. Gilbert M. Joseph and Daniel Nugent (Durham: Duke University Press, 1994).

the capital city of Tenochtitlán/Mexico—and the gulf coast. For any aspiring hegemon in Mexico—from Aztec emperors coveting tropical fruits and feathers to Spanish colonial authorities hoping to secure the lifeline to Europe—control of the Puebla-Tlaxcala Valley was the sine qua non.

Although it has always been the focus of keen attention from the capital city, the Puebla-Tlaxcala Valley has never been easy to control, mainly because of a daunting topography. Two famous and formidable volcanoes separate it from the Valley of Mexico: the cone-shaped Popocatépetl ("Smoking Mountain") and its rugged companion, Ixtaccíhuatl ("Sleeping Woman"). Between them and to their north are rough mountain passes that have seen everything from foot paths to superhighways. Off to the east, the plain is interrupted by the elegantly shaped volcano "La Malinche"; east of that the high plains stretch to yet another neovolcanic ridge, at which point the land begins a precipitous drop toward the steamy coast of Veracruz. To the south, the valley gives way gradually to the hot lands of southern Puebla and Morelos.

The valley floor is impressively flat, ruffled only by occasional hills and mounds, and scarred by narrow gulleys and canyons carved by the heavy summer rains. Even the lowest hills afford a view of the vastness of the plain—a view that, it seems, might go on forever or melt into haze but for its abrupt encounter with the belt of dark coniferous woods around the base of the volcanoes. Fruit and hardwood trees grow amid the fields, and neat rows of old and brittle eucalyptus trees line the roads and rivers and boundaries. The air at seven thousand feet is thin. Temperatures are always mild, frosts infrequent and unpredictable, and little but the persistent summer rainfall sets one season apart from another.

The great volcanoes that dominate the landscape have for centuries provided not only volcanic soil and living water for farmers and settlers, but also inspiration for poets and travelers, as well as refuge for bandits, rebels, and revolutionaries. The Atoyac River, which flows down the rugged eastern slopes of Ixtaccíhuatl, has long been both a key attraction and the object of fierce conflict for generations of villagers and landowners.[9]

Before the Spaniards came, the valley was the scene of almost constant armed strife between the several indigenous groups of the region and between those groups and their hated rivals, the Aztecs of the Valley of Mexico. When the Spaniards arrived, the Tlaxcaltecas and Huejotzincas of the Puebla-Tlaxcala Valley placed their armies at the disposition of the Spaniards, so intense was their hatred of the Aztecs. When the Spaniards won that war, the lords of the valley gladly adopted the conquerors' religion and confidently awaited their reward.

Those lords never quite became a privileged caste, however, a role to be monopolized by European settlers who flooded into the colonies hopeful of striking it rich in the new land. Many of those settlers were arrogant and impatient characters who survived largely by preying on the Indian communities. The imperial administrators of the day hoped to ward off ugliness by building a new city remote from established Indian settlements. They would invite only poor and industrious Spaniards to live there, humble family farmers who would raise those products that the Spanish population demanded: grapes for wine, olives for olive oil, and especially wheat for bread.

So began the city of Puebla, the urban center of the valley, which according to legend was laid out by angels descended from heaven for that purpose — hence its name, "Puebla de los Angeles." For a time, the City of the Angels attracted just the sort of ambitious commoner the city fathers had envisioned: recently arrived humble souls, scrimping to buy a few acres and hauling their produce in carts to the city markets.[10] But commerce changed as the colony grew because more settlers meant greater demand for European goods. Small farmers could not keep pace, and the Indians, who did the bulk of the heavy agricultural labor, were maddeningly indifferent to wheat and grew it only when coerced, so eventually the viceroy took to granting plots on the condition that the grantees raise wheat.

There was no shortage of land in those days. The nearly constant strife that had torn the area before the conquest meant that Indian towns were concentrated on the defensible slopes at the feet of the volcanoes, leaving much land on the valley floor free for the taking. And those Indians who *did* live on the valley floor were no great obstacle to aspiring land barons, for they died at an alarming rate. A century after the Spanish conquest, the Indian population of the valley was barely one-tenth what it had been in 1520. The survivors were taken from their forlorn little villages and moved to central, easily supervised settlements. Several villages, including San Jerónimo Tianguismanalco (which three centuries later would emerge as Rosalie Evans's nemesis) were created from the remnants of other villages. Ambitious Spaniards took advantage of these circumstances to claim newly vacant lands, ignoring royal rulings that Indian lands were strictly off limits to them.[11]

Land was not only abundant, but increasingly valuable. Raising wheat, in fact, proved a profitable enough investment to attract the attention of the big players in colonial agriculture. Gradually, these powerful and well-connected land grabbers moved in to buy up and consolidate the small parcels of land that had been the property of Indian towns or of small truck farmers.[12] They were able to get much land for a pittance by exploiting the growing desperation of the Indians and by often resorting to outright fraud. Spaniards would occupy lands to which they had no legal title, take land in excess of that granted them by the king or viceroy, or carry out transactions among themselves without bother-

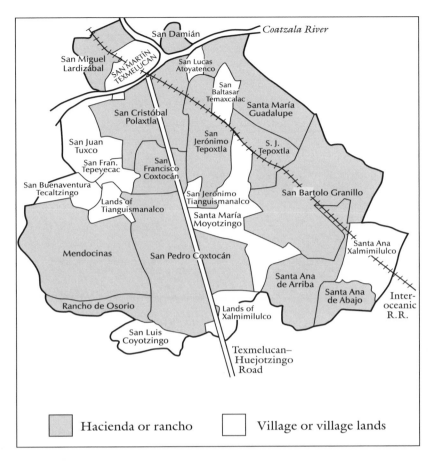

2. Area around the Hacienda of San Pedro Coxtocán, c. 1920, Hacienda and Villages.
Source: Various agrarian maps from the Departamento de Asuntos Agrarios y de Colonización, Puebla, Mexico.

ing to notify the Indian owners, who technically enjoyed the right to state their objections.

The hacienda San Pedro Coxtocán, which Rosalie and Harry Evans bought in 1906, was created out of erstwhile marshland by a certain Benito de Sandianés, who petitioned the crown in 1602 for approximately two thousand acres, supposedly for his own use. Sandianés was no farmer, but rather a speculator, pure and simple. Through influential connections in the provincial government, he was licensed to sell his new property, and he found a buyer that same year, 1602.

Transactions of this kind were hard to control, for they could yield profits up to 300 percent.[13] The upshot of it all was that by 1620 land tenure in the Puebla-Tlaxcala Valley had acquired the pattern it would retain—with only minor variations — until the 1920s: small, nearly landless villages were surrounded on all sides by massive haciendas, wretched islands of humanity amid a sea of wheat.

The considerable demand for labor on the wheat estates was met by Indians, who were recruited with varying degrees of cunning or force. Royal officials and compassionate friars tried to secure special protections for them — including their own system of courts, their own carefully codified set of duties and privileges, and lands that they were to own communally and that could under no circumstances be taken from them. Such efforts, although well intentioned, had the ironic effect of re-creating the Indians as a permanent subcaste — separate, protected, and dependent. They became the laboring class of the new society.

MODERN TIMES

By the end of the nineteenth century, the situation of the agrarian communities of the Puebla-Tlaxcala Valley remained harsh, but it had changed profoundly in many respects. The people of the valley were not nearly as racially distinct from the rest of Mexican society as they had once been because racial mixing was well enough advanced that *mestizos* (mixed-race persons) formed an overwhelming majority. Culturally, too, the people were far more mestizo than Indian as even the Nahuatl language, though still widely spoken, steadily lost ground. Moreover, liberal politicians of the mid–nineteenth century subscribed to enlightened notions of the equality of all citizens, prescribing an end to ranks and hierarchies and special protections and privileges — all that weighty baggage of a misguided colonial epoch — that divided societies and impeded the building of nations. They were appalled at the existence of a permanent subclass in their midst and were convinced that the salvation of the Indian communities lay in obliterating cultural and ethnic distinctions: race would become irrelevant, and Indians would become individual citizens who, finally freed from their ancient torpor, would march shoulder to shoulder with their fellow Mexicans into a brilliant future.

It did not work out that way. Race continued to loom large in deciding who would do the work and who would give the orders, and the vast majority of rural dwellers, whether or not they fit any precise racial or cultural criteria, were "Indians" as far as the landlords were concerned.

To be sure, not all Indians were humble farmhands. The social and occupational structure of the region was complex. In the late nineteenth century, the valley underwent a commercial boom and fantastic population growth. A handful of villagers managed to purchase small plots from bankrupt haciendas at wildly inflated prices — prices that very few villagers could afford to pay.[14] This trend created new problems by exacerbating class antagonisms in the villages as those villagers who managed to buy land — known as *fraccionistas* — became the object of nearly universal scorn. Landless villagers regarded them as a privileged, homegrown kulak class and begrudged them their relative good fortune.[15] Large landowners considered them an uneducated and unworthy class that stood in the way of modernization because they eschewed modern technology, took little interest in new farming methods, competed with more substantial farmers for labor, and contributed to overproduction.[16] Some landlords also resented the fraccionistas for setting a poor example for fellow villagers because as landowners in their own right they had no incentive to sell their labor to the haciendas. Ironically, their ranks would be swelled later through the deliberate machinations of landowners out to undercut the agrarian reform.

A small group of rural folk managed to attach themselves permanently to a hacienda — living on the hacienda grounds, drawing a regular wage, and enjoying relatively privileged circumstances. Yet another tiny group found work in the region's booming textile industry, moving to the factory towns of Puebla, Atlixco, and San Martín Texmelucan, where they lived in monotonous tract homes and worked under onerous, closely supervised conditions. There they were influenced by radical new notions that inflamed the incipient union movement throughout Mexico in the first decade of the twentieth century. Later, they would provide valuable leadership and ideological orientation to the revolutionary movement. During the Díaz regime, however, the organized militancy of industrial workers found little echo in the countryside. The diversity of the agricultural workforce made organization difficult, and given the tyranny of nature and the urgency of agriculture, landlords and authorities deemed it an evil to be avoided at all cost.[17]

Most of the rural poor of the Puebla-Tlaxcala Valley made up an agricultural proletariat, known generically as *jornaleros,* or hired hands. Their lot was as monotonous as it was harsh. They hired themselves out by the day or week, working from *sol a sol* (sunup to sundown), an average of twelve hours per day, for a wage of 25 to 30 centavos. In times when labor was relatively scarce, the individual jornalero had some bargaining power, but as population boomed in the late nineteenth century, that bargaining power eroded steadily until his only advantage was mobility: if he found conditions too difficult on one estate, he could always seek work on another. Some jornaleros would walk many miles from their home village to put in their day's work, always in the hope that competition for labor might be to their advantage. Unfortunately for them, the haciendas were well coordinated enough, and the villagers so lacking in options, that labor conditions varied only slightly from one hacienda to the next. Hacendados could use their new telephone lines to manage the workforce, rotating workers among haciendas as it suited them or blacklisting troublemakers. "They didn't pay me well," complained one hacienda hand, years later. "And naturally, being on my own account, I always thought to get more. But no matter where I went, on whatever hacienda, the wage was the same."[18]

In the countryside, the power of the landlords, though mediated through administrators and political bosses, was astonishing. Luis Sánchez Pontón, who would serve briefly as state governor in 1920, was shocked into political activism after working in the Texmelucan Valley as a young lawyer before the revolution. The villages seemed to be little more than labor pools for the haciendas, and there was not much an idealistic lawyer could accomplish on behalf of his Indian defendants: "It is impossible for you to counter the influence of [the hacendados and political bosses]," a local judge told him; "I could give you a verdict in favor of your defendants, those Indians, but it would be meaningless."[19]

The jornaleros had few options and limited horizons. Although the railroads built in the late nineteenth century wrought dramatic changes in the local economy and society, they did little to broaden the jornaleros' outlook. A farmhand's daily wage of thirty centavos would take him less than twelve miles down the iron road, so the poor traveled as they always had, on foot, carrying their wares on their backs or on the backs of mules.[20]

Children learned early on just how limited their horizons would be. They were put to work pasturing animals or guiding them during the plowing. In planting season they would scatter seeds, and during the harvest they would run behind the reaping machines, scaring birds away from the cut wheat.[21] Schools rarely existed, despite occasional flurries of interest in the subject on the part of politicians. When the Puebla legislature tried in 1884 to have the hacendados finance schools on their haciendas, the hacendados howled that such utopian plans could be afforded only by those landlords who owned estates "the size of certain independent nations of Europe."[22] So the number of schools in the region remained stagnant or declined even as the population boomed.[23] In those places that had schools, most families so depended on their children's labor that absenteeism was chronic.[24] Instruction, when it happened, was rudimentary at best, carried on in rooms equipped with little more than a primer and a blackboard.[25] When Luis Cabrera — later a leading student of the agrarian question — taught school on a Tlaxcala hacienda in 1895, he was warned by the administrator to teach only reading, writing, and Christian doctrine, and absolutely to avoid any mention of arithmetic or "matters of civic instruction that . . . are good for nothing."[26]

Although reformers and critics had long decried the rude lot of the rural worker, that lot appears to have changed very little over the course of the centuries.[27] Sanitary conditions were grim, a major reason why the average life expectancy in the state of Puebla was only thirty years in 1895 and twenty-five in 1910.[28] For the average village family, home was a single-room dwelling with a roof of grass or dried cactus leaves, walls of mud or stone, which allowed no ventilation, and a door that consisted of a board propped against an opening. The women spent their days grinding corn and cooking over a fire that filled the small room with heat and smoke.

The clothes worn by the adults were ragged and few; the children often went naked. Their diet consisted almost exclusively of corn, beans, and chile peppers, supplemented by hens' eggs, wild fruits and plants — mesquite berries, yucca blossoms, the nopal cactus — and, on very rare occasions, some meat. A contemporary study of nutrition among rural workers found that on average they would have had to increase their caloric intake by 70 percent just to replace energy used in routine muscular exertions.[29] Often the only drinking water was rain collected in open pools, which grew stagnant and toxic. Dead animals were seldom buried or disposed of, but left where they fell to be picked apart by ravenous dogs or carrion birds. Animal carcasses could often be found floating in the village water supply. One dismayed observer noted that "one recognizes the proximity of a workers' town . . . by the abundance of fecal matter scattered about in public view."[30] Drunkenness was endemic, and domestic and civil disputes that ended tragically could often be attributed to the nefarious effects of pulque, which some haciendas provided in partial payment of wages.

Not surprisingly, the villages were breeding grounds for disease. Mothers nursing their infants before the smoky hearth passed a variety of ailments to their young. Gangrene and streptococcal infections, smallpox, stomach viruses and parasites, malaria, and eruptive fevers were common. The role of village nurse often fell, by tradition, to the wife of the hacendado, whether or not she had any expertise in the field. Such amateur care would be supplemented by that of local *curanderos,* healers who specialized in combinations of magical and herbal remedies, and of *componedores,* who hoped to pass for surgeons. Some of these self-appointed experts still practiced the discredited art of bloodletting, but more typically they would apply poultices to fractured or dislocated limbs; clean open wounds with fetid water, chamois skins, or spider webs; and — perhaps their most exotic cure — treat head injuries by covering their patients' heads with blankets and dragging them by the feet. Such individuals could, if sufficiently clever and unscrupulous, do more than contribute to the villagers' poor health. In 1909, for instance, a man appeared in the village of Atoyatenco claiming the ability to cure illness, relocate hills, widen *barrancas,* and cause crops to flourish or fail. For such services, of course, he demanded and received money from the gullible.[31]

Because of their poor nutrition, abominable health care, and fondness for strong drink, villagers earned their reputation for sloth and indifference. The hacendados claimed that few workers were capable of putting in a solid work week. On Saturdays they often failed to show up, complained the landowners, and on Mondays they would sleep off hangovers. One hacendado calculated that if he subtracted these unauthorized absences, together with Sundays and officially recognized holidays, the loss would amount to nearly half of the working year. Even when they did show up, the workers displayed an exasperating lack of enthusiasm for their tasks. *Mayordomos* (overseers) would be sent from house to house before dawn to rouse the peons from their slumber, for they were unlikely to come out of their own volition. "[The campesino's] work is impaired," said one hacendado,

> because from start to finish he preoccupies himself with a single idea: that of obtaining his wage with the least effort. If he's plowing, each time he completes a furrow, the cleaning of the plow strikes him as a plausible motive to suspend work, and he devotes himself to that cleaning with a calm capable of exhausting the most patient overseer. If one entrusts him with a machine, before studying how to use it he inquires cunningly as to the means of destroying it; and it is not unusual that he will refuse to use it when he sees that its automatic movement impedes the leisure he loves so well. For this reason he hates harvesting machines; for this reason he abhors working with mules who carry him along at a rapid pace, and is more content with the ox, with its slow and measured gait. He never worries about improving his work but only about passing the time, and when he is deficiently supervised he works very little and very badly.[32]

From this description, it requires little insight to see that the hacendados were dealing with something other than garden-variety laziness, which would have appeared far less deliberate and certainly less creative. The workers' indifference was a more or less conscious statement of protest.[33] In their unimaginative way, most hacendados chose to deal with this "stupendous apathy" by hiring more — and more brutal — supervisors. A complex and costly chain of command developed — *bracero, ayudante, capitán, mayordomo,* and finally *administrador* — which, far from genuinely combatting the workers' low productivity, merely contributed another incentive to flee or to resist by some relatively safe means.

Only rarely, when a clear chance presented itself, would the workers resort to open violence,[34] but the landowners were always keenly conscious of this latent threat.

THE LANDLORDS' OTHER BURDENS

For all the brutality of the system they upheld, in some sense the landowners of the Puebla-Tlaxcala Valley were themselves victims. Apart from a brief period in the seventeenth century, wheat farming had never been a source of secure fortunes in the valley. Among the recent victims of the vicissitudes of valley agriculture was Don Fernando G. Mendizábal, who had owned San Pedro Coxtocán before it was purchased by Harry Evans. At the time of his death in 1896, Mendizábal's farm was heavily mortgaged to Harry Evans's employer, the Bank of London and Mexico. His heirs had been unable or unwilling to keep the place up, so Harry Evans had only to take over the lien in the possession of his bank.[35]

Mendizábal had first entered the wheat market at a time when the markets for all agricultural products were gravely depressed. Local people were few and poor, usually managing to scrape by on what they were able to grow for themselves. Dilapidated roads, decrepit ports, and unstable political conditions effectively prevented shipping wheat to other regions or lands. Credit was scarce and costly, furnished by a weakened Catholic Church or unscrupulous usurers. Landlords came to dread years of abundance, when they would be obliged to sell their crops for a fraction of what they cost to grow.[36]

Belying the popular image of the Mexican landowner as a resolutely medieval character who rejected anything that smacked of "progress," the landowners of the San Martín Valley of Puebla agreed with the liberal prescription, which saw little wrong with Mexican agriculture that modern capitalism could not solve. Through the Agricultural Society of San Martín Texmelucan (founded in 1860), they proposed the confiscation of lands held inactive by the church and peasant communities; improvements in harbors, communication facilities, and transportation technologies; revised taxation; easier credit; and reforms to attract foreign investment and stimulate foreign trade. Like all good liberals, the society's members hoped to transform Mexican agriculture from a backward colonial system into a dynamic capitalist one.

With a notorious legislative assault beginning in 1856, the government made great strides in reducing the amount of land controlled by the church and peasant villages.[37] However, the liberals reasoned that such strides would mean little real progress if not accompanied by a great leap forward in transportation and communication infrastructure, which would enable the stepped-up production to circulate. Throughout the early nineteenth century, Puebla's landlords dreamed deliriously of steel rails and mighty steam engines, or of somehow making a viable waterway of the diminutive Atoyac River. Puebla congressman Manuel María Zamacona put it most baldly: "The iron rails will resolve all the political, social and economic questions that could not be resolved by the abnegation and the blood of two generations."[38]

The first of the long dreamed of railroads—the Mexican Railway—connected Mexico City with the port of Veracruz and was completed in 1872 to the jubilation of the landowners of the Puebla-Tlaxcala Valley. It was soon joined by an alternate east-west route, the Interoceanic. Subsequent years brought the completion of a host of north-south connections and feeder lines until the Puebla-Tlaxcala Valley was connected to almost every corner of the republic.

The celebrations occasioned by the new era of railroads were short-lived. By 1889, a British observer noted that all along the route of the Mexican Railway "the country . . . does not appear to have undergone any alteration from the advent of the iron road, the towns and villages seem to retain the same original aspect, and hardly anywhere does one remark any business activity directly traceable to the railway itself."[39] This disappointment was largely owing to the fact that shipping costs were notoriously high, the result of high construction costs, unfavorable exchange rates, federal budget shortfalls, and corruption.[40] Indeed, freight rates were so prohibitive that some farmers preferred to let their crops rot in the fields rather than pay them. As one critic observed, a railway "that could be beaten in point of cheapness by pack animals is naturally not the railway to develop a country."[41]

In fact, the railroads did bring prosperity to some, but not in the ways the landlords had envisioned. In central Mexico, the price of land traversed by the railroads rose to dizzying heights, higher than far more productive lands in Argentina or the United States.[42] In the Puebla-Tlaxcala Valley, the value of rural properties more than doubled between 1879 and 1906.[43] The greed of the powerful rose in step with the land's market value, accompanied by all the usual distortions in land tenure patterns.

High prices for land and shipping sent landowners searching for crops that promised the highest value per weight and the most secure return on investment. In much of Mexico, bulky basic grains gave way to cash crops for export — such as henequen fiber, rubber, and coffee. Mexico's powerful classes played increasingly to a foreign audience,[44] which was, for the most part, bad news for grain farmers. Between 1877 and 1910, production of crops for export more than tripled, whereas the production of domestic foodstuffs declined, remained stagnant, or grew only insignificantly.[45] Corn, the crop most precious to the greatest number of Mexicans, was the least precious to the new agricultural empresarios and so was banished to the poorest land and left to satisfy itself with rainwater, while the better-quality, irrigated lands were given over to crops that promised better returns.[46]

Wheat lay uncomfortably between these extremes, neither a glamorous export crop, nor so humble a grain as corn. Its consumers were, by and large, city folk who scorned the lowly tortilla, and because it was also a cash crop that needed high-quality irrigated land, most Mexican peasants could not have grown it on their own account even had they been so inclined. On the other hand, its value remained relatively low in relation to its bulk, thus making its potential as an exportable commodity uncertain indeed.

No one really doubted that Mexico's future lay in exports, so it is not surprising that for a brief while during the early 1880s the farmers of the San Martín

Texmelucan Valley contemplated a scheme to sell their wheat on the docks of Liverpool, but the valley's farmers lacked faith in the operation and protested that their crops were already committed to markets in Puebla and Mexico City. Beset by the vicissitudes of the highland climate, where late rains, hailstorms, and early freezes were common, Mexico was not ecologically equipped, experts argued, to compete with wheat-growing giants such as the United States, Canada, and Argentina. The abrupt shift between the pervasive dampness of the rainy season and the dryness of the winter made the highland fields ideal breeding grounds for the traditional scourge of the highland cereal farmer: the infamous *chahuixtle,* a microscopic parasitic fungus that spread rapidly, turned whole fields a noxious rust color, and destroyed the grain.[47]

Nature's caprices were exacerbated by human abuse. The arid soil of the plateau had been cultivated for centuries without being replenished with vital nutrients. Artificial irrigation was essential for wheat, yet water was scarce and growing scarcer, its access governed by regulations that were positively byzantine. The destruction of woodlands, which had been going on for hundreds of years, continued despite efforts to regulate it. As young trees fell before the ax, soil eroded, grew barren, and was abandoned. A German agronomist who visited the region at the turn of the century described whole fields turned to desert, where only hardy and undemanding varieties of agave grew. He saw crops that were "true caricatures of plants" — mature corn stalks only a foot tall and fields of barley with so few sprouting plants that they resembled a "human skull on the verge of total baldness."[48] Some claimed the rainy season was actually growing shorter and that deforestation and drought caused previously unknown epidemic fevers among Indian workers of the Texmelucan Valley.[49]

All of these natural disadvantages — coupled with the primitive tools, ancient farming methods, and the fabled lethargy of the local workers — made exporting wheat a quixotic notion at best. The wheat farmers of the Texmelucan Valley were not fatalistic in the face of these challenges, however. They were, for instance, positively enamored of the prospect of mechanizing their operations, but there were obstacles to this scheme. The harvest often had to be carried out during the later months of the rainy season, when deep mud bogged down the machines and rendered them inoperable.[50] Farm machinery was not manufactured in Mexico, and only the wealthiest farmers had the wherewithal to import it. Even those well-heeled Mexican wheat farmers who did manage to import harvesting machines were soon complaining that they lacked the twine needed to bind the harvested sheaves.[51]

Although nature had not been as generous as Mexican farmers might have wished, in the end it was foreign competition that most profoundly distorted the Mexican wheat economy. Wheat production in the United States tripled in

the three decades after 1860 so that by the late 1880s it single-handedly produced nearly a quarter of all of the world's wheat.[52] Mechanization and abundant water made it possible for U.S. wheat growers to sell their produce at
prices that would have proved ruinous for the Mexicans. At the same time,
Argentina emerged as a major wheat exporter, claiming a large share of the
British market. New wheat producers from France to the Ukraine weighed in to
supply Europe. Mexico's only strong suits in the wheat game quickly became
the superior class of its grains and the cheapness of its workforce, which in certain extraordinary circumstances — say, extremely poor harvests in the United
States or some other part of the world — might make wheat a temporarily viable
export for the country.[53]

Uncompetitive on world markets and inefficient in any case, Mexico's wheat
growers made the most of their monopoly of the domestic market. Especially
after the turn of the century, wheat farmers used their considerable political
influence to protect the three key advantages that ensured their monopoly and
their profits: low property taxes, high tariff duties, and cheap labor. With those
blessings secured, they could carry on their operations without regard to global
market conditions. Between 1877 and 1910, Mexico's population and the demand for wheat grew dramatically,[54] but wheat production remained stagnant,
so the price more than doubled. In some years, Mexican consumers would pay
twice the price for Mexican wheat as their U.S. counterparts would pay for U.S.
wheat.[55]

Landowners also used their clout to see that taxes would not eat heavily into
their profits. Most property taxes were based on assessments carried out before
the railroads had caused property values to skyrocket. If reassessments were
required, hacendados would greet the tax inspectors with a feast of barbecued
goat and the finest pulque, making sure that they left feeling mellow and sati-
ated, content to leave well enough alone.[56] Critics and reformers charged that
landlords profited at the expense of the national treasury, but the landlords
make it clear that they needed low taxes to survive.

In the matter of protectionist tariffs against cereal imports, Mexican wheat
farmers never relaxed their vigilance. Even when sporadic agricultural crises
obliged the government to subsidize the duty-free import of foodstuffs, the
wheat growers would howl in protest, portraying themselves as victims of
the vilest betrayal. In 1885, Fernando G. Mendizábal of San Pedro Coxtocán
charged the government with using the "pretext" of aiding the "needy classes"
to import wheat and flour, even though the imports spelled doom for the
farmers of the San Martín Valley. Wheat, cried Mendizábal, was irrelevant to the
needy classes because they ate only corn, which at the moment was cheap and
abundant. Mendizábal warned that even the decent folk might one day have to
learn to love corn in order to safeguard the interests of Mexico's wheat farmers,

for "a good hunger knows no bad bread."[57] Yet corn production, too, barely kept pace with population growth.[58]

Distorted though it may have been, the Mexican wheat game was capable of yielding very handsome profits indeed. One government agronomist calculated that a U.S. small farmer with his modern farm machinery was capable of producing three times the amount of wheat per acre as the Mexican farmer, who relied on manual labor alone. It would cost the U.S. farmer slightly more to produce his grain, but the Mexican farmer's big bonanza came in the final transaction: his grain would fetch more than one and a half times the price per bushel as the U.S. farmer's grain. Thus, the Mexican farmer could realize $48 per hectare of grain, which, when production costs were subtracted, yielded a profit of $27.89, nearly 50 percent. The U.S. farmer's profit—26.5 percent—seemed paltry by comparison.[59]

The promise of such profits naturally attracted big players and squeezed out the small-timers. The successful turn-of-the-century wheat farmer would have to count on political influence sufficient to maintain tax and tariff benefits, as well as on ample capital to cope with capricious market and ecological conditions. The banking system was personalistic and sloppy, making credit available only to those with serious clout.[60] Farmers who lacked credit or who borrowed unwisely were left to the mercy of nature and speculators. The survivors were men of means and connections. Harry Evans managed by virtue of his formal affiliation with one of Mexico's oldest banks; others counted on family fortunes or on close-knit networks with very diverse interests and investments. By far the most successful empresarios in the Puebla-Tlaxcala Valley were the Spaniards, who farmed wheat in conjunction with other mercantile and industrial pursuits. The Spanish community in the region was, as the Spanish minister boasted, "a vast family whose cohesion efficaciously contributes to the sound conservation of the memory and traditions of the Fatherland."[61] Virtually a commercial society, the community served to distribute the shocks of local commerce and to apportion credit to members in good standing. The leaders of the community were men like Félix Pérez, a cotton merchant and textile magnate who owned eight haciendas in the Puebla-Tlaxcala Valley during the late nineteenth century, including the Hacienda San Cristóbal Polaxtla, whose workers would soon emerge among the most zealous leaders of the agrarian movement. The largest and most valuable property in the region belonged to Pérez's son-in-law, a Spanish immigrant named Marcelino G. Presno. He owned, among other properties, the Hacienda y Molino de Guadalupe, a veritable agricultural-industrial complex that, in addition to its farming operations, boasted a flour mill, a sawmill, a furniture and box factory, a china factory, three small cotton textile factories, and extensive woodlands exploited for timber.[62] The rise of such entrepreneurs signaled a gradual process of monopolization of the area's wheat economy by men with diversified investments and the resources to involve themselves in the market at all of its stages — from securing the capital to growing the grain, milling the flour, and baking and selling the bread.

The older agricultural elite — men such as Fernando G. Mendizábal — were pushed to the wall. Mendizábal died in 1896 with his hacienda heavily mortgaged to the Bank of London and Mexico, where the lien was taken over by Harry Evans a decade later. Some lost their land to usurers and speculators, whereas others sought to make the best of the situation by dividing their lands into very small plots and selling them to the wealthier residents of the neighboring villages.

By 1910, Harry and Rosalie Evans must have been aware that their new vocation had its share of challenges. It is unlikely, however, that they fully sensed the tensions that plagued their portion of the Mexican countryside. On the very eve of the revolution, the political and social landscape appeared as placid as the fields of wheat that blanketed the valley floor. Perhaps the Evanses were aware of the ripples that had troubled that placid surface, the great peasant rebellions that had rocked the region in the 1860s and 1870s, but such disturbances seemed safely tucked away in the distant past, and now the system functioned as naturally and predictably as the highland weather.

For certain, they saw little connection between the few vexations inherent in their new situation and the woes of the venerable dictator, Díaz. The activities of upstarts such as Francisco I. Madero and Aquiles Serdán were surely as remote from their concerns as the workaday life they had left behind in Puebla. The farming life agreed with them.

Three

The Master may destroy the mould
　With cunning hand, if time it be;
But woe, if, raging uncontroll'd,
　The glowing bronze itself should free!
—Friedrich von Schiller, "The Song of the Bell"

———

OSALIE EVANS spent the winter of 1910–1911 in the United States caring for her father, who had slipped suddenly into dementia. It was difficult to find nurses who showed the proper compassion and respect. Most seemed simply to assume that Mr. Caden had always been a crazy old man. Rosalie was badly unnerved, for most of the time her father only muttered incoherently and seemed barely to recognize her. Back in Mexico, Harry too had his hands full. In the fall, the region had been hit hard by frosts that wiped out nearly half of the wheat crop of the San Martín Valley. Next to such troubles, a little political agitation seemed a passing thing: "I hope the political situation clears," wrote Rosalie in March, "so we can go abroad this summer. I would like to forget myself with you in some strange place."[1]

THE REVOLUTION BEGINS

A trip abroad did not seem so far-fetched a prospect. Although there had been some distressing activity lately, it appeared to be nothing the great dictator could not handle. The elections in June of 1910 had gone off without a hitch, once all pretense toward fairness was jettisoned: Madero supporters were harrassed and banished from the voter rolls; federal troops patrolled streets and polling places, arresting opposition voters or forcing their votes at bayonet point. When it was over, Díaz claimed a commanding victory.

In Puebla, the movement led by Aquiles Serdán gained momentum for a time, especially at the state college and in the factories, but governor Mucio P. Martínez ruthlessly kept it in check by ordering the arrest and deportation of labor leaders and the scattering of student demonstrations. Nor was official hostility the only threat to the movement. It was further undercut by its own heterogeneity. Illiterate farm and factory hands, dissident hacendados, urban artisans, urbane lawyers, anarchists, die-hard liberals, students, and professors — all agreed that the old regime had to go, but were likely to agree on little else.

Even so, the revolutionary movement struggled along, waiting for the day — November 20, 1910 — that Francisco I. Madero, from his San Antonio exile, had declared the revolution should begin. In Puebla, planning was meticulous and ambitious: the state prisons were to be emptied; factory workers would burn rails and bridges; and peasant armies would converge on the city of Puebla from all of the cardinal points. Unfortunately for the plotters, the authorities learned of the intended rebellion and reacted energetically. Police and government troops locked workers in their factories, placed armed guards at all strategic routes, blockaded the railway stations, and raided homes of suspected conspirators, sometimes tipped off to stockpiles of weapons by the rebels' own nervous kin. Most of the conspirators fled the city.[2]

Aquiles Serdán did not flee. On November 18, 1910, two days before the rebellion was set to begin, he and about thirty loyal confederates holed up in Serdán's home. Soon police and federal soldiers began their assault. After three hours of pitched fighting, most of the home's defenders were dead, including Serdán himself, who was dispatched with an unceremonious shot to the head after being discovered hiding under the floorboards of his living room.[3] The authorities installed his corpse in front of the police station, a grim warning to any who aspired to see the rebellion through.

Uprisings in the countryside were equally ill-starred, even if the results were less brutal. Peasant soldiers set fire to the bridge of the Interoceanic Railway at Santa Cruz, Tlaxcala, and sniped at trains carrying federal reinforcements to Puebla, but to little effect. At the national level, too, the revolution seemed to sputter like damp gunpowder. Despite the Puebla disaster, Francisco I. Madero himself rode across the Rio Grande at Ciudad Porfirio Díaz (now Piedras Negras) on the night of November 19, but the small contingent he had counted on to help him take the little border town was nowhere to be found. He went splashing back across the river in despair.

Although it all seemed little more than a grim comedy of errors, appearances were deceiving. The revolution had thus far failed only in realizing the aim of its progenitors, who had envisioned a narrow political revolution — a small urban elite seizing power with a quick strike to the nation's jugular. Almost imperceptibly, however, the revolution came alive in the countryside, among people with little patience for parliamentary procedure, little interest in candidates and votes, and scant faith in politicians. The revolution's leaders had expected their rural contacts to carry out their logistical chores, deferring dutifully to their urban overlords. It would be some time before the urban rebels noticed that the countryside was slipping out of their control.

The unofficial headquarters of rural rebellion was the state of Morelos, just south of Mexico City. There, villagers whose lives and lands had been disrupted or destroyed by burgeoning sugar plantations made early contact with Madero, secured some vague promises of land reform, then took up arms under the leadership of a farmer and a horse trader named Emiliano Zapata.[4]

When the shooting started, the campesinos of the Puebla-Tlaxcala Valley joined in eagerly and gave vent to long-simmering destructive impulses: felling telephone and telegraph wires, invading haciendas, making off with horses, pistols, and machetes.[5] Throughout the country, in the wide-open deserts, plains, and valleys, the start of the revolution obeyed a rural rhythm, like snow melting in the sierra or seeds sprouting under rocky ground — frustratingly slow, improvised, and desultory, but nevertheless unstoppable. Coming out onto their terraces at night and straining their eyes, the city people of Puebla could see the glint of rebel campfires on the slopes of the great volcanoes, and they would wonder at that world of which they knew so little, but which was closing in on them so rapidly.

San Pedro Coxtocán was not spared the rebels' wrath. On May 20, 1911, revolutionaries entered the property and carried off a horse, several rifles, and a sum of money. Loyal employees tried frantically to round up the livestock before they fled to the city, leaving the estate in rebel hands. Harry Evans complained via the British embassy and was soon rewarded with the assurance that the authorities were resolved to prevent brigandage, but by the time he received his reply, the authorities themselves had changed. Porfirio Díaz resigned on May 25, leaving the capital to Madero's forces.[7]

"Mr. Madero has unleashed a tiger," Díaz is reported to have said just before boarding the ship that would carry him to his European exile. "Now let's see if he can control it."[8]

CONTROLLING THE TIGER

Controlling the unleashed tiger did indeed prove a challenge. Disbanding the peasant armies and confiscating their weapons would be no simple task because the revolution, brief and inconclusive though it had been so far, appeared to have inspired a new attitude among a population marginalized for centuries. The sudden relaxation of control finally allowed them to give vent to long pent up frustrations, and it was unlikely that anything so profoundly felt could be dismissed by fiat. In the city of Puebla, anger found an outlet in a popular wave of anti-Spanish xenophobia. Signs on storefronts urged death to the Spaniards (or *gachupines,* in popular parlance), and even the most gallant Spanish bullfighters — normally revered figures — were mocked and insulted.[9] In south-western Tlaxcala, the rebel army styled itself the "Xicohténcatl Brigade," taking the name of the Tlaxcalan chief who had fiercely resisted Hernán Cortés and his Spanish conquistadores. It was as if the Indians of the Puebla-Tlaxcala Valley were out to exact revenge for wrongs four centuries old.

Madero and his urban supporters did their best to contain the situation. Zapatista rebels, who had encroached upon Puebla from the south, received word as early as May 24, 1911, that henceforth any "act of hostility against the haciendas" would be judged an "act of war."[10] On May 29, rebel troops waited impatiently in Cholula, the northwestern gateway to Puebla City, expecting to make a triumphant entry into the state capital, but were bewildered when they found themselves impeded by soldiers of the old regime. The confrontation turned violent, and the clash was followed by disorderly street marches conducted by revolutionary sympathizers chanting for long life to Madero and Aquiles Serdán, death to the rich and to the Spaniards. Such street marches soon became regular events, terrorizing the more moderate elements in the city.[11] In early spring of 1911, rebel bands still operated in the countryside, but soon the authorities categorically declared such groups to be bandits who would be exterminated accordingly.[12] Many people who had fancied themselves heroes were now officially outlaws.

In Puebla City, the "revolutionary regime" came to look much like the old one. With Madero's approval, a conservative Catholic lawyer became governor, although he had connections to the government of Mucio P. Martínez. The judiciary remained intact, but the command of the region's revolutionary army went to a wealthy industrialist and sugar planter. The new powers in the state subscribed to a political philosophy that was quite influential in the upper echelons of the Madero government: social reform, they reasoned, was a long-term goal that could be addressed — if it were to be addressed at all — only once law and order were definitively established. The rural rebels, who had fought for Madero and demanded immediate land reform, felt betrayed. What incentive would the government have to go through with reforms if those who needed them most desperately and demanded them most stridently were to surrender their only solid bargaining chip — namely, their weapons and their rudimentary military organizations?

The nature of the Madero regime became still clearer to the rural rebels in July 1911, when Madero visited Puebla City. By that time, he was running for president while a conservative interim regime held power in Mexico City. Tensions ran high in the days prior to the candidate's arrival. General Abraham Martínez, Zapata's chief of staff and official representative of the Interior Ministry, arrested several prominent Puebla citizens and charged them of plotting Maderos' assassination. Puebla's elites cried foul, demanding that General Martínez himself be arrested. The city divided into camps, and hostilities erupted on July 12, the day before Madero was scheduled to arrive, when federal troops attacked bands of rebels holed up in the city's bullring. Door-to-door street fighting raged throughout the night, and the sun rose on city streets strewn with corpses, most of them rebels killed by the federal troops of Colonel Aureliano Blanquet.

It would have been a tense and tragic situation in any case, but candidate Madero handled it with stunning ineptitude, blaming the rebels entirely for the fight and publicly commending Colonel Blanquet for his "loyalty and courage," all but promising him a promotion. When told that nearly a hundred rebel corpses lingered unburied in the municipal cemetery, Madero just shrugged and said it was a problem for local authorities, who proceeded to shove most of the bodies into mass graves. The final insult came in a parade on July 18, which featured a woman, supposed to represent Mexico, riding in an automobile, holding aloft a banner depicting two children — one made up as a federal soldier, the other as a "Maderista rebel," the two joined in a warm fraternal embrace.[13]

Although it would be some months before the counterrevolution was formally declared, hostilities were under way almost before the smoke cleared from the Puebla episode. Rebel troops fanned out from Puebla City as full-fledged outlaws and were soon engaged in new clashes in the countryside. In the most notorious instance, rebels attacked a Spanish-owned textile mill near Puebla City, killing four German employees and one Spanish, and sparking a tense international incident.[14] To the south, Zapatistas raided a large sugar plantation at Atencingo, killing several Spanish administrators.[15] In the national congress, conservative orators viewed such incidents with panic, declaring Zapata and his minions to be nothing less than "the subsoil which has risen up and wants to blot out all the lights of the surface."[16] Under the influence of interior secretary Alberto García Granados — who owned a hacienda only a few miles south of the Evanses' San Pedro Coxtocán — the interim powers in Mexico City unleashed one of their most ruthless officers, General Victoriano Huerta, to deal decisively with rural unrest.

Such hostility had the ironic effect of helping to transform what had been an inchoate rural uprising into a relatively cohesive and intransigent peasant army, but the transformation was hardly inevitable. If analysts of peasant politics agree on anything, it is that the outlook for spontaneous mobilization and solidarity among the rural poor is, under normal circumstances, dim. In Mexico, the immense power of the landowners and the utter dependence of the rural poor upon them generally had led many of the latter to conclude, logically, that their best hope for winning better treatment or small favors lay in deference, obedience, and loyalty to the *patrón,* even if feigned. Little could be gained from cooperation with fellow villagers, and the landowners further complicated the problem by fomenting a paternalistic culture, styling themselves the fount of all favors and the arbiters of all justice. The prospects for concerted action were further undercut by the fact that decades of increasing commercialism and economic diversification had introduced new class and occupational differences into most villages, blurring matters of interest, allegiance, and antagonism. All this meant that however deeply villagers may have been aware of and resented the injustice of their lot, they had a difficult time seeing themselves and the landowners as distinct and mutually antagonistic "classes."[17]

At this particular time, however, solidarity was practically thrust upon the villagers of central Mexico by official hostility, which made it apparent that it would be suicidal to lay down their weapons. To that were added the firm and charismatic leadership of Emiliano Zapata[18] and the attractiveness of the sweeping plan for reform that his headquarters issued in November 1911. The "Plan of Ayala" disavowed Madero's government and promised to return all stolen lands, waters, and woodlands to their rightful owners, the villagers. Enemies of the revolution—a category that the Zapatistas defined broadly—would be relieved of their properties, but all other properties would be subject to expropriation only if they were judged to be monopolies that deprived the people of a livelihood.[19] From that point on, Zapata would cling to the Plan of Ayala as though it were a sacred text, the betrayal of which placed one beyond any hope of redemption.

TEN TRAGIC DAYS

Rosalie and Harry Evans observed these events with a certain incredulity, but still without a great deal of alarm. Rosalie had wished that the political situation would clear so she and Harry could go abroad for the summer. When that wish went unfulfilled, the couple decided to go abroad anyway, hoping that Mexico would right itself in their absence. While Madero and Zapata thrust and parried, Rosalie Evans lived at the opera, "getting all the Wagner I can." Perhaps it was prescience, perhaps only a powerful nostalgia brought on by so many recent losses, but in the midst of her "intellectual spree" Rosalie was preoccupied with impermanence and a world that seemed to be slipping away. Visiting Goethe's Weimar home, she was saddened that so little remained of the great man. "It seemed like a crushing testimonial against all hope of immortality," she wrote, "that such a spirit should quietly fade into the past." At a monastery in Milan, she remarked that to her the most ornate sacred relics seemed little more than showy baubles.[20]

It would have done nothing to improve her mood had she known that while she and Harry waited for a ship to carry them back across the Atlantic, revolutionaries were busy drafting plans that would destroy life as they knew it. The Evanses were well aware of the trouble in Mexico, of course. Rosalie's sister, Daisy, wrote to warn them not to sail directly to Veracruz, for Mexico was still too unsettled, so they sailed instead to New York, arriving on December 5, 1911. Within days, Harry was once again soliciting protection for his hacienda from the British legation. He had reports that other haciendas in the vicinity were being raided and that some three hundred Zapatista rebels were in the mountains only a short ride from San Pedro Coxtocán.

Harry Evans had few doubts as to his own benevolence as a landlord or that his goodwill was reciprocated, but he was nevertheless reconciled to spending some time away from the hacienda — mostly in Puebla and Mexico City — while the situation settled. Claiming that he was on excellent terms with "the people of the place," Evans allowed that he would require only a small contingent of ten to fifteen soldiers for about two weeks while he gathered his grain harvest and removed what was left in the living quarters.[21] Within a few weeks, Harry had the assurance he sought: the current Mexican government wished to protect the haciendas. The secretary of war, he was told, had given orders to the zone military commander to "take steps for the protection of the property in question."[22]

Harry's insistence on the absolute goodwill that reigned between himself and the villagers was mostly wishful thinking, however, just as his faith in the authorities' ability to halt the perilous spiral was misplaced. By the end of March 1912, the U.S. ambassador reported alarmedly that many of the federal troops garrisoned in Puebla were deserting the government and that the state was "rapidly approaching a condition of anarchy."[23] The mountainous north of the state was rocked by a rebellion led by a grizzled, hard-drinking, bewhiskered octogenarian federal army veteran named Higinio Aguilar, who appeared to be attracting followers with embarrassing ease.[24] In the center of the state, factory workers added to the tumult by declaring a general strike, forcing twenty-four textile plants out of operation.[25]

Most foreigners based in Puebla, including Harry and Rosalie Evans, fled to Mexico City, where they hoped to find strength in numbers. That spring they waited and planned, wisely expecting the worst and meeting regularly at the British Club to discuss survival strategies. Ads in the English-language *Mexican Herald* counseled foreigners to lay in a generous supply of candles and lanterns, a week's supply of food, and two blankets, as well as to stay in their homes in case of trouble and to avoid "riotous mobs." In case of extreme emergency, they were to gather with their fellow foreigners in designated "concentration homes."[26] In May, the U.S. ambassador made a U.S. Navy ship available to spirit away refugees, giving British second priority after Americans.

So far, Mexico City had remained an island of tranquility whose residents only read and chattered with alarm and disgust about the upheavals convulsing the rest of the country. The wealthy and frivolous drowned their fears and uncertainties in a sort of desperate abandon, and the capital's normally staid restaurants opened midnight cabarets to cater to their whims.[27] Others, however, were actively plotting to put an end to Madero's faltering experiment with democracy and to reimpose the iron-fisted regime they reckoned Mexico needed. Coincidentally, in early 1913 two strong potential leaders of such a regime were in prison in Mexico City: Félix Díaz, nephew of the deposed dictator, was awaiting trial for a failed October uprising in Veracruz, and General Bernardo Reyes, who had served Díaz as secretary of war and had run unsuccessfully against Madero in 1911, was awaiting trial for the abortive uprising with which he had greeted his loss at the polls.[28]

Díaz and Reyes were liberated by their supporters, and they launched their bid for power on Sunday, February 9, 1913, with an attack on the National Palace. Reyes was killed that same morning, but Díaz and his followers occupied the national armory and laid in for a protracted seige. For the next week and half — the "Ten Tragic Days," as the episode would soon be known — Mexico City was torn by fierce street fighting. Well-heeled foreigners like Harry and Rosalie Evans remained sequestered in their homes, listening to the nearby boom of cannon and the pop of Maussers and rapid-fire guns, taking advantage of lulls in the shooting to replenish their provisions. When most of the city's streetlamps were destroyed, neighbors took turns patrolling their blocks by moonlight to ward off looting and incursions of combatants into the "neutral zone." By the following Saturday, stray bullets had shattered windows and splintered the walls of homes in even the most exclusive neighborhoods. On Sunday, a week after the battle had begun, the shooting stopped long enough for frightened noncombatants to depart. The streets were filled with rubble, jumbles of wire, dead horses, and dead people, and a harsh wind scattered dust and disease in all directions. The train stations were packed with frenzied refugees, some waiting for the afternoon train to Puebla, most waiting for the night train to Veracruz.[29]

Harry and Rosalie Evans left no record of their actions or whereabouts during this time, although they were probably in Mexico City for at least some portion of it. It seems probable, too, that they were among those who welcomed the outcome of the bloody episode, for when the smoke cleared, Mexico's new president was General Victoriano Huerta, the man who had headed the government's harshest effort to liquidate the Zapatista rebels. Huerta had an unsavory reputation as a gambler, womanizer, and heavy drinker, but he was also a champion of law and order and had little patience for talk of radical social reforms. He assured Mexico that "from now on peace and prosperity will reign."[30] As if to prove that assurance, Mexico City returned to normal with a speed and thoroughness that astonished residents. Within a couple of days, the dirt and debris and tangled wires had been removed along with the corpses of people and animals. The streetcars ran, and the streetlights burned.

Four days later, almost certainly on orders from the top, Madero and his vice president were "shot while trying to escape."

EXILE

It was far too late, however, for such a facile attempt to turn back the clock and restore an old-style regime. No sooner had General Huerta settled into the National Palace than his armed and active enemies were legion. Zapata continued his rebellion in the south, and in the north, leadership of the anti-Huerta struggle was seized by Governor Venustiano Carranza of Coahuila—an avuncular, bespectacled man with a long white beard. A wealthy and fairly conservative landowner, Carranza clearly had little in common with Zapata or with many of the other popular leaders who joined the fight against Huerta. But as long as Huerta was in power, they could agree on at least one thing. That allowed them, for the moment, to cooperate tolerably well.

In his effort to hang on to power against daunting odds, Huerta systematically subordinated civilian to military concerns, increasing the size of the federal army from fifty thousand troops to a quarter million and peopling it with ragged recruits rounded up from bullfights or late-night cantinas. Such soldiers had little stomach for defending the regime; some units surrendered wholesale without firing a shot. This costly military effort lost Huerta much support even from his most probable allies because many of the rich citizens came to feel they were unfairly hit with emergency taxes and forced loans.[31]

In early 1914, the anti-Huerta forces got a boost from an unexpected source. President Woodrow Wilson of the United States declared Huerta's regime "a government of butchers" and resolved to eradicate it by placing "an insuperable stumbling block" in the dictator's way.[32] In April, he found a suitable pretext to occupy the port of Veracruz, which would enable the United States to cut off the flow of arms and customs revenues to the Huerta government. To Wilson's surprise, the move was met with considerable resistance, and more than two hundred people—most of them Mexican—died in street fighting. Carranza and Zapata both loudly decried the intervention, but they were not above capitalizing when Huerta was forced to concentrate his forces in order to rattle sabers against the invaders. By July, Huerta recognized the futility of his predicament, resigned the presidency, and sailed off to European exile.[33]

President Wilson's actions also had the effect of shifting popular Mexican xenophobia away from Spaniards, who theretofore had suffered disproportionately, toward Americans and Britons (who were often conflated in the popular mind). Mobs looted American-owned businesses, demolished a statue of George Washington in Mexico City, attacked U.S. citizens, and desecrated U.S. flags.

At this point, Harry and Rosalie Evans, heeding the advice of their countries' diplomats, decided to abandon Mexico for an indeterminate exile. On May 9, 1914, they caught the train from Mexico City to Veracruz. A mile and half out of town the tracks had been destroyed, and the refugees had to hike five miles to another car. The next day, they sailed from Veracruz to Havana, eventually making their way to New York where they were met by Rosalie's sisters, Daisy and Edith, and Daisy's husband Jerdone. Soon they all sailed together for Europe, where they would remain until September. While in Europe they received such discouraging news from Mexico that they scarcely noticed how Europe was itself on the brink of war. The ship they sailed to the United States on, the *Royal Edward,* would soon be transformed into a transport ship and sunk in combat. They passed the remaining months of 1914 in Washington, D.C., and Chevy Chase, Maryland, taking leisurely nature walks and museum tours.[34]

OMINOUS SIGNS

The remnants of Huerta's regime in Mexico City surrendered to Carranza's army, commanded by General Alvaro Obregón, on August 13, 1914. Tlaxcala surrendered to General Pablo González on August 20, and Puebla followed suit three days later.

The Poblanos were bemused by the spectacle of an invading army, uncertain of the meaning of this latest turn of events. One wealthy man who had been influential in the old regime and who represented the city's archconservatives watched with unabashed amusement as the northern generals reviewed the troops of their "Army of the East." It was, he later recalled, "the drollest and most original parade" he had ever seen. A long steel tube wrapped with wire served as a cannon. Swarthy soldiers sporting the clothing of the landed gentry, some on tall horses, others on "liliputian" mounts, marched in two rows through the streets of Puebla City, in the shadows of elegant colonial cathedrals. Between them rolled hundreds of carts and carriages loaded with loot from haciendas and churches. Their weapons "seemed the provenance of some museum," ranging from catapults and Moroccan muskets to .30-.30s and Maussers.[35] After watching the parade unmolested for several hours, the observer was stunned to learn that this parody of an army had declared him an "enemy of the people" and had ordered his arrest. He barely managed to escape to Havana.

In the countryside of the Puebla-Tlaxcala Valley, few haciendas remained in operation under their owners. Like the Evanses, most landlords had fled, usually leaving behind a trusted administrator and some dubious sharecropping contracts, and hoping for the best. Those haciendas floated in a legal limbo, and while the various factions to the revolution debated just how revolutionary the revolution should be in this respect, they fell into the de facto possession of army officers, agrarian leaders, peasant land invaders, or brigands. Nearly all of them were sacked for food or treasures. Raiders took furniture, fixtures, and artworks from the residences; looted wheat, corn, chile, and beans from the granaries; slaughtered livestock and smashed agricultural machinery; tore down mighty truss beams and girders and added them to their stocks of firewood; and heaped flagstones, garden walls, and roofing tiles onto their piles of building materials. Although the looting clearly reflected the villagers' very practical, very desperate need for provisions, it was also undertaken with a certain gleeful abandon. The Spanish foreign minister described it, with admirable under-statement, as "a marked persecution of anyone who possesses something of fortune."[36]

For all the fearsome rhetoric and impromptu radicalism, no one could say precisely what this revolution was about. The Carrancistas left little doubt that they regarded themselves as the winners of the fight against Huerta and that they intended to take control, but Carranza had yet to commit himself on the issue of social reform. There were indisputable radicals within his coalition, but there were also people of every other ideological stripe. The "plan" Carranza had issued to justify his actions against Huerta had very narrowly defined his revolution's objectives — namely, to overthrow the dictator — but was silent on other pressing matters, even though by now it was apparent that the revolution was a far cry from a routine barracks revolt. The changes that mattered now were primarily social and economic. The disparity in objectives, exacerbated by dramatic regional differences that had grown more dramatic during the years of fighting, made it unlikely that any single banner would win universal allegiance.

The signs were ominous from the moment Carranza's army marched into Mexico City. Carranza dispatched two top aides — Antonio I. Villarreal and Luis Cabrera — both with impeccable credentials on reform issues, to explore the prospects for bringing Emiliano Zapata and his armies into their coalition. The southerners pointedly rebuffed the emissaries. Apart from their leader's deep-seated personal antipathy toward Carranza himself, the Zapatistas, it seemed, were profoundly cynical toward and distrustful of government in general. Zapata's official proclamation in response to the Carrancistas' overtures made it clear that freedom of the press, free elections, proper legal proceedings — "all those beautiful democratic principles, all those great words that gave such joy to our fathers and grandfathers" — had "lost their magic for the people." What use was freedom of the press to people who could not read, or free elections to people who did not know the candidates, or proper legal procedures to people who had seldom dealt with courts or legal codes? Revolutions might come and go, but still "the people continue to suffer from poverty and endless disappointments."[37]

THE FIGHT OF THE REGIONS

Despite their mutual suspicions and hostilities, the revolutionary factions agreed to meet in a convention in the northern city of Aguascalientes. Tempers were short and debates heated — the debaters headstrong and clearly in the grip of what one of the most impassioned of them would later call "a revolutionary psychosis."[38] The convention failed despite the sincere efforts of some representatives to find common ground. Carranza, objecting to the strong-arm tactics of his northern rival Pancho Villa, disavowed the convention and ordered his representatives to withdraw. The breakdown of the convention ostensibly left two major contenders to fight a renewed bout of civil war: the "Conventionist" forces, made up of the followers of Villa and Zapata, and the "Constitutionalist" forces of Carranza. The forces of the Villa-Zapata alliance marched on Mexico City to install their man in power, while Carranza abandoned the capital to establish his own provisional government in Veracruz.

In Puebla, as elsewhere in Mexico, the war entered a new phase of unprecedented violence. Most of the factories in the state were sacked for anything that might prove valuable, including even the belts on the machines.[39] The Conventionist forces took Puebla without much of a fight in late December 1914 and turned their immediate attention to looting weapons and cash from businesses and private homes. In early January of 1915, determined Constitutionalist forces under General Alvaro Obregón routed the outnumbered and outgunned armies of Zapata after ferocious street fighting.[40] Prospects for the success of the Conventionist forces were greatly weakened by the profound contrast in the social makeup of the respective armies: the rough-and-tumble cowboys, itinerant workers, miners, muleskinners, and hardscrabble dirt farmers of Villa's north made strange bedfellows with peasants of the south who had lived from the same soil for countless generations. They shared a deep-seated suspicion of government, the rich, and outsiders in general, but not much else. The clash of egos between Villa and Zapata did nothing to enhance the alliance's prospects either, so cracks in the convention's solidarity were not long in appearing. Villa's failure to deliver promised artillery and transport for the siege of Puebla was a costly case in point.[41]

The weaknesses in the Villa-Zapata alliance are notorious, but less often remarked is the fact that neither Villa's nor Zapata's armies were tightly knit: even the smallest fragments of each coalition's fabric tended to fray. Not surprisingly, therefore, Zapata soon encountered problems with his allies in Puebla.

The situation in the Puebla-Tlaxcala region was in many ways strikingly different from the situation in Morelos, the heartland of the Zapatistas' agrarian rebellion. In Morelos, factories were few and primarily devoted to making light consumer goods closely linked to agriculture — such as processed sugar, rum, and cigarettes.[42] The state's principal city, Cuernavaca, was only a short distance from Mexico City and seemed more an appendage of the national capital than a capital in its own right. Mexico City's elites were Morelos's elites: they controlled most of its farms, mills, and markets and held the top jobs in state government. In short, the economy was relatively simple, and local powers were relatively weak and dependent.[43]

The Puebla-Tlaxcala Valley, by contrast, was separated from the national capital by formidable volcanoes, which seemed almost symbolic of a political and cultural divide that had endured since before the Spanish conquest. Puebla's elites were mostly well-heeled Spaniards who identified themselves more with their own region — which they seemed to view as a reasonable facsimile of Spain itself — than with Mexico City. Moreover, by virtue of the existence of the city of Puebla and the abundance of railroad connections, the Puebla-Tlaxcala Valley was among the most heavily industrialized regions in the country as both the nation's premier textile manufacturing region and far and away the national leader in electrical-generating capacity. Apart from these assets, the city boasted numerous smaller industries, such as flour milling and the manufacturing of china, soap, and building materials. This sophisticated commercial-industrial economy flourished amid a predominantly agricultural milieu.

The peasant movement that arose in Morelos was thus relatively more coherent than that of the Puebla-Tlaxcala Valley. Although the Morelos leaders were quite heterogeneous,[44] the people who followed them tended to be either landless sugarcane workers or on their way to becoming landless sugarcane workers. There were few poles of power: the sugar planters and the national elite were one and the same, so when push came to shove the movement had little trouble naming its enemy. In the Puebla-Tlaxcala Valley, however, power was spread among industrialists, managers, hacendados, administrators, and a host of middlemen. The rank and file consisted of a wide array of occupational groups: hired hands, sharecroppers, smallholders, muleskinners, petty merchants, construction workers, factory hands, railroad workers, domestic servants. Many members of the movement had worked in several of these capacities, and identities were thus in flux: the boom in textile manufacturing was recent enough that many factory workers had once been farmhands, and few were more than a generation removed from the peasant village.[45]

The different characters of the two regions made for different types of popular movements and complicated the prospects for an interregional alliance. The Morelos Zapatistas were relatively cohesive, solidary, and uncompromisingly committed to land reform. The Puebla rebels were torn between admiration for the Zapatistas' vision of land reform and a nagging feeling that such a posture was atavistic: what was really needed was not land to the tiller, but reforms that would protect the rights of workers and guarantee them certain minimum rewards.

The unpromising alliance between the rebel groups of Morelos and Puebla worked well enough as long as the local groups had the usurper Huerta as their common enemy. With the breakdown of the convention and the fateful split among revolutionary factions, the alliance was weakened by hitherto unde-tected stresses and strains. No one embodied the tortured ambiguity of the Puebla-Tlaxcala Valley's social and economic structure more than the man who was about to become the region's outstanding rebel leader, General Domingo Arenas.

DOMINGO ARENAS

Domingo Arenas hailed from Zacatelco, Tlaxcala. In 1910, Zacatelco was a relatively large village of five thousand souls on the Mexican Railway line about sixteen miles southeast of San Martín Texmelucan.[46] Arenas was then twenty-two years old, the son of a poor campesino family. He had only two years of formal schooling, but experience had taught him much about the social and economic forces at work in his home region. At various times, he had tended sheep for his family, worked as a field hand on local haciendas, sold bread and tortillas in local towns and factories, and manned the spindles in nearby textile mills. At the outset of the revolution, his charisma and ambition attracted the attention of the leaders of the Maderista movement, who set him to drilling raw recruits from the villages around Zacatelco in anticipation of the uprising. Fate dealt perversely with the young Arenas, however: one day during drills a young soldier's rifle fired accidentally, killing one man and wounding Arenas in the left arm. With no immediate medical attention, the wound festered, and his arm was later amputated in a Tlaxcala hospital, earning Arenas a nickname he would carry through his few remaining years — "El Manco" ("the One-Armed Man").[47]

Arenas's revolutionary commitment continued to cost him dearly. In the early days of the fighting, Tlaxcalan authorities sought to curb his political activity by jailing his wife and young son and holding them for more than a year. Arenas himself was imprisoned in Puebla City for political reasons from May 1912 to May 1913. Upon his release, he joined the rebel forces in the war against Huerta and distinguished himself in fighting throughout Tlaxcala, Puebla, Veracruz, Hidalgo, Morelos, and Mexico state. By the start of 1914, he had attained the rank of general. When his immediate superior, General Felipe

Villegas, was killed in action, Arenas succeeded him to the command of the Xicohténcatl Brigade.

When the fight against Huerta was won and incipient dissension in the rebel ranks became apparent, Arenas prevaricated. He obliged when the Constitutionalist commanders ordered him to inventory properties of enemies of the revolution, which were to be taken over by the government, and was likewise agreeable when Máximo Rojas, a man with antecedents similar to his own, was named interim governor of Tlaxcala. But he had trouble accepting the growing indications that the northern revolutionaries were contemplating a government of occupation in his home region. Local troops, tested and hardened by years of war, were crowded out by Yaquí Indians who made up a large part of the Constitutionalist army. Still worse, among all the leaders of the anti-Huerta struggle, Rojas was the only one the Constitutionalists acknowledged as a general. Even Rojas, it seemed, was taken for a toady. When Carranza visited Tlaxcala and Puebla in early November, the swarthy, diminutive Rojas seemed to lurk rather obsequiously in the long shadows of the first chief and his lanky, light-complected Coahuilan confidant, Francisco Coss. The supreme commander of the Army of the Northeast, General Pablo González, drove the point home by demoting Domingo Arenas to the rank of colonel. Upon hearing the news, Arenas made a dramatic show of removing the brass Mexican eagle from his hat and hurling it disgustedly into the dirt.[48]

For a few weeks after that, "El Manco" continued to feign cooperation with the northerners, but he had decided his course by the end of October, even before the convention had made the revolutionary schism official. On October 28, he wrote to Zapata that "since 1910 when I rose in arms against bad government, the banner I held aloft and continue to hold aloft is yours." Arenas guessed that he could count on eight hundred cavalry and three hundred infantry, but that the business of raising troops would be made easier if Zapata could send ammunition and paper currency.[49] Although scarcely noticeable at the time, something ominous was evident even in these early contacts. Zapata expressed satisfaction at Arenas's defection from the Constitutionalist ranks, but he had little ammunition to spare, and he flatly refused to send paper money "because he found this means of maintaining troops repugnant."[50] Revolutionary soldiers should serve for ideals, not for cash.

Arenas formally announced his rebellion against Carranza on November 12, and before long the one-armed man was the dominant power throughout much of the rural Puebla-Tlaxcala Valley. It was with his help that the Zapatistas were able to take the city of Puebla in the closing days of 1914 in a series of fierce battles that left Arenas severely wounded. The victory was, as already noted, fleeting: on January 5, 1915, Carranza's armies struck them a blow from which they would never recover, effectively demolishing any hopes for peace in Mexico.

While the Evanses endured their fretful exile in Charleston, South Carolina, living on constantly dwindling savings and some meager dividends, the factional struggle turned chaotic and unimaginably violent. Landowners like the Evanses despaired not only that their properties were imperiled, but also that there seemed to be no authority to which they might complain. Harry appealed for help from the British legation, but the reply he received was not encouraging: "I believe you will not doubt my good will to assist you," wrote the chargé d'affaires, "but my difficulty is how to do so, as it is now some weeks since there has been any Ministry of Foreign Affairs in the country, whilst Authorities in power have been changing with a rapidity which is truly bewildering."[51]

The Poblanos quickly proved themselves a source of constant annoyance to Emiliano Zapata. Telegrams from villagers of that state seemed to bring only news of rivalry, rancor, and opportunism — complaints that Zapata's own generals and soldiers were extorting their money, stealing and killing their livestock, burning their crops, and generally terrorizing everyone. One village pleaded with Zapata to withdraw his forces, then send weapons to the villagers so that they could do their own fighting.[52]

Zapata did his best to keep control, decreeing summary justice for any soldiers who harrassed noncombatants, but the locals of the Puebla-Tlaxcala Valley began to look more and more like potential enemies. To the locals, on the other hand, the Zapatistas looked more and more like foreign invaders. Lacking outside funding for their rebellion, the Zapatistas lived as predators on the haciendas, appropriating crops, oxen, sheep, forage, and firewood. They raided factories and mills for fabric and yarn to make cheap cotton clothing and for wheat and flour to feed the troops or to distribute among the poor. The Constitutionalists, hoping to impair the guerrillas' ability to live off the land, burned crops and killed livestock. When the Zapatistas retaliated, villagers were caught in the cross fire.[53] It is hardly surprising, given this style of warfare, that the majority of noncombatant villagers found much fault with both parties.

Some potential for long-term improvement did exist, however, for the bitter factional struggle drew much attention to the rural areas. It was becoming increasingly apparent that the hearts and minds of peasants would be crucial weapons in the fight. The success of Zapata's movement in winning adherents suggested that promises of land and local autonomy were the currency needed to purchase those hearts and minds, so the factions went into the business of minting such promises.

In truth, for the present, rural folk were not much in the market for ideals: the simple struggle for survival commanded their greatest attention. Although the object of the war may have been to end the misery of the common people of the country, it was those very people who suffered the most. Their hunger was acute, especially in 1915 when late frosts wiped out much of Puebla's corn crop.[54] Money was available—a chaotic jumble of paper notes issued by the various factions—but its value was uncertain, and there was nothing much to buy anyway. The Puebla-Tlaxcala Valley, as the British legation explained regretfully to an anxious Harry Evans in May 1915, was "nominally" controlled by the Constitutionalists, but "it is not in their power. Their writs do not run."[55]

So the economy reverted to the primitive: people bartered for whatever they could get or combed the woods and hills in search of herbs and edible plants. Winning hearts and minds in this milieu would be no easy thing. The Zapatistas seemed to have the advantage, but Carranza was far from ready to admit defeat. He sent his most trusted men to govern the territories he controlled, with instructions to do "everything possible to gain the support and friendship of the people."[56] Many of those leaders undertook the task with remarkable energy, sincerity, and imagination. Successive governors of Puebla vied with one another to pass progressive legislation designed to appeal to the common people—setting price controls, forgiving the debts of hacienda peons, quadrupling wages, passing new labor codes, building schools and clinics, revising tax schedules, restricting the church and clergy, and more.[57] Of course, there was a large element of fiction in their actions because few citizens were either impressed or troubled by the pompous decrees of a government that might be toppled at any moment. Writer Martín Luis Guzmán describes a Constitutionalist general who "with every twenty words . . . outlined a plan which, if put into effect, would have changed the face of the earth."[58]

On January 6, 1915, Carranza issued a law that might indeed have changed the face of at least a portion of the earth because it called for a radical redistribution of property and wealth in Mexico. The Law of January 6 was authored primarily by Luis Cabrera, one of the men Carranza had sent to make peace with the Zapatistas in August of 1914. By 1915, some considered Cabrera to be nothing less than "the brains of the revolution."[59] In 1912, he had defied Madero by insisting that sending his armies to impose "law and order" was not the way to peace, which would never come, he said, so long as the agrarian problem remained unsolved. In that 1912 speech, Cabrera presented Congress with a vision of Mexico's future that clashed with the legacy of Mexican liberalism. For decades, the most progressive elements in Mexican politics had held that the way to the future was lighted by northern Europe and the United States, those countries where secular science, individualism, and private property had triumphed. According to those liberal thinkers, the enemy was Mexico's colonial heritage, peopled by savage Indians, benighted peasants, reactionary priests, unreconstructed monarchists, acquisitive oligarchs—all of those elements that seemed so thoroughly antimodern.

Although Cabrera tepidly embraced some elements of the liberal agenda, he also invoked a decidedly romantic view of his country's past and of its rural population. The year 1856 appeared to him as the end of an idyllic era during which Indian villages had lived comfortably with the same lands that had been guaranteed them under colonial law, evolving efficient, small-scale democracies. The liberal agrarian legislation of that year had stripped the Indians of their lands, leaving them an impoverished and dependent people. At the same time, the liberal laws had been a boon to the oversized, inefficient, parasitic hacienda — for Cabrera and his ilk, the "emblem of all that the Revolution opposed."[60] Cabrera's idea was to confiscate the bulk of lands from the large haciendas, reducing them to "small properties," which could be intensively and efficiently farmed. The rest of those lands would become communal *ejidos,* to be distributed among the villages near the hacienda boundaries. Theoretically, the *ejidatarios* (as the beneficiaries of the land grants were known) would eventually increase their holdings to rival those of the ex-haciendas, and the ideal of the medium-sized property would triumph.

The ejido was supposed to be transitional. For the time being, however, it was a curious and ambiguous concept of property that would never be quite clarified: the land would be administered by the community, worked by individuals on individual plots — all within limits set by the state, which technically remained the land's owner. The ejidatarios could not sell the land and could lose their right to it by failing to cultivate it for two years running. Three quarters of a century later, many ejidatarios were still unclear as to who actually owned the land they worked.[61]

As far as the villagers of the Puebla-Tlaxcala Valley were concerned, the law's most important provision was not the one that called for "restitution" to the villages of lands seized by the haciendas since 1856. The law took account of the fact that many villages had not lost their lands since 1856 or if they had, would find it impossible to prove. Any village, then, that could prove it lacked sufficient land to satisfy the needs of its residents was eligible for land in the form of *dotación* (an outright grant).

The circumstances under which the law was promulgated were hardly conducive to careful and thorough reasoning. There was, after all, a war on, and the Law of January 6 was intended largely as a weapon in that war. The law failed to address a number of critical issues — such as how and to what extent expropriated landowners would be compensated. The fine points of agrarian reform procedure would emerge subsequently in an endless stream of decrees and circulars, giving the not inaccurate impression that the government was making up the details as it went along.

Some of the law's ambiguities were probably intentional. Although Carranza allowed the law to be promulgated in his government's name, he was himself a large landowner with little enthusiasm for agrarian reform. He not only decried the despoiling of the rich, but, like most large landowners of the day, he doubted the capacity of the poor to make good use of any lands they received. Aides who worked on the agrarian problem in his government held the impression that he wished to proceed very slowly on the issue so as to avoid "confusing and agitating the people."[62] The law was an expedient and as such probably did give a major boost to Carranza's military and political fortunes. While he reaped these benefits, however, Carranza was also issuing further circulars that seemed designed to make the agrarian reform process as slow and tortuous as possible.[63]

Indeed, even in its original conception, the law had provisions that were sure to make it a clumsy vehicle. For one thing, although the local communities were responsible for beginning the reform process by creating committees, drawing up petitions, and requesting inspections, there was never any doubt that the federal government had made itself the ultimate arbiter in agrarian matters. All grants were to be considered "provisional" until approved by the president of the republic himself, a byzantine agrarian bureaucracy ensuring that the process would be slow. Worse still, landowners who felt wronged were explicitly offered recourse to the courts, where within a year they could appeal for *amparo,* or a stay of execution. Not surprisingly, the landowners were quick to avail themselves of the option, and the volume of their claims promised to slow the agrarian reform to a sluggish crawl.

The Constitutionalist governments of Puebla and Tlaxcala went dutifully through the motions of carrying out their agrarian reform, setting up their state agrarian commissions and taking up petitions for land with much fanfare.[64] But, for the moment, the Constitutionalists did not control enough of the Puebla-Tlaxcala Valley to make a real difference. The Zapatistas still had thousands of men operating in Puebla in 1915, and between guerrilla actions they went through the motions of carrying out an agrarian reform of their own under a law expedited October 26, 1915, and overseen by Domingo Arenas.

EL MANCO'S TREASON

While Arenas carried out the Zapatistas' law, the Constitutionalists were demolishing Villa's forces in the north. By the end of the summer of 1915 it was clear that Villa had only a feeble capacity for continued resistance.[65] In October, the Constitutionalists capped their military success with a diplomatic one by securing political recognition from the United States. With that recognition came greater access to arms and an embargo on the same to their enemies. With Villa under control and a renewed confidence, Carranza's best generals were again free to turn their full attention to securing the vital Mexico City–Veracruz axis.

The campaign quickly bore fruit. By the end of 1915, Arenas had ceased to be a serious military threat to the Constitutionalists, for he effectively controlled only a small region at the feet of the volcanoes.[66] Lacking the strength for frontal assaults, the Puebla Zapatistas instead launched savage terrorist attacks against the trains, blowing them up with dynamite bombs or contact mines, then following up with volleys of rifle fire.[67] It was a costly irritation for the Constitutionalists, one they were resolved to contain.

As Arenas's military fortunes declined, so did his relations with his Zapatista allies. Zapata seemed to lack confidence in the wiry one-armed general: by early 1916, Arenas was practically begging Zapata to send him funds to help feed and pay his troops, who were, he said, "in constant combat." Although he admitted to having lost control of the railroads, he boasted that he could still be useful in obstructing road traffic through the mountain passes.[68] But by September of 1916, as Zapata's movement lived some of its darkest hours, Arenas's defection was in the air. He complained constantly that Zapata's other chiefs were abusive and corrupt, confiscating haciendas only to run them as personal fiefs. He continued, however, to profess personal loyalty to Zapata and to his Plan of Ayala. That plan, he assured Zapata with a considerable flourish, "shall triumph, because it is not merely the energies of all of the aborigines that are arrayed against our enemy; but also the hurricane winds of the Puebla mountains, the freezing gusts from the volcanoes, even the alpine birds of prey. We Indians must win, because through the course of generations we have assimilated the strength of the wild beasts of the woods, the hardness of immovable basalt, the resistance of the roots that bear up beneath the rolling boulder, and the divine tenderness of the song of the forests."[69]

In August of 1915, Carranza announced that any Zapatista who surrendered would receive full amnesty. Some took the offer, others were sorely tempted, and everyone began to look like a potential traitor. Zapata's coolness and troubled relations with his comrades gave Arenas ample grounds for his impending betrayal. These "push" factors were joined by a "pull" factor, though: the Constitutionalists really *needed* Arenas. With him on their side, they could practically eliminate the Zapatista threat to the railroads while securing control of the railroads from other predators. In order to attract Arenas, they were prepared to offer him "unification" on his own terms, rather than an ignominious "surrender." Arenas was able to demand not only recognition of his rank, but also recognition of his military land grants and considerable autonomy in carrying further his regional agrarian reform.

On December 1, 1915, Arenas met with General Cesáreo Castro near the town of Huejotzingo — only a few miles from the Evans hacienda — and signed a pact "unifying" his forces with those of the Carrancistas. He tried to persuade Zapata that he had not "surrendered" but was in fact advancing the cause

General Domingo Arenas—"We Indians must win." *Credit:* Mario Ramírez Rancaño, *Domingo y Cirilo Arenas en la Revolución Mexicana* (Mexico City: Centro de Estudios Históricos del Agrarismo en México, 1991).

through subterfuge.[70] Of course, the notion that he could act as a double agent behind Constitutionalist lines was far-fetched, and Zapata did not buy it. The betrayal came at an especially bad moment, for the Zapatistas were once again very much on the defensive militarily. Worst of all, in January of 1917 the Constitutionalists lived up to their name by issuing a new constitution, one that contained an agrarian reform article that went even further than the Law of January 6. In setting itself up as a legitimate champion of agrarianism, the Constitutionalist government stole much of the Zapatistas' thunder. On December 15, Zapata's headquarters issued a manifesto charging that Arenas had sold out the Plan of Ayala "for the thirty coins of Judas" and formally sentenced him to death, together with anyone who continued to follow him after January 5, 1917.

For their part, many Constitutionalists found the cocky little general annoying. The tenacious Zapatistas had managed to survive years of the Constitutionalists' massive weaponry and their most prestigious strategists, yet Arenas had no sooner switched sides than he was boasting that he could pacify Morelos within six months if only he were provided with "foodstuffs instead of machine guns, clothing . . . seeds, agricultural machinery and livestock . . . two hundred engineers to survey lands, and three hundred schoolteachers with materials for three hundred schools."[71] Not only was he insufferably arrogant, but perhaps really a closet Zapatista. For the moment, however, he was untouchable. The day of reckoning would come, and some urged that his loyalty be tested by fire.

THE NEW MASTERS

Whichever side Arenas was really on — he himself probably did not quite know for sure — he was bad news for the local landlords. In early December 1916, Arenas established his headquarters in the city of San Martín Texmelucan, a two-and-a-half-mile ride from the Evans hacienda, San Pedro Coxtocán. From there, he devoted his attention to doing what others had done before: raiding haciendas, carving up hacienda lands, and making presents of those lands to the peasants. For the landowners, the problem was that Arenas, unlike his predecessors, was not an outlaw. He had the full backing of the municipal government of San Martín, which gave him provisions and set him up in an office in the municipal palace. Even the local church supplied him with food, money, and furniture.[72] By May, he had put himself in charge of the judiciary at the district seat of Huejotzingo and was entertaining complaints from the local villagers.[73] The landowners could control some matters with bribes to key state officials and military men,[74] but in the Texmelucan Valley and southwestern Tlaxcala, Arenas had his way, and he devoted himself passionately to the cause of seizing and distributing land. The landowners later described his land reform methods derisively: "A military chief, acting alone and ignorant of the case, with no calculations of any kind and at his whim, ascends to the church tower of a village, and with a looking glass surveys all of the land he is able to see; and that is how he sets the grant."[75]

The Arenista land reform was hardly free from error and abuse. Like their fellow Constitutionalists, Arenas's forces sometimes confiscated properties with high commercial potential and worked them directly and rapaciously to raise war funds. Corruption, irregularity, and arbitrariness reared their ugly heads, foreshadowing some of the meanness that would later attend more enduring land reform efforts. Unscrupulous officers enriched themselves at the expense of the communities or used their control of lands to reward friends and punish enemies. Villagers who had acquired small plots prior to the revolution or who had made sharecropping arrangements with hacendados in violation of the interests of would-be squatters were singled out for special vengeance.

For many, however, the period of Arenista dominance seemed almost too good to be true. As one Arenista recalled many years later, the word from Arenas's headquarters was, "those who wish to go on fighting, fine; those who don't, cultivate the land. And it was a dream, at last we really felt ourselves the new masters."[76] Arenas shared this optimism. In February 1917 he wrote to a friend that at last "passions have dissipated, energies have grown more serene, and people who yesterday went mad over matters of petty detail . . . today join with us in a sublime embrace of brotherhood, to form the bases of a new Mexico."[77]

Yet there was always something anarchic and unreal about Arenas's agrarian reform, as if the villagers knew their tenure as masters of the land would not last. Arenas tried to allay their fears with inspirational remarks on the promises of the revolution and exhortations on no longer submitting humbly to oppression.[78] Hacienda invasions were often spontaneous acts by villagers taking advantage of the landlords' absence to sow their corn and beans on hacienda lands, but the villagers never quite shook the disquieting sense that the entire enterprise was spurious and irregular — that the landlords would return soon and the government would betray them. For now, though, they simply worked the lands without waiting for commissions and courts to decide on the legitimacy of their ownership and without holding back a share of the crop for the hacienda. It was generally understood that, for the moment, the land was owned by all the villagers in common, and its fruits were to be distributed according to each family's needs.[79] Arenas talked of founding schools and tried to bring everyone into the fold — including even the *acasillados,* former dependent hacienda workers who were technically excluded from the agrarian reform — by forming agricultural colonies. Even occasional Zapatista envoys were compelled to confess that Arenas was doing well. In Arenas territory, said one, "there is no reason to go on fighting."[80]

THE DEATH OF EL MANCO

The villagers were right in supposing this lotus land to be fleeting. As Constitutionalist officials constantly reminded them, all of those land grants were merely "military" in nature and thus would have to be reviewed by many people, up to the president himself, before they were assured. The days of the Arenista land reform — like the days of General Arenas himself — were numbered.

Arenas's land reform was a gamble on long odds. His power depended on the continued external threat to the railroads; once that was brought under control, he would be expendable.[81] He hoped he would be able to effect irreversible changes before he lost his bailiwick. Some Constitutionalist officers took Arenas's zeal for land reform as evidence that he held treason in his heart, so they sought to test his loyalty by ordering him to fight the Zapatistas. Occasionally, Arenas would obey, at one point very nearly killing Emiliano Zapata's brother Eufemio, and at another igniting the southern leader's wrath by allegedly stealing his favorite horse.[82]

Some landowners, meanwhile, began to pioneer methods of obfuscation, subterfuge, and force that they hoped would regain them a sure hold on their lands. Many took advantage of the general confusion of the moment to cut deals with the few villagers who had the means to buy land and were suspicious of the whole notion of land reform.[83] Others, like the resourceful Spaniard Marcelino Presno, sought to evade constitutional restrictions on the amount of acreage an individual could own by "selling" his various estates to family members and granting himself power of attorney for all of them. The maneuver was obvious chicanery — two of his sons were still minors (a remarkable fact in view of Presno's advanced age) when they supposedly purchased their enormous estates — but legally unassailable.[84] Some landowners, including Harry Evans, had signed sharecropping contracts before fleeing the land, hoping that when they eventually returned, they could make a brief for the inviolability of those contracts, using them as grounds to eject squatters and to counteract the effects of the impromptu agrarian reform.

In short, Arenas had his share of challengers. Ironically, the most deadly were his own former allies and fellow *agraristas,* the Zapatistas. Arenas played a dangerous game, professing unswerving loyalty to the Constitutionalists even while teasing the Zapatistas with hints that he might rejoin them. Eventually, top Arenista and Zapatista chiefs arranged to meet on August 30, 1917, at a deserted village on Popocatépetl's lonely slopes. The agenda was uncertain. The

Zapatistas claimed Arenas wished to formalize his promise to rejoin their forces, whereas the Arenistas claimed their chief went to the meeting in order to accept the surrender of several top Zapatista officers.

There is no telling what the meeting was supposed to be about, just as there is no telling what in fact took place there. The only certainty is that, at the end of it, Domingo Arenas was dead. Perhaps he showed up, hat in hand as if to surrender, but with his men hidden in a perfidious ambush. Perhaps — as the Arenistas told it — he showed up to the meeting the picture of ingenuousness, with warm greetings for all and no suspicion of the treachery that awaited him, only to be gunned down by mounted Zapatista riflemen. Perhaps he died — as some versions have it — in hand-to-hand combat with Zapatista general Gildardo Magaña. One especially lurid account maintains that his head was cut off and sent to Zapata's headquarters at Tlaltizapan, Morelos, while a Zapatista general calmly disemboweled the remainder of the body, fed the entrails to the dogs, stuffed the ravaged carcass with lime and hay, and hung it from a tree until it rotted.[85]

In the end, there is no great urgency to name the true villains of the episode, for none of the factions in the struggle had a monopoly on virtue. Arenas's political influence was about to end in any case. Had he not been killed on Popocatépetl, his influence would gradually have been sapped by a regime indisposed to sanction freewheeling reforms that left bureaucrats and top officials playing catch-up.

Not surprisingly, both the Zapatistas and Carrancistas tried to capitalize on Arenas's death. In late September, Zapata issued appeals to ex-Arenistas, written in both Spanish and Náhuatl, assuring them that they were not to blame for having been duped by their late leader's false promises or for having been cowed by the threats of a man so "bloody and cruel." They would be offered safe conduct and complete amnesty if they wished to join the "Liberating Army of the South."[86] A few took the offer, but most probably found the temptation eminently resistible, for Zapata's movement was moribund. In December, the Zapatistas were chased from their mountain retreat at Tochimilco by Domingo Arenas's avenging younger brother, Cirilo, who had inherited command of the "Arenas Division" of the Constitutionalist Army.[87]

For its part, the government hoped that Arenas's death would clear the way for the stable constitutional regime they had in mind. In Puebla, the long era of government by northern interlopers came to an end with the election that summer of native son Alfonso Cabrera, the younger brother of Carranza's ideologue, Luis Cabrera. To Cabrera would fall the thankless task of trying to "normalize" Arenas's military land grants, which essentially meant handing them back to the landowners while the bureaucrats deliberated. At the end of Cabrera's first six months in office, only 38 out of 283 petitions for land had been approved by the state agrarian commission, and of those only 12 were approved by Carranza.[88] As the Constitutionalists' bureaucratic monster lumbered into action, the government decreed that firearms must be licensed, a clear sign that it meant to end the feast of vultures.[89] Under these circumstances, villagers had to decide whether to cast their lot with the lost cause of Zapatismo or humbly to ask the bureaucrats for definitive title to the lands that Arenas had given them — or at least some portion of those lands.

While the villagers prepared their petitions, entertained inspectors and engineers, and waited for word, landowners such as Harry Evans returned, hoping that the new order would treat them kindly. He made little headway in reestablishing his landownership, however, before he died suddenly in November of 1917.

Harry's widow would now enter the picture, resolved to take up the fight.

Four

"Sir abbot, and ye men of lawe,
Now have I holde my daye,
Now shall I have my londe agayne,
For ought that you can saye."
—*A Lytell Geste of Robyn Hode*

WHEN ROSALIE EVANS left for Mexico on January 3, 1918, she took some comfort in the knowledge that her undertaking would be hazardous. "I have wondered," she confessed to her husband's ghost, "if that would not be a justifiable case of suicide. I even fear it would be misunderstood as cowardice as I so long to die."[1]

Mexico was clearly capable of accommodating a death wish. The train Mrs. Evans and her servant rode on was packed with rude men, licentious women, and a conductor who hounded them with insults. Outside, the spectacle was bleaker still. Rebels had torn up whole sections of track, putting the train twelve hours behind schedule, and poverty and desolation were everywhere. "A sweeping wind is driving dust along," Mrs. Evans observed sadly, "and at every station ragged children and forlorn gaunt women sell their normal *dulces* and *tortas compuestas.*"[2]

She returned to a Mexico different from the one she had known before the war, made stranger still by the fact that Harry was not waiting for her there. She tried to reach him, spending hours praying by the grave that mourners had covered with violets or waiting patiently in the hospital room where he had died. Her efforts bore fruit one late night in the death room. She awoke at midnight, feeling surrounded by "something like electricity, but it had a body, for each pressure I gave with the hand was given again. Yet it seemed all over me." An ethereal Harry sat in a chair, and talked to her for hours. "Though your answer was not clear," she wrote to Harry later, "when I asked you if you would come often you said it would be difficult. I then cried out, 'but in the years to come will it be harder?,' and I think you answered 'yes' but of that I am not sure as I was waking and you were leaving me."[3]

Mrs. Evans's preoccupation with death and the spirit world was not so exotic among her contemporaries. A good portion of the real world had been devastated by the unprecedented brutality of World War I, and in a world so suddenly filled with bereft people, the grieving widow had much company. As people sought solace from fortune-tellers and mediums, contacting the departed became a growth industry. In Britain, authorities dusted off the old Witchcraft and Vagrancy Acts to prosecute charlatans, and such respectable figures as Arthur Conan Doyle and the physicist Sir Oliver Lodge declared their conversion to spiritualism and carried their message throughout the world.[4] In Mexico, even a hardened character like Diego Kennedy, an American hacendado and standard bearer of the intransigent landlords of Tlaxcala, found solace in the unseen world. Mrs. Evans sought his advice only reluctantly, having earlier been repelled by his rigid demeanor. Her predilection was partly confirmed when he offered no condolences on her husband's death. But he warmed to the topic of necromancy, acknowledging that his mother was a practicing spiritualist and offering to put Mrs. Evans in touch with a medium.[5]

Mrs. Evans was encouraged. If the daunting chasm separating life and death could be spanned, then how great a challenge could it be to fight off a corrupt government and hordes of peasants to regain her property?

MEXICO, 1918

It was not only the absence of Harry that made Mexico so much more frightening than it had once been. Crime was rampant and spared few. Factory owners claimed they could not pay their workers because the couriers who moved the payroll funds from bank to factory were routinely robbed. Milkmen left off making rounds after being repeatedly relieved of their jugs, mules, and carts. On Mrs. Evans's first trip to Puebla City after she returned to Mexico, robbers leaned brazenly through the windows while the train waited to leave the station, trying to snatch passengers' luggage. At the junction at Apizaco, conductors warned passengers to hug their bags close, for they expected a rebel attack and would have to douse the lights for three hours or so. Robbers, they warned, were in their element in the darkness.[6]

The high incidence of crime, coupled with the penury of the state treasury, brought services practically to a standstill. Uncollected garbage piled up in the streets of Puebla and Cholula. Trolleys and streetcars ran at their peril over degenerated roads, tracks, and bridges. The city's central streets, once the promenade of Puebla's fashionable aristocracy, were now the haunt of beggars, soldiers, and growing numbers of prostitutes who openly plied their trade. Clinics reported alarming increases in venereal disease and alcoholism.

Then, in the winter of 1918, the Spanish influenza besieged this already weakened organism. Puebla City suffered mortality twenty times Mexico City's. Rosalie Evans described it as "a deserted city, so many people had died of the plague."[7] Public health workers confessed themselves unable to count the corpses, and by November more than a hundred corpses lay piled in the municipal cemetery, unburied for want of space. Hard on the heels of the influenza epidemic came the ravages of tuberculosis, typhus, and famine. In the rural villages, where conditions were notoriously unsanitary and treatment facilities nonexistent, conditions were far worse. "The mountains looked bare and cold," wrote Rosalie Evans in November. "A mist hung over the cities — the cities of the dead. The ground was parched and a few Indians crouched by fires in the open, coughing."[8] Small carts reconnoitered the dirt streets of the villages, collecting the dead and dying. Survivors still swear they saw people who were still barely breathing thrown into mass graves.[9]

CONFLICT AT THE GRASS ROOTS

In the villages, the germs of deadly disease were joined by those of incipient internal conflict, although years later the villagers would look back on the early days of the agrarian reform and recall only blissful solidarity. From the outset, the legal process of petitioning for land was daunting. In San Lucas Atoyatenco, on the eastern border of San Martín Texmelucan, some 214 families sent the National Agrarian Commission a petition containing titles to lands they claimed they had rightfully owned since colonial days — lands that had been "publicly and notoriously" usurped around 1860 by the surrounding haciendas and *ranchos*. But after examining the titles, the commission's department of paleography declared them to be forgeries.[10] Two other villages bordering on San Pedro Coxtocán — Santa María Moyotzingo and San Jerónimo Tianguismanalco — also initially claimed *despojo* (despoilment) and asked for "restitution," but were similarly embarrassed in their efforts to substantiate their claims.[11] Some villagers began to doubt the competence of their representatives.

Although the federal government reserved for itself the role of ultimate arbiter, it insisted that all petitions for land be made on the initiative of the villagers themselves, which entailed a degree of pressure and unaccustomed responsibility that made conflict inevitable. From the outset, some villagers demurred on the land question, whereas others were zealous in support of reform. The villages had little experience with elections and committees, so agrarian matters often fell into the hands of the most brazen or the least scrupulous individuals.

Along with the charges of ineptitude came charges of gross malfeasance. In Santa María Moyotzingo, the largest of the villages surrounding San Pedro, Vicente Pérez, the original president of the village's *comité particular ejecutivo* ("special executive committee") oversaw the informal distribution of large chunks of San Pedro Coxtocán and three other estates among the villagers. In June 1917, however, Pérez was ousted from his post by angry villagers who charged him with favoring family and friends in the distribution of land and with collecting a variety of unauthorized fees.[12]

In such circumstances, there was widespread skepticism among the villagers, which a few enterprising hacendados — such as Harry Evans's friend, the indefatigable old Spaniard Marcelino Presno — did their best to exploit. Using a few still loyal former hacienda servants as their mouthpiece, they spread the word that the government's agrarian reform was a ruse and that anyone simple enough to fall for it would "suffer disastrous consequences in their person and interests." Ricardo García, an agrarian engineer sent to scout out several villages in April 1918, was met with near homicidal rage when he tried to take an agrarian census of the village of Santa Ana Xalmimilulco. Pure coincidence saved him: it so happened that General Cirilo Arenas — younger brother of the late General Domingo Arenas, who had joined the government side and been rewarded with military command of the zone of San Martín Texmelucan — was in town that day. Cirilo managed to calm aroused passions by explaining to the villagers that the "Superior Government" was "generously fulfilling the revolutionary principles" and that they need fear no harmful effects should they cooperate with García.[13]

It must have been singularly confusing, then, when Cirilo himself rose in arms against Carranza's government only a few weeks later. He had been only fifteen years old at the start of the revolution, and in the spring of 1918 he was not yet twenty-three. He had both of his arms, as well as his brother's famous name and passion for agrarianism, and he had unarguably survived a baptism by fire, but he seems to have lacked his brother's charisma, savvy, and instinct for command. The Constitutionalists expected to neutralize him with little trouble. They rolled back and obstructed land distributions,[14] and gradually supplanted the locals who made up the Arenas Division (now under Cirilo's command) with outsiders. In early May, Constitutionalist forces headed for San Martín Texmelucan with orders to complete the disarmament of the Arenas Division, but when they arrived, they found the city deserted: Cirilo Arenas and his men had already taken to the mountains. Having seen how the wind was blowing, Cirilo had decided not to stick around to find out just what the first chief had in mind.[15] Carranza, predictably enough, sent two of his northern generals — Manuel Laveaga and Clotilde Sosa — together with their Yaquí foot soldiers to take charge of the situation.[16]

Cirilo Arenas and his men would spend the next several years living on the slopes of the great volcanoes. It was a rugged life. Ill-clad, the rebels suffered the cold and heat, the thin air, and all the hardships to be found at over ten thousand feet of altitude. They slept in small caves or in the open fields, drank from thin streams or from rainwater that formed in puddles in the roads and fields, ate whatever they could cultivate, kill, or commandeer. As time went on, some realized that it was easier to make deals with the hacendados than to risk life and limb in daring raids. Some turned enforcers, protecting properties from other rebels in exchange for cash or supplies. Others occasionally kidnapped employees of recalcitrant haciendas for ransom. The mountainside was crowded, and the mountain rebels had a subculture all their own.[17]

In addition, the uncertain life of the mountain rebel did not make for secure alliances. Cirilo Arenas was at first welcomed enthusiastically by the Zapatistas, desperation helping to erase the memory of old betrayals. In fact, Zapata predicted hopefully that with Arenas and others swelling the rebel ranks, the Constitutionalists would be defeated within a month and the people would at last be able to reclaim the sovereignty "so villanously disavowed by the despotic Old Man with the ridiculous whiskers."[18] This collection of so many disparate rebels — some fighting to restore old privilege, others aiming to assuage local grievances against the northerners' predatory style, still others holding out stubbornly for an ideal — needed more than their common hatred of a "despotic old man" to unite them, however, and Arenas soon found himself drifting in and out of unlikely and brittle alliances, as his brother had done before him.

To noncombatant villagers, such shifting alliances must have been dizzying. The various factions vied with one another to exploit their confusion. The Zapatistas distributed fliers assuring the people that the Constitutionalists had no intention of giving them land. Had they not heard such false promises from every government since Madero's? The villagers, said the Zapatistas, should seize the day "and proceed without delay to redistribute [land] among their inhabitants, for once peace arrives and the government is established, we risk being made victims of the intrigues of the rich."[19]

For most villagers of the Puebla-Tlaxcala Valley, the Zapatistas were hardly an ideal alternative. The kinds of lawlessness they counseled might indeed have serious repercussions should they come out the losers. Apart from advising the villagers to court disaster, the Zapatistas were also a party to the dangerous cross fire in which noncombatant villagers were caught, and despite their inspirational rhetoric, they did not deal gently with opponents or fence-sitters.

Yet the pressure to decide among the bewildering array of rebel factions was growing less imperative by the day for the villagers of the Puebla-Tlaxcala Valley. Rebellions of the sort led by Zapata or the Arenas brothers were becoming anachronistic. Many prominent radical agrarian agitators had not followed their erstwhile leaders into rebellion but, claiming the agrarian mantle for themselves, had determined to try their luck in more conventional political channels. By 1918, they were championing the agrarian cause in the national Congress. Others within the rebel ranks waited anxiously for an opportunity to lay down their arms without suffering too great a humiliation.

A VISIT TO SAN PEDRO

When Rosalie Evans returned to Mexico, she found the villagers in an uncertain mood. She added one more voice to a devil's chorus of people claiming to have the interests of ordinary Mexicans at heart. The trouble, of course, was in knowing whom to believe.

Mrs. Evans spent the months from January to May bickering with bureaucrats, tax collectors, and politicians so that eventually her frustations in the realm of Mexican officialdom persuaded her of the need to visit her hacienda in person—a bold move "for a woman," as some patronizingly pointed out. In fact, it would have been a bold move for anyone, and few hacendados of the region were willing to risk it. It was not just the obstinacy of the bureaucrats that drove Mrs. Evans to this extreme. Her firm, almost religious resolve had not weakened since January, when, newly widowed, she had chosen to confront her grief aggressively. "I seem to be back again in my fourteenth year,"[20] she had told her sister then, "with an unhampered spirit that has at last established a most imperfect communication with the world it then stood for. The intervening years have disappeared . . . , and even the uncertainties of it all no longer daunt me. At last all fever, nervousness, bodily earthly fear have left me. I have no desire yet to live apart from my kind, and in coming here I have done right."[21]

Privately, she would also admit that fighting for a cause was still only part of the story. Frankly, danger had its attractions. "Sometimes," she confessed to her diary, "I wonder what urges me to make the struggle. It is more as if I am on a Sacred Crusade than anything else. But when I calmly think, there is nothing noble in fighting for your own. I suppose the risks I take excite me."[22] And risk held an additional attraction. A few days prior to her visit to the hacienda, authorities announced they had cause to believe that the San Martín–Puebla train, on which Mrs. Evans was riding, might be robbed. "I hoped nothing would happen to anyone," she confessed in a note to her late husband, "but I had the keenest desire for a bullet to strike me, and join you in a flash."[23]

By the time she visited San Pedro Coxtocán in May of 1918, Mrs. Evans was no neophyte businesswoman. Although Harry had usually managed the family's investments, she had learned much from writing his business correspondence while he dictated. She had also availed herself of the wisdom of her fellow hacendados, although they were slow in coming to take her seriously. Diego Kennedy—the American hacendado who had long advocated strong and often violent measures against land reform and who had even fronted the landlords' syndicate in a bid for the Tlaxcalan state governorship in 1912—told her that the hacendados "each have a man, unknown to the Indians, watching," and advised her to send an undercover agent of her own to scout out the villages. She sent her gardener José María—"who I know used to love me and I hear he's never robbed the place"; he reported that other landowners were doing their best to bypass the government by drawing up "secret" or "private" contracts with the villagers or with local military commanders. Kennedy had mentioned nothing of these arrangements, but when she confronted him, he confirmed the information.[24] Essentially, these "contracts" meant buying allies with bribes, but in a time when laws and lawmakers could make only the shakiest claims to legitimacy, few scrupled to observe only the most decorous conduct.

Harry's manservant Maurilio, whom Mrs. Evans was grooming for the job of administrator, reported that the news of her impending visit had been greeted with "much rejoicing, no opposition from the Indians."[25] Heartened by such reports, she thought to ask the villagers to give her half of the crop instead of the fifth she had originally intended, but as she rode out from Puebla to San Martín, it became clear to her that the villagers would not immediately be so accommodating. "The Indians are in appearance as you know them," Mrs. Evans reported to her sister, "but are no longer apathetic, they are insolent and aggressive. We no longer protest, as they are backed by the governor and would be only too glad to attack us. I pretended to see nothing—there were about two hundred Indians and we were five! When we reached San Martín I began to realize as never before what the revolution really meant. For reasons of their own the Indians are now making the most of their power, as they are unrestrained."[26]

Mrs. Evans was proud of her understanding of the "natives" and scornful of the ignorance of her fellow hacendados: "All those men have been in business for years," she wrote, "but they don't understand the natives and never will." She likened her own understanding of Indians to a game of chess, a straightforward contest of wit and nerve and Machiavellian calculation. A fitting comparison, in a way. Her relations with the villagers, like most relations between parties of drastically unequal power, were founded upon a variety of masks and fictions, feints and intrigues. The villagers—most of whom had served long years as hacienda peons, victims of abuse on the job and of desperate poverty at home— had developed coping mechanisms. The mask of docility Rosalie Evans so admired was a posture that combined feigned ineptitude and exaggerated humility so effectively that neither the weak nor the powerful could easily distinguish between performance and essence.

For the landowners of Mexico, few myths were as warmly cherished as the myth that portrayed Indians as eternal children. In their zeal to simplify, they collapsed time and space, lumping countless generations of disparate people into a single category with common characteristics. Upon reading Washington Irving's biography of Christopher Columbus, Rosalie Evans was struck by the author's description of Indians with their "indolent and holiday life" in a "state of primeval innocence." She marveled at how little the "natives" had changed over the centuries — "scant clothing, simple credulous minds, and only brave in numbers."[27] Other commentators reinforced this impression: "They are happy-go-lucky," wrote one traveler, "and are unconcerned for the future. [T]hey do not possess self-control and are always willing to follow a leader who understands how to make an appeal to their prejudices or fanaticism."[28]

Many landowners would despair at ever modifying these supposed character traits of the Indians, yet, ironically, they also took great comfort in them. Because the Indians were childlike and utterly dependent, they must then need external support and guidance. If left to their own devices, they would surrender to their instincts, revert to primordial savagery, and lack the initiative even to feed themselves. Indeed, many landowners suspected that cash wages were wasted on the Indians because they could not be trusted with something so refined and mysterious as money.

In their own view, the landowners bore the burden of saving the Indians from their own bestial nature, but they could take nothing for granted. Constant vigilance was needed to keep the Indians, with their "simple and credulous" nature, from being led astray by agitators out to exploit their "prejudices or fanaticism." Better that they should trust their fates to those who were more enlightened and had their best interests at heart. To credit the Indians with any initiative of their own would have been tantamount to confessing that landlord dominance was built on a hypocritical paternalism, sometimes supplemented by force and terror. Landlords preferred to believe it was ordered by nature.

Rosalie Evans was particularly insistent on sustaining landlord apologetics. As a woman, she was supposed to abhor brutality and uphold the noblest values of civilization. In November of 1918, when accommodating local authorities offered to have her deceitful administrator shot, they were mightily amused by her histrionics: she would rather lose her farm, she protested, than have a man killed on her behalf. She was deeply committed to the notion that it was her womanly duty to act as a civilizing influence, and this duty dovetailed nicely with her imperatives as a landlord: if the Indians behaved, she would help them and be "an active source of good among them." If left "unrestrained," they were on the road to ruin. She reinforced this idea with her constant, almost provocative use of the possessive in referring to the Indians as if they were a commodity like the land ("my land," "my villages," "my Indians"). Whatever reality and worth these things had, she believed, were realized only through her.

The rural poor of Mexico were accustomed to being viewed as a breed apart, citizens of the nation in theory only. The old tension between caste and class had never been resolved, even though the pace of economic life had quickened and mobility had increased. Some villagers would leave home in search of work in the factories or cities, and the old village ties were loosening. It remained unclear, however, whether Indian and white were simply fellow citizens of unequal attainments, or ward and protector. If much had changed, much also remained the same. Universal education and the protonationalist propaganda championed by the liberals had not filtered down to the village level in sufficient measure to fully erase old customs and identities. Many of the villagers of the Puebla-Tlaxcala Valley still spoke Náhuatl as well as Spanish, and the studied docility of the stereotyped peasant—the shuffling feet, hat in hand, hunched shoulders, and monotonous assurances that they were just ignorant country people—might still, some reckoned, be a safe and necessary posture.

In short, the rules were in flux. Who could say how far it was safe to go? The "unrestrained" villagers were indeed making the most of their power—albeit, paradoxically, within limits. Aggressive impulses, which for so long had been exercised mostly within the relative safety of their own communities and displaced onto fellow villagers, were now being turned very tentatively outward.[29] The villagers tested the water carefully, which helps to account for the erratic behavior Mrs. Evans would come to find so exasperating. They might be docile individually yet bold in groups, momentarily meek yet quickly incited. They did not know which authorities, if any, could legitimately be deferred to and which could be defied. The game they had to play was a delicate one, for too much obeisance to the wrong authority could imperil one's standing within the community, even while too little could invite reprisals from above.

Thus, in that spring of 1918, as a fine crop of wheat ripened in the fields, the villagers of the region awaited Mrs. Evans with a strange mixture of uncertainty, defiance, and fatalism. Although they had a sense that the landlords' power might be attenuated, they felt that prudence was still essential: the new bosses, after all, might turn out to be as bad as the old ones, or worse. There was also great internal dissension; those villagers intent on getting land were well aware that among them dwelt every shade of spy and collaborationist. Nevertheless, the hardliners maintained that because the villagers were the ones who had planted and cultivated the wheat nearing harvest, they should keep it if they could. To that end, most villagers simply played it by ear, employing a combination of vigilantism, deference, intrigue, and any other weapons they might find in their meager armory.

Of course, Mrs. Evans was not convinced that the villagers, no matter how "insolent and aggressive" they may have been, were entirely relevant. As she rode out to San Pedro that day in May of 1918 for the first time in seven years, she wondered who held the real power. The "natives" blended so completely with the flora and fauna of the place as to be practically invisible. Although a family of campesinos was occupying the main house, and the land had been kept in cultivation the entire time Mrs. Evans had been away, she was able to come to the bizarre conclusion that "no one has set foot on [the land] for two years."[30]

Mrs. Evans supposed that all depended on Carranza's general on the scene, Miguel Laveaga. No wild-eyed radical agrarian, Laveaga was a landlord in his own right and the scion of a wealthy landed family from the state of Durango. A Carranza loyalist, he had fronted the official ticket in the 1916 race for governor in his home state, but lost.[31] Like many military men, he probably hoped to parlay his loyalty to the winning faction into protection for, and perhaps an increase in, his own fortune. At the moment, his task was to secure trouble spots for the government, and the Puebla-Tlaxcala Valley had once again lapsed into turmoil. But it was no mere military adventure. His most pressing duty, he soon discovered, was to adjudicate agrarian politics.

For the moment, the most vexing problem was deciding who should get the hacienda's wheat crop. Carranza had already undercut the authority of local military commanders and state politicians — and indefinitely prolonged the land distribution process — by decreeing that his own approval was necessary to make provisional grants definitive.[32] At the end of October 1917, he followed that decree with a circular, which stated that in order to prevent shortages of essential foodstuffs, "all the fruits and products be respected and guaranteed as the legitimate and exclusive property of those who sowed and cultivated the lands." The law had been widely promulgated by Cirilo Arenas in November of 1917, along with a note in large type encouraging villagers to seek military support in staking their claims. The law, however, contained a crucial exception for "cases where there are sharecropping contracts that have been negotiated between the cultivators and those who call themselves owners of the lands," even if the lands were occupied legally pursuant to a grant of provisional possession.[33] Most landlords — including Harry Evans — had anticipated such a moment back in 1914, and had signed sharecropping contracts with some of the villagers before abandoning their properties to the fortunes of war. Now they were back, arguing that the contracts were still in force.[34] Legally, all this meant that the status quo would prevail. In practice, it meant that no one was quite sure who the lands or the crops belonged to, an uncertainty that put much power into the hands of men like Laveaga.

Some of the villagers, surprised by Mrs. Evans's audacity in visiting the hacienda, initially agreed to surrender half of the wheat crop to her. Others, upon hearing of the agreement, took up their weapons and invaded the lands, declaring that the entire crop was theirs. According to Maurilio, Mrs. Evans's scout and would-be administrator, they also killed a man and left his body in the doorway of the main house as a warning to any who might wish to favor the landlords' interests.[35]

The situation demanded tact, diplomacy, and impartiality—traits in which General Laveaga was sadly lacking. Maurilio, the loyal servant, informed Mrs. Evans that Laveaga was the only one who could save the situation, and he urged her to accompany him to Polaxtla—Marcelino Presno's magnificent hacienda, which the general had made his headquarters—to parlay with the powerful man. "The whole valley is waiting for him," reported Maurilio. Villagers queued up in hopes he would back their claims, whereas hacendados hoped to get protection in exchange for pay. None of them was entirely sure he was really the man to see or if he had the power to dispose what they proposed.

General Laveaga, according to Mrs. Evans, held sway at Polaxtla as in "the court of a primitive king." He was over six feet tall and massively built, sitting regally at a table built to seat more than two hundred, an ironic reminder of the halcyon days when hacienda homes were meant for entertaining on a grand scale. There was much about the hacienda itself—from its fortresslike walls and vast holdings, to the Virgin of Guadalupe carved in stone above the main entrance—that harkened back to an earlier time. The general allowed few to sit with him at the huge table, so deputations of villagers and anxious hacendados lined the walls of the long hall, waiting while the general dined.[36]

Laveaga used Mrs. Evans's appearance as his cue for a show of chivalry. Yielding the head of the table to "the English lady," he remarked to her that he had attended school in California as a boy and that if she did not mind, they would speak English. "You should have seen the faces of the audience fall," wrote Mrs. Evans. Laveaga's choice of language was a calculated insult to the villagers, one made more aggravating by the leisurely and obsequious manner in which he treated "the English lady" to accounts of his California boyhood while everyone else stood by uncomprehendingly, growing impatient and angry. Mrs. Evans played along, offering the general "whatever he thought just in payment" if he would give her protection and guarantee her a large share of the crop. He refused any payment, but instead summoned the agrarian representative of the village of San Mateo Capultitlán, a tiny village on San Pedro's southern border, and ordered him to surrender half of the wheat crop to Mrs. Evans. The villagers argued, offering to make the señora a "present" when the crop was in, but Laveaga was firm: "The señora is not a *limosnera* (beggar) on her own hacienda."

With that, the general rose and rallied his troops for a foray in search of the

General Miguel Laveaga — "It was like being in the court of a primitive king." *Credit:* Gustavo Casasola, *Historia gráfica de la Revolución Mexicana, 1900–1970,* 2d ed. (Mexico City: Editorial Trillas, S.A. de C.V., 1973).

Arenistas. Mrs. Evans walked off through the fields in the direction of San Martín. "I do not know what occurred to him," she later recounted; "he must have feared for me, for in a few minutes he rode back, got off his horse, sent the men off with a colonel, and walked with me to San Martín, where he ordered a special [rail] car for me. All the way we were followed by about fifty petitioners who now walked up and down the [train station] platform waiting for a chance to speak to the general as he sat smoking cigarettes and talking to me." While he was at it, Laveaga even offered to intervene on Mrs. Evans's behalf with the state governor to ensure she would not have to pay her property taxes.[37]

Though it filled Mrs. Evans with optimism, Laveaga's performance was just that. Local military commanders had considerable authority and discretion, but nothing like the power Laveaga pretended to wield. Even a general — especially one charged with pacifying a troubled region — could not afford to ignore the most basic elements of tact and diplomacy. The villagers and the hacendados were not the only ones vying for the crops. Laveaga's own Yaquí soldiers were still largely dependent on the crops and livestock they could appropriate from the haciendas for their own sustenance, and they were not pleased by their commander's generosity. If the general persisted in accommodating the hacendados, a few zealous villagers might be tempted to follow the example of Cirilo Arenas and take to the hills under arms, or they might recall the Zapatistas' advice and take the law into their own hands. Nor was Laveaga's influence with the governor nearly as strong as he claimed. The general himself was merely a guest at the gaming table, one who knew neither the players nor the stakes and who had clearly overplayed his hand.

Maurilio began gathering the hacienda's share of the wheat and storing it in the hacienda's granary (despite Mrs. Evans's instructions that he take it to San Martín). Within days, a warrant was issued for his arrest, and some villagers threatened to kill him. When he reported this to his employer in Puebla, she took the first train to San Martín and again confronted Laveaga. Laveaga continued his bluff, offering to "make the Indians understand that I owned the place or hang them all," but he backed down when he arrived on the hacienda grounds. There, he took to disputing ownership of the chile pepper crop with a group of angry agraristas.

It is impossible to know from Mrs. Evans's account precisely what happened, but after her visit to the hacienda she knew that she had lost Laveaga's favor. Later that day he told the villagers not to surrender any wheat to Maurilio, and the next day an article appeared in the local newspaper celebrating the way General Laveaga had favored the claims of the Indians over those of the "wealthy oppressors," the byline indicating that article was penned by the general himself.[38]

For reasons that were never made clear, Laveaga was transferred out of the region the day after his newspaper article appeared.

FRUSTRATIONS AND VICTORIES

Unable to fathom what forces lurked behind the bewildering series of triumphs and disappointments she was experiencing—and unwilling to admit that the villagers had any real volition in the matter—Mrs. Evans searched for the man who really controlled the gaming table. The governor of Puebla, Alfonso Cabrera, was a likely suspect—the Indians, she had noted, were "backed by the governor"—so he was the man she turned to after her disappointment with Laveaga.

She went to see him along with William Hardacker, the British vice-consul at Puebla. Cabrera kept her waiting for four hours and then declined to see her, his minions suggesting that she return the next day at the same time. She did and again was kept waiting for four hours. When Cabrera finally saw her, she was not surprised when he told her, "not politely, but insolently, . . . that my hacienda *justly* belonged to the Indians, the revolution had been for them, and that I should have none of the crop."[39]

Mrs. Evans, with her scant faith in Mexican authorities, took this to mean that Cabrera was on the take and opposed her only because he intended to have his own share of her hacienda's profits. She became obstreperous, threatening to go over Cabrera's head and appeal her case directly to President Carranza— not the last time that she would make a scene in the office of a high official. It was impolitic, but it worked: she was given an order authorizing her to take half of the crop and to pay no taxes on the hacienda for the year. Such writs did not run, however, and the next day Maurilio reported that the villagers were once again harvesting wheat with no intention of surrendering any of it to Mrs. Evans.

In fact, Cabrera was not the hidden hand that Mrs. Evans at first thought him to be, though he would likely have found her assessment of his power flattering. A physician by training, Cabrera was a man of little charisma and practically no political experience, renowned for his haughty and autocratic temperament. Like Mrs. Evans, he was busy struggling to gain some sense of control over his domain. The first Puebla native to govern that state since 1884, he was also a civilian who became governor in early 1917, a time when most Mexican states were governed by military men. First Chief Carranza would have favored a military man for the post, and the state's military zone commander—General Cesáreo Castro—seconded that preference, judging himself to be the very man for the job. For the moment, however, Castro—like Carranza, a native of the northern state of Coahuila—was prevented from becoming governor by a newly minted provision in the state's constitution declaring that the position must be held by a Puebla native.

Castro was not discouraged. In addition to having his soldiers dress as workers and peasants and attack Cabrera's supporters in the streets, he also threw the armed weight of the military behind opposition candidates in municipal elections and favored the interests of the state's landowners whenever he had the chance. Carranza made little effort to rein Castro in, on the grounds that he would provide a useful counterweight to the civilian governor. Carranza wished to reward the civilian, antimilitarist wing of his coalition — a group headed by the Puebla governor's brother, the redoubtable ideologue Luis Cabrera — but always within manageable limits.

Tensions between soldiers and civilians, as well as between the state and central governments, were in fact only the beginning of Cabrera's headaches. He was faced, too, with obstreperous conservatives, just now returning to Puebla in force, and with subregions of his state — notably the northwestern mountains — dominated by local warlords who had no intention of bowing to the governor's will. As if that were not enough, he was confronted by a disgruntled, aroused labor movement and the intransigent industrialists who meant to keep their workers in line.

Few men had the political skills to navigate in such troubled waters. Nearly everyone in the state seemed to sense that the moment was ripe for something, and no one wished to see that moment pass without a complete triumph for their side. On the one hand, popular apathy now might mean the entrenchment of old or new oligarchs and thus a sudden stifling of the people's voices; on the other, if the old oligarchs could not set some fast rules for the game, forces from below might upset the whole social order. The contest was not merely a vertical one: flagging energies now might also favor the assertion of one region's interests over those of another. Although Cabrera did his best to gain control, in the end his government seemed just one more party involved in the many-sided contest. In addition to founding his own "Popular Law Party," which was charged with imposing loyal candidates in state, district, and municipal offices, he also created a new armed force, the "regional corp," officially intended to combat banditry but also clearly intended as a counterweight to the regular army. If Cabrera did indeed "back the Indians," his motives were as much tactical as ideological: a matter of trying to keep his legions of enemies in check.[40]

The maddeningly arbitrary operations of the government were, in short, a reflection not of Governor Cabrera's absolute control but rather of his lack of it. Of course, Cabrera's relative lack of clout did not greatly improve Mrs. Evans's situation. In the midst of all her troubles, she was slapped with a tax bill for three thousand pesos. Taxation was a strategy favored by more tepid reformers.

General Antonio Villarreal, who would soon be appointed secretary of agriculture, even advocated it as a matter of official policy: "We should," he argued, "gradually fight against the big landowners through indirect means, such as taxes, until they find it impossible to hold big extensions of land and start to get rid of them as quickly as possible."[41] The idea of being fed a steady diet of fiscal harrassment did not sit well with Mrs. Evans, who for the time being was unable to draw on her husband's New York bank account and had no other income. It would be several days before the harvest was finished and the wheat could be marketed, assuming she could get a share of the wheat. Her sister Daisy gave her enough to pay the rent on her apartment in Mexico City and the wages of her servants, with a bit leftover so she could think of relocating to Puebla, but one thousand pesos did not come close to covering her expenses for the hacienda, so she was practically reduced to begging for credit. A former colleague of Harry's, the president of the Mexico City branch of the Canadian Bank, saved the day by lending her eight thousand pesos interest free, taking it on faith that she would soon be declared executrix of her husband's will, that San Pedro would yield a splendid wheat crop, and that she would somehow be able to fanagle at least a hefty portion of that crop.

Mrs. Evans's tax troubles were not over, however. On June 15 the state tax collector caught up with her in the Puebla City office of William Hardacker, Britain's vice-consul, and presented her with a bill for immediate payment of the tax. Maurilio, it seemed, had forged her signature to a document stating that she agreed to pay the tax sooner than she had intended, before half of the wheat crop had been gathered. She simply refused to pay the tax, however, and the episode turned out to be of little consequence, but so many trials had increased her already pronounced paranoia. She returned to Hardacker's office and angrily berated him for failing to present her case more effectively to the governor. The consul was livid: "If you are so important," he told her, "I wash my hands of your affairs. I have too much of my own to attend to to see these people continually."[42]

Mrs. Evans was still harsher with Maurilio. The young would-be administrator had already earned her wrath by storing the gathered wheat at the hacienda, where villagers could come by night and steal it back, rather than at San Martín as she had ordered. She acknowledged, however, that perhaps it was stupidity rather than malice that had caused his betrayal: "Maurilio was a carpenter, you know," she told her sister, "but with the naiveté of his race feels he can at once be [a farmer]."[43] Although she continued to maintain for a while that she believed Maurilio meant well, she no longer trusted him — "the minute you give a man like that a little power he loses his head" — and within two weeks she had replaced him with Eduardo Guerrero, a man recommended by her neighbor, the Mexican hacendado Ignacio Ovando. Guerrero went to live on the hacienda, and Maurilio took to plotting revenge.

Eduardo Guerrero was, according to Mrs. Evans, "ugly and commonplace," a swarthy man of about thirty, with "fierce black mustaches."[44] Although he came highly recommended by Ovando, Mrs. Evans distrusted him from the start, believing physical courage to be his only redeeming feature. For the moment he served her well, however, risking great danger by agreeing to sleep on the hacienda and supervising the harvest resplendent in his full *charro* regalia. Although the city of San Martín was now "squalid beyond description and full of drunken soldiers," when Mrs. Evans visited the hacienda grounds and settled down to watch the harvest, it was as if the revolution had never happened. This was a world where a gentleman on horseback still commanded respect from the near-naked Indians.

"We heard the music far off," Mrs Evans recounted. "When we got to the great corral we pushed open the gate and saw a busy, wild-looking crowd; the music was pure Indian, a great tom-tom drum beaten on by bones, yet in perfect time. In the middle of the yard the modern threshing-machine, and the Indians working it, mostly with only cloths tied around their waists, their bare legs black and muscular." In the midst of it all was Guerrero, in his element. "Once or twice," Mrs. Evans observed, "bitter disputes ended in real fights, when the wiry things surrounded him, but he always controlled them and without murder." And finally the goal at the heart of all these disputes was realized: "The wheat was finally delivered."[45]

In her short struggle, Rosalie Evans had acquired her share of enemies. By now they included Laveaga, Cabrera, the British consul, Maurilio, and numerous villagers, especially the family that had taken up residence in the hacienda buildings and that she had personally, unceremoniously ejected. Soon enough she would add Guerrero to the list. She was certain that Guerrero was stealing wheat, a practice that had nearly acquired the force of custom in the Puebla-Tlaxcala Valley. "There are about a dozen haciendas in the valley, all except Ovando's in the hands of unscrupulous young administrators, who, for risking their lives, are stealing a good half of what is produced." Guerrero, however, was stealing more than was seemly, and Mrs. Evans was sure he intended to gradually take over the entire operation.[46]

By the end of 1918 she had replaced him with thirty-two-year-old Jesús Bermejillo — a slender, strikingly handsome, highly educated Spaniard with aristocratic bloodlines (he was first cousin of the Duke of Alba, whose distant ancestor had laid waste to the Netherlands). Like Mrs. Evans herself, he spoke several languages and had a taste for danger. Coming in the wake of Maurilio and Guerrero, he seemed almost too good to be true: in addition to possessing honesty, courage, and sophistication, he was (in the words of one man who knew him) "very decorative to have around at parties."[47]

Despite the slow accumulation of foes, it seemed Mrs. Evans's efforts had begun to bear fruit. In June 1918, after her success with the wheat crop, she was visited in her Puebla hotel by the father-in-law of the agrarian leader of San Mateo Capultitlán, the village that had earlier disputed ownership of the chile crop with General Laveaga — and, according to Mrs. Evans, "the richest man in the village." Even so, his appearance embarrassed her. "I wish you could have seen him," she told her sister, "just like the old beggars you see on the streets, a long beard, ragged, dirty linen clothes and barefoot. I saw the other hotel guests regard me, for I have no sitting-room and received him in the rotunda." She expected an argument, but instead got total surrender: "*Niña,*" he told her, "I am your humble servant. I want to tell you I have never hurt your hacienda and I want to know if you will sign a contract for half the corn with me. I will no longer appeal to the governor."[48] The man's poverty aroused no compassion in her; she merely congratulated herself for provoking the total capitulation: "I know no such radical change has taken place in their hearts and that it is only fear of me, as I succeeded with the wheat; they are now disheartened and we are encouraged."

A still greater triumph arrived that same month (June 1918) in the form of a telegram from President Carranza himself, offering her his full support.[49] Governor Cabrera did his best to ignore Carranza's orders and continued to work through his tax collector to seize the land. The village of San Jerónimo Tianguismanalco, meanwhile, tried to assert its provisional possession of the 122 hectares of land, which had been upheld by the state agrarian commission in January.[50] Still under the close tutelage of Ovando — a man whose claim to expertise in understanding the psychology of the villagers merits some credibility[51] — Mrs. Evans yielded diplomatically on the issue of the chile crop, but haggled with the villagers from Tianguismanalco for a full half of the corn. In the autumn of 1918 Juan Peña, the agrarian leader of Tianguismanalco, offered to split the crop with her "if the governor can not get an order from Carranza in our favor."

At this point, Mrs. Evans triumphantly produced her telegram from Carranza and "deliberately handed it to my enemy Juan Peña. You should have seen them. They spoke in their own Indian language, they hung over one another's shoulders, their faces changed utterly, they began calling me *niña* in a conciliatory voice. Juan Peña handed me back the paper and said: '*Niña,* we are all going to Puebla and hear from the governor himself what this means. We are afraid we are deceived.' "[52]

The greatest boon to Mrs. Evans's cause was the unqualified support she received in September 1918 from Manuel Aguirre Berlanga, Carranza's blond-haired, bespectacled interior secretary. She nearly got herself shot by Aguirre Berlanga's bodyguards when she burst precipitously into his hotel room demanding justice. Despite the considerable fright she caused him, Aguirre Berlanga became her advocate: "Señora," he promised, "I will not only make the pueblo of Tianguis retire but I will give you an order for the complete return of your hacienda, and a safe conduct from General Castro, when you have to visit it."[53] He was good as his word: within days she had a paper formally returning possession of San Pedro to her, complete with specific orders to that effect addressed to Governor Cabrera and General Cesáreo Castro. A clerk for Aguirre Berlanga politely offered to have Guerrero shot for stealing from her.

Sixty-two years old, a Carranza loyalist with little sympathy for agrarian reform, General Castro, for his part, was delighted to help. "He fairly chuckled and asked what I wanted him to do," Mrs. Evans reported; "he was at my disposal." She only wanted him, she said, to gather the villager leaders and make them sign away all their claims on the hacienda. "I then said I did not need his aid to get half the corn, as the Indians had agreed with me. I am sorry for the poor creatures and bear them no malice; they will steal my land if they can, but I want no revenge."

"Is the hacienda now mine?" she asked Castro.

With a genial smile, the old general replied: "It always was."[54]

LANDLORD MACHINATIONS

Although Rosalie Evans would probably have been loath to admit it, she had something very important in common with the villagers of Tianguismanalco who felt themselves deceived upon seeing an order from the president of the republic supporting the claims of the landlord. Like them, she clung to the notion that someone high up in the government was at least *capable* of coming to her rescue, just as they were capable of endless harrassment. She was pessimistic regarding what she might ultimately expect from the likes of Carranza and Cabrera, but she was confident at least that "when a serious government comes in I shall get [the hacienda] back."[55]

Other landlords who had not enjoyed quite the same success in garnering such enthusiastic support from the likes of Carranza, Aguirre Berlanga, and Castro were less sanguine about and less trusting in the official channels. Their strategies varied. The most obvious recourse was to naked force, the approach taken by Rosalie Evans's immediate neighbor, Clara Teruel, the widow of an extremely wealthy Spaniard named Manuel Echave. When the villagers of Santa María Moyotzingo tried to claim provisional possession of the lands of Mrs. Echave's hacienda, San Jerónimo Tepoxtla, she had her administrator and several armed men carry out the harvest under threat of violence. Eventually, she

General Cesáreo Castro—"He was at my disposal."
Credit: Gustavo Casasola, *Historia gráfica de la Revolución Mexicana, 1900–1970,* 2d ed. (Mexico City: Editorial Trillas, S.A. de C.V., 1973).

too won the backing of General Castro, even without express orders from Carranza. The villagers of Moyotzingo accused her of "showing in all of her actions bad faith toward the poor, to the degree of using the military authorities who cannot negotiate rationally because they are in league with the *latifundistas* [landowners]."[56]

A far more damaging strategy in the long run was the landlords' own version of agrarian reform. According to this scheme, the landlords would voluntarily subdivide their properties and sell them directly to the villagers for a "just and equitable price." The benefits of this approach, they declared, would be enormous. Villagers would be helped by generous repayment schedules and low interest rates. Also, by eliminating the government and its agrarian bureaucracy, the nation would save hundreds of thousands of pesos per year, and the villagers would not be subject to new tyrannies (because the agrarian committees within the villages, asserted the landlords, were as brutal and arbitrary as any hacendado or *jefe político*). Plus, the villagers would have a healthier appreciation for the lands they received if they had to pay for them, and the landlords would not be entirely reduced to misery.[57]

Surely there was some truth to the landlords' claims. Government agrarian policy was always confused, its bureaucracy inefficient, and local agrarian committees could indeed devolve into minidespotisms. Still, the notion of placing the landlords in charge of the entire land reform process was too much like trusting the fox to guard the henhouse. Besides, it would rob the federal government of its role as the ultimate source of largesse — a role of which it was supremely jealous. In any event, the landlords' proposal was never seriously entertained.

Many landlords nevertheless put the proposal informally into operation, and not necessarily always in bad faith. Captain Frank Ruhl, an aging Englishman with investments in just about everything Mexico had to offer, decided late in the revolution that agriculture was too risky for a man of his years and that he would trust his fortune to the eventual recovery of the mining sector. Accordingly, in 1918 he sold his entire hacienda, San Simón, which was immediately northwest of San Pedro Coxtocán, to a group of villagers from San Buenaventura Tecaltzingo and San Juan Tuxco, who in turn divided the land into small lots averaging approximately three thousand square meters.[58] Such transactions were nothing new. Several haciendas of the region had disappeared even before the revolution began, sold off by hacendados weary of the uncertainties of Mexican cereal farming.

Of course, the existence of a class of small landowners within the villages had long been troublesome, but prior to 1918 landowners sold their haciendas mostly because they wished to quit the farming game, and their intent was not to stir up trouble. With the coming of the agrarian reform, however, land sales became a weapon of landlord resistance, and some hacendados acquired a real talent for fomenting antagonism. Take, for example, the tiny villages of Xaltepetlapa, and Tlanicontla, west of Huejotzingo, which had been disputing each other's boundaries ever since a road had been built between them. A man named Espuro, who owned an hacienda in the area, sold a portion of his estate on very generous terms to the villagers of Tlanicontla. When the villagers of Xaltepetlapa received their lands in the form of a government grant of ejidos, old resentments bubbled up anew, and Espuro missed few opportunities to add fuel to the fire. By the late 1920s, he was able to sit back and watch the two little towns destroy each other.[59]

Most landlords did not have such handy preexisting hostilities to exploit, but they had similar intentions. In 1919, Marcelino Presno sold one hundred hectares of land from his hacienda, San Bartolo Granillo, to a group of about forty villagers of Santa Ana Xalmimilulco. The transaction was recognized as valid by the secretary of agriculture and development, even though it included lands that had already been petitioned for and granted provisionally to the village. When the village agrarian leaders complained, both Presno and his fraccionistas were able to present themselves as champions of the humble. Would the agrarian authorities, they asked, despoil some villagers who had purchased lands honorably and in good faith in order to give lands to other, less worthy individuals?[60]

Presno did not neglect to mention that he would be happy to sell more of his land. In fact, he sent representatives into the villages to promote the idea, as did Clara Teruel de Echave, who had her administrator, Filiberto Bañuelos, spread the rumor in the villages that he alone was authorized to grant lands. His frequent appearance in the company of soldiers lent some credibility to his claim that he wielded more power than the government agrarian commissions.[61] Those villagers who were not seduced by such maneuvers believed that the fraccionistas would serve as lackeys for the landlords, obstructing the agrarian reform at every turn. Moreover, given the fraccionistas' considerable debt to the hacienda, their position would not differ greatly from that now occupied by sharecroppers, and the door would always be open for the hacienda to reclaim the land some time in the future, once the agrarian agitation had subsided.[62]

Other individuals also hoped to profit from the current agitation, and their strategies were decidedly devious. William Hardacker, the British vice-consul who came to be counted among Mrs. Evans's great enemies, engaged in widespread lending with a view toward foreclosing on exasperated and bankrupt landlords. Mrs. Evans was not merely being paranoid in her interpretation of his intentions: "Hardacker," she wrote, "has twenty years of good business standing. But the revolution has hurt him, his interest being in machinery and factories. He has lost heavily. I come along, a delicate woman owning a large and valuable property [which had been] confiscated. He sees his opportunity —

by lending me a few thousand dollars it will soon be in his hands. By his petty official position and long knowledge of Mexicans he will get it back . . . , and by the *appearance* of generosity become owner of a rich estate and rehabilitate himself without loss of credit."[63]

In this, Hardacker took his cue from his close friend and colleague—the U.S. vice-consul at Puebla, William O. Jenkins, a man whose love of money and flair for wheeling and dealing kept him embroiled in almost constant controversy. Even Mrs. Evans, who normally admired winners, considered him "an awful character."[64] Jenkins had been in Mexico since 1902 and over the years had acquired a stocking factory, a good deal of urban real estate, the city bullring, and the train station. He also had interests in several clothing and textile factories and was a partner in Diego Kennedy's tractor-importing concern.

It took the shocks of revolution, however, to transform Jenkins into the great financial predator he became. During the siege of Puebla in January of 1915, he had found twenty-seven dead men lying in front of his home, most of them with their heads shattered like melons from being shot with expanding bullets at close range. Later that day, he was arrested by Constitutionalist soldiers, charged with having shot the men himself, and only an eleventh-hour intervention from higher-ups saved him from the firing squad—an experience that left him badly unnerved and determined to abandon Mexico and his fortune at once.[65] He remained in Mexico, but it seems his natural misanthropy was reinforced. Although in subsequent years he became renowned for his philanthropy, in this period he was apparently capable of shocking ruthlessness. His most celebrated caper came in October of 1919, when he was kidnapped by armed rebels who demanded ransom from the Carranza government. The government later claimed that Jenkins had been in league with his kidnappers in a scheme to discredit Carranza and, if possible, bring on U.S. intervention.

Apart from other creative maneuvers like this one, Jenkins found ways to grow richer from the revolution. Like his friend and colleague Hardacker, Jenkins stepped up his speculatory activities at a time when many rural proprietors were panicked and eager to sell at bargain prices, and so was able to supplement his already considerable wealth with haciendas in every corner of Mexico. By the 1950s, he was practically unrivaled as the wealthiest man in Mexico.[66]

THE AGUA PRIETA REBELLION

The various strategies adopted by the landlords to hold on to their lands— sometimes with help from military men and politicians—kept the villagers constantly off balance. By October of 1919, the agrarian leaders of the village of Moyotzingo complained to the state agrarian commission: so many of their requests had gone unheeded that now "all of the residents of the village consider agrarian matters anulled, and so are committing many outrages, even despoiling other villagers of the area."[67]

If the landlords were not exactly looking forward to a secure and brilliant future, they could at least take some comfort in the obvious disarray of the agrarian revolution. In April of 1919, Emiliano Zapata was killed in a treacherous ambush orchestrated by Carranza and General Pablo González. What remained of Zapata's movement was a shambles. General Fortino Ayaquica, Zapata's leading representative in Puebla, surrendered in December of 1919,[68] preceded and followed by the surrender of many lesser lights.

Little remained of the Arenista movement. During the summer of 1918, Cirilo Arenas and his men had still been capable of mounting pitched battles with Constitutionalist armies.[69] By mid-1919, however, the Arenistas survived mostly by attacking unguarded villages and haciendas, although they would still blow up an occasional bridge or train.[70] In the villages they would raid homes — stealing clothing, kitchen utensils, food, and anything else they could carry away with them to their mountain retreat.[71] In both the villages and haciendas, they would kidnap anyone they thought might yield a meaningful ransom. In July, they abducted the mayordomo of San Pedro Coxtocán and demanded three hundred pesos ransom, which Mrs. Evans refused to pay. The Arenistas had little bargaining power, however, so they released the man unharmed. Mrs. Evans sent them eighty pesos to show her gratitude, and they wrote back thanking her and vowing to allow the harvest to proceed.[72]

Cirilo and his men had by now allied themselves with so many different — and often disreputable — factions that they lost any ideological coherence they might once have claimed. Many old Arenistas and Zapatistas, including the leader of the Arenistas' old political wing, the Partido Liberal Tlaxcalteca, now publicly denounced Cirilo and his men as "bandits."[73]

Cirilo's end came in early 1920, when he was spotted entering a movie theater in Puebla City. Although he insisted he had come to Puebla to surrender, a court martial was unforgiving. He faced a firing squad at five o'clock on the morning of March 7, 1920.

Ironically, the men Cirilo Arenas had sought, at least in theory, to overthrow and who in the end refused him clemency soon joined him in ignominy. General Alvaro Obregón, Carranza's most brilliant general, announced his candidacy for the presidency in June of 1919. Carranza, fearing Obregón's power and his supposed radical tendencies, tried to impose his own, more lackluster candidate. In favor of Carranza's man, Alfonso Cabrera tried to use his state bureaucrats and paramilitary regional corp to harrass the opposition candidates.[74]

Under the banner of their "Plan of Agua Prieta," Obregón and his powerful partisans launched a rebellion in May of 1920 that sent Carranza fleeing toward the coast. He sought safety in the sierra of Puebla, but was assassinated in a thatch-roofed hut in the high mountain village of Tlaxcalantongo by Obregón's partisans on May 21, 1920. Cabrera also fled for the sierra, but like Carranza he found no solace and was eventually captured at the Guatemalan border carrying only a blanket and a snakeskin bag filled with gold coins.[75]

A DISTURBING DREAM

Rosalie Evans had changed greatly since January of 1918, when she had come to Mexico resolved to fight the good fight and to dedicate the struggle to her late husband's memory. By March of 1919 it seems she had become involved romantically with her new administrator, Jesús Bermejillo, although she kept him at a distance with the assurance that he would never replace Harry in her affections.

The memory of her late husband was not now as comforting as it once had been, however. At the end of March 1919, Mrs. Evans awoke with a start at three in the morning and scribbled down the details of a terrible nightmare. In it, she arrived at a house where Harry lay sick in a small room, guarded by a young Yaquí boy. She offered the boy a bribe so he would let her in to see Harry. The gesture only angered him, and he tormented her by waving a pistol over Harry's head. Rosalie shot the boy, but the shot did not kill him. She ran for help, but by the time she returned to the house, she found that the Yaquí boy had eaten six of Harry's fingers. "Unnerved and in a dreadful state," she moved Harry to the couple's old home in Puebla. The Yaquí boy was there waiting and would not leave. When she went to sit with Harry, she found him covered with a shroud, and when she pulled the sheet back, he woke with a start and said, "Rosalie, why did you do that?"[76]

The dream frightened her badly, but so many other things that might once have frightened or repelled her were now practically amusing. In April of 1919 the passengers on the train from Mexico City to Puebla had passed by a pine tree from which dangled the ravaged corpses of seven men. Mrs. Evans expressed fascination instead of horror: "You see," she wrote to her sister, "they had been shot in the fight and hung afterward, and they looked like those wax and cloth Indians we used to buy in Puebla, not horrible to me, but strange large manikins."[77]

"I am afraid my year has wrought its work," she wrote to her sister then. "I never believed before that people could change, become some one else, and I think that is what I have done. I look in the glass and I do not know if it is visible to others — but it is to me. . . . Harry no longer holds me by the hand. I stand alone. I can not say if he will come back. . . . Good-bye, far-off sister."[78]

Five

At certain revolutions all the damn'd
Are brought: and feel by turns the bitter change
Of fierce extreams.
— John Milton, *Paradise Lost*

⬩⬩⬩

S MEXICO'S new rulers took control of the government in early
1920, Rosalie Evans was nervously optimistic and not at all charita-
ble toward the ousted regime, despite the favors it had done her. "It
hardly seems fair," she wrote of Carranza and his entourage, even as they fled for
their lives, "to let them escape after four years of robbery and murder, without
punishment." Her harsh feelings were inspired partly by Carranza's eleventh-
hour efforts to salvage what he could of popular sympathies by renewing the
agrarian reform initiative. These efforts did not amount to much — a few new
inspections, a handful of hastily confirmed provisional grants, some hostile
notices mailed to landowners — and they proved too little, too late. In fact, they
further embittered the landlords, even while they handed the new regime a
sobering reminder that agrarian reform was an issue it would neglect at its
peril.[1] It was difficult for anyone to predict quite how that new regime would
read this cautionary tale.

THE NEW RULERS DEBATE THE AGRARIAN QUESTION

Mrs. Evans's hopes for the new regime were based on odd reasoning. Whereas
Carranza and Luis Cabrera "simply sit at home in great luxury and think of laws
to rob the people," she thought, "[the new leaders] at least have been out
pillaging for themselves, and so have been exposed a *little*."[2]

Even that faint praise was surprising given the reputation of the new regime's
top leader, General Alvaro Obregón. A passing glance should have suggested
that he had been exposed more than a little, for only a pinned-up sleeve showed

General Alvaro Obregón and Family, c. 1920. *Credit:* Gustavo Casasola, *Historia gráfica de la Revolución Mexicana, 1900–1970,* 2d ed. (Mexico City: Editorial Trillas, S.A. de C.V., 1973).

where his right arm should have been, that appendage having been shot off by the Villistas in 1915. Of course, heroic limblessness was a solid political asset in Mexico, visible proof of sacrifice for the fatherland. The great nineteenth-century dictator Santa Anna was so zealous on the point that he held an elaborate state funeral for his amputated leg.[3]

Obregón's reputation was not founded solely on symbolism, however. He had long been considered the most prominent radical within Carrancista ranks — a leading advocate of agrarian and labor legislation, which had rankled the first chief. Obregón knew well what a powerful political tool land reform could be. He had used it himself in recruiting Yaquí and Mayo Indians to fight against the Villistas and Zapatistas, and had endorsed its use in pacifying regions such as Morelos and the Puebla-Tlaxcala Valley, where rural unrest was strongest. Landlords shuddered at the sight of his peasant supporters, with their wide sombreros and loose white cotton clothes, riding on his campaign car or chanting "vivas" through city streets. They must have been likewise unsettled by the fact that Adolfo de la Huerta, who was keeping the presidential chair warm for his friend and fellow Sonoran, was distributing land at an unprecedented pace. By the time his six-month term ended in November of 1920, de la Huerta had distributed more land than Carranza had in three years.[4]

Mrs. Evans's optimism regarding the new regime was not entirely unfounded, for Obregón was a consummate politician. He was more pragmatic than idealistic, and he was skilled at the arts of manipulation. A large farmer himself, he had built a veritable agrocommercial empire around his garbanzo farms in Sonora. Unlike many of his contemporaries, he had moved beyond his local roots and adopted a comprehensive view of the country's problems — becoming very well aware that the precarious supply of foodstuffs in a country devastated by war, together with the unfortunate shortfall in the Mexican treasury, argued against hasty actions and counterbalanced demands for immediate and drastic social reform. A radical reform might cause severe food shortages, increase the country's dependence on imports, and possibly earn the wrath of U.S. policymakers weighing the prospect of granting official recognition to Obregón's regime. The latter was hardly a matter indifference because U.S. recognition of the Obregón government would be a necessary prerequisite to getting loans that were desperately needed to rebuild the country. Obregón knew that ruling revolutionary Mexico called for a careful blend of coercion and conciliation. All of the contending parties demanded their rewards, so the real trick was to placate any one group without alienating all the others.

In October of 1920, one month before he assumed office, Obregón took to the floor of Congress to expound on the agrarian problem and to refute claims from both the left and the right. On the left was Zapatista ideologue Antonio Díaz Soto y Gama, who saw no excuse for failing to seize and distribute land immediately. "Even the most obdurate reactionaries," he argued, "acknowledge that the Revolution has but one problem: the Agrarian Problem. . . . It is a question of carrying into practice the most solemn, the highest and most sacred promise of the Revolution"[5] — a not so subtle reminder to Obregón that delays in land distribution had already contributed mightily to the unraveling of three regimes and that agrarian rebels would not take kindly to yet another rebuff.

On the right was General Francisco Serrano, formerly Obregón's chief of staff and currently undersecretary of war and the navy. Serrano complained that the agrarian reform would sink the rich without elevating the poor; that it would cost more, financially and socially, to divide the big estates than to leave them intact; and that, in any case, most estates had been legally acquired, so confiscation would amount to robbery.

Behind each of these orators stood hosts of powerful phantoms. Whereas the Zapatista spokesman alluded ominously to the restive masses behind him, Serrano claimed numerous allies among foreign observers and in the press. The national daily *Excélsior* printed a steady stream of anti-agrarian editorials, rehearsing a list of well-worn arguments. Small farmers, it said, would not be able to match large ones in mechanizing and modernizing their operations. If they had land, they would use it crudely to meet their own needs, blithely disregarding the needs of the ever-growing urban population. And finally, offering the most cherished argument of landlords like Rosalie Evans, the paper maintained that the Indians simply did not *want* land: "If the mass of the population, rural included, does not want land," ran one editorial, "goodbye agrarian problem!"[6]

In this milieu, Obregón was the voice of moderation, and he gave nearly everyone cause for hope. His performance was certainly reassuring to landowners. Mrs. Evans was so convinced of his sincerity that, six weeks after the debate in Congress, when she was notified that some 1,500 acres of her land had been definitively confiscated, she easily convinced herself that the notice was a mistake — "perhaps a simple distraction, quite understandable."[7] Few felt threatened by Obregón's thumbnail sketch of the great villains of Mexican agriculture, for these very same villains had been trotted out by generations of reformers and were, of course, the benighted landowners who "disregarded the evolution of agriculture," clinging to their old ways out of some inexplicable obstinacy, eschewing the blessings of modernity.

Landowners like Rosalie Evans and her neighbors felt they could breathe easy, for surely they did not fit that stereotype. They had, in fact, worked hard to bring in modern machinery, study the latest advances in seeds and fertilizers, lower shipping costs, secure credit, and actively participate in the processing and marketing of their grains — all the things Obregón was now recommending. Indeed, there were probably few landowners in the country who felt the president-elect could possibly have been referring to them when he denounced the antimodern landlord. True, most Mexican grain farmers had trouble competing with the U.S. counterparts, and the profitability of their operations was still founded on low wages, low property taxes, and high import duties, but these problems were due to unfortunate structural defects in the national and international agricultural economy. The landlords were content in the knowledge that Obregón thought, as they did, that the solution to those problems was not to split their lands up among poor and ignorant Indians.

In fact, Obregón was quite explicit on the last point: a precipitous division of the estates would be disastrous. The objective for the moment must be to avoid shortfalls in production and a disruption of markets that would end in famine. The long-term objective would be the creation of that middle class of small farmers so long dreamt of. In the meantime, however, the proper strategies were to attack only those farmers who remained obstinately antimodern; to allow the rest space and facilities to modernize their operations and raise the wages they paid to their laborers; and simultaneously to educate the rural masses, imparting both basic literacy and technical training.

Díaz Soto y Gama was not pleased, although he may be have been somewhat mollified by repeated claims that the regime planned to do whatever it did "with absolute radicalism." He could not resist pointing out the faulty syllogism at the heart of Obregón's arguments: "The objective," he said, "is to destroy the big estates. But the big estates cannot be destroyed unless small properties are first created. But small properties are not yet formed, so therefore the big estates cannot be destroyed." For him, the big estates were "monsters" that must be slain before progress could take place.

The great stumbling block to agrarian reform, however, was that the politicians, like generations of landowners and observers before them, had scant faith in Mexico's rural masses. One Obregonista congressman admitted that "the great majority of our peasants are hungry" and acknowledged that many of them did indeed hunger for land. At the same time, however, he seconded the anti-agrarista argument that there was a limit to the amount of land the peasants could productively use. Therefore, although the country people were hungry, "if anybody presents a bill to compel them to eat twenty-five loaves of bread in an hour, I will oppose it."[8]

So much for ideology. In practical terms, this debate meant little change in official agrarian policy. Obregón issued a lengthy "Law of Ejidos" within days of his inauguration, but that document only succeeded in further muddying the waters.[9] Complicated and confusing, it did not alter the most objectionable feature of Carranza's policy: the president's personal approval would still be required to convert provisional grants into definitive ones. Theoretically, at least, concentration of power in his own hands would give Obregón the flexibility he needed to play to several crowds. He could present himself as a radical populist and lofty benefactor, even while avoiding any doctrinaire commitments that might compromise his image as an enlightened modernizer.

The law also maintained the most frustrating ambiguities of earlier laws. The hopeful petitioners and anxious landlords of the Puebla-Tlaxcala Valley found in it only the haziest hint as to how the whole process should work. So far, only one grant of lands from San Pedro Coxtocán—one given to the village of Santa María Moyotzingo—had been confirmed by the president, but was promptly appealed through the courts. Two other grants—to San Jerónimo Tianguismanalco and San Francisco Tepeyecac—had been approved by the state government and agrarian commission, and thus were deemed "provisional." The problem was that no one seemed to know exactly what "provisional" meant, and while petitions plodded through the bureaucratic labyrinth, crops continued to ripen in the fields, demanding immediate and undivided attention. It was unclear not only who should get the crop, but also who had the authority to decide the matter. In the end, the only thing that was assured was conflict.

JOSÉ MARÍA SÁNCHEZ

Ambiguity at the top translated into conflict and confusion everywhere else. In revolutionary Mexico, few at any level put much stock in the notion of the abstract rule of law, as Rosalie Evans was learning to her great exasperation, for faith in such notions could imply a perilous relaxation of vigilance. Even federal deputies wore firearms openly in the chamber. One congressman from Michoacán, varying this practice, kept an enormous pistol—which he nicknamed "the Constitution"–tucked discreetly away in his briefcase. The man's fellow deputies, astonished at seeing no weapon displayed on his person, would advise him to arm himself at once for his own protection, to which the man would reply imperiously, "I need no protection except 'the Constitution,' which I always carry in my briefcase!"[10]

The most optimistic individuals found reassurance in the fact that by 1920 the worst of the armed conflict had ended, and the difficult task of state building had begun. A darker assessment, however, suggested that the contending parties had merely reversed von Clausewitz's dictum and were continuing the war through political means. Nourished by ten years of armed conflict, political passions remained heated. For the federal government, state-level politics quickly became an exasperating cacophony, where zealous defenses of state sovereignty clashed with calls to adjudicate intractible wrangles—a no-win situation because most political skirmishes ended in bitter denunciations either of the federal government's aloofness or of its bullying favoritism. In any case, the echo of Obregón's inaugural address had not yet faded before Puebla's political scene turned violent.

Obregón's favored candidate in the Puebla gubernatorial elections of December 1920 was José María Sánchez, a political ruffian who would set the fervid tone of the state's political life in the first half of the 1920s. He towered above his colleagues, and not just figuratively: his six-foot stature — prodigious in his time and place — earned him the nickname "the Giant of Chachapa." Chachapa was the homely village just east of Puebla City where Sánchez was raised and where, according to his own account, he first tasted the degradation of life as a hacienda laborer. Some well-to-do residents of Puebla City in 1920 insisted that, not so many years before, they used to see Sánchez driving carts loaded with sand and other construction materials.[11]

The revolution had offered him escape from grinding toil. He cast his lot first with the Zapatistas and at some point found his way into the Constitutionalist ranks. Although he claimed the rank of general, it was never clear precisely where that commission came from. His military career is lost in obscurity, but in any case it was apparent that he intended civilian politics to be his game. By 1917 he was serving as deputy to federal Congress, where he hitched his fortunes to those of Obregón. By 1919 he was serving as Obregón's unofficial representative in Puebla, where he first gained attention by decrying Carrancista impositions.

Sánchez was a new breed of politician. In the old Mexico of Porfirio Díaz, men sometimes rose from poverty to high political office, but in those days would adopt a new set of manners upon arriving there. Sánchez, by contrast, not only made no apologies for his humble beginnings, but seemed to imply that gentility was an egregious character flaw. He was no diplomatist or conciliator: he was a loud, abrasive, arrogant, and supremely self-confident man who found the hatred of his enemies positively invigorating. He once thanked a group of reporters for their heated diatribes against him, explaining that on any day the papers failed to attack him, he could not enjoy his breakfast.[12] "Of course," he wrote in the preface to a book on socialism, "I have never even considered my useless political enemies, who for reasons of hatred, rancor, and — why not say it? — my own superiority, see only evil . . . in everything I do. Such is the characteristic attribute of ill-intentioned and inferior beings, whose unhealthy instincts compel them to lash out as a consequence of their own impotence."[13]

Sánchez's confidence came largely from his image as a champion of the common folk, but even the common folk found him hard to take at times. When delegations of peasants and workers came to see him, he would greet them with his left hand "for reasons of hygiene." When the delegations objected to this insult, he condescended to use his right hand — but wore a glove. And he entertained no audience without a loaded pistol placed menacingly on his desktop.[14]

José María Sánchez — "a new breed of politician." *Credit:* Gustavo Casasola, *Historia gráfica de la Revolución Mexicana, 1900–1970,* 2d ed. (Mexico City: Editorial Trillas, S.A. de C.V., 1973).

Eccentric, volatile, feared and despised though he may have been, Sánchez
understood well the political arts of his day. In the period before the gubernatorial elections, the interim state government was seeking actively to break up
a wave of violent strikes that swept Puebla's textile industry. At the same time,
villagers were fearful and uncertain about the return of the old landowners,
wondering nervously who would win the new government's support. Sánchez
presented himself to these groups as their salvation, exploiting fears and inqui-
etudes to forge a formidable popular coalition.[15] His rival candidates presented
anemic competition: a wizened, white-whiskered, dipsomaniacal, octogenarian

general named Higinio Aguilar campaigned on behalf of the propertied classes, and Rafael Lara Grajales represented the urban moderates of the sort who had conducted the Madero revolution a decade before. All factions resorted to wholesale fraud and violence in their campaigns, and the election ended — in what would be the standard outcome of elections throughout the decade — with both Sánchez and Lara Grajales claiming victory and setting up rival legislatures.

This sort of thing was embarrassing to Obregón, who feared the unfortunate precedent it might set for other states. He was also concerned about the impression potential creditors overseas might get from seeing armed camps squaring off in the main plaza of one of Mexico's most elegant cities. Accordingly, the president, although making a show of impartiality, sent emissaries to examine the voting and to discover that José María Sánchez was in fact the winner. By the time Sánchez took office in June of 1921, a full six months after the elections, the state treasury was empty, the state was eighteen paychecks in arrears to its employees; city services were practically nonexistent; crime was still rampant; and a good part of the state's politically active citizens viewed their new leader with horror. With Sánchez in the governor's chair, the revolution in Puebla veered sharply leftward.[16] His forays into radical legislation provoked rioting and mayhem, and ended with the governor himself on the lam.

MANUEL P. MONTES

Sánchez's inauguration as governor happened to coincide with the harvest season, and agrarian activists were emboldened to renew their offensive. In early May 1921, as Sánchez prepared to take office, they shot and gravely wounded a young Spaniard who rented Santa María Coxtocán, a smaller property annexed to San Pedro. Mrs. Evans had the unpleasant duty of rescuing him in her buggy while his face turned "such wonderful colors, purple, yellow, crimson, then a ghastly livid hue, and his eyes grew dim — made me think of a dying bird."[17] Some days later the activists raided San Juan Tetla, a property that U.S. consul William O. Jenkins rented to a Spaniard named Fernando Arizmendi — a friend of Mrs. Evans and a bold, chivalrous character whose brother had been killed two years earlier by Cirilo Arenas's men. When Arizmendi confronted the raiders, most likely expecting them to flee at his approach, he found them uncharacteristically bellicose. They explained that they had orders from a certain General Manuel P. Montes, then opened fire, killing a foreman and wounding Arizmendi's horse.[18]

The name of Manuel P. Montes was gaining notoriety in the Texmelucan Valley. Around the same time that Montes's men killed Jenkins's foreman, May of 1921, Mrs. Evans gained her first impression of the man from a circular he sent to the villages — reviving the old Zapatista war cries, inciting villagers to

Manuel P. Montes — "He was short and square, with the cruelest little black eyes." *Credit:* Julio Cuadros Caldos, *Mexico-Soviet* (Puebla: Santiago Loyo, 1926).

take lands by force, and chiding them that only cowardice would prevent their doing so. Mrs. Evans had barely received this missive when its author appeared before her in the flesh. "He was dressed in a black frock coat, and a bull fighter hat," Mrs. Evans recounted. "[He] is short and square, with the cruelest little black eyes, like a snake ready to strike." This first meeting was unpromising. Montes tried to exhort the gathered villagers, who on this occasion were un-armed, to take the crop by force. Mrs. Evans, according to her own account, "outspoke him, calling him a coward, assassin and my whole wicked vocabulary of insults. He trembled with rage, but I got my hand on my pistol and *he* ran."[19]

The episode heralded a disheartening turn of events for Mrs. Evans. The relative calm she had been enjoying during the early months of the Obregón administration caused the growing radicalism of mid-1921 to catch her un-awares. Although she would later develop a healthy fear of such tranquil inter-ludes, she nevertheless always held to the conviction that the villagers wanted only to be left alone so they could go on working for the haciendas. Rather like pondwater, they would remain inert unless disturbed by some alien force. She probably had cause and effect backwards, however the villagers' radicalism was not so much provoked by the presence of outside interference as held in check by its absence. A radical posture would be merely reckless without some as-surance of outside support. The government's will was inscrutable and unpre-dictable, however, and so was the will of its chief tool for enforcing agrarian reform, the federal army. In this unsettled situation, bold and decisive men like José María Sánchez and Manuel P. Montes could upset the fragile equilibrium Mrs. Evans found so reassuring.

The federal army — which villagers looked to for clues regarding their govern-ment's sympathies — was a barely coherent collection of opportunists and ad-venturers whom the federal government, for the moment, could only dream of controlling. Whether from ideological conviction or simple greed, officers often backed the landowners against invasions whether or not they had been ordered to do so. In fact, the archconservatives seemed to have a lock on Puebla's top military post. General Cesáreo Castro, the man who had helped Rosalie Evans in the fall of 1918, had stayed loyal to Carranza and was currently adjusting to exile in the United States, but his successor as chief of military operations for the region was General Fortunato Maycotte, a man cut from the same cloth. Both hailed from Coahuila, both were rigid military men with mustaches that curled up at the ends, and both were frank enemies of radical social reforms. From the start of his tenure in the state, Maycotte fought with Governor Sánchez just as Castro had wrangled with Cabrera.

Whereas the top leadership was split, most of the rank-and-file soldiers gar-risoned in the key district towns were merely bemused. By and large, they were young men far from home and disoriented upon finding themselves in places

General Fortunato Maycotte—"From the start he fought with Sánchez." *Credit:* Gustavo Casasola, *Historia gráfica de la Revolución Mexicana, 1900–1970,* 2d ed. (Mexico City: Editorial Trillas, S.A. de C.V., 1973).

where they had no interests to defend, no reputation to uphold, no family to please. Weapons, alcohol, marijuana, and guarantees of impunity made them bold and volatile. With no dog of their own in the fight, they waited for some hint or direction.[20] Officers in charge of local garrisons would sometimes distribute soldiers among haciendas that gladly housed and fed them, saving the army the cost of their upkeep. The army's budget was small, and the soldiers were hungry. As Mrs. Evans discovered, their loyalty could be bought with coffee, tortillas, and beans[21] — hardly the loyal minions of a secure and resolute government.

As long as they were uncertain of the federal government's ability to enforce its will — or of precisely what that will *was* — and as long as they lacked forceful local leadership, land hungry villagers could mount only the most tentative actions. In June 1920, for instance, "the creatures" (as Mrs. Evans called them) threw a piece of iron into Mrs. Evans's threshing machine. In September, villagers from Tianguismanalco showed up on San Pedro's land to measure off a field they had been granted provisionally more than two years earlier. When Mrs. Evans confronted them, their leader, Francisco Rosas, answered impolitely. With that, Mrs. Evans turned violent for the first time, making her horse "plunge about, scattering the men right and left," while she drew her pistol and threatened that if the villagers did not leave at once she would shoot Rosas. They left, but returned in force a week later to once again measure the field. This time, Mrs. Evans restricted herself to calm persuasions, explaining that the grant needed definitive approval of the president before the villagers could begin to work it.[22] Clearly confused by the tricky agrarian legislation, they left once again without a fight.

Ambiguous episodes of this kind impressed Mrs. Evans. "I have not a single enemy," she wrote in December of 1920 at the very moment that José María Sánchez was being elected governor; "the *agrarios* are as if they were not. I know the hydras are lurking in their adobe dens, but while they lie dormant and hidden I bask in the sun and renew my strength." For a time, it was just as it had been in the old days, some workers even doffing their hats as she passed and greeting her with an "Ave María." "If the treacherous government continues to support me," she wrote hopefully, "I shall have no further trouble."[23]

Her hope was fantasy, of course, for treacherous governments are, after all, treacherous. With Sánchez's inauguration and Manuel P. Montes's escalating activities, a new spirit of radicalism was in the air. Suddenly, the federal army — the most prominent menace to ambitious agrarian reformers — was countered by a newly invigorated paramilitary force known as the *regionales,* the "regional corp," apparently a descendant of the force created by Governor Alfonso Cabrera for his own defense against the anticipated treachery of General Cesáreo Castro. In the Sánchez government, however, they became agrarista shock troops under the immediate command of the village agrarian committee president. The various units were orchestrated, however, by a new breed of local firebrand, the agrarian *caciques,* local bosses who staked their claim to power on their success in delivering land to the people. Most were ex-Zapatista or Arenista officers, and they operated in every district of the state: Fortino Ayaquica in Atlixco, Honorato Teutli in Cholula, Francisco Barbosa and Pedro Luna Galicia in Tehuacán, and Ricardo Reyes Martínez in Tepexi de Rodríguez. Braced by Sánchez's ascension to power, these men grew ruthless in their ambitions, motivated by a complicated mixture of self-aggrandizement and idealism. Although the agrarian cacique had a host of ancestors in Mexico's political cosmos, he was a new species because his power was so clearly and so single-mindedly predicated upon the promise of delivering land to the tiller. As sketched by one anthropologist, he was ambitious, jealous of his power, egotistical, violent, energetic, cunning, acquisitive, and coldly self-assured.[24] The successful agrarian cacique was so dogged and single-minded as to be undeterred even by a rather high degree of popular diffidence. Neutrality became a dangerous posture.

By early 1921, Manuel P. Montes was clearly emerging as the unrivaled agrarian cacique of the San Martín Texmelucan Valley. He did not cut an impressive figure — standing barely five feet tall, his mustachioed countenance marred by the signs of a childhood bout with smallpox.[25] His quarrel with the haciendas had begun practically upon his birth in 1881 in El Moral. At that time, El Moral was officially a *barrio,* or "neighborhood," located on the banks of the Coatzala River, which runs south of the city of San Martín Texmelucan. In 1910, it had a population of forty-seven grown men and their families, only nine of whom were able to read and write. Although it was officially an appendage of San Martín Texmelucan, its most important connection was to the entity to the south, the hacienda Polaxtla. Whereas other villages in the region were surrounded on all sides by haciendas and not so directly subject to any one of them, El Moral — squeezed between city and hacienda — was almost wholly dominated by Polaxtla. The villagers would alternately list their residence as "the barrio of El Moral" or "the hacienda Polaxtla"; it amounted to the same thing.

Polaxtla had an evil reputation of long standing. One of the largest haciendas of the region and one of the first acquired by Félix Pérez, a Spanish cotton merchant who went on to control a large portion of the economy of the Texmelucan Valley in the late nineteenth century, the hacienda produced the usual wheat, corn, beans, and chile peppers, and also enjoyed a monopoly in the region on the elaboration of pulque. Montes had worked on Polaxtla as a boy and continued to work there even after he acquired the trade of *albañil,* or mason. According to him, the labor regimen on the hacienda was harsh, and the administrators and foremen were quick to resort to cruel punishments.

Montes's political beginnings were fairly typical of local caciques. Owing to the fact that his family was, by barrio standards, fairly prominent, he learned to read and write, which translated into a measure of power in El Moral. By 1907, he was the barrio's *inspector suplente,* a petty official who would register the villagers to vote, bail them out of jail, relay the news of the day, make their case before the local authorities, help the sick and injured find medical care, and generally act as a mediator between them and the world outside — or, at times, a bulwark between them and the hacienda Polaxtla.[26]

With the outbreak of the revolution in 1910, Montes joined the movement headed locally by an ex-Methodist preacher named Benigno Zenteno. From there, he moved into the camp of Domingo Arenas, following him in and out of his various alliances, and standing in his shadow in late 1916 when the Tlaxcalan leader "unified" his forces with those of the Carrancistas.[27] He built up an extensive clientele as a tireless propagandist for Arenas's agrarian reform.[28] A disaffected secretary later claimed that Montes did not earn his general's rank through military exploits, for he never actively participated in combat.[29] It was as if all along he had been grooming himself to take over the political wing of the movement once the fighting stopped. His campaign, which began in earnest after Arenas's death, was based on a single-minded determination to seize and divide up the estates and to keep Arenas's land grants intact.[30]

By 1919, "Colonel" Montes was the district of Huejotzingo's alternate to the national Congress, and the next year he was deputy in his own right. Like José María Sánchez, he linked his fortunes to those of Obregón. One account even has him participating in the treacherous assassination of Carranza in May of 1920, being taken prisoner, and escaping in time to welcome the triumphant Obregonistas into Puebla.[31] On July 10, 1921 — with the help of Cristino Vázquez and Lorenzo Meza, organizers from the Regional Confederation of Mexican Workers (CROM) who had won their spurs in the factories of San Martín Texmelucan — Montes formed the Confederación Social Campesina "Domingo Arenas" (hereafter referred to as the Domingo Arenas Confederation), with its headquarters in El Moral.[32] CROM would later evolve into a tool for breaking the power of the agrarian caciques, but at this early stage cooperation between field and factory workers was still possible.

THE SAN LUCAS MASSACRE

Montes masterminded most of the bold actions taken throughout the valley in the spring and autumn of 1921, but he devoted special attention to exacting vengeance against Polaxtla, the old nemesis of El Moral. Since Montes's childhood, the hacienda had been passed from Félix Pérez to his son-in-law, Marcelino Presno, who had in turn "sold" it to his married daughter, Natalia Presno y Pérez de Navia Osorio. In contrast to several of the supposed "buyers" of Presno's properties, Natalia Presno had at least attained the age of reason, but she took little interest in the hacienda, spending most of her time in Europe. The task of defending the property against agrarista incursions fell to Presno's proxy, a Spanish lawyer named Victoriano Alvarez, and to the administrator he hired, a young Spaniard named Antonio Arroyo.

Montes's first victory in his fight with Polaxtla came on April 13, 1918, when he had El Moral upgraded from a barrio to a pueblo, which made it legally eligible to receive an ejido. Bolder action followed in December of 1920, when the villagers of El Moral invaded Polaxtla's lands and, in defiance of agrarian and municipal authorities, built a small squatter settlement of makeshift adobe huts. Victoriano Alvarez demanded that the federal government forcibly evict them and destroy their huts, but he got no satisfaction. In early 1921, the State Agrarian Commission approved a grant of 222 acres of Polaxtla's land to El Moral. Alvarez grew weary of pleading with the federal government for help and resorted to private arrangements: he armed the hacienda's employees and instructed them to drive off agrarians and their engineers by force; he brought in scab workers, who endured threats and harrassment from the Montistas while they gathered in most of the wheat crop; and he made a pact with the garrison commander at San Martín, Colonel Ernesto Piña of the southern state of Oaxaca, securing his unstinting support.

Conflict developed along with the agricultural cycle. When villagers tried to gather the corn harvest in October of 1921, Antonio Arroyo and several armed men warned them off at gunpoint. The confrontation gave way to a gun battle, which left one man wounded and the home of Manuel P. Montes pocked with holes from bullets fired from the hacienda's parapets. Soldiers became field hands and harvested the remaining corn for the hacienda. Montes protested the attack to National Agrarian Party president Antonio Díaz Soto y Gama, who in turn used the incident to upbraid President Obregón for his tepid commitment to agrarian reform, furiously charging that Obregón's own top military commanders — men such as Castro and Maycotte — were leagued with the privileged classes. Men "who yesterday were soldiers of the revolution have today become instruments of the people's worst enemies."[33]

After the corn harvest, the conflict only worsened. The villagers of El Moral, joined by those of San Lucas Atoyatenco on Polaxtla's southern border, plowed the land of their provisional grant and planted wheat, but lawyer Alvarez immediately sent his loyal ox teams, guarded by soldiers of Colonel Piña's 180th Cavalry regiment, to plow over the seeds. In the meantime, Colonel Piña and several hacienda employees skirted the hacienda's boundaries in an automobile, threatening any who approached the disputed land.

On Monday, November 28, 1921, the border between San Lucas Atoyatenco and Polaxtla became the scene of a showdown, although accounts of what happened there conflict absolutely. Alvarez claimed that three hundred armed villagers, led by soldiers of the regional corp, attacked the hacienda, intending to steal the cavalry's horses and to kill the loyal field hands; federal troops fired on them to repel the assault. The agraristas, however, claimed that the federal troops launched an unprovoked attack on the village of San Lucas, and they called for stern punishment of Marcelino Presno and his "bourgeois hyenas." Regardless of which account comes closest to the truth, the fact remains that after forty-five minutes of shooting, six agraristas lay dead, and many more were wounded or jailed.[34] The martyrs of the "San Lucas Massacre" were honored in a *corrido* (ballad), and their sacrifice would be commemorated in yearly celebrations.

Unfortunately, support for the villagers at the topmost levels was as unpredictable as always and at that moment was diminishing. Obregón approved orders for the arrest of Colonel Piña and administrator Antonio Arroyo, but his support for the agrarian raiders was qualified. By the end of January 1922, he was pressuring Governor Sánchez to provide protection to the hacienda and to prevent the villagers from interfering with the harvest. Meanwhile, although José María Sánchez continued to back the people of El Moral, he had problems of his own.

SÁNCHEZ AT BAY

Sánchez's radical designs — and his reckless, autocratic style of carrying them out — proved his undoing. Since taking office, he had distinguished himself as an author of controversial legislation, beginning with a decree that all livestock must be branded and registered with the state government. Ranchers loudly decried what they derisively called the "Goat Law" as an unwarranted interference in private life and commerce.[35] The "Goat Law" controversy was soon forgotten, however, amid the howls of protest surrounding Sánchez's legislative pièce de résistance — the "Ley de Patente," or "License Law," which aimed to solve the perennial problem of government penury by taxing virtually everything. It featured a bulky list of some 284 different kinds of companies, together with the rates at which each could be taxed. Any business not specifically mentioned could be taxed "by analogy." Rates were determined by a board appointed by the governor, and the governor retained the right to revise or veto any of the board's decisions. The governor also accorded himself the power to adjudicate any disputes arising from the law. In other words, Sánchez gave himself — theoretically, at least — the power of life and death over the state's commerce.[36]

The protests were immediate and heated. Although the conservative press of the city largely coordinated the protests because it had good reason to fear that Sánchez would use the law to tax them into submission, people from all social classes also joined in. In mid-October, some ten to fifteen thousand protestors marched through the streets, escorted by troops provided by General Maycotte. When the marchers arrived at the main plaza, Sánchez supporters fired down on them from the cathedral tower. The rally turned so violent that Governor Sánchez was obliged to escape through the back door of the government palace and to avoid the city for several weeks.

President Obregón continued to back his protege, but Sánchez's support in his home state was waning. He tried desperately to shore up his most reliable base of strength by sanctioning land invasions of the kind led by Montes against Polaxtla and by passing a new labor code—measures that earned him a bit of international notoriety. The *New York Tribune* reported in December that workers and peasants in Puebla were seizing land and factories "with the avowed intention of establishing a soviet." Sánchez, the red and black banner fluttering from his car, was cheered by workers as he toured the factories. The Spanish government, meanwhile, took up the cry of Puebla's Spanish industrialists, merchants, and factory owners, and threatened to cut off its relations with Mexico.[37]

Increasingly, however, the governor's most intransigent enemies were to be found in the state Congress. Enraged at Sánchez's efforts to override their authority and frightened by verbal and physical abuse that he and his people occasionally heaped upon them, many of the congressional deputies withdrew their support. In mid-February, the growing tension led to a fistfight in the halls of Congress between a Sanchista deputy named Tranquilino Alonso and an anti-Sanchista deputy named Antonio Moro. The fight was broken up, but Moro's younger brother, Alfonso, later stalked Tranquilino Alonso and shot him dead.

The killing of deputy Alonso triggered a series of events that brought Sánchez's brief, tumultuous career as governor to an end. The chief of Puebla's police, General Arturo Camarillo, captured young Alfonso Moro a few blocks away from the spot where Alonso had been shot. The police roughed him up and locked him in a jail cell, then went off to look for brother Antonio. At the Moro home, they found a third Moro brother, Fernando, a family man looking forward to a promising career in medicine. Camarillo and his men took Fernando Moro into the street, where they riddled him with bullets in full view of his neighbors and family. Back at the police station, Camarillo ordered Alfonso Moro taken from his cell and shot.

The cold-blooded killing of the Moro brothers shocked Puebla society and was universally blamed on Governor Sánchez. The scandal was one that neither Sánchez nor his patron, Obregón, could live down. The state legislature, which moved its operations to a railroad junction town thirty miles northeast of

Puebla City, issued orders for Sánchez's arrest. Realizing the hopelessness of his situation, Sánchez asked the federal Congress to grant him indefinite leave from his post as governor.

Soon after, he left Mexico on an extended tour of Europe and the Soviet Union, hoping the situation might grow calm in his absence. While Sánchez held the ambiguous status of "governor on indefinite leave," he was replaced by a federal deputy named Froylán C. Manjarrez.[38]

DISARMING THE REGIONALES

The removal of Sánchez effectively deprived men like Manuel P. Montes of their most secure patron. Sánchez's successor won lavish praise from the conservative press when, shortly after taking office, he announced that his government, in collaboration with the federal army, would undertake to demobilize all "irregular" forces — namely, the agrarista regionales.[39] In this announcement, the interim governor was merely following orders from President Obregón himself, who had received volumes of complaints from his military zone commanders of agrarista attacks on haciendas. Obregón warned Manjarrez that his administration would continue to support the agrarian reform, but only so long as it was carried out in an orderly, legal manner.[40]

The federal soldiers were happy to oblige. In fact, they had begun disarming the regionales even without orders from above. The regular army men resented the regionales as rivals and potential adversaries, and so were generally unsentimental in dealing with them. The captain of the detachment stationed on Mrs. Evans's hacienda, for instance, scarcely blinked before he ordered the summary execution of a regional soldier he claimed had barged drunkenly into his tent, demanding the deference that was his due and randomly shooting off his pistol. Only the timely intervention of the municipal president of the young man's home village spared his life.[41] Professional soldiers not only feared these volatile characters, but they also disliked having to police the many disputes occasioned by the presence of zealous and self-important amateur soldiers within the villages.[42]

To be sure, as fierce partisans in village politics, the regionales earned much local enmity, for the agrarian reform caused bitter feuds among the villagers. Some of the poorest villagers, pleading hunger and desperation, signed work contracts with the haciendas. When a young Tlaxcalan named Daniel Rodríguez, for instance, took a job guarding some woodlands of the hacienda San Juan Tetla against the rapacious axes of the villagers, a group of regionales broke into his home and beat him senseless in front of his family.[43] Other field hands who violated labor boycotts or who went to work on disputed lands made themselves vulnerable to similar reprisals.

Some conflicts were of recent vintage, others venerable feuds. In both cases, the regionales became factional hatchet men and avengers. The landlords' practice of *fraccionamiento,* in particular, gave rise to fierce intravillage disputes. In Santa Ana Xalmimilulco, for instance, Serapio Pérez and Genaro Solís nearly killed each other in an endless dispute over less than 4 acres of land. Genaro Solís was a committed agrarista, a former Zapatista lieutenant colonel who had hated Serapio Pérez since anyone could remember. When the revolution ended and the armies demobilized, Solís went home anticipating his reward. Unfortunately, the plot of land he claimed as his portion of the village's grant was also claimed by Pérez, who insisted that he had bought it in 1919 from Marcelino Presno. The plot—known as "La Posta"—took on an almost symbolic dimension as it was disputed in nearly every conceivable fashion. No sooner would one man sow the land than the other would appear to tear up the seedlings. The agraristas and regionales united around Solís, whereas the fraccionistas backed Pérez. And so the feud continued for years.[44]

The true origins of disputes were not always so easy to discern. Although conflict at least appeared to obey the logic of an ambiguous class war, fights often as not contained elements of mystery that even their protagonists were hard-pressed to clarify. In February of 1922 a young officer of the regionales in the village of Tepatlaxco had his hand blown off by a grenade. He explained that when he and several fellow soldiers tried to post copies of Governor Sánchez's new labor code on the street corners, a group of their fellow villagers had followed them, tooting on harmonicas and shouting, "Long live the counterrevolution and the industrialists, death to the party of the ragged bums! ["muera el partido de los los encuerados"]. The officer swore he was at a loss to understand this attitude because his tormentors had been his close friends before he donned the uniform of the regional corp. The tormentors, for their part, charged that the regionales were constantly getting drunk and terrorizing their fellow citizens. The wounded officer, they explained implausibly, had been waving a grenade threateningly at them when the grenade accidentally exploded.[45]

MONTES AT BAY

For Manuel P. Montes, the fall of José María Sánchez and the campaign to disarm the regionales were decidedly bad news. He was keenly aware of his need for allies higher up, just as he was aware of the growing resentment from below aimed at himself and his followers, but he could not easily denounce all of his critics as reactionaries and stooges of the hacendados. Not a few dissenters were found among veteran Arenistas. At the moment, he needed all the support he could possibly get because he was set to run for federal Congress in July.

Confronted with such adversity, Montes—who was always alive to the value of symbol and ceremony—made a sudden, stunning announcement. The remains of General Domingo Arenas, he claimed, had been found near Zapata's old headquarters at Tlaltizapan, Morelos, and he, Montes, intended to bring them to San Martín Texmelucan, where they would be honored prior to being shipped to Arenas's hometown for burial. The announcement was met with some incredulity, for among the few points nearly all accounts of Arenas's demise agreed on was that the corpse had been desecrated and disposed of unceremoniously. Some even said that the body had never made it to Morelos but had been cast into a ravine near Tochimilco. In fact, Cirilo Arenas himself had written to Zapata in October of 1918 to ask that his brother's remains be returned to him for a proper burial. Although there is no record of the response, it seems likely that Zapata would have obliged Cirilo's request had it been within his power to do so, for at that time he was desperate for allies and would have jumped at the chance to win one with so small a favor.[46] The corpse lingered in absolute obscurity, however, until it was supposedly unearthed by Montes's agents. There was some grumbling, both then and later, that this claim was pure chicanery, but it gave Montes the symbolic boost he needed. Thus, on February 19, 1922, Montes's agraristas, led by fully armed soldiers of the regional corp, marched through the streets of San Martín bearing the mortal remains of someone they claimed had in life been Domingo Arenas.[47]

Clearly, Montes intended to hammer home the point that he was the rightful political heir to Domingo Arenas. Hoping simultaneously to reinforce the zeal of his followers, he made the point by nurturing a cult of agrarian struggles, so the number of martyrs and occasions grew exponentially. A "Campesino Congress" in August was followed immediately by a rally to commemorate the fifth anniversary of the death of Domingo Arenas, which was followed by yet another rally in honor of September 16, Mexico's Independence Day. Soon after, another rally was held to commemorate the San Lucas Massacre of September 28, 1921. Local authorities unwittingly cast themselves as philistines when they tried to rein in these rallies. Although the municipal president of San Martín grudgingly allowed the rallies to proceed, he did so with the provisos that the marchers carry no weapons and that "you will not make subversive speeches or hurl insults at people, associations, or nations."[48]

Together with his ceremonial efforts, Montes continued to lead sporadic land invasions, which were made somewhat less risky by the fact that Colonel Piña had been replaced in San Martín by an officer who was less sympathetic to the landlords. In May, some three hundred armed agraristas bearing red and black flags occupied Polaxtla, gathered the harvest, and refused to surrender any of it to the hacienda.[49] But these populist tactics did not win everyone over. Villagers who were reluctant to participate in such mass actions as rallies and hacienda invasions were harrassed ruthlessly by their local regionales. The occurrence of such harrassment was recorded when some villagers of Tianguismanalco went to the courts with tales of arbitrary arrests and incarcerations, beatings, and threats.[50]

The federal election was the crucible. On June 1, the church bell of Tianguismanalco began to chime, calling the villagers to gather in front of the municipal president's office for a town meeting. As the villagers arrived in the main square, they were handed ballots already marked in favor of Manuel P. Montes and told that if they did not cast those ballots, they would get no land. In Xaltepetlapa, local election officials showed up at nine o'clock in the morning to set up the polling booth, only to find the Montistas already there, instructing citizens how to vote. Despite such maneuvers, the official tallies gave the election by a wide margin to Montes's opponent, Roberto Casas Alatriste. Not surprisingly, Casas Alatriste belonged to the Cooperatista Party, whose Puebla contingent was headed by Governor Manjarrez. Upon hearing the official results, Montes, with some twenty-five armed men, rode from village to village threatening election officials and voters and stealing ballot boxes. One of Casas Alatriste's first acts as federal deputy was to demand that local civil and military authorities immediately disarm what remained of Montes's regionales.[51] Montes tried to retaliate for his humiliation at the polls by ordering all of the unions affiliated with the State Syndicalist Confederation out on strike.[52]

Both military and civilian authorities grew bolder in their efforts to curtail Montes. A rally on Independence Day gave way to a dance in the main square of El Moral, which was in full swing at eight o'clock that night when federal soldiers arrived. The stomp of boots and the click of weapons silenced the music and halted the dancing. The soldiers demanded to know which one of the revelers was Montes. When the cacique stepped forward, the officer in charge struck him in the face with his pistol, leaving a gaping wound across his cheek that would heal into a menacing scar.

The other soldiers cocked their weapons and threatened to kill anyone who moved. Unmoved by Montes's heated protestations that he had friends in high places, including the president of the republic, they arrested twenty-six revelers without explaining the charges, tied their hands, and marched them off to San Martín under guard. A group of them sacked the municipal president's office, taking special pains to smash the all-important presidential seal, the symbol of local authority. Upon passing by Montes's home, the soldiers banged on the door and threatened to shoot it in if it were not opened immediately. Montes's eighteen-year-old daughter timidly obliged. On the pretext of searching for weapons, they ransacked the house, tearing through dresser drawers and wardrobes and jewelry boxes, scattering riding gear, kitchen utensils, and tools. They also riddled the headboard of Montes's bed with bullets, burned a red and black flag that hung on the wall of the room where the Domingo Arenas Confederation held its sessions, and hit Montes's aged mother in the head, knocking her to the floor—all the while hurling insults against Obregón and "certain functionaries of the current administration."[53] Montes and the others were then taken to Puebla City, where they were released almost immediately.

A "REIGN OF TERROR"

The vengeance visited upon Montes gives some indication of the anxious state of mind that prevailed among the local authorities, who feared, among other things, the return of José María Sánchez, who had become a formidable bugbear for the state's conservatives. No sooner had Sánchez abandoned Mexican soil than the rumors began to fly that he would soon return to lead an armed rebellion against the Manjarrez government. A local newspaper went so far as to describe a "latent rebellion" led by Sánchez and fueled by the agrarista shock troops of men like Montes.[54] Sánchez's supporters did their best to keep up the state of agitation by announcing that they were in constant telegraphic communication with the general, who continually assured them that very soon he would be back in Puebla to reassume his rightful office. As elections for municipal authorities approached in November, the rumor mills sowed panic with their predictions of a major Sanchista insurrection, even though the most that was actually uncovered was a small and easily dismantled plot in Atayatempan, a minor village some twenty miles southeast of Puebla City.[55]

As 1922 drew to a close, the authorities in San Martín Texmelucan decried a Montista "reign of terror." The most notorious episode in that reign was the murder of twenty-two-year-old Dionisio García in the village of San Buenaventura Tecaltzingo, which was an uncommonly tense village, a weathercock testing the divisive winds of local agrarian politics. Located about only three-and-a-half miles southwest of San Martín and even closer to the Montista stronghold of El Moral, it was among the first villages Montes had successfully recruited upon the founding of the Domingo Arenas Confederation in the summer of 1921. The town's García family (no relation to Dionisio) soon came to be counted among Montes's staunchest allies in the region. Pascual García became village president, his son Jesús the commander of the village regionales, and his other son, Gumaro, second in command to Montes at his El Moral headquarters.

The García clan had its share of mortal enemies in Tecaltzingo, however, where the fraccionistas were also well represented. In 1919, the Englishman Francis Ruhl had divided his entire hacienda, San Simón, and had sold it in small lots to the villagers of Tecaltzingo and its neighbor, San Juan Tuxco. Meanwhile, the wily Mexican hacendado Ignacio Ovando—Mrs. Evans's men-

tor until he had the bad grace to recommend to her a corrupt administrator[56] —
had actively recruited allies in Tecaltzingo with sharecropping contracts that
promised favorable treatment to those who explicitly renounced their petition
for a government land grant.[57] Most menacing of all was General Antonio Martínez — a federal army officer and an unabashed partisan of the landowners —
who owned a *rancho* (midsized property) practically within Tecaltzingo's town
limits. Martínez had favored the hacendados with soldiers and weapons, and,
according to some villagers, he and his men had sacked the homes of known
agraristas, confiscated their weapons, arrested them arbitrarily, and tortured
them in the barracks at San Martín.[58]

Martínez's presence in the village created quite an uncomfortable situation
for the Montistas of Tecaltzingo, but one that they dealt with tit for tat. Jesús
García and his regionales used the same terrorist tactics to help neutral or
wavering villagers make up their minds. According to their enemies, the Garcías
had declared "war without quarter" against anyone not affiliated with Montes.

With so many enemies occupying so small a town, the tension could hardly
be contained. It had already exploded once in September of 1921 into a bloody
riot that left several wounded on both sides and that was broken up only upon
the arrival of Martínez's federals.[59] Despite Jesús García's challenge on that
occasion that the agraristas and their antagonists have it out once and for all —
"que de una vez se rompa el cohete" — the tension only increased. By November
of 1922, the villagers of Tecaltzingo were so badly polarized that the warring
factions nearly forgot their adversaries and focused their ire on the irresolute —
people such as Dionisio García. An orchestra violinist, Dionisio had little interest in obtaining land and was loath to part with the money the Montistas
demanded in dues for joining the Domingo Arenas Confederation. For months
he had refused to sign a statement of adherence to the confederation, all the
while enduring constant threats and harrassment. On November 15, he traveled
to San Martín to buy rosin for his violin bow, where he was once again confronted by an angry group of Montistas, but was able to return to Tecaltzingo.
His mother last saw him playing marbles in the street with three local children.
An hour later she learned that he had been shot in the head by Jesús García, who
immediately spread the word that Dionisio's fate should serve as a warning to all
fence-sitters.[60]

GHOSTS AT SAN PEDRO

While Sánchez plotted his return from the Soviet Union and Montes whipped
his coalition into fighting shape, Rosalie Evans planned for her annual round of
Christmas parties in Mexico City. "My Indians are all peaceful just now," she

reported. She had regained a measure of calm and confidence recently, a feeling helped along by the cool air of the volcanoes, where she had been going each morning with her eight dogs to supervise the gathering of wood to power the threshing machine. "The brilliant sun," she wrote, "the strong pine odor and lying on the grass watching the small white clouds glide overhead, have brightened the darkest corners of my heart."[60] She bought a black crepe gown with flowing transparent sleeves and a black silk hat, and hoped to make an impression.

She also had moments of foreboding, however. On December 12, the heirs of Fernando and Mónica Mendizábal, San Pedro's former owners, had insisted on removing their grandparents' remains from their burial site under the floor of the hacienda's chapel. Although buried twenty-six years before, the bodies "were perfect in form, though mummified in part." The Mendizábal grandsons were poorly prepared for this eventuality, as they had brought along nothing but a couple of small boxes to transport the bone fragments and ashes they had expected to find. So, to the horror of the hacienda servants who looked on, they "tore the flesh off with their hands—parchment-like of course—and broke the bones to the size of the boxes!" Having torn up the chapel floor and desecrated the corpses of their forebears, the grandsons ate dinner, drank some beer, and "drove rollicking off to Puebla."[62]

In the estimation of the hacienda servants and employees, such disrespect toward the long dead was far worse than any depredations the agraristas could devise: "The four peons who had been forced to help them were all ill in bed. One had lost his sight and begged for herbs from [Doña Mónica's] garden to restore it." Shortly thereafter, Mrs. Evans's cook reported that she had heard screaming as she was preparing for bed, "as of some one who had gone mad." The watchmen and maids became agitated—declaring that they could not sleep, "the spirits sobbed so." A few days later, Mrs. Evans herself heard the screaming and dreamed she saw the dead landlords of San Pedro standing at the foot of her bed. Still later, she and her cook heard something outside and opened the window, admitting an invisible sobbing banshee. Even so sober a man as General James A. Ryan, agent of the Texas Oil Company and a guest at San Pedro, heard the ghostly sounds, which did not end until Mrs. Evans ordered a mass said over the restored graves of the Mendizábals.[63]

Yet, as Mrs. Evans readied herself for society that Christmas season of 1922, it was not unquiet shades that weighed most heavily on her mind. On November 9, President Obregón ordered the definitive grant of lands to San Jerónimo Tianguismanalco and San Francisco Tepeyecac, and she received the order in mid-December, bringing to nearly two thousand the number of acres that had been legally confiscated from the hacienda and leaving only 739 acres in undisputed legal possession of the estate.

The confiscation order and the haunting of San Pedro did not strike Mrs. Evans as altogether unrelated. "When I opened Obregon's orders, unsuspectingly," she confessed, "the first thing I thought of was the sobbing spirit."[64]

Six

The grand principles of right and wrong operate in
the same way between nations as between individuals;
fair and open conduct, and inviolable faith, however
they may appear adverse to present purposes, are the
only kind of policy that will ensure ultimate and
honorable success.
—Washington Irving, *Life and Voyages of Columbus*

B Y THE START of 1923, the number of Rosalie Evans's enemies had
grown considerably. Still, she thought she knew who her friends
were. Anglo-Saxons—especially those who had made their mark in
society—fared far better in her estimation than their Mexican counterparts. She
considered most Mexicans so ill-bred that among them even the pretense of
sophistication was pathetic. The foreign secretary, Alberto J. Pani, for instance,
had the distinction of being "the only one of the new government who attempts
society," yet he was also a "little, unctuous, very prosperous (since the revolution) black Mexican, with an agreeable manner—said to be a perfect fraud."[1] In
short, Mexicans—especially those who were not prosperous or whose fortunes
were of recent vintage—were "by nature" treacherous, but white Americans
and Europeans would have to prove themselves so.

Mrs. Evans's racial assumption led her to make some of her most regrettable
errors in judgment, for the community of foreigners with interests in Mexico was neither righteous nor solidary. Some considered Mrs. Evans and her
struggle an obstacle and an embarrassment. One such individual was General
James A. Ryan, the man who had heard noisy ghosts while a guest at San Pedro.
Ryan was a West Point graduate whose colorful career included hunts for
Geronimo and Pancho Villa.[2] After retiring from the U.S. Army, Ryan went to
Mexico as a representative of the Texas Oil Company, a task that brought him
into contact with influential individuals in both U.S. and Mexican officialdom.
He was especially zealous in urging Americans and Mexicans to discuss the U.S.
diplomatic recognition of Mexico. In the meantime, he carefully built up his
reputation as the man to see to get things done in Mexico.

Rosalie Evans was among those won over by his posturing. The day before Christmas 1922 and shortly after receiving notice of the definitive confiscation of San Pedro's lands, she dressed carefully to pay General Ryan a visit. Mrs. Rosemary Ryan presented her with a red coral comb and generous flattery ("No one," Mrs. Ryan told her, "had hair like mine, nor knew how to wear combs as I did"), and General Ryan spoke the very words she had most hoped to hear. "I can get you an interview with Obregón," he promised, when she told him of the Mexican president's decree. "You shan't lose that place."[3]

AN INTERVIEW WITH THE PRESIDENT

By 1923, Mrs. Evans was predisposed to think ill of Obregón, although her mind was not altogether closed on the topic. She had met him once before — in 1920, shortly after he had moved into his new office at Chapultepec Palace. On that occasion, Obregón had given a cordial reception to her and the British chargé d'affaires, Herbert Ashley Cunard Cummins. As Mrs. Evans recalled it, the scene at the palace was warm, with Mrs. Obregón sitting gingerly on the edge of a Louis Quinze chair, the Obregón children playing on the floor with "gorgeous French toys," and the courtyard full of "new automobiles, limousines, coupés and touring cars of expensive foreign makes."[4] Obregón, perhaps flush with new power and content amid this scene of deluxe domesticity, had promised protection for Mrs. Evans and her hacienda — one reason why she interpreted so many of her subsequent experiences as the vilest betrayal.

Ryan was in fact able to secure Mrs. Evans an interview with the president in 1923. Later, in a decidedly self-serving account, he would insist that the interview he had arranged was a smashing success.[5] It was really a catastrophe, however. If Mrs. Evans entered the interview thinking Obregón was "a very bad man" (as even Ryan admitted), she left it thinking of him as "a poor brute," of whom she had "rather a sort of horror as of a *chien enragé* that should be killed."[6] Nor did Obregón warm to Mrs. Evans, who certainly bore her share of the blame for the disastrous dialogue. Upon being ushered into Obregón's office, she lost no time in committing her first faux pas by reminding him that she had met him previously in the company of the British chargé d'affaires, Mr. Cummins, although she knew Obregón had come to loathe Cummins and had repeatedly urged the British government to remove him from Mexico. She should not have been surprised, then, when Obregón "merely rolled his round eyes to the ceiling and made no reply."

From this inauspicious opening, the interview degenerated even further. Obregón insisted that he was too busy to intervene personally in Mrs. Evans's affairs, but he offered to send an inspector. Mrs. Evans hotly rejected his offer on the grounds that agrarian inspectors were notoriously sympathetic toward the

Foreign Minister Alberto Pani — "The only one of the new government who attempts society." *Credit:* Gustavo Casasola, *Historia gráfica de la Revolución Mexicana, 1900–1970,* 2d ed. (Mexico City: Editorial Trillas, S.A. de C.V., 1973).

agrarians, and they would only rouse the rabble against her. After locking horns for a while longer, Mrs. Evans became obstreperous.

"I felt toward him suddenly," she recalled later, "as I did toward any of the other bandits who have tried to rob me — and whom I have defied. . . . The point I remember clearly was that I accused him, saying: 'Señor, do you realize I am asking you no favor — no concession? The land is my own, left me by my husband, paid for by him — and you are deliberately inciting your people against me, to rob a woman — a foreigner — a widow — in your own country.'"

This was hardly the sort of speech calculated to endear her to a politician accustomed to deference, although he may have been flattered that in making her attack so personal she seemed to credit him with a degree of power bordering on omnipotence. Privately, she retracted even that compliment. "Had he the power of the sultan of Turkey," she remarked, "I should now be in a little sack down a deep well" (168–169).

MRS. EVANS AND THE "WOMAN QUESTION"

Mrs. Evans's approach to her interview with Obregón was admirably bold and forthright, but as diplomacy it left much to be desired. Had her purpose been to bring the president's wrath down upon her, she could not have designed a more effective speech. Her blunder is indicative of her tortuous approach to many of the realities of postrevolutionary Mexico. Age-old habits of thought still retained much power in Mexico, but at the same time many Mexicans felt a strong disposition to challenge even the most sacrosanct notions. Back in 1914, at the Revolutionary Convention of Aguascalientes, the Zapatista firebrand Antonio Díaz Soto y Gama had gone so far as to denounce and desecrate the Mexican flag, suggesting that it stood for slavery and oppression. He had nearly been lynched for this heresy, but the point remained: no one could be certain quite how far the boundaries could be probed. The old ways were clear enough: they included an informal hierarchy in which men were above women, whites above Indians, the rich lorded it over the poor, and foreigners — especially wealthy white ones — were accorded much deference. To all of these precepts, challenges floated in the air. In this uncertain atmosphere, Mrs. Evans quite simply saw that some things could be worked to her advantage, whereas others were clearly against her.

Her nationality was hardly an asset. There was much resentment — even scapegoating — of foreigners, who according to the black legend of Porfirian Mexico had long monopolized Mexico's most valuable resources and exploited them for their own exclusive betterment. Her race could be either an advantage or a disadvantage. One strain of thought held Indians and mestizos to be superior to whites and considered them the true essence of the nation, but this notion was the romantic caprice of urban intellectuals and had yet to make any great inroads into the calcified racism of Mexican society. "Indians," as Mrs. Evans noted, were certainly "making the most of their power," but there was no clear understanding as to just how much power they had to make the most of.

Gender was the trickiest issue of all. Rosalie Evans was keenly aware of her gender, and she looked constantly for ways to make it an asset rather than a liability—no mean feat. Like any war, the Mexican revolution placed a premium on such "masculine" traits as courage, strength, and ruthlessness. A war-torn Mexico was a world where a woman was simply assumed to be out of place. Once in 1918, when her administrator had warned her not to go near her hacienda, Mrs. Evans was defiant. "He thinks I will not dare to go down," she huffed. "They put in the papers, in dead earnest: 'No one killed to-day but one señora and two children.' Only men count. We are back to the days of force, and women being the weaker are relegated to their ancient position" (72). She went to the hacienda despite the warning, and her luck held. On another occasion, when one of her mayordomos was kidnapped by Cirilo Arenas's men and held for three hundred pesos ransom, she responded in a way that indicates both her awareness of society's expectations and her determination to resist them. "You see," she explained, "my part was to burst into tears and give the money for fear the man would be shot—as did the administrator of San Juan Tetla a few months ago, but that was an administrator, and besides three hundred pesos was exorbitant for a major-domo [sic], so I held out." Luck held on this occasion, too, and the rebels released her employee. "You do not know what a triumph that was," Mrs. Evans told her sister, "and how important" (120). Her defiance on this occasion was similar to the defiance with which she treated Obregón: a simple resolve not to be cowed into submission by threats of violence to which she, as a woman, was supposed to be innately vulnerable.

It would have been difficult for anyone to sustain such a performance in a culture where certain habits of thought were so deeply ingrained: women, after all, have a place in the collective psyche as the guardians of civilization. To them falls the task of transmitting "culture," of educating the young in proper manners and standards of decency. Women are supposed to abhor violence, and to moderate men's basest instincts. For all her bold defiance of stereotypes, Rosalie Evans subscribed to these notions and never wished to behave like a man among men. Some confusion was bound to arise from this contradiction: a matter of signals mixed and crossed. A splendid example took place in April of 1919, when she found herself sitting down to a game of chess with a Carrancista officer named Villareal, who was in charge of her sector for the moment. "I dared not decline as San Pedro is at his mercy," Mrs. Evans wrote later.

It was a curious sight—we played in the *patio* of the *molino* [mill]. A crowd assembled to watch us, peering over one another's shoulder, haciendados [*sic*], men of the *molino,* and federal officers. During an interval, Villareal, who is rather a dandy in appearance, told me the following pleasant story: The day before, he had directed his lieutenants to put nine captured rebels—Zapatistas, I believe—in a small hut with only one window, and he shot them one by one—"with my own hand, Señora," he said, waving a small white effeminate hand, which might have been a pretty hand but for a sort of sore or eruption between each finger. That and the story of the cowardly murders made it hard work to finish that game of chess. Only the safety of San Pedro could have made me do it. I beat him—impolitic, I know—but the only way I could punish him. (111)

Noble, feminine ends were thus served by a kind of bravado that bordered on machismo—a subtle contradiction that would become a hallmark of Mrs. Evans's style. Not surprisingly, most of the Mexican men with whom Mrs. Evans came into contact did not respond well to such strategies, and this was certainly true of Obregón. Indeed, Mrs. Evans's comportment during her interview with Obregón seemed especially calculated to give offense. After all, Obregón had become president of Mexico at a time when leadership tended to go to the most intrepid, the most audacious, the toughest and most resolute. In other words, for the moment Obregón was the supreme *macho,* and as such he was bound to live by certain codes. Men were supposed to be virile enough to dominate women, yet chivalrous enough to protect them from harm. By subjecting the president to a merciless browbeating in his own office, Mrs. Evans seemed strongly to suggest that Obregón came up short on both counts.

Although Obregón left no record of his most private thoughts, they might be inferred from a terse telegram he sent to Mrs. Evans a few days later: "After studying your case carefully have reached the conclusion I will not modify the decision in your affairs. The resolution is final."

MR. CUMMINS

Mrs. Evans was livid when she read this telegram and remained so even after Obregón sent her a longer letter—which she failed to preserve—explaining his reasoning in the matter. "I do not mean to obey Obregón's orders," she said, announcing a fateful decision. "I shall go down on Thursday and mean to pull up the stakes [the agraristas] have set. They say they will shoot me or put me in prison. Neither do I seem to mind in the least. . . . If one has a soul (as I do believe)—you should sacrifice your body rather than submit to robbery and imposition! . . . [T]his I know will be the final fight. I saw it in Obregón's brutal face" (171–172).

The decision to pull up the stakes marking the land grants to the villagers was only one part of Mrs. Evans's new and defiant resolution. Just before she received the telegram announcing Obregón's negative decision in her case, Mrs. Evans had described her tumultuous interview to General Ryan, who listened with a clouded expression, then casually gave her some of the worst advice she would ever hear. "Repeat this to your legation and no one else," he said. "It may become an international question" (170).

Mrs. Evans thus took her case to the British legation. She had taken her husband's British citizenship upon marriage and had chosen not to renounce it after his death.[7] Her choice of nationality would seem appropriate later, for she found much to admire in the truculent approach of Britain's top diplomat in Mexico, chargé d'affaires Cummins. She soon came to regard the men of the British legation as her "most trusted advisers" and consulted with them shortly after her interview with Obregón. They encouraged her in her resolve to disobey the president's orders and elected to inform Obregón that the British government would hold him responsible if anything happened to her. This advice seemed almost a calculated bid to exhaust any sympathy and patience that Mrs. Evans might have hoped for from Mexican officials. Scolding the president of the republic in his own office was impolitic, but it was not necessarily fatal. After all, the revolution had not been fought in the name of male prerogative, even if rampant machismo was among its lamentable by-products. Among the most cherished of the revolution's slogans, however — those brief and poignant phrases used to explain and justify a decade of fratricidal bloodletting — were "land and liberty" and "Mexico for the Mexicans." Material improvement of the working masses was joined by a demand for national self-assertion, and anyone who emerged to head a government born of the revolution was bound to be jealous of his credentials in achieving those aims. Now, it appeared, Rosalie Evans and her British allies were resolved to oppose the betterment of the rural masses by undermining national sovereignty — which, in any case, would be the symbolic effect of their bold demand for exemption from the agrarian reform laws.

Adding greatly to the general tensions between Mexico and Great Britain was the personal enmity that prevailed between chargé d'affaires Cummins and the majority of Mexico's top officials. Herbert Ashley Cunard Cummins — Cunard to his friends — was fifty-two years old in 1923, a large, ruddy-faced man with a receding hairline, white mustache, and a pompously stiff bearing that befitted a self-proclaimed champion of private property and the unimpeachable rightness of all that was Anglo-Saxon. He had graduated from Christ College at Finchley and been made a knight of the Order of St. George and St. Michael, and had

H. A. Cunard Cummins — "All depends on Mr. Cummins." *Credit: The Rosalie Evans Letters from Mexico.*

become an officer in the Order of the British Empire.[8] Rosalie Evans's passionate ethnocentrism found a hearty echo in Cummins. "I like to help you," he once told her; "you are a credit to us and show what fine English-American blood can do."[9]

Cummins had been in Mexico since the start of the revolution in 1910, serving first as vice-consul at Gómez Palacio, Durango, where for a time he managed a boot factory that eventually went bankrupt. He went on to serve at Ciudad Juárez; then, despite his poor track record in business, he served in Mexico City as commercial attaché of the British legation. In 1917, while Great Britain weighed the prospect of recognizing the Carranza government, Cummins was elevated to chargé d'affaires (or, as Mexican officials were fond of emphasizing, the "mere guardian of the archives of the British legation in Mexico City" with no recognized diplomatic standing).[10] At one point, he had scandalized conservative Mexican sensibilities by living openly with a mistress,[11] but by the time Rosalie Evans met him, he was considered eccentric and reclusive by his fellow Britons. He lived a bachelor's life in the colony of San Angel, surrounded by a butler named Merton, three Chinese servants, a house full of canaries, a garden full of peacocks, and an assortment of pet snakes.[12]

Cummins's long years in Mexico, and especially his tenure in some of the country's most troubled regions, lent him much credibility among his superiors in the British foreign office, who even credited him with having penetrated deep into the Mexican psyche. Plutarco Elías Calles, who would emerge as Mexico's strongman during the late 1920s and early 1930s, once claimed to know more about cricket than Cummins knew about Mexico.[13] Such skepticism was understandable, for Cummins found within the Mexican soul nothing but corruption, venality, ignorance, mendacity, and cupidity. Cummins's distaste for things Mexican even led him to dismiss a few kindred spirits. Once, for instance, with a bit of sardonic self-deprecation, a Mexican newspaper editorialist bemoaned the violence reigning in his country: "We kill because we are assassins [*matoides*], and we fail to respect the rights of others because we are ignorant of the first rules of civilisation." The irony was lost on Cummins. "At last," he gloated, "Mexicans admit that they are unfit to govern themselves."[14]

During his time in Mexico, Cummins had found much to criticize. In his dispatches to the foreign office, he had lambasted every Mexican government since Madero's for failing to discipline unruly elements and provide strong protection for the propertied classes.[15] In 1917, he had incurred the wrath of the Carranza regime by ardently backing a series of planned coups designed to bring to power "white men by blood and education."[16] In 1919, he had further angered the Mexican government by inciting a prominent British businessman to spurn all offers of indemnity for expropriated properties.[17] Nor had he lost much time in alienating the Sonorans who now headed the government. Thinking they might be the malleable and subservient leaders he had so long anticipated, he asked Obregón to grant the interim presidency to Alfredo Róbles Domínguez, a conservative Catholic whom Obregón regarded as a stooge for foreign capital.[18]

Cummins accorded Mexico's agrarian problem the same enthusiastic misreading he gave to its political situation. He seconded Mrs. Evans's view that the peasants themselves had little influence in agrarian matters, glossing over the thorny contradictions inherent in his analysis. "From the beginning of the revolution," he informed the foreign office, "its leaders appreciated that promises of land — and loot and other forms of reward — afforded the surest means of gathering recruits among the peasants of the villages. . . . It also created in the mind of the ignorant labourer beliefs that he had long been the object of exploitation and oppression, and it aroused the desired degree of enmity against the landowners and the more prosperous inhabitants of the republic." The revolution's leaders, according to Cummins, had been so successful at persuading the peasants they were miserable that by now vapid revolutionary slogans about land and liberty were sufficient to excite a Pavlovian yearning in souls too simple to know their own wants. "And yet it is well known," Cummins assured his superiors, "that no general demand for land has ever existed among the peasantry."

According to Cummins, in addition to being unnecessary, the agrarian reform was solely to blame for the current sorry condition of Mexican agriculture: "Great quantities of grain and other agricultural products are now being imported from the United States, whereas the country should produce for exportation a large margin beyond the needs of the inhabitants."[19] This assertion was fantasy, of course. Even in the golden days of the Porfiriato, large wheat farmers had never ceased to bewail their lack of competetiveness in world markets and had worked to content themselves with a captive domestic market.[20] Moreover, overproduction of wheat was fast becoming a serious social problem for the United States, and it seems unlikely that Mexico could have resisted opening its markets to wheat imports in any case. Mexican wheat growing had been moribund even before the revolution, and by now the patient was in extremis.

Obregón had several times pleaded vainly with the British foreign office to send a less hostile representative. Its acquiescence was unlikely, however, in view of the old-style conservatism that had prevailed in there since 1919, when George Nathaniel Curzon had taken the reins as foreign secretary. Lord Curzon was a former viceroy of India and ex-chancellor of Oxford, a man of boundless ambition and splenetic temperament. So profound was his faith in the goodness and permanence of the British Empire that, while viceroy, he had banned the singing of "Onward, Christian Soldiers" because it contained the line, "Thrones and crowns may perish."[21] He did an expert job of ignoring the fact that his vision of British power and prestige was anachronistic. By 1923, Britain was a much weakened military power: its dominions were beset by incipient independence movements, its wartime coalition government had collapsed, and industrial workers had become a political force to be reckoned with.[22]

Mexico, for Curzon, was emblematic of the divided and disorderly postwar world that he found so hard to credit or accommodate. Its real importance was slight, for Britain's share of trade with Mexico had declined steadily since the 1870s, and the United States was emerging as the unrivaled economic and strategic power throughout North America and the Caribbean. By 1922, it was selling ten times as much to Mexico as Great Britain and buying four times as much from Mexico.[23] For Great Britain, Mexico's importance was more symbolic than actual: it was a testing ground, a chance for defining attitudes and probing the vulnerabilities of the postwar world order. If the British let themselves be kicked around by Mexico, other more vital regions might begin seeing chinks in their imperial armor. Mexico was, in short, as good a place as any to stand on ceremony and make the most of what remained of British prestige and influence. Die-hard imperialists such as Cummins and Curzon eagerly adopted Rosalie Evans as a symbol of all they stood for.

Anglo-Mexican relations were complicated by the fact that those relations were not, strictly speaking, bilateral. In the aftermath of World War I, Great Britain and other European powers reluctantly acknowledged U.S. dominance in the Western Hemisphere, agreeing even to recognize the Monroe Doctrine in the covenant of the new League of Nations. For Mexico, meanwhile, friendly relations with Great Britain were desirable not so much in themselves but because British approval could only enhance Mexico's chances at the more coveted prize of recognition from the United States, a prerequisite to obtaining the loans Mexico desperately needed. The United States had emerged from the war as the the world's leading creditor nation and for the moment was determined to use its economic power to achieve political goals. Charles Evans Hughes, the U.S. secretary of state, made it clear to Mexico that loans would be contingent upon diplomatic recognition, and that recognition, in turn, would be tied to acceptable behavior — namely, to Mexico's willingness to repay its existing debts and to refrain from confiscating American-owned properties under the terms of the Mexican Constitution of 1917. Given the enormity of U.S. influence in the region, it was unlikely that bankers and capitalists of any nationality would defy the U.S. stance. In few cases have diplomacy and the dollar been more intimately intertwined.[24]

The conditions laid out by the United States for resuming diplomatic relations were, however, in the Mexican view "inconsistent with national dignity."[25] Indeed, agreeing to them would have amounted to political suicide because it would have granted the United States veto power over the Mexican Constitution. Although a few interested parties, such as General James Ryan, worked feverishly behind the scenes to break the impasse, hardliners in the British foreign office quietly hoped that the United States would take a rigorous stand against Mexican economic nationalism. If the United States succeeded in securing important concessions, they reasoned, perhaps Britain might win similar courtesies.

Unfortunately for the hardliners, the impasse was not unbreakable. When the U.S. State Department announced that it intended to work primarily through a committee of international bankers, the Mexicans realized that an understanding with the bankers was now a precondition for recognition and loans. And when, in the summer of 1922, an agreement was forged on the repayment of the debt, the Americans acquired a stake in the stability of the regime.[26] They began to understand that the revolution could not be undone and that excessive demands on Obregón might well doom his regime, thus ending any hope for future business dealings. In the eyes of key U.S. officials, Obregón was suddenly transformed from a Bolshevik bully into a bulwark against far more fearsome radicalism.

By the start of 1923, then, U.S.-Mexican relations were uncharacteristically cheerful, even if latent tensions simmered just below the surface. For the moment, talk of intervention in Mexico was couched in cumbrous martial metaphors: "If Mexico is conquered now," gushed the *New York Globe,* "it will be by American capital." The editorialist envisioned a future where American investment would transform a troubled and exotic Mexico into just another southwestern appendage of the United States, complete with clean streets and schools, "jazz music and motion pictures, radio and safety razors, soap and silk shirts, derby hats and commercialized baseball." Henry Ford, meanwhile, announced his plans to "flivvervene": "Let me invade Mexico with factories," he barked, "and give the people something to do!"[27]

Cunard Cummins seemed to be either oblivious to these trends or so mystified that he could not concede their reality. In late 1922, while U.S. capitalists, diplomats, and journalists oozed good-neighborliness toward the southern republic, he was pondering ways in which his pet projects might become the catalysts for international hostilities. Since his earliest days in Mexico, he had taken a powerful interest in a British-American cotton concern called Tlahualilo. The company's battle for water rights in the fertile Laguna district of Durango and Coahuila dated back to 1883. In 1922, President Obregón proposed to end the interminable wrangling by expropriating the entire property, which, for Cummins, was unthinkable. He urged the foreign office to view the company's fortunes as a test "to measure the seriousness with which the Mexican Government are approaching negotiations for recognition."[28]

Threats to a large, wealthy multinational company in which Cummins had a longstanding personal interest did not really arouse much popular American and British indignation, however. Rosalie Evans's case, on the other hand, was made to order. Once Mrs. Evans placed herself under Cummins's tutelage, she quickly replaced the Tlahualilo Company as his favorite case in point. Soon, he was treating his foreign office superiors to almost lurid accounts of the elegant "lady, who Fate has treated so harshly" and who was now being "reduced to a state bordering upon poverty."[29] The principle regarding the inviolability of private property was the same as in the Tlahualilo case, but the Evans case had a good deal more romance and drama, and was thus capable of winning greater admiration and sympathy.

Cummins played the Evans story to the hilt, often with scant regard for the truth. Some of those who read of the case, for instance, reckoned that since Harry Evans was an Englishman who died in 1917, it was logical to assume that he had sacrificed himself for his country in the Great War. Cummins and Mrs. Evans did nothing to correct this impression and, indeed, often encouraged it in subtle ways, as when Mrs. Evans wrote that her hacienda had been invaded by agrarians "during the Carranza regime and while my husband was in Europe" (in fact, she had been in Europe with him, and he had not been in uniform).[30] Cummins also began regaling the foreign office with breathless accounts of Mrs. Evans's exploits in defense of her property, such as the time in late January when she and her men repaired an irrigation dam that had been vandalized by the agrarians, or how under cover of darkness they would pull up the stakes marking the boundaries of the land grants. Cummins's admiration was plain and undoubtedly genuine, but so too was his determination to fan flames. One could never know, he told the foreign office clerks forebodingly, what this "highly nervous, but courageous and resolute woman" might do.[31] Although he claimed that he had repeatedly urged her to exercise prudence, his implication was unmistakable: the British should force the issue now, before the wild Mrs. Evans brought down an ugly crisis on their heads by killing or being killed.

Gradually, the relationship between Cummins and Mrs. Evans became symbiotic. Mrs. Evans was Cummins's symbolic loaded weapon, his last best hope for winning redress of British grievances, and in turn the personal interest and efforts of His Majesty's representative gave legitimacy and a kind of nobility to Mrs. Evans's lonely defiance, reinforcing her long-held conviction that nothing less than "civilization" was at stake: "All depends on Mr. Cummins," she wrote.[32]

As Cummins increasingly devoted himself to Mrs. Evans's cause, his communications both to his own superiors and to Mexican authorities grew more shrill and belligerent. "There is no argument but force that will restrain these immoral and uncultured people," he explained to Lord Curzon in February 1923; the Mexicans had come to believe that "the important nations" were too preoccupied in Europe to punish them for their misdeeds — a misapprehension that Cummins now hoped to correct. With a view toward fully alerting Mexican authorities to the great displeasure of the British government, Cummins "added words" to a note to Foreign Secretary Pani "from which they may infer that the silence hitherto preserved regarding their ill-doings may now be broken." He warned his superiors to keep up their guard against smooth-talking Mexicans, who only hoped by disingenuous means to "learn to what degree foreign Powers will continue to suffer their nationals to be despoiled." The British, however, must betray no hint of vulnerability. Indeed, the Mexicans, like small children, would one day be grateful to the stern disciplinarians who "check them in their wrongdoing." Cummins believed that the ideal solution to the problem would be for Great Britain and other "important European powers" to urge the United States to armed intervention. He was convinced that U.S. restraint was owing entirely to fear of alienating public opinion in Latin America, but if the United States acted at the behest of the great European powers, "they would be relieved of any charge that they were inspired by ulterior or selfish motives."[33]

This "solution" was a stunning misreading of the tenor of the times, for at that very moment the United States was preparing to send a commission to begin negotiations for formal recognition of the Obregón regime. Cummins, however, was sure that all the nonsense in the U.S. press about "invading" Mexico with factories and fistfuls of dollars was a mere smokescreen for more heroic intentions, and Rosalie Evans agreed. "The United States," she wrote, "will find it impossible to have an openly hostile Bolshevik country next door."[34] One thing was certain: neither Mrs. Evans nor H.A.C. Cummins would allow any U.S. commission to leave Mexico without getting a generous earful of their views.

MRS. EVANS SNAGS A FLAG

While pursuing her ends through diplomatic channels, Mrs. Evans did not neglect her own hands-on efforts to regain the hacienda. Despite those efforts, her plight steadily worsened. She met repeatedly with Foreign Secretary Pani and Agriculture Secretary Ramón P. de Negri — "an intelligent-looking old Indian, of the Juárez type," who took a conciliatory approach, offering to purchase the lands slated for expropriation.[35] Mrs. Evans flatly refused to sell any portion of the hacienda, but she agreed at least to consider selling the entire estate — only for cash and at her valuation, though.

It was unlikely the Mexicans would agree to her terms. After all, if their government had had the ready cash to pay generously for its expropriations, agrarian reform would not have been such a strenuous proposition. As it happened, however, Mexico had only recently agreed to an onerous schedule of debt repayment and was currently searching desperately for loans. Even if it managed to secure such loans, other projects — such as the creation of banks and ambitious development schemes — would take precedence over compensating landowners for confiscated property.

The landlords' prospects were not enhanced by the fact that, for many influential individuals in the new government, they were among the great villains of the revolution. Because they were widely viewed as exploiters of labor and bastions of a discredited regime, the matter of compensating them for their losses rated low on the government's list of priorities. Redeeming the rural poor played far better politically. Moreover, the landlords had for many years grounded their economic viability on absurdly low property valuations for tax purposes. Mrs. Evans herself admitted that "in the old days the tax value was nominal and never considered."[36] This practice, in fact, was a key point in the indictment of the hacienda system: critics had long charged the hacendados with wielding undue political influence in order to cheat the national treasury and ensure their own profits. The landlords now looked silly as they fumed over government offers to compensate them at no more than 10 percent more than the fiscal value of their properties. They also found little sympathy when they groaned bitterly about the government's plan to pay them with slow-to-mature agrarian bonds, even though nearly everyone recognized that those bonds were — as one U.S. newspaper put it–"worth about as much to the bale as Russian rubles."[37] Relatively few Mexicans were vexed to see the great landowners hoist with their own petard.

Mrs. Evans's talks with Pani and de Negri were typical of what had long since become an exasperating routine, one in which she achieved only a dizzying string of pyrrhic victories. Pani offered to deal with Mrs. Evans only if she would forgo seeking aid from Cummins, who, he informed her, was "persona non grata." The Latin struck her as enormously amusing, apparently owing to what she perceived as a discrepancy between the highfalutin phrase and the upstart official who uttered it. De Negri made a more favorable impression, despite his devious offer to purchase a strip of land that would have split the irrigation system — rendering it, and hence the land, useless. He was at least gracious enough to introduce her to Froylán Manjarrez, the relative moderate who had replaced José María Sánchez as governor of Puebla. Although Manjarrez was, according to Mrs. Evans, "just a common young man who looks half negro, and does impossible things," he seemed agreeable enough when de Negri ordered him to protect her until Obregón made a firm decision in the case.[38]

Mrs. Evans soon learned once again that such promises were worth little. Only days after her reassuring conference with de Negri, her administrator, Jesús Bermejillo, reported that agrarians had again invaded her land and were measuring it for distribution.[39] She threatened the authorities that if the invaders were not immediately ejected she would "go at once to San Pedro and knock down the monuments." It was a serious threat. When she arrived at the hacienda, she was incensed to find red flags — "a defiance of all that's good or spiritual in life" — fluttering around the boundaries of her land. Forgetting all counsels of patience and prudence, she set herself immediately to pulling the flags down. One flag, which waved imperiously atop a small hill, was a particular affront, not only for its elevation but because it was the most difficult to remove. In a dramatic dash, Mrs. Evans rode up the side of the mound, grabbed the flagstaff in passing, and broke it off with the weight of the horse. "It was really exhilarating," she recounted later. "I have never stormed a citadel or captured a flag before — and it whistled in my ears as I dashed down. . . . The *agrarios* fired on me, but even that only added excitement and pleasure."[40]

The flag-capturing episode became the stuff of tall tales once Mrs. Evans began her publicity campaign in earnest. She was, of course, not entirely the solitary heroine she styled herself in some of her accounts, for this melodrama was played out under the watchful gaze of federal troops and her own armed supporters who "planned to charge [the agraristas] with a volley if they came near, but they never did." Many of Mrs. Evans's supporters were backing out or confessing their impotence, however, so she was in fact becoming ever more solitary. Cummins's representations on her behalf only worsened her position, and her champions in the foreign office were sympathetic but unnerved by her boldness. "A brave woman," remarked Charles Dodd, a foreign office secretary, upon hearing of her exploits, "but if she killed anyone, we should find it hard to protect her."[41] A few weeks later, another secretary lamented: "The case is so hopeless that I am not sure that Mrs. Evans should not be told plainly that we cannot effectively help her."[42]

TALKS AT BUCARELI STREET

Still worse than Cummins's impotence and the foreign office's lukewarm support was growing coolness toward Mrs. Evans among her peers. She had long counted on "kindness and sympathy from all the social set." That situation began to change noticeably in May 1923, however, when the group of U.S. commissioners arrived in Mexico and, after settling into an address on Bucareli Street, embarked on serious talks aimed at extending official recognition to the Obregón regime. The so-called "Bucareli talks" had much support in the foreign business community, where those individuals with ready cash envisioned handsome profits to be made once stability and international harmony were secured. Mrs. Evans increasingly discovered that some of her friends, "for some petty personal business," favored U.S. recognition and resented her stubborn protests.[43] As if that attitude were not enough to make her feel helpless and alone, quite a few Spaniards — from the close-knit community that had so dominated industry and commercial agriculture in the Puebla-Tlaxcala Valley — had come to despair of ever winning in the face of daunting challenges and tepid support from their own government. Heeding the advice of pessimists among them, many pulled up stakes.[44] Even those Spaniards who retained their properties were reluctant to visit them, preferring to leave the dirty work of protecting them to intrepid foremen and administrators. By mid-1923, of nearly twenty landowners with haciendas in the region, only Mrs. Evans and two Mexican landlords were still fighting.[45]

In late March, when Obregón had once again confirmed his decision not to revoke his order of expropriation of San Pedro's lands, Mrs. Evans succumbed to a rare moment of abject despair. "To-night," she wrote on March 22, "is the first time I have given up. I have no recourse left. . . . My work of five years given over to the rabble, the men who have trusted in me deceived and cheated, and I can't stop it! I shall oppose it, risk myself, what gain? Failure — the word that has never existed for me. San Pedro is not just my hacienda, it's part of me as my very body." The setback, Mrs. Evans believed, was not hers alone. Indeed, the more desperate and hopeless her struggle became, the more noble it seemed: "This has been like a sacred crusade, I did not mind dying the minute I won out. My hope has been that the final result of the fight might be the establishment of a moral administration in Mexico. If that can be done and the political life of Mexico be somewhat purified and the continuance of injustice and oppression be prevented — even if only to a relative degree — I shall regard my life as well spent and well given — if lose it I must."[46]

Within days, however, her mood had changed, and she resolved once again to fight to the last. She claimed — not for the first time, but now more convincingly than before — that she had evidence of a plan to kill her. The government and the "agitators" would have her shot "and say the Indians did it, as I was reckless."[47] She could not let so contemptible a government off lightly.

POLITICAL DISCORD AND A CAMPESINO CONGRESS

For all Mrs. Evans's crusading, the political life of Mexico was by no means being "purified," but rather grew murkier and more menacing by the day. At issue was the approaching presidential election. Obregón favored his interior minister and fellow Sonoran, Plutarco Elías Calles, who also had the support of most of the country's more radical labor and agrarian parties. The opposition was gradually coalescing into the Cooperatista Party, which presented a vague platform that appealed to many prominent conservatives and moderates, particularly within the military. For the moment, the Cooperatistas were somewhat weakened by the fact that they had no standard-bearer for the coming elections.

Efforts to persuade the logical favorite, Finance Minister Adolfo de la Huerta, had so far borne no fruit.

The situation was particularly volatile in Puebla, where Froylán Manjarrez—a kingpin and former president of the Cooperatista Party—occupied the governor's chair. Candidate Calles charged that Manjarrez changed electoral laws to ensure the victory of his partisans and that he was running the state government as a political party. As was usually the case, tensions at the top were echoed at the local level. In Santa Ana Xalmimilulco, which had long been plagued by sharp divisions between agraristas and fraccionistas, the enemies of agrarian reform styled themselves Cooperatistas and made a bid to capture the town government. The agraristas, in response, staged a violent mutiny. Although Governor Manjarrez tried to adjudicate, his brother David, who headed the State Agrarian Commission and who investigated the Xalmimilulco dispute, was a frank partisan of the anti-agrarista faction. The governor was probably quite moderate, but his regime was easily tarred with the anti-agrarista label, a reputation difficult to live down.[48]

In early May of 1923, as the politics turned increasingly volatile, the agrarians decided to flex some muscle by holding their "Second Campesino Congress." More than one thousand representatives—agrarian leaders in their three-piece suits, as well as rank-and-file farmworkers in their loose white clothes and immense sombreros—marched with workers in the May Day Parade and then crowded into the amphitheater of the National Preparatory School in Mexico City to hear impassioned oratory, debate the contentious issues of the day, and adopt a series of radical resolutions. Although those resolutions had little impact in the long run, they gave the agrarian movement an evanescent boost.

The Campesino Congress stopped short of advocating "direct action" against the landlords, but it did recommend relieving them of every material and legal protection they had left. It asked that all paramilitary forces acting on behalf of the landlords be dissolved; that campesinos be granted the explicit right to bear arms "of any sort, for their security and legitimate defense"; that the army be prevented from intervening in the agrarian reform on behalf of the landowners; that all persons imprisoned for crimes of a "social order" be pardoned; and that all abuses committed against agrarista comrades be documented. Responding to machinations of the sort championed by Marcelino Presno in the Puebla-Tlaxcala Valley, they also demanded that landlords be enjoined from making "simulated distributions" or sales of land to villagers after a land grant petition had been submitted.

Most importantly, the Campesino Congress sought to strip the landowners of what they maintained was their only legal recourse against the arbitrary abuses of agrarian officials: when threatened with expropriation, they could—and almost always did—appeal for *amparo*, or injunction, against the acts of agrarian officials. Under the terms of amparo, the land would remain in the landowner's possession while the courts — all the way up the Supreme Court of the Nation — ruled on the legality of the expropriation. To the landlords, amparo seemed the last vestige of civilization in the entire agrarian reform process.

For the champions of agrarian reform, however, amparo was more insidious than armed force. The court system was cluttered, complex, highly politicized, and unpredictable. Because the revolution had not abolished the infrastructure of the judiciary, many judges currently sitting on the courts had been trained under the old regime and still clung to its values — which did not necessarily translate into ideologial repugnance for radical reform, however. Ironically, among the most salient values of the old regime had been judicial subservience to the will of the executive, which helps to explain why in regions where the president or a powerful governor strongly favored land grants — regions such as the Puebla-Tlaxcala Valley — rulings nearly always went against the landowners. In view of constantly shifting political priorities, this tendency gave agrarista partisans little comfort, however, because even in those regions where rulings tended to favor agrarian reform, land distribution was interminably delayed while cases wound their way through severely backlogged courts.[49] For all their talk of fairness and legality, landlords came to use and abuse the request for amparo as a simple and fairly reliable stalling tactic. Salvador Cancino, Mrs. Evans's lawyer, practically made his living by requesting delays and postponements of scheduled hearings on the theory that as long as his cases went unheard, they could not be decided negatively. Even on those occasions when negative verdicts were finally arrived at — as happened several times in Mrs. Evans's own case — the lawyer's task was simply to appeal the decision. And so on indefinitely.

The Campesino Congress now proposed that amparo, in agrarian matters, be relegated to the realm of theory. Any judge who granted amparo in a case of restitution or grant of land, the delegates said, should be arrested, as should any landowner who "unjustifiably" petitioned for amparo. It was the duty of all campesinos to denounce amparos to the National Agrarian Party (PNA).

The congress ended with stirring words and exhortations: "The villages will never," the delegates declared, "for any reason or under any pretext, give back a single inch of the land," and they were "willing to shed [their] blood if necessary to ensure that [their] aspirations and rights are not mocked." President Obregón's own remarks to the congress sounded like a ringing endorsement of the PNA position, although clearly a strong political agenda undergirded his remarks. Describing the congress as "one of the greatest historical political events" in Mexico since the revolution, Obregón declared that his administration hoped that the people and their government would merge to form a single organism. Public officials, said Obregón, should no longer consider themselves leaders, but faithful interpreters of popular aspirations. The agrarian reform faced opposition from powerful interests both from within and from outside the country, and the government needed but one thing to solve the problem: "the frank and absolute support and confidence of the popular classes."[50]

This declaration was a far cry from the measured rhetoric Obregón had used to expound on the agrarian problem in October of 1921. But then, the times were dangerous, and politics made its ineluctable demands. Of course, there was also little danger that the suggestions of the Campesino Congress would actually be taken up in the Chamber of Deputies, which was dominated by the relatively moderate Cooperatistas. Indeed, the PNA even had some difficulty getting its resolutions published because the Cooperatistas controlled the printers' union.

The congress had its effects, just the same, however, and Rosalie Evans would feel those effects soon enough.

Seven

Let us advise, and to this hazard draw
With Speed what force is left, and all imploy
In our defence, lest unawares we lose
This our high place, our Sanctuarie, our Hill.
— John Milton, *Paradise Lost*

URING THE WEEK of the Campesino Congress, Rosalie Evans had guests at San Pedro. Anita Morgan, the wife of an employee of a U.S. trading firm in Mexico City, had been staying at the hacienda with her two young children for a week without incident. Lulled into a sense of safety, Mrs. Evans had planned a trip to Mexico City, presumably to seek a word with the U.S. commissioners to the Bucareli talks, but before she left San Martín, alarming news reached her from the hacienda. She canceled her ticket and rushed to San Pedro's defense.

A STRIKE AT SAN PEDRO

The San Martín delegation to the Campesino Congress, led by Manuel P. Montes, had left Mexico City on May 5 in a car fitted up specially for the occasion and arrived home just in time for the start of another season's wheat harvest. Encouraged to defiance by the congress and by Obregón's show of support, the agraristas of the Domingo Arenas Confederation immediately declared a strike against the six haciendas still operating in the valley. Their single demand was that harvest workers' wages be raised from sixty-five to eighty-five centavos per day. A job action of this sort was merely an expedient, of course, because the confederation was pledged to the ultimate destruction of the hacienda system and the delivery of hacienda lands to the villages. Increased wages were desirable, but in reality the most important aim of the strike was probably to mount an overwhelming show of strength in order to intimidate even the most recalcitrant hacendado holdouts. With an army of about 150 haphazardly armed men, the agraristas first attacked the haciendas San Miguel Lardizábal and Espíritu Santo, killing an administrator and a mayordomo.[1]

Early on the morning of May 11, an agrarista army invaded San Pedro Coxtocán, taking prisoner nine of the peons who had been cutting wheat in the hacienda's fields. Mrs. Evans ordered Anita Morgan to stand ready to ride to San Martín to telegraph for help, then she herself rode out with Bermejillo and her loyal employees to meet the invaders. When she was quick to refuse their demand for a wage hike, which would be "ruinous to the hacienda," the strikers, in no mood to quibble or compromise, threatened to kill her or destroy her crop if she continued to resist. They then marched off, leaving her to meditate on their warnings.

By means of "threats and entreaties," Mrs. Evans found ten men to continue the harvest. When five strikers later loped back onto the property, Mrs. Evans rode out with her dogs to perform what would soon come to seem an annoying and absurd chore, albeit an extremely hazardous one. "I was trying to knock the strikers off the bank that divided the field from the road," she recounted, "defending myself with my whip—I mean whirling it about, giving them no chance to get my bridle. I was beside myself with rage and kept myself from firing on them by the greatest effort. [Jesús Bermejillo] joined me and we routed them."[2]

While in the field she managed to dash off telegrams to Obregón, Pani, and Cummins, sending Anita Morgan to San Martín to transmit them. After a brief, desperate preamble, she asked: "Please order an end to this intolerable situation, allowing me to work my fincas without these continual threats of death and confiscation."[3] The next day, agraristas blocked the road to the hacienda so effectively that workers could not enter the grounds, and the hacienda servants had to crawl stealthily through the tall grass to do the marketing in San Martín. In her telegram that day, Mrs. Evans was more specific about her demands: "Situation worse. Urgently need soldiers."[4]

The presence on the hacienda of a U.S. citizen, Anita Morgan, was fortuitous because it enabled Mrs. Evans to appeal for protection to the U.S. chargé d'affaires, George Summerlin (who had earlier favorably impressed Mrs. Evans as "a gentleman, a Harvard graduate"). Given the delicate state of U.S.-Mexican relations, with the commissioners just sitting down at Bucareli Street to haggle over the recognition question, Mrs. Evans's telegram got prompt results. By midnight on May 12, a detachment of soldiers arrived, and word came that the U.S. embassy was sending its third secretary, Benjamin Muse, to investigate.

Ben Muse was a twenty-five-year-old Virginian with a round face, a whisp of mustache, and a barely functional command of Spanish. Nevertheless, he was a careful, open-minded, and reasonably thorough investigator. His first impression was that the notorious Texmelucan Valley was an anticlimax after his harrowing eight-hour drive over the mountains in the dark with a chauffeur who did not know the way. The apparent calm that he observed made it difficult to credit the "steady fire of complaints" about lawlessness and anarchy he heard from Mrs. Evans's friends at the El Pilar textile plant, who met him on his arrival. Anita Morgan and her children were safe and sound, and her husband too had somehow made it to the hacienda unharmed. Muse noted that the hacienda buildings had sustained no damage and that the "house of Mrs. Evans was admirably built for defense and could be held by half a dozen well-armed men against an indefinite number of native skirmishers." The detachment sent in response to Mrs. Evans's urgent telegrams was on the scene, and the colonel who commanded it was an "intelligent, agreeable gentleman" whose only real defect was that he carried indecipherable orders. "Both the property owners and the marauders carry official documents and encouraging messages from persons high in the present regime," Muse reported. "[The colonel] told Mrs. Evans frankly that he did not know definitely whether his superiors wished him to protect her or to aid the men who were attacking her property."[5]

Despite the apparent tranquility of the scene, Muse could not help but notice that Mrs. Evans and her party, including the handful of field-workers who showed up, were quite agitated, so the morning after his arrival he paid a visit to the agrarista headquarters in the village of San Jerónimo Tianguismanalco, where he received eager assurances that the syndicate had committed no violence and had no intention of doing so. A simple strike was on, the agraristas explained, and if Muse wished to return later that afternoon, they would give him a more detailed presentation of their case.

By lunchtime, Muse was frankly nonplussed. What he had seen so far of Mexico's vaunted agrarian reform was comical. As he ate his lunch, he was aware that Mrs. Evans and her friends were in another room trembling with anticipation of imminent violence; strikers were plotting strategy in a nearby village; and the colonel of the guard was trying to decide which way to point his guns if it came to a showdown. Just then, the tension was broken by the most patent absurdity of all. An old man showed up at the door, claiming to be an itinerant land appraiser in the employ of the state government. He said he knew nothing of strikes or troubles in the area and, in fact, had not even targeted San Pedro specifically. He was merely making his leisurely way from one hacienda to the next, fixing a value for each of them because they would all be confiscated in time.

It was, of course, an odd coincidence that an appraiser should happen to arrive at this moment of high tension and when a U.S. official was present, but then, the appraiser himself was just odd enough to make the coincidence plausible. His most notable characteristics were his confused and doddering manner and the "large and lugubrious ear-trumpet" he carried to compensate for near total deafness. Muse found himself wondering about some papers the old man had laid out distractedly on the table and was amazed at how easily his curiosity was satisfied: Mrs. Evans and the others distracted the old man by shouting into his ear trumpet, while Muse surreptitiously copied the documents. Their contents left the young American aghast: they were all form letters that contained blank spaces where the name of the property, its owner, and its assessed value were to be filled in. "In brief," Muse mused, "this subordinate government employee with a very minor intelligence was empowered to start the process for the seizing of any property he chose and its bestowal upon any one he chose in the State of Puebla. Its value . . . was to be determined by him alone."

Still more surprises awaited. After lunch, Muse kept his appointment in Tianguismanalco, where he discovered a crowd of people filling the pews of the village church and still more loitering around the door. They were, he was told, agrarian "syndicalists" from three villages, convening in his honor. Muse was nervous, but somewhat reassured to note that he seemed to be the only one present who was armed, nor did those assembled make any move to disarm him — except figuratively, by maintaining "a most friendly atmosphere of camaraderie." Impressed by Montes's apparent command of "Bolshevist theory," he also sympathized with the villagers' frustration when they showed him a bewildering collection of documents that seemed to justify every conceivable position on agrarian reform. He listened in horror as Montes charged that Mrs. Evans was the greater proponent of violence: she had, according to Montes, tried to bribe federal army officers into killing him and several other enemies.

The agraristas behaved well until near the end of the gathering, when they insisted that Muse sign two copies of the meeting's minutes, which a pair of secretaries had been laboriously handwriting all the while. Muse refused on the grounds that "no parliamentary rules required the signature of minutes in this documentary form." Strange that he should be surprised by this lapse in proper parliamentary procedure, but he clearly thought the point worth insisting on, even after the assembled agraristas began to shout angrily, and one of them grabbed his wrist. Muse eventually compromised by signing another document that merely affirmed he had been present at the meeting. He then elbowed his way out of the church into pitch darkness and still more excitement. The young man who had been serving as his guide for the duration of his visit crept up behind him and whispered that his life was in serious danger: the agraristas had prepared an ambush. The guide took him on a circuitous route to a place where Mrs. Evans and several others waited to rescue him.

"Poor Mr. Muse!" Mrs. Evans wrote. "He could not take it in."[6]

Although she sympathized with Muse in his befuddlement, Mrs. Evans nevertheless fretted about what sort of report he would make to the Americans. She had little difficulty persuading him that Montes's charges against her were false — "you know," she huffed, "my pride is *not* having killed Manuel Montes two years ago when he led the men against me!" — but she was far less successful in convincing him of the grand conspiracy against her. He was, she feared, inclined to take the "erroneous view, natural and not unintelligent, that they were in a state of anarchy down there."[7]

In fact, Muse had been impressed by the speed with which the federal government sent troops in response to Mrs. Evans's entreaties and by the mysteriously sudden acquiescence of the field hands to the meager terms she offered them to settle the strike. These actions did not, however, necessarily indicate to him that everything happening in the valley sprang directly from the fecund imagination of President Obregón. Rather, his report conveyed the impression that agrarian reform in the Texmelucan Valley was a matter of confusion and ineptitude, symbolized less by the fearsome Manuel Montes than by the weird old appraiser with his ungainly ear trumpet and absurd form letters. Such a view, Mrs. Evans realized, could do incalculable damage to her cause, for if the Americans were to get the impression that the situation in San Martín was simply out of control, they might also fall for certain other arguments the Mexicans had been making insistently for some time. Foreign Minister Pani, for instance, had patiently explained to the Americans that agrarian reform was being carried out with the aims "of being certain of obtaining at once the general pacification of the country and of avoiding the greater and truly irreparable damages of civil war." He conceded that some of the agrarian agitators with whom the government dealt were violent opportunists, but, he said, all was justified because in the end nothing could contain "the popular desire for lands" or "the noble enthusiasm, almost explosive, of some agrarians." In short, the price for continuing to ignore the poor and their demand for land would be more years of instability and upheaval, a prospect the Americans abhorred. It followed that sacrificing the interests of the likes of Mrs. Evans was a lamentable but ultimately small price to pay for peace.[8]

Hoping to correct this misapprehension, Mrs. Evans did everything in her power to capture the personal attention of the U.S. commissioners to the Bucareli talks. In a memorandum she sent them, she allowed herself to bend the truth a bit. She led the commissioners to believe that her husband had been killed in World War I; she asserted once again that the villagers of her region had plenty of land for their needs and no interest in acquiring more; and she swore that no village adjoined her land, when in fact the agrarian maps clearly showed no fewer than five villages sharing their boundaries with the hacienda. Although she oversimplified and distorted the issues, her intent was to impose herself on the commissioners' attention and to persuade them that "recognition without guarantees for life and property is a base abandonment of [their] own countrymen."[9] The commissioners, however, were more interested in petroleum than in land, and for the time being they seemed comfortable enough with Pani's arguments on the vital domestic importance of agrarian reform.

Mrs. Evans might well have remained merely another intriguing irritation for the U.S. commissioners if Mexico hadn't still been capable of delivering a few surprises, even to seasoned veterans. In late May, she wrote to her sister that the agrarians "act on definite orders from Mexico City. Proof? While American commissioners are here [the agrarians] are afraid to go further. . . . Obregón has promised them the land after the delegates go." But her "proof" evaporated a little more than two weeks later when — with the U.S. commissioners still in town and haggling — Obregón suddenly issued a sweeping decree that all of San Pedro Coxtocán and its neighbor, Polaxtla, were to be confiscated on grounds of "public utility." The decree explained that the land was to be used for a military-agricultural colony.[10]

This decree is among the most mysterious episodes of the entire San Pedro affair. Mrs. Evans and her allies logically assumed the decree to be grounded in the well-known links between the Obregón administration and the agrarians of San Martín; in fact, however, Obregón had made his decree without their knowledge or consent. The prospect of a military colony on San Pedro and Polaxtla lands was not at all welcomed by Montes and his followers, for it would usurp their ejidos and threaten them with a strong and decidedly unwelcome federal military presence in their district (which may have been among Obregón's intentions). In late August, the Domingo Arenas Confederation sent an angry telegram to the president demanding that he revoke his decree. They also reported alarmedly that the minister of war in Obregón's cabinet, General Francisco Serrano, together with some cronies — all federal generals — had recently been touring the region looking for haciendas to buy and that one of those generals had lingered in the area, treating the agraristas to brutal threats.[11]

The decree risked alienating the agraristas at a time when Obregón had every reason to cultivate their support, but the fact that he took this risk was less surprising than the way in which the decree played so neatly into Mrs. Evans's hands — a fact she realized soon after the initial shock had worn off. In the face of Obregón's capriciousness, her first move was predictable enough: she went straight to Cummins, supplying him with a handy pretext for insisting that the U.S. commissioners, Charles Beecher Warren and John Barton Payne, pay her some attention.

Beyond demanding that attention, no one seemed to know quite what to do.

Charles B. Warren (*left*) and John Barton Payne (*right*) — "fat, standoffish, large, and impressive." *Credit:* Gustavo Casasola, *Historia gráfica de la Revolución Mexicana, 1900–1970,* 2d ed. (Mexico City: Editorial Trillas, S.A. de C.V., 1973).

The hardliners in the British foreign office hoped their goverment might pressure the United States to have their commissioners "make of [Mrs. Evans's case] a grievance which must be addressed before recognition can be thought of." Others deemed it undignified for Britain to fight its battles by proxy, but had no other ideas. "I'm afraid," wrote Rowland Sperling, the assistant foreign secretary, "there is no reason why Mrs. Evans should receive preferential treatment and can only suggest that Mr. Cummins should lodge a claim in the same way as has been done in other cases."[12]

The U.S. commissioners, meanwhile, were dollar diplomats par excellence who failed to see Mrs. Evans's case as one of stark and absolute morality. Mrs. Evans had spotted them earlier at a tea, and her first impression was not favorable. "Warren and Payne," she sniffed, "fat, standoffish, large and impressive, looking like stage bankers."[13] In fact, both were the sort of upstart bourgeois types that left her cold. Payne, who hailed from rural West Virginia, had made his reputation as a Chicago superior court judge, counsel for shipping and railroad commissions, and Woodrow Wilson's interior secretary. He made a terrible first impression on Mrs. Evans, who thought he "looked and acted like a rough old Southern lawyer, used to cross-questioning negro offenders."

Charles B. Warren seemed more sympathetic. A lawyer, a former banker, and former manager of a Michigan sugar company, he was also a major player in Republican Party politics (he is perhaps best remembered as the man who delivered to Warren G. Harding the surprising news that he had been elected president). He had been rewarded for his efforts with various appointments, most recently as U.S. ambassador to Japan.[14] Outwardly, he appeared to share at least some of Mrs. Evans's moral outrage; a friend supposedly heard him say that if he were "that lady's representative, they would go over my dead body before they would get her place."[15] When Mrs. Evans recounted some of the many frustrations and treacheries the Mexicans had subjected her to, Warren was reassuring: "Don't judge by the past, go in confidence," he said. "I am sure you will be satisfied." She was unsure what to make of this. Perhaps he was merely one of those annoyingly pragmatic American business types who imagined that everything could be fixed with some winning combination of tact, bluff, hard work, and money. If so, she reckoned that Mexico would disabuse him soon enough. Then again, he just might be the champion she had been waiting for, a Cummins with clout.

Warren did manage to impress her when he went to the trouble of interviewing Governor Manjarrez about her hacienda. His report was encouraging: Manjarrez had happily informed him that the people of the Huejotzingo district had no need of land, that the president had no intention of founding a military-agricultural colony, and that someone had "forced Obregón's hand." San Pedro Coxtocán had become nothing more than booty to be doled out to some influential general or other, Manjarrez assured Warren, even allowing himself to speculate a bit as to who the "mystery man" might be, with Generals Antonio Villareal and Francisco Serrano topping the list.[16]

Warren, Cummins, and Mrs. Evans found this information oddly satisfying. Warren congratulated himself on his intrepidness and efficiency, and told Mrs. Evans that Manjarrez's admissions would effectively render Obregón's decree unenforceable. Cummins was effusive in his praise for Warren, who, he said, defended Mrs. Evans "in terms so frank that were his goodwill and influence less essential to [the Mexicans] at the moment, his words would have been resented and a serious incident have arisen."[17] Manjarrez's assertions also seemed to vindicate Mrs. Evans's long held contention that Obregón had it in for her personally and that his motives were far from pure. If she and her diplomatic allies could somehow show Manjarrez's contentions to be true, then the world could be fully alerted to this gross miscarriage of justice, and her cause would receive a hearty boost.

It seems not to have occurred to any of them to question the accuracy of Manjarrez's claims or his motives in making them. As a leader of the Cooperatista Party, Manjarrez had ample reason for wishing to undercut the legitimacy of the Obregón regime with the U.S. commissioners—especially at that moment, late July of 1923, when a showdown was impending between the Cooperatistas and the Calles faction, which had the full backing of the Obregón government. In Puebla, Governor Manjarrez was at pains to prevent a full resurgence of agrarian might under the auspices of political predators like Manuel P. Montes and José María Sánchez. Sooner or later, Obregón would have to choose sides. Manjarrez may have wished to plant seeds of doubt in the minds of the U.S. commissioners, thus hindering U.S. recognition of Obregón and favoring his own party's interests.

Mrs. Evans had her lawyer challenge the legality of Obregón's decree, a case fairly easily argued on the grounds that it overstepped the president's constitutional authority. Warren did not make it an official grievance, but he took up the matter with Mexican officials in the same "extra-official" spirit in which the entire Bucareli conference was being held. He alerted those officials that the Evans case "interested" him, and that "if six months from now they start again . . . I shall resent it." Also, the United States would be officially displeased should a private individual occupy the hacienda. Still, he told Mrs. Evans frankly that he could not "prevent the government from molesting you or even killing you in ambush," and he pressed her to promise that if he could get a solid and fair offer for the place, she would accept it. Even in the face of this pressure, Mrs. Evans remained noncommittal: "Mr. Warren, I am afraid to answer," she said. "I know your advice is right."[18]

We will never know how she would ultimately have responded to such an offer of purchase because no offer was ever made. The best Warren could do was to secure a promise from Agriculture Secretary de Negri not to touch the hacienda for the time being. The U.S. legation also helped Mrs. Evans unofficially by steering the cable editor of the *Chicago Tribune* in her direction, thinking that if all else failed she could threaten the government with damning international publicity. "Published right," Mr. Cummins was heard to say, "this lady's story will make the world weep." The reporters interviewed Mrs. Evans, photographed her with her dogs, and urged her to allow them to go to press at once with the lurid tale of the pretty widow besieged by Mexican bandits. Mrs. Evans, however, urged them to sit on the story for a while. "I don't want to make [the world] weep just yet if I can help it," she told her sister. If the world wept and forgot—evanescence being among the drawbacks of periodical journalism—she would be no better off. Blackmail, however, seemed promising. "I am getting on nicely," she wrote, "with my history pigeon-holed in an editor's drawer, to come out dramatically in case of destruction or confiscation."[19]

Obregón's decree confiscating San Pedro was never revoked, but it also was never enforced. It simply remained on the books, a hypothetical sword of

"Published right, this lady's story will make the world weep." *Credit: The Rosalie Evans Letters from Mexico.*

Damocles waiting to fall on hacendado and ejidatario alike, and no entirely plausible explanation for its existence was ever offered. The charge that it was intended as a gift to some "mystery man" who had "forced Obregón's hand" was not too outlandish. However, the chief suspect, War Minister Serrano, was probably innocent, even though he made an attractive villain. A well-known gambler and racketeer, he was an Obregón protegé who, it was rumored, had once received funds from the national treasury to cover an embarrassing debt from a single night's gaming.[20] If he sometimes defended landowners' interests, it was most likely in anticipation of worming his own devious way into their ranks. It is true that he and some cronies were seen motoring around the San Martín Texmelucan Valley scouting out real estate, but when Montes and his agraristas complained about these activities, Serrano got a sound scolding from Obregón. In response, he pleaded lamely that he had thought the haciendas Polaxtla and San Pedro Coxtocán were not needed for ejidos, but because he had been alerted to the difficulties, he and his friends meant to abandon their land-buying schemes.[21]

A more likely mystery man was José María Sánchez, just back from the Soviet Union and busily plotting his political resurrection. Eventually, Mrs. Evans became convinced of his guilt, even though he never tried actually to take the hacienda and even threatened to sue Mrs. Evans for "calumny" when she publicly made the charge.[22]

Even if it were true, however, that Obregón meant to use the hacienda as plum to buy the loyalty of some potentially disruptive individual, it seems peculiar that he would choose to force the issue of Mrs. Evans and her hacienda at a moment when his regime was on the verge of winning the long sought recognition from the United States. The official explanation, revealed much later, was that the decree was intended as a special favor to Mrs. Evans. According to the terms of Obregón's decree on indemnification, land that was expropriated for ejidos could be paid for only with agrarian bonds. Land expropriated for "public utility," on the other hand, was to be paid for in cash.[23] This explanation seems reasonable enough. The regime would have had ample motive to address the volatile Evans problem by throwing a bundle of cash at it. The problem with this explanation, however, is that Mrs. Evans swore repeatedly that she never received an offer of payment of any amount or on any terms, and Obregón never tried to square things with the U.S. commissioners by explaining his motives.

It is possible, of course, that Obregón issued the decree in order to thumb his nose at Cummins and the hardliners by pointing up their impotence. If so, it would have been a risky gambit with Mexico's diplomatic and economic future at stake. Obregón never explained the move, though, so the motivations behind it must remain a mystery.

In the end, neither Obregón's decree nor Mrs. Evans's appeals much influenced the course of history. In late August, the U.S. and Mexican commissioners to the Bucareli talks announced that they had arrived at an agreement hailed by the *New York Times* as "one of the most important steps in American foreign policy in recent years."[24] The agreement's key elements dealt with oil lands, which were exempted from confiscation pending certain conditions. The commissioners could claim far less success in the matter of agricultural lands, however. Essentially, the agreement said that although the United States did not accept the *principle* behind the practice of paying for expropriated lands with agrarian bonds (instead of with cash), it would informally encourage landowners to take whatever the Mexican government offered. After that, if landowners felt themselves wronged, they were free to make their cases before the newly established General Claims Commission, which might take up to three years to render a decision.[25] Cummins took a predictably dim view of the pact, but he mercifully spared Mrs. Evans the details.

Ignorant of the pact's fine print but apprised of its spirit, Rosalie Evans was furious but resigned. Just as she felt that the Mexican government was behind all her woes and could easily end them with a word or the sweep of a pen, she also felt that the United States and Great Britain were quite capable of imposing their will upon Mexico if only they had the backbone for it. She berated Warren and Payne for asserting "a definite policy and noble aims," but then dropping it all in order to "play to the gallery." The Mexicans, she was sure, would not live up to their end of the agreement in any case, but would "only rejoice that they have once more won out against the Gringoes. All the upstarts and the new people will make rapid fortunes while the bubble lasts." In the end, she lamented, it seemed "like a slap in the face of civilization."

She left Mexico City for San Pedro so that she would not have to hear the "bells ringing, whistles blowing, disgraceful rejoicings of the Recognitionists over their triumph."[26] On the hacienda, she busied herself "putting agrarios off," a task that was coming to seem like a routine eradication of irksome pests. While visiting in November 1923, her sister recalled watching her in action as she rode out — followed by her pack of barking dogs and singing "Nous sommes les enfants de Gascogne" — to chase invaders. She cut an impressive figure, mounted and well armed, spurring and whirling her horse to intimidate and terrify interlopers.[27]

Montes and his agraristas had by no means given up and had even taken to invading some lands they had not petitioned for through the usual channels — an indication that they had come to regard the "usual channels" as hopelessly gummed up. Governor Manjarrez ordered Montes's arrest, but like many other such orders, this one was never carried out.[28]

In late September 1923, Montes's agraristas invaded San Pedro Coxtocán in force. They hastily planted the newly plowed fields in hopes that the grain would sprout quickly because, according to the current law, the harvest would belong to whoever planted the ground.

The captain of the federal army detachment on the hacienda told Mrs. Evans he had orders only to protect her, not to interfere with the agrarians. Mrs. Evans galloped defiantly to the fields with her expanding pack of dogs, taunting the captain with a reminder that he would be held responsible if she were killed. Near the road, she encountered an army of "some hundred miscreants — sticks, stones and old shotguns their weapons," intent on punishing her field hands.[29] Although she had always prided herself on her patience, this time she determined that, if goaded, she would shoot. The ploy worked: the captain, seeing the inevitability of a bloody episode, arrived on the scene just in time to find her facing the angry agrarista army with her pistol drawn, and he reluctantly agreed to "keep them off" if she put down the gun.

The next day, Mrs. Evans was pleased to note that her workers were uncharacteristically happy. "I have never seen them laugh and whistle at their work before, not like Indians but merry plow boys! There is a spark of spirit in the breast of the rudest. They knew they had acted bravely and I suppose felt the blessing of a good conscience."[30]

Their happiness may have been occasioned by a good conscience or perhaps by the knowledge that, for the moment, they were safe from attack. In either case, Mrs. Evans's observation was a telling one, for it indicates that even the willing workers of the haciendas were generally a dispirited lot. Otherwise, good cheer would have seemed nothing remarkable. Notwithstanding Mrs. Evans's long held conviction that Mexico's Indian villagers realized the limits of their ambitions and capabilities as hacienda employees, her own observations suggest that there was little beyond fear and dull economic compulsion to attract them.

THE DE LA HUERTA REBELLION

While Mrs. Evans sparred with invading agraristas, the illusion of political stability in Mexico, which had so impressed the U.S. commissioners and the eager investors who stood behind them, evaporated. An electoral dispute in the state of San Luis Potosí turned ugly, and Obregón's apparent efforts at impartiality only angered both sides. At the same time, Plutarco Elías Calles resigned his cabinet post to pursue the presidency with the resounding support of radical labor and agrarian groups. The Cooperatistas, still thrashing about for a candidate, decried the impending imposition of Calles and stockpiled weapons in case words and ballots failed.

As the Cooperatistas searched for a standard-bearer, Finance Minister Adolfo de la Huerta fortuitously discovered a host of new causes to resent the Obregón regime. By the autumn of 1923, it took only a little prodding to persuade him to make a bid for the presidency, and one fateful September night, Puebla governor Froylán Manjarrez typed de la Huerta's resignation from the Obregón cabinet.[31]

The Domingo Arenas Confederation—despite its dissatisfaction with the pace of the government's agrarian reform—unequivocally backed Calles. "Heart of country beats with you," they told their man by telegraph, making clear a willingness to "combat any element opposing your candidacy with the same faith with which we fought against Porfirio Díaz, Huerta, and Carranza." They did not sound like constituents gearing up for routine electioneering, and Calles accepted their support in still more ominous terms: "My revolutionary spirit takes strength from seeing workers and peasants place themselves enthusiastically and decidedly at my side to combat the reaction. It is assured that the camps will be divided and that the reaction will fight us with all its weight and strength; but I want you to know that at the head of all the revolutionaries of the Republic, I will fight that reaction, feeling proud to have it for my enemy."[32]

As usually happened in Mexican political struggles, the battle lines were drawn even in the smallest villages. In the tiny village of Tianguizolco, just west of Huejotzingo, early one morning in late October, a group of twenty-five agraristas draped a red and black flag over the church tower and reconnoitered the streets, shooting into the air and shouting "¡Viva Calles!" When some villagers tried to interfere, they were berated as "Adolfistas" and thrashed for refusing to sign statements of adhesion to the Montista organization.[33] Throughout the region, the cry of "Viva Calles" became a challenge to any who would stand in the way of land distribution—or of the increasing power of Manuel P. Montes.

By November 23, when de la Huerta formally announced his candidacy, it was apparent that the election would be neither free nor fair nor peaceful. It was also clear that de la Huerta had no chance of winning. The campaign had already taken a violent turn. Obregón used his bully pulpit to denounce the "complete material and moral bankruptcy" of de la Huerta's handling of the treasury, and Calles whipped his agrarian and labor partisans into a frenzy. In Puebla City, meanwhile, Governor Manjarrez did all he could to promote de la Huerta's candidacy. The state's Department of Labor sent out pro–de la Huerta circulars and pressured factory workers into signing petitions in de la Huerta's favor. The State Agrarian Commission also made active propaganda. Villagers who arrived in the city to celebrate the "Fiesta del Arbol," normally an innocent annual tree-planting ceremony, found themselves herded into a theater where the Great Cooperatista Convention was busy postulating de la Huerta's candidacy.[34]

Puebla, as a result, became a special target for the Callistas. On Sunday, November 18, Calles and his followers, in the words of an unsympathetic observer, "fell upon the City of Puebla like a tornado . . . , threw the city into a state of pandemonium for a day, and departed leaving dozens of wounded inhabitants in their train."[35] As agraristas flooded into the city, walking or riding in special railroad cars, the roads and rails became rowdy battlegrounds. While two merchants were leading horses and mules from the hacienda Polaxtla passed the village of Moyotzingo on Monday afternoon, they were set upon by more than sixty men shouting "Viva Calles," hurling rocks, and trying to steal their animals.[36] A carload of Spaniards out for a country drive met up with a trainload of Callistas who showered them with stones when they failed to echo the partisan rallying cry. Callistas from Atlixco fired random shots at a baseball field where a game was in progress, severely wounding one player.[37]

The Callistas paraded through the streets of Puebla while their opponents jeered. At one point, a group of railroad workers took a shot at Calles himself, narrowly missing him. Legend has it that Calles was so nonchalant about the attack that he refused even to sit down in the automobile. The sense of passionate invulnerability was reinforced by agrarista leader Antonio Díaz Soto y Gama (later to become a bitter enemy of Calles), who harangued the crowd with a curious metaphor: "Words are women and deeds are men," he told them. "We men should stand for Calles, for he is stingy with words and generous with deeds. If reason does not bring us the victory, force will!"[38]

In the last days of November, the military chief of the state of Guerrero, Rómulo Figueroa, rose in arms against the government. As government troops tried to put the rebellion down, other rebellions flared in the south and east of the country. Upon hearing compelling rumors of his imminent arrest and possible assassination, Adolfo de la Huerta fled Mexico City for Veracruz. Governor Manjarrez was arrested on December 7 and taken prisoner to Mexico City, where he was soon released on the condition that he leave Mexico. Soon the rebellion was joined by well over half of the federal army's generals, among them a veritable who's who of Puebla's former governors and military chiefs — Francisco Coss, Cesáreo Castro, Fortunato Maycotte. Even General Miguel Laveaga, the man who had overdone his show of chivalry toward Mrs. Evans in 1918, figured prominently among the rebels.

To replace Manjarrez as acting governor of Puebla, the federal senate named a young left-wing intellectual from the northern mountain region of Puebla — Vicente Lombardo Toledano. Although Lombardo Toledano would later become a dominant figure in Mexico's postrevolutionary labor movement, in

1923 he was little known and inexperienced, an odd choice for such a crucial post. Clearly, this appointment was a political plum to the Regional Confederation of Mexican Workers (CROM), an organization in which Lombardo Toledano was a rising star.

To Lombardo Toledano fell the difficult task of raising troops to fight the Delahuertistas (as the rebels were soon known) — difficult because most professional soldiers followed their leaders into rebellion. The state's military zone commander, Juan Andreu Almazán, refused to obey Lombardo Toledano's orders to take his troops to the railroad junction at Apizaco on the grounds that they could not be trusted. He was right. The entire regiment soon deserted to join the rebellion.

At the same time, there was irrefutable intelligence that General Fortunato Maycotte was leading rebellious troops from Oaxaca in a march on Mexico City and that he would reach Puebla within days. With professional soldiers in such short supply, Obregón and Calles heeded the words of a confidential agent, Octavio Paz, who told them that the agraristas of the Puebla-Tlaxcala Valley — the "region of the volcanoes" — had held a rally in Huejotzingo, during which they had offered "5000 men to fight the rebels, sell-outs, reactionaries, [and] latifundists." All they asked in return was that the goverment disarm the hacendados and support them in their land claims.[39] In these perilous circumstances, this struck Obregón as a reasonable bargain. As Mexico's leading military strategist, he took personal charge of the government's anti-insurgent campaign. He first ordered all government forces to evacuate Puebla and join the protective cordon ringing Mexico City, then all campesinos of the region to be armed and mobilized.

To lead this ad hoc army, Obregón chose none other than General José María Sánchez. Technically, Sánchez was still wanted in Puebla for the murder of the Moro brothers nearly three years earlier. The amnesty granted him the day after his indictment had been invalidated by a superior court in Puebla, and Sánchez currently had pending a request for "amparo" against that decision. There was still an active warrant for his arrest, and the man who had killed the Moro brothers, allegedly at Sánchez's behest, was awaiting execution in the state penitentiary.[40]

Yet Sánchez did not behave like a wanted criminal. He had returned from the USSR in late 1922 and within months had published a book recounting his impressions and explaining socialist theory in broad strokes. (Many thought it improbable that he had actually written the book himself, however, given his minimal education.)[41] Throughout 1923, Sánchez and his partisans nurtured rumors that he would soon resume the governor's chair — by force, if necessary. Although the prominence of his enemies in the Puebla state government obliged him to keep a low profile for most of 1923,[42] the outbreak of the de la

Huerta rebellion gave him a fresh start. When Sánchez's most intractable and powerful enemies followed Governor Manjarrez into ignominy or rebellion, suddenly his services were in demand. He struck a good bargain: he would organize powerful campesino contingents to fight for the government in exchange for the resurrection of his battered political career. Of course, he could hardly mobilize the state's agraristas on his own, so he leaned heavily on regional caciques for help. In the Texmelucan region, of course, control of the mobilization fell to Rosalie Evans's archenemy, Manuel P. Montes.

SAN PEDRO IN FLAMES

For Rosalie Evans, the outbreak of the rebellion interrupted a pleasant visit from her sister, Daisy Pettus, who retreated to California at the first hint of trouble. Mrs. Evans remained on the hacienda until December 10, when she received a call from Ben Muse, who had become a good friend and a regular visitor to the hacienda. That Monday he was uncharacteristically glum. "Since war began," he told Mrs. Evans, "I have given up society." War? From the limited news reports she had had in her rural retreat, she had not guessed it would amount to more than a series of trifling skirmishes.[43]

Mrs. Evans and Cummins greeted news of the rebellion with mixed feelings. Cummins reported "a hope among thinking people that events may so shape themselves that both Calles and de la Huerta may be eliminated, and General Angel Flores [the radically anti-agrarian governor of Sinaloa] by some fortune of circumstances become the next President"[44] — clearly long-term optimistic predictions, however. In the meantime, Mrs. Evans had to consider the frightening prospect of five thousand angry agraristas under arms, which was enough to persuade her to abandon the hacienda for the relative security of Mexico City — an unwelcome choice because in Mexico City she was forced to subsist for several days on a diet of rumors. On December 14, the day Puebla City was evacuated, she heard that Manuel Montes had seized complete control of the Texmelucan region.

On Sunday, December 16, she took the Interoceanic train for San Martín and found the line cut at Nanacamilpa, Tlaxcala, about fifteen miles shy of her destination. With customary audacity, she sought out the supreme commander of the large army of factory workers and campesinos she found there, readying themselves for action. She found him — General Juan Andreu Almazán — on the steps of his military train, "a hard young man, heavy and sulky." Almazán moaned about the treachery and disloyalty that had forced him to arm the agrarians and place Manuel Montes at their head. "I am betrayed by traitors," he told her angrily, "and I am going to arm the countryside."[45] He refused her request for a horse and safe-conduct to visit her estate, but he said he would order Montes to respect her hacienda. He also allowed her to send a man to scout out the situation. Mrs. Evans was impressed enough to ask Cummins to send the British government's official thanks to Almazán, but she returned to Mexico City only reluctantly and uneasily.

Three days after her meeting with Almazán, she received a telephone call confirming her worst fears: the man she had sent to San Pedro reported seeing the hacienda in flames and her administrator, Jesús Bermejillo, fighting for his life against agrarista attackers.

The next morning she determined at all odds to get to the hacienda, although it entailed a grueling train ride through the war-torn region — Almazán's troops were even then massing to retake Puebla City. She could get no farther than San Martín, where officers only mocked her pleas for a horse and soldiers. She waited nervously at the El Pilar factory for rumors to trickle in. Everyone now agreed that the hacienda buildings had been torched and were still smoldering. Some said Bermejillo and the dogs were dead. Others held that they had escaped.

When she finally made it to the hacienda a few days later, she learned that the dogs had been found cowering in the corner of a burned-out barn, "howling their poor dog hearts out," but that was the only good news. Only two rooms were relatively unscathed — the rest burned and the roof above them collapsed. Furniture, gold mirrors, paintings, clocks — nearly all of her most cherished possessions — had been charred or stolen. Livestock had been rustled or killed, the chapel garden was withered and parched, and blackened splinters of the once mighty roof beams littered the ground along with rubble from the sturdy walls that now supported nothing.

With the indominatable spirit that so exasperated her enemies, Mrs. Evans did not ponder the tragedy for long. Almost mechanically, she began to pick up debris, wipe away soot and ash, and dig up and replant the garden.[46]

It was clear what had happened. Before marching off to Puebla where they would participate in the retaking of the city on December 21, the freshly armed agrarista armies had taken the opportunity to issue yet another warning to those landowners who resisted the land reform — the most destructive warning yet. The uprising gave them a chance at vengeance when neither Mrs. Evans, nor her men, nor federal troops would be there to drive them off. Indeed, for the moment the agraristas *were* federal troops. It appeared as if they were only now heeding the advice that the Zapatistas had tried to give them years earlier: take full advantage of violent upheaval, for peace means retrenchment and retrogression.

Obregón and Calles were undoubtedly aware that their reliance on agrarista troops would entail a day of reckoning. Sure enough, they would soon grow weary of the steady stream of letters and telegrams from disgruntled peasants that opened with unsubtle reminders of how villagers had shed their blood defending the government. For now, however, they were resolved to exploit every possible advantage to maintain power, and their resolve paid immediate dividends. In the battle of Puebla, some ten thousand government troops fought against forty-five hundred Delahuertista rebels. Within a few early morning hours, the battle was over and the corpses of nearly seven hundred rebels lay in the streets of Puebla, many of them most likely victims of mass execution by government forces. After gathering up weapons and ammunition from the dead, the agraristas under Sánchez and Montes went off in several directions to fight other battles.[47]

It did not take Rosalie Evans long to realize both her ultimate horror and her only hope. The Obregón regime was basking in the warm afterglow of its accords with the United States. Charles Evans Hughes, U.S. secretary of state, declared the rebellion to be "subversive of all constitutional and orderly procedure" and authorized the shipment of arms and supplies to the Mexican government.[48] Chargé d'affaires George Summerlin candidly acknowledged that some of the weapons being sold by the United States were ending up in the hands of labor and agrarista volunteers, but it seemed a price worth paying for the maintenance of "order" in Mexico.[49]

The fact that the country of her birth was now aiding and abetting her enemies was almost too much for Mrs. Evans to bear. Her enemies were using U.S. weapons to sack and destroy her property, and the "civilized world" had as yet failed to express its outrage. She immediately recalled the newspaper story about her case that she had kept under wraps for several months. If foreign citizens were not appropriately outraged, she figured, it was simply because they did not have the facts. She would have to go public.

She told her sister to contact the *Chicago Tribune* and authorize publication of her story. "Lose no time," she ordered, as she sat forlornly in the old textile mill in San Martín on Christmas Eve 1923, listening to amateur soldiers carousing in the streets and firing their weapons merrily. "I am as anxious to speak as heretofore to be silent. . . . I believe in the justice of America and Great Britain, indeed I want to appeal to the justice of the civilized world — that through me, though ruined, they may pause before the Senate ratifies a treaty with such a goverment."[50]

Eight

When you wake up, say to yourself — To-day I
shall encounter meddling, ingratitude, violence,
cunning, jealousy, self-seeking; all of them
the results of men not knowing what is good and
what is evil.
— Marcus Aurelius, *Meditations*

ROSALIE EVANS began 1924 sick in bed in her Mexico City home, laid low by the stress of the preceding weeks. She was haunted by the image of her beloved hacienda reduced to a smoldering ruin, and she fretted for the life of her administrator, partner, and confidant, Jesús Bermejillo, who had last been seen battling for his life amid the flames and was now rumored to be running with the rebels. Friends remarked how her long dark hair had turned rapidly and completely white, and even Mr. Cummins was alarmed at "the nervous condition to which the weight of her cares has reduced this British subject, illustrated by an inclination to inflict bodily harm upon Mexican Authorities and to reject counsels of moderation."[1]

Yet, never one to wallow long in despair, the ailing Mrs. Evans plotted her next move. "My mind," she wrote, "is bent on publicity."

She was not the only one thinking along these lines. In London, foreign office clerks scribbled their thoughts in the margins of Cummins's telegram recounting the sacking and burning of San Pedro. "A disgraceful story," said one. "[O]ne of our worst cases," said another, "and it is painful to think that we are in reality powerless to assist." Yet another anonymous hand asked parenthetically, "Has the story been published?" It may have been Lord Curzon himself who brought this discussion around to its logical conclusion: "Would it not be worthwhile to publish the tale? It is an effective answer to those who are always clamoring for recognition."[2]

By New Year's Day 1924, Rosalie Evans was heartily reinforced in her resolve: "My most trusted advisers say my duty now is to publish quickly," she reported.

"I am going to prevent, if I can—preposterous as it is—the shipment of more arms to the criminals."[3]

MRS. EVANS GOES PUBLIC

So on January 6, 1924, Mrs. Evans made her debut in the headlines, first of the *Chicago Tribune* and then in newspapers throughout the English-speaking world. The story was an unquestioning rehearsal of Mrs. Evans's own account, including her speculation—reported as fact—that Obregón had promised San Pedro to José María Sánchez as a reward for his loyalty. The article was fairly sober in tone, though it lingered briefly on the episode in early 1923 when Mrs. Evans had pulled up the red flags planted by Montes and his men. "Mrs. Evans advanced to remove these," ran the copy. "Riflemen opened fire on her from a distance. She continued, however, and returned with the flags under fire."[4]

The story would not long remain so prosaic in the telling. By July, the *Syracuse Herald* had recreated Rosalie Evans as a "brave and pretty war widow" who was "believed to have in her veins the blood of the redoubtable Douglases" of Scotland. In this version, Mrs. Evans and six greenhorn followers perform a series of fantastic, dime-novel feats. At one point, they steal out into the darkness to confront an army of 150 bandits, taking "the greasers completely by surprise, [so] they fled in panic." In perhaps the only sentence in a lengthy feature that contained any truth, the *Herald* stated that "Innumerable stories are now being retailed, regarding the amazing adventures of this heroic woman and of her hairbreadth escapes from death at the hands of her cowardly besiegers."[5]

Mrs. Evans's brush with fame came at an improbable moment. In Great Britain, balloting in the House of Commons in early December had resulted in the formation of the country's first Labour Party government, fronted by J. Ramsay MacDonald, the son of a Scottish coal-mining family. MacDonald was hardly a radical,[6] and his sphere of action was in any case circumscribed by his party's minority status in Parliament. Neither was he an old-style conservative like Lord Curzon, however, which became especially significant when he decided to act as his own foreign secretary and shortly thereafter announced, amid warm words about "neighborliness among nations," that his government would grant diplomatic recognition to the Soviet Union. The conservative hardliners were not alone in objecting. Rafael Nieto, the Mexican ambassador to Sweden who had been negotiating for British recognition, angrily broke off discussions, complaining that Mexico was less radical and hence more deserving of recognition than the USSR. "Mexico can wait indefinitely and patiently," he fumed, "for a policy which she thinks is just and moral."[7]

Many British businessmen, noting a certain hypocrisy in their country's international dealings, also felt that Mexico deserved recognition. Vincent York of the Mexican Railway had nothing but praise for Obregón's efforts to uplift the masses and meet his country's international obligations. "The whole of the British Colony in Mexico are unanimously in favor of recognition," he wrote, in sharp contrast to Mrs. Evans's version, "and complain bitterly that it has been so long withheld." Lord Asquith, the venerable Liberal, told the House of Lords that he "need not dilate on the value of trade that would be brought about by recognition of a great and rich country like Mexico." The only obstacles to that, he noted, "were the difficulties connected with private claims, among which that of Rosalia Emilia [*sic*] Caden Evans bulks rather large."[8]

Mrs. Evans thus figured, almost literally, as a final bulwark between Britain's old-style imperialist intransigence and the most accommodating vision of the postwar world championed by the Labourites. Lord Curzon continued to expound his views in the House of Lords, characterizing Mexico as "one of the most disorderly countries in the world." Among its lesser defects, Mexico was a poor credit risk. To prove this, Curzon needed only recall the brief Huerta government of 1913–1914 when, "in the gushing good humour which is recommended by the noble Lord [Asquith], a loan was made to that gentleman," but repudiated by subsequent revolutionary governments. Then there was the matter of the continuing confiscation of foreign property, especially Mrs. Evans's lands. "That was a desperate and deplorable case of gross ill-usage," Lord Curzon remarked, "and when I left office it was wholly unrecognized, uncompensated, and still remaining to be solved."[9] MacDonald, as both prime minister and foreign secretary, would have liked to grant recognition to Mexico, but by publicizing Mrs. Evans's plight, Curzon and Cummins had thrown down a gauntlet: such a policy, they implied, would be entertained only by cowards or fools. Mrs. Evans was quite conscious of her utility: "I am too tempting a weapon not to grasp," she wrote. "Wielded right, I may be a deciding factor."[10]

Obregón was not indifferent to the matter of British recognition, even when U.S. recognition was practically assured. He was eager for any and all foreign investment—especially because the de la Huerta rebellion was bleeding Mexico's treasury, disrupting production, and destroying infrastructure. Britain's hostility also obstructed Mexico's entrance into the League of Nations, which Obregón thought crucial to enhancing Mexico's global credibility. There was still at least some danger that British hostility might jeopardize Mexico's newfound friendship with the United States and Senate ratification of the recognition treaty. That friendship was already paying dividends in the form of five thousand Enfield rifles, five million rounds of .30 calibre ammunition, and eight De Haviland airplanes—all U.S. Army surplus. A ban had also been placed on all public and private arms sales to the rebels. Although some historians later maintained that the government forces would have prevailed anyway, thanks to

the weakness of their opponents, at the time the U.S. connection was something Obregón would not readily risk.[11]

Mrs. Evans was not alone in her criticism of U.S. support for Obregón.
Caustic commentators pointed out that by opting on principle to back nearly
any established government against any "unwarrantable uprisings,"[12] the United
States was betraying its own revolutionary roots. Senator Hiram Johnson of
California accused the U.S. government of telling Latin Americans, "If you dare
fight for what you deem to be right, if you raise your hand against oppression
and wrong, the most powerful nation of the world will come to the aid of those
you think your oppressors and will maintain existing power."[13]

Few, of course, could agree on who in Mexico represented "oppression and
wrong," and this was the debate that Rosalie Evans joined with a vengeance.
Now that her story had been publicized by the *Tribune* article, Cummins and
others encouraged her to write up her own account,[14] although they warned her
that she risked expulsion or worse — she would, after all, be committing herself
to an act of blatant subversion and would be preventing British recognition in
the bargain. Mrs. Evans nevertheless took up her pen zealously. Her writing was
more turgid than she might have wished, despite some time spent tutoring
herself in "newspaper English." "If they want to have me speak," she declared,
"it will have to be in old-time phrases, picked up in childhood from English
classics."[15]

The result of her efforts was published in the *Chicago Tribune* on February 26.
Hers was a minority opinion, however, and perhaps for that reason it was
tucked away on page 13, amid ads for Liquid Arvon Dandruff Formula and
Compton's Pictured Encyclopedias. More conspicuous pages contained ap-
proving coverage of Mexican government victories and the adventures of a
commercial mission to Mexico headed by J. Ham Lewis, former senator and
current Chicago business tycoon, who predicted "a great future for the southern republic."[16] In any case, it would be a challenge to catch the attention of a
reading public weary of war and reeling from revelations of corruption in their
own government. Moreover, by the time the article appeared, the Mexican
government's victory over the rebellion was a foregone conclusion. Even Mrs.
Evans was surprised to learn that her article had been published.

In the article, she began her diatribe with a denunciation of the U.S. State
Department for its "recognition without sufficient guaranties [*sic*] for life or
property, not only of American citizens, but of thousands of unfortunate Mexicans and foreigners, who, owing to their faith in the just enforcement of the
Monroe Doctrine, have patiently awaited the vindication of their claims when
the United States recognized Mexico." This decision was not only "the gravest
error ever committed by the American government in relation to [Mexico]",
but also a direct cause of the de la Huerta rebellion. Seizure of property, she

maintained, had nothing to do with uplifting the impoverished masses. She illustrated the point with the claim that her neighboring hacienda, Polaxtla, had been confiscated on the pretext of helping the poor villagers, but was now being run by a nephew of President Obregón and a cousin of the minister of war. (She made this charge frequently, but according to agrarian reform records, Polaxtla, even though reduced to a "small property," remained in the family of Marcelino Presno until well into the 1930s.)

Mrs. Evans hoped to ignite the xenophobic and isolationist sentiments she took to be latent in American society: "They know in the state department [that] the most dangerous elements in that most dangerous organization, the I.W.W. [Industrial Workers of the World], are planning and plotting with the criminal elements, encouraged by Obregón and Calles, to establish bolshevism in Mexico." The U.S. government claimed that its arms sales to Mexico would discourage war and uphold law and order, but "do they realize," Mrs. Evans asked, "in selling arms to the Obregón government they are arming the I.W.W.s not only of Mexico but from all over the world who have taken refuge here, and this on the border of their own country?"

Mrs. Evans saved her most dangerous point for last. The State Department asserted that Obregón's regime was a responsible one because it promised to repay its foreign debt, but Mrs. Evans credited this laudable posture to none other than the rebel leader, Adolfo de la Huerta, who had negotiated a debt-servicing agreement with international bankers in 1922: "The department of state's appreciation of the government that is complying with its obligations turns out, upon investigation, to be merited by the revolutionaries who are to be killed with American rifles, aeroplanes, and bombs."[17]

Mrs. Evans's public statement was a risky business. Obregón was touchy about foreigners who engaged in pro-rebel activities. Vicente Lombardo Toledano had barely stepped into the governor's office of Puebla before he received Obregón's orders to "open a minute investigation of foreigners who in different ways supported the subversive movement in the state."[18] Obregón also had agents smoking out foreign connections to rebel funding, under the threat of constitutional Article 33, which prescribed summary expulsion for "pernicious foreigners." On February 23 the government deported John Frederick Wright, the *Chicago Tribune*'s Mexico City correspondent, for writing articles about Mrs. Evans that were "objectionable to the government" and for his "persistent misinterpretation of political news." This move was an embarrassment because Wright was actually quite friendly to the Obregón regime. The objectionable article was a report on Mrs. Evans written by Ralph Cameron, another *Tribune* correspondent. Wright's expulsion proved fateful, however: the *Tribune* retaliated by publishing Mrs. Evans's own article.[19] Although Mrs. Evans wrote to *Excélsior,* Mexico's most prominent daily, explaining the government's error, the government apparently decided that saving face was more important than expelling the right foreigner.[20]

Mrs. Evans could not have imagined that her activities would go undetected. Sure enough, the very day her article was published, a certain Enrique Mexía of Gary, Indiana, concerned that the Mexican president know "the enemies in [his] own house," clipped the article from the *Tribune* and sent it to Obregón.[21]

Mrs. Evans's temerity in writing the article can only be explained by her boundless faith that virtue would win out in the end. "You would laugh," she wrote her sister in early February, "if you knew how I put myself to sleep last night, and well asleep as I used to do when afraid of the dark as a child: 'God's above the devil—God's above the devil.'"[22]

TROUBLE FOR CUMMINS

Obregón no doubt considered Mrs. Evans a "pernicious foreigner," but at the same time he feared the political damage that might result from her deportation. To be sure, some of Mrs. Evans's closest friends urged her to take any offer and get out.[23] Whereas many in the foreign community thought her a major pest, she also had many sympathizers. The slight, frail, middle-aged woman, cosmopolitan and well educated, seemed badly miscast in the role of villain and oppressor. For much of the audience, Obregón was the natural heavy, and attacks on the widow Evans would do nothing to improve his image. (Mrs. Evans appreciated his quandary: "Beware of women and children," she wrote, "we are dangerous to harm."[24]) Obregón was by no means unconcerned about his image overseas: he paid a press agency in New York to enhance it, and his regime rolled out the red carpet for any visiting journalist whose opinions promised to be at all sympathetic. One British journalist, Dr. E. J. Dillon, was even set up in an office in Chapultepec Castle, where he churned out a series of books and articles that were embarrassingly effusive in their praise of Obregón. Such writers could be relied upon to inform at least a small circle of readers of the pressing need for agrarian reform and of the patriotic zeal with which the Obregón regime was carrying it out, but they could not seriously be expected to neutralize a powerful symbol like Mrs. Evans.[25]

If Mrs. Evans was untouchable for the moment, Cunard Cummins was quite another matter. Cummins was an irascible character—loved by those whose interests he championed with unrestrained ardor, but disliked by a number of important operators in Mexico who felt he did far more harm than good. His dispatches in the wake of the Bucareli talks were so hostile to Mexico that even the foreign office asked him to moderate his tone a bit so as not to interfere with the normalization in U.S.-Mexican relations.[26] He never minced words in his denunciations of the "bolshevik" Calles, and with the outbreak of the de la

Huerta rebellion he recommended that Great Britain recognize the rebels as belligerents and thus clear the way for shipments of arms to them.[27]

The Mexican government had longed for years to be rid of Cummins. In early 1924, when the Labour Party came to power in England, Obregón thought he saw an opening for a better relationship between the two countries. Labour, after all, should be sympathetic to a kindred regime. Cummins did not miss the opportunity to turn this interpretation to the Mexicans' disadvantage by reporting that, due to "the want of opportunity and the lack of understanding of the world's affairs," the benighted Mexicans had allowed themselves to be deceived by the term "Labour." That word, he noted, "calls to mind in Mexico conditions very different from those it represents in England," inspiring hopes for a government less "zealous of British rights and prestige."[28] Cummins's view was partly wishful thinking, however, for in fact the Mexicans had not greatly misread the new prime minister's disposition. MacDonald would surely have welcomed a relaxation of tensions with Mexico,[29] but then, as one editorialist remarked, "in more than one quarter of the globe those elements which the Labour Party would like to praise for well-doing and advancement have been evincing a stubborn evil genius for doing the opposite."[30] Caught between the troublesome behavior of the radical regimes and the intransigence of British conservatives, MacDonald had to negotiate a foreign policy minefield. By the end of 1924, he would be badly embarrassed by the Cummins-Evans episode, and his gestures of goodwill toward the Soviet Union would contribute directly to the collapse of his government.

The "Cummins affair" began to heat up on January 15, 1923. After receiving a pair of harsh notes from Cummins regarding the treatment of Mrs. Evans and the Tlahualilo Company, Mexico's new foreign secretary, General Aaron Sáenz, announced he was suspending all correspondence with the British representative. He explained that Cummins had consistently made false and malicious reports to his superiors, sent discourteous notes to the Mexican government, and shown "obvious disrespect" for Mexican officials in personal meetings. In short, he was the "principal obstacle" to the renewal of Anglo-Mexican relations.[31] Cummins's basic dishonesty, said Sáenz, was evidenced by his claim that the Mexican government had sent federal troops to destroy the Evans hacienda — a patent falsehood because Sáenz himself had personally ordered protection for Mrs. Evans and her property.[32] Although Sáenz did not mention it, at least some circumstantial evidence revealed that Cummins's reports were having their intended effect — as, for instance, in early March when British bankers canceled plans for a loan to Mexico "owing to [the] Reds."[33]

By mid-April, MacDonald could no longer ignore the torrent of Mexican complaints about Cummins. He announced that he would soon send a seasoned diplomat, Thomas Hohler, to investigate the situation and render an "independent" opinion. Hohler was an odd choice, for he and Cummins were old friends and coreligionists. They had been business partners in Torreón early in the revolution, and it had been Hohler who recommended Cummins for the job of commercial attaché in Mexico City back in 1916.[34] At the very least, he might be able to express the views he shared with Cummins in a less antagonizing tone.

The Mexicans seemed satisfied with Hohler, however, and inquired only as to the date of his arrival so they would know when to roll out the red carpet.[35] Unfortunately, tensions in Mexico would come to a head long before the so-called "Hohler Mission" could even set sail.

SÁNCHEZ AND MONTES RETURN

Troubles with England were not paramount in the thoughts of either Obregón or Calles, who found plenty of internal problems to worry about. Although it is true that by late winter they had the rebellion well in hand,[36] Lord Curzon's sardonic prediction that the rebellion would be "followed by a general sniping by everybody at everybody else without any humbug or hypocrisy" turned out to be woefully accurate.[37]

Episodes of armed violence in 1920s Mexico were more than merely cathartic: they were extraordinary opportunities to adjust the balance of power and hence to remake the world. Antonio Villareal, former agriculture minister and current rebel leader, shrugged off the notion of a peaceful transmission of power as hopelessly quixotic. "In real Mexican politics," he said, "when an election is peaceful, there has been no election. . . . The transmission of the Executive Power in Mexico has never been accomplished peaceably except under a dictatorial regime."[38] In other words, the strong had imposed their will upon the weak for so long that it had become an ingrained habit. Institutions of power — the courts, the polls, the government commissions — were only as yielding and useful as the people in control wished to make them. Public power was an all-or-nothing proposition: one either controlled the courts, polls, and political offices, or was trampled by those who did. One imposed or was imposed upon. If the usual channels worked smoothly, they were probably working in someone else's favor.

For many Mexicans, then, violence meant hope. This notion found an echo in the very vocabulary of politics, which provided that in moments of disruption, the president or inner circle of senators could decree any state government out of existence by declaring that public powers had "disappeared." Such moments were to be sought out or hastened along, for when power disappeared, it left nothing but a seductive void to be filled by anyone with the requisite ambition. These were times when what could not be won through negotiation could be taken by force; when paths that had once seemed hopelessly blocked could be cleared; and when all enemies could be peremptorily cast into outer darkness.

The "disappearance" of public power in Puebla brought on by the outbreak of the rebellion and the defection of Governor Manjarrez had resulted in an appointment that satisfied almost no one. Vicente Lombardo Toledano was not a bad governor, even if his plans for moralization and redemption through education were overly idealistic under the circumstances. The problem was that the young labor leader so obviously owed his appointment to political patronage: Obregón had appointed him mostly to appease Calles, who in turn relied on CROM's support. Not surprisingly, the imposition of Lombardo Toledano was roundly denounced in Puebla as a violation of state sovereignty.[39] Moreover, many individuals felt themselves entitled to fill the void in state power, and for the moment none was more active or insistent than José María Sánchez.

Ironically, Sánchez's claim rested less on the fact that, technically, he was already the state's governor, than on his recent role in defending the Obregón regime. He had led two battalions of volunteer troops to the banks of the Lerma River near Ocotlán, Jalisco, playing a part in the decisive battle against the Delahuertistas. He did not hesitate to style himself "the hero of Ocotlán" and to demand that he be rewarded accordingly. His partisans, who came to dominate the state legislature once all the rebel elements had been expelled, worked assiduously to undercut the authority of Governor Lombardo Toledano and to demand a replacement. Their efforts were rewarded in March, when power "disappeared" once again, and the vacancy was filled by a federal deputy named Alberto Guerrero, who seems to have understood that he was to be a stand-in for José María Sánchez.

The return of Sánchez inspired hopes and expectations in the ranks of the state's popular movements that could not possibly be fulfilled. He arrived in Puebla in March, fresh from the battlefields of Jalisco, to find delegations of workers and peasants already lined up to demand municipal posts and seats in the state and federal congresses. Everyone wanted a reward, be it in the form of land, power, or booty.

Rosalie Evans had good reason to be alarmed at these developments. Sánchez was closely identified with *agrarismo,* and his power rested largely on the shoulders of such local agrarian leaders as Mrs. Evans's arch foe, Manuel P. Montes. Not surprisingly, Montes was among those who felt entitled to a hefty boost in personal power and patronage. Fearing just such a development, Mrs. Evans spent much of January and February pleading with sympathetic military men to do what they could to prevent Montes from returning to the area. She hoped that her presumed power to influence American opinion might sway these men in her favor.

Her hopes were dashed in early March, however, when she boarded the Mexico City train in Puebla and saw Montes jump off the train from Veracruz, "received with flags waving, music and shouting." She immediately sent word to the detachment of soldiers stationed on San Pedro to double the guard.[40]

UNCERTAIN SOLDIERS

Doubling the guard would not be nearly enough to save the hacienda or Mrs. Evans now, for her situation had changed profoundly for the worse. She was notoriously identified with the losing side of the rebellion by virtue of both her own propaganda campaign and the fact that her former administrator, Jesús Bermejillo, had become a ranking officer in the rebel army. Worse still, although conservative federal army men such as Castro and Maycotte had at one time protected landowners from zealous agraristas, they had more recently seconded the rebellion and were thus weakened and discredited by the rebels' impending defeat.[41] Worst of all, the agraristas of Huejotzingo were now well armed and feeling themselves the creditors of a long overdue account. With that great void in state power beckoning, their return in the wake of the rebellion touched off an all-out struggle in which the stakes were high and scruples forgotten. It would take more than a handful of poorly trained soldiers to tame these forces, even had those soldiers generously supported the landowners.

In fact, the soldiers were growing increasingly diffident. Mrs. Evans had always grudgingly counted on their aid, although they do not loom large in her own account of her struggles. If she mentioned them at all, they seemed either a part of the scenery or a necessary evil. She could not bring herself to be grateful to them, in part because she took their support as her due and in part because she never learned to trust those ragged men who, despite their billets, were of a similar race and class as her antagonists. Some, according to Mrs. Evans, were "yet in early infancy — that is as far as their sturdy little black bodies are concerned — but their souls are warped as pine knots."[42] In the farm's hierarchy, the rank-and-file soldier rated lower than animals. Mrs. Evans scolded one soldier who had dared to sit on her porch and threaten one of her dogs. "You are here to protect me," she said. "You are never allowed in the house — now leave it."[43]

Menacing and objectionable though the soldiers may have been, Mrs. Evans would sorely miss them when they finally withdrew their protection. Until the spring of 1924, she had continued to receive government orders and warnings from villagers casually, confident the worst could be postponed indefinitely through the usual legal appeals and stalling tactics. She began to notice the change in late March, when the villagers of San Lorenzo Chiautzingo — a relatively large town on the banks of the Xochiac River, which fed San Pedro's irrigation from the south — built a sand dike that diverted the hacienda's water

Federal Soldiers at San Pedro — "She could not bring herself to be grateful." *Credit:* Rosalie Evans Papers (#2895), Special Collections Department, University of Virginia Library.

onto their ejidal lands. When she rode over to investigate, she was met by the village president, who defiantly explained that the villagers claimed the water because they were Mexicans and that if she wanted a fight, she would have one. She tried to trample the man with her horse, but he escaped into the church, where he gathered the villagers by furiously ringing the church bell. Once assembled, however, the villagers refused to fire on her even though many of them were armed — thereby impressing Mrs. Evans because she believed it was proof of their sympathy for her position. She was dismayed, however, that the soldiers of the guard stood by dumbly. Chiautzingo sent some thirty armed men to guard their dam, and Mrs. Evans's telegrams to Cummins, Obregón, and the governor of Puebla got no results. "These beasts are doing it intentionally," she complained, "my wheat withering."[44]

"I am going to follow my own inspirations," she wrote, in what could serve as the tragic epigraph for her last months, when nearly all outside aid deserted her. Lately, she had taken to carrying a small edition of the meditations of Marcus Aurelius that had belonged to her mother, trying to absorb its counsels of patience, equanimity, and serenity in the face of provocation. Although she admired such sentiments, they proved overly demanding in the real world of Mexico.

"Forgive me," she wrote her sister, "for throwing out sparks and destroying the creeping, crawling things. Ah! the hypocrisy, how I hate it!" The object of her wrath on this occasion was the colonel of the detachment at San Pedro, who refused her order to destroy the dam built by the villagers of Chiautzingo and advised her to take up the matter with the civil authorities. "Then I exploded," she recounted, giving the colonel such an earful of taunts, insults, and threats that in the end he backed down. That night he took a squad of soldiers and peons to smash the dam. "I would have no further trouble," she wrote hopefully. In fact, although the wheat was saved, the real trouble was only beginning.[45] This occasion was virtually the last time she would receive active support from the soldiers.

GEORGE CAMP

Increasingly unable to rely on the soldiers, Mrs. Evans came to put more faith the ministrations of private supporters, most notably a thirty-year-old Texan named George "Jack" Camp. Although a native of San Antonio, Texas, Camp had lived in Mexico as a child and had longed to return. After serving as a lieutenant in France during World War I and spending some years in India, he had found his way to Mexico City, where he established a small contracting business with a friend he had met while an engineering student at MIT. He was small and thin, with reddish hair, a ruddy complexion, and a volatile nature. "Trouble," he said, "has always been a magnet to me."[46]

Camp learned of Mrs. Evans from Zelia Nuttall, a well-known archaeologist and paragon of Mexico City's foreign society. Mrs. Nuttall had been edgy about Mexico City's rising crime rate and had persuaded Camp to stay at her home — a sturdy mansion that had originally belonged to the conquistador, Pedro de Alvarado — to protect her and her property. During that time, she had peaked Camp's interest with stories of her friend, the intrepid Rosalie Evans. From the first, Camp was captivated and eager to make Mrs. Evans's acquaintance. Mrs. Evans inspired his profound admiration because she shared his fervent belief in the sacredness of property rights and a willingness to use force to defend them. Camp also learned that Mrs. Evans was without an administrator. It seemed unlikely that Jesús Bermejillo would return to take up his old job: at that moment he was in Oaxaca, serving as chief of staff for Antonio Martínez, the rebel general.

Starting in late January, Camp began paying frequent visits to San Pedro, where he was always warmly welcomed. Mrs. Evans never formally hired him as administrator. She did not have to: Camp was a willing and eager recruit because defending her gave him the opportunity to indulge both his passion for firearms and his disdain for Mexicans.

TROUBLE AT THE GRASS ROOTS

Mrs. Evans could also still count on a few allies among the villagers, although not nearly as many as she imagined. The villagers of Chiautzingo who refused to shoot at her probably restrained themselves at least as much from prudence as from sympathy. Even the most hardened agraristas may have realized that the murder of a prominent foreign woman would be counterproductive given the likely fallout. It may also have been true—as some friends of Mrs. Evans claimed—that many villagers held the hacendada to be "more of a spirit than a human," a witch woman whose lands were magically protected from hail and drought, who performed miraculous feats, and who might wreak posthumous vengeance against anyone who harmed her.[47]

If true, such a belief would be unsurprising. At first glance, it might seem that the villagers would resent Mrs. Evans for her flamboyant violation of their norms and expectations regarding the proper behavior of women and widows, but this view would be a misreading of the case. Certainly, they had notions regarding appropriate gender roles, but these notions were bound up with issues of ethnicity, nationality, and class. That is, women of the villages were expected to behave in fairly prescribed ways, but the rules did not apply to a wealthy foreign woman. Even if they had, Mrs. Evans's transgression of these rules was so extreme that she would have been judged either a lunatic or a saint. In fact, she was a figure of authority from before the revolution, a key part of the system that had long infantilized villagers, so they were uncertain whether harming her would be a matter of eliminating the vestiges of the old system or of committing reckless folly.

In any case, harming a woman would not have been a laudable act for a macho man. Mrs. Evans consciously styled herself a maternal figure, a woman of authority who was caring but stern. Thus, harming or killing such a woman was no testament to a man's valor, but quite the contrary: it would be tantamount to a cowardly act of matricide. Mrs. Evans must have set off a riot of conflicting emotions, especially among the male villagers. The villagers did not really *want* to kill her, but her continued, high-profile defiance was at the same time an intolerable affront, a suggestion that the men of the villages were incapable of defending their own. Attributing supernatural powers to her—not an uncommon response to widows, who presumably had been freed from the overlordship of men—was a convenient rationalization. How better to resolve such a conflict than by blaming the unseen and the inexplicable?

There is also the more prosaic point that many villagers admired Mrs. Evans for her courage, and some even liked her personally. Field hands almost always regarded the hacienda owner—normally a remote and exalted personage—more highly than they did the administrators and mayordomos with whom they came into close and frequent contact. The villagers were also fully capable of recognizing and admiring courage. One elderly villager in 1992 went so far as figuratively to endow the intransigent widow with male attributes: "Tenía huevos," he recalled, almost reverently.[48]

For her part, Mrs. Evans tended to interpret all opposition to the agraristas as support for her, seldom troubling to distinguish among the many reasons for it. In fact, disaffection with Montes or agrarismo usually implied neither a great love for the hacienda system nor a studied objection to bettering the lot of the poor. In the wake of the rebellion, anguished cries were heard from a variety of fence-sitters, grudge bearers, malcontents, and factionalists on the outs—all of whom were horrified that the old paramilitary "regional corp," which Governor Manjarrez had made some headway in disbanding, was finding a new lease on life.[49] In the spring, a large group of citizens from San Buenaventura Tecaltzingo complained of abuses that made them wonder if the revolution had accomplished anything toward freeing them from the grip of harsh and corrupt local powers. The Montista village president arrested and jailed innocent villagers according to his drunken whims, forcing them to perform hard labor on public projects. Brandishing "national armaments," the agraristas now threatened and terrorized with abandon any who failed to join their crusade, damning them as "Delahuertistas," the new favorite epithet.

"They despise us," wrote the beleaguered dissenters of Tecaltzingo, "for the crime of not wishing to enter fully into their agrarista labor. [We refrain from supporting agrarismo] for the simple reason that we do not know if it is a good thing. Understanding our own ignorance, and not wanting to get involved in anything, we have decided to remain neutral, and it is for this reason that they shower us with curses and abuse . . . although we have never obstructed them in their activities and on the contrary have respected them and left them in complete freedom."[50]

Other villagers charged that Manuel Montes represented himself as the only source of land. He would deny lands to political enemies or make sure they got inferior plots; his people confiscated crops, collected unauthorized taxes, and kidnapped, threatened, or killed any who did not unconditionally obey his orders.[51]

Nor were the village agrarian leaders that Montes imposed always paragons of virtue. An extreme—but unfortunately, not atypical—example of such a leader was Antonio García, president of the agrarian committee of the village of San Gregorio Aztotoacán, a few miles west of San Martín Texmelucan. García had presided over his village's ejidal grant in 1920, taking a hefty portion of that ejido for himself and using it to grow maguey without ever informing his fellow ejidatarios about the destination of the field's profits. He rented ejidal plots to some villagers — ignoring the fact that ejidal land was supposed to be the common property of them all — and even "sold" some ejidal plots without entering the transactions into the district tax records. He sometimes charged his fellow villagers for irrigation water and frequently collected fees on the pretext of having to travel to Puebla or Mexico City to transact some agrarian business or other, entering only a minor portion of these sums into the account books. Doubling as chief of the village's corp of regionales, he threatened dissidents with violent reprisal. "It is not fair," complained the embittered villagers of San Gregorio, "that we have escaped the clutches of the hacendados who exploited our sweat and labor, only to fall into the hands of an individual like Antonio García."

But when a group of villagers persuaded the state agrarian commission to have him removed from office, García unleashed a reign of terror that obliged several citizens to leave their homes and spend several nights crouched among the cornfields. At a meeting, several villagers rose up to challenge García, whereupon García's brother, the municipal president of the nearby village of San Salvador el Verde, opened fire, killing two villagers and wounding several others.[52] Bad agrarian leaders, once installed, were not easy to remove.

Not all those who opposed Montes were indifferent toward the land issue, however. After all, Montes's abuses were only able to flourish in the shade of official ineptitude. Growing resentment of the Montistas was accompanied by a corresponding impatience with the indecisiveness and ineffectuality of the state and national governments, which had supposedly granted land to the villages without supplying the resolute force that might make those grants a reality. This phenomenon had not only permitted Rosalie Evans to keep up her resistance for so long, but also in effect created the agrarista monster that so vexed villagers and landowners alike. With the federal forces waffling and often turning their guns against villagers who hoped to occupy their lands peacefully, there arose a logical need for a countervailing force. Men like Montes staked their credibility and hopes for power on their ability to deliver land, whether it be in connivance with or defiance of the government and its army.[53]

THE BATTLE FOR EL ROSARIO

In April of 1924, the immediate object of the contest was a field of about 350 acres that had been granted in March to San Jerónimo Tianguismanalco and San Francisco Tepeyecac. The land in question was one of the Evans hacienda's northernmost fields, a piece of ground known as "El Rosario," located at the foot of Coxtocán Hill. Seventeen years before, Harry Evans had bored his elaborate irrigation tunnels into that hill, so the loss of El Rosario also meant the loss of a good portion of the water that had once made San Pedro one of the most valuable properties in the valley. When the summer of 1924 was blessed with copious rainfall, the loss of the irrigation tunnel did not prove fatal to the year's wheat crop, but that bit of good fortune did not make the loss more tolerable for Mrs. Evans, who already envisioned the withering of future crops and who, in any case, felt a certain sentimental fondness for her late husband's engineering feat. She was as resolved not to part with the field as the villagers were to take it.

She was acutely aware of the Mexican law mandating that a crop belonged to the party who sowed it. Once El Rosario had been legally expropriated, her strategy was to gather one crop, then quickly plow and replant the field before the villagers realized what was happening. It was a cynical interpretation of the law, to be sure, but such maneuvers were not expressly forbidden. They were not easy to perform, however. Few field hands were willing to take on the task of plowing and planting, especially after the first four men who tried were immediately taken prisoner by a band of armed agraristas. Mrs. Evans fumed that she had "not a grain of patience left."

The villagers of San Jerónimo Tianguismanalco were also running short of patience. Like Mrs. Evans, they were coming to the conclusions that they were on their own and that force was the only remedy. On April 22, with crude eloquence they informed the state agrarian commission of their "absolute desperation" at the "derisive behavior the English subject, Rosalía Caden viuda de Evans." She had, they charged, ignored presidential decrees and repeated orders from the state and national agrarian commissions. Now, they said, it was time to take forceful measures: "We have spent a year and month of continuous gestures; a year and a month of trusting in the Law and in the authorities; and we have arrived at the conclusion that there is no law and no authority but force and unreason. If the current situtation continues, then we believe it our duty to aid the Government in making its orders respected." Finally, in no uncertain terms, they demanded that federal troops be withdrawn from the hacienda.[54]

It was the strongest statement the villagers had yet made against Mrs. Evans, and it got results. A week later a letter went out from General Benigno Serratos, acting chief of military operations in Puebla, to the officer in charge of the detachment on San Pedro. Unlike so many previous orders, these were clear and unambiguous. The captain and his troops, said Serratos, were to "abstain from interfering with anything that the agrarian committees of either village do in order to carry forward the orders of this office, which intends to grant the villages real and effective possession of the lands they have been granted."[55]

Either by curious coincidence or devious design, the boy Mrs. Evans sent to San Martín to collect her mail took Serratos's order from the post office box, apparently thinking it was intended for Mrs. Evans. She thus learned of the new situation before the captain of the detachment and made appeals at once to all of the old channels — especially to Cummins, whom she visited in Mexico City. "I feel the government in Mexico City won't dare back such an order when Cummins shows it," she said.[56]

Upon learning of the Serratos order, Cummins expressed all the outrage appropriate to the occasion, but there was little he could do. The Mexican government had been returning his letters for months, and now he was a lame duck of sorts, only waiting for Thomas Hohler to arrive. He suggested that Mrs. Evans appeal to Charles Warren, the chief negotiator of the Bucareli accords who had since been named U.S. ambassador to Mexico.

Warren had grown markedly cool toward Mrs. Evans, however, in the year since she had first brought herself to his attention. He had urged her to sell her hacienda for the first serious offer, and she had muttered some words that might at least have passed for acquiescence. The Mexican government told Warren that they had offered her one hundred thousand pesos; she had refused it, though, and had demanded at least five times that amount. Mrs. Evans denied ever hearing such an offer, but agreed that she would indeed have refused it had it been made. Warren now accused her tersely of overvaluing her hacienda and demanding special treatment. "Take my word," he told her in exasperation, "be *grateful* if you get anything — and previous confiscation *before* they discuss payment."

Mrs. Evans had no intention of heeding this sort of advice. "I tell you I have changed since they burned San Pedro," she told her sister. "I am in deadly earnest now to win. . . . I told [Warren], voluntarily I would not give up — must either be removed as a prisoner or killed." Cummins was equally contumacious, threatening Warren "that if harm befell her His Majesty's Government would . . . take a very serious view of the matter"; this, he said, was no idle threat, for Lord Curzon had taken a personal interest in the case.[57] Warren, duly impressed, softened his tone and promised once again to do what he could.

The matter took on greater urgency when Mrs. Evans returned to the hacienda and found that in her absence the villagers of San Jerónimo Tianguismanalco and San Francisco Tepeyecac had held a ceremony — replete with brass band, feasting, and the waving of red flags — to divide up El Rosario.[58] She immediately wired the news to Cummins, not neglecting to mention that she intended to drive the invaders off the next day. Cummins was, of course, aware that driving off invaders would be nothing new for Mrs. Evans, but he thought it would be far more dangerous this time because the ceremony granting possession had been carried out with orders from Mexico City and in the presence of military brass and high-level civilian officials. Such pomp and ceremony would, he feared, persuade the villagers that this time the government —

"thoroughly incensed by what they described as Mrs. Evans's continued defiance of their authority" — meant business.

Not content to wait for news and hope for the best, Cummins climbed into an automobile chauffered by George Camp, and the two men drove much of the night along the narrow, rugged road over the high mountain pass at Río Frio, arriving unannounced at San Pedro at five in morning. They were shivering in the kitchen when Mrs. Evans awoke, pleasantly surprised, and warmed them with coffee. Cummins halfheartedly urged her to be prudent, but she was adept by now at reading his mixed signals — the way he would utter his warnings of terrible danger with a gleam of admiration in his eye.

Mrs. Evans spoke restively. Moderation was no good, she said. Most of the foreign landowners in Mexico had listened to counsels of moderation and had been ruined or killed for it, even while "foreign Governments had done nothing to call a halt to the robberies and murders being committed by a band of criminals that ruled in Mexico merely because they had rifles, and that, therefore, it rested with the individual to submit or resist, that evidently no man would resist, but a woman would, that it was a matter of principle which she would not abandon."[59] She echoed Cummins's sentiments precisely, so without much of a fight he gave up his attempts to calm her. "It was evident," he concluded, "that no persuasions would induce Mrs. Evans to leave her property," and in any case, her arguments "contain[ed] truths not easily gainsaid."

Having won her point, Mrs. Evans rode with Camp to El Rosario, where some seventy or eighty mostly unarmed agrarians were busy measuring or harvesting. Cummins stood behind a tree and watched as Mrs. Evans and Camp threatened and cajoled, occasionally spurring their horses and pointing their guns. The men in the field appeared to have little heart for a confrontation, which Cummins was quick to interpret as cowardice coupled with a fatalistic longing to return to their old situation as hacienda dependents. For the hacienda's defenders — Mrs. Evans, Cummins, Camp — such interpretations were as consistent as they were smug. Behavior that could be seen as cautious, prudent, or simply decent was the surest evidence of what they had contended all along: the villagers must either be perfectly content with their lot or too pusillanimous to do anything about it.

Of course, the villagers' reticence could also be explained by the fact that Camp and Mrs. Evans were heavily armed and accompanied by two soldiers. Even though the soldiers only watched, giving little indication which side they would back in a pinch, the villagers no doubt reasoned that the safest posture, under the circumstances, was the sort of taciturn deference that earned them such contempt from characters like Cummins.[60] The agrarian authorities of the villages, meanwhile, took the credit for counseling the villagers to maintain a pacific attitude in the face of repeated provocation.[61]

Nine

Lord, let me know my end
  and the number of my days;
tell me how short my life must be . . .
Man . . . is but a puff of wind,
he moves like a phantom;
the riches he piles up are no more than vapour,
he does not know who will enjoy them.
And now, Lord, what do I wait for?
— Psalm 39

⟨⟨⟨

ALTHOUGH THE CONFRONTATION over El Rosario remained for the most part a tense standoff, it had its casualties. At one point, Mrs. Evans reined her horse precipitously while racing toward the house. The horse bucked and threw her so that she landed hard, striking her head against a stone bridge. Although badly bruised, she refused to seek medical attention in the city for fear that the agrarians would take advantage of her absence, however brief. According to George Camp, she made a remarkable recovery from this trauma, adding further to the villagers' suspicions that she enjoyed supernatural protection.

A second casualty of the incident would not heal so readily, however, and would dramatically increase Mrs. Evans's isolation and vulnerability: as a result of his conduct during the campesinos' strike of early May, Cunard Cummins finally provided Mexican officials with the excuse they had been waiting for to boot him out of the country. With her lone champion gone and the countryside in arms, Mrs. Evans would gird herself for the final fight.

EL CASO CUMMINS

Mexican officials charged that Cummins had visited Mrs. Evans only to encourage her in her subversion and that he had protested the recent treatment of her in terms that set a new standard for insolence. Cummins's letter described the whole Evans affair as "incredible to his Majesty's Government," for "not only the Constitution and law of Mexico . . . , but surely the laws of man, forbid the persecution and despoiling of a woman alone in the world and defenceless." He placed the blame for all of Mrs. Evans's woes directly on the Mexican government and army, strongly implying that Obregón himself bore the lion's share of that blame.[1]

Foreign Secretary Sáenz telegraphed the British foreign office that although "Mexico has no desire to create a fresh conflict with England, nor that Sir T. Hohler's mission should be cancelled; it cannot . . . tolerate [the] insolent attitude of Mr. Cummins." He asked the British to withdraw Cummins voluntarily, but threatened to expel him if they refused. Under pressure from conservatives and from the public — which was responding predictably to Mrs. Evans's publicity campaign — Ramsay MacDonald stood behind Cummins, adding that any precipitous action against him would force Britain to cancel the Hohler mission. That cancellation would mean, he did not have to add, a complete rupture in British-Mexican relations.[2]

Already this war of words had gone too far for either side to back down gracefully, no matter how badly Alvaro Obregón and Ramsay MacDonald may have wished to avoid such unpleasantness. On June 4, Obregón gave Cummins a week to leave the country, after which he would be forceably removed. Mrs. Evans was so intent on seeing Cummins before his expulsion that, together with Camp, she made a wild ride through the waterlogged countryside, north to Tlaxcala and then south to Atlixco (a circuitous route designed to keep the agrarians from learning she had left). From Atlixco, she caught a train for Mexico City, made her way to the legation, and, mud-splattered from head to foot, she chatted with her mentor and protector for the last time.[3]

Cummins refused to leave Mexico unless ordered to do so by the British government. He shut himself up in the legation building and waited. Mexican troops surrounded the legation to impede the delivery of food, while the Mexico City authorities cut telephone service and threatened to cut off the light and water. Six people, including servants, remained inside the legation, with supplies of food that Cummins reckoned could be made to last for four days. To supplement the supplies, Cummins's admirers braved the police cordon to toss a few morsels over the fence.[4] In all, it made for a rather silly spectacle, and some reporters made the most of it. One newspaper wag ridiculed Cummins for his aristocratic ways, wondering whether, in the absence of water, he would use wine or ginger ale to bathe and shave. "Because Mr. Herbert Ashley Cunard Cummins, representative of His Majesty's Government, might die of hunger, but with three day's growth of beard? Never!"[5]

Finally conceding the futility of the situation, Prime Minister MacDonald asked U.S. officials to oversee the withdrawal of Cummins from Mexico and to take charge of the legation and its archives — a task the U.S. officials agreed to only with great reluctance because Britain had become rather unpopular of late. MacDonald received hearty cheers from the conservatives in Parliament as he read Cummins's letters and declared the Mexican government's behavior "inexcusable."

When reporters asked the prime minister what had become of Mrs. Evans in the midst of all this, he replied: "I am not quite sure. The whole story is an exceedingly romantic one."[6] Cummins did his bit to deepen the romance by leaving a trail of titillating newspaper interviews all along his lengthy route back to London. In El Paso, he declared the Evans story "one of the outstanding events of the century."[7] Mrs. Evans was "one of the most wonderful women I have ever heard of," he told reporters on the docks of Southampton. "She said she would shoot as many agrarians as possible before they robbed her."

"And," he added, "she is a first-rate shot."[8]

OLD-STYLE DIPLOMACY LOSES GROUND

More than anything previous, the expulsion of H.A.C. Cummins attracted the world's attention to the plight of Mrs. Evans. Her sister Daisy made the most of this publicity windfall, even going so far as to push a resolution at both the Republican and Democratic national conventions that urged the U.S. government to "protect Anglo-Saxons in barbarian countries."[9]

The diplomatic imbroglio did not clinch the debate, however, for a strong current of opinion was not notably kind either to Cummins or Great Britain. "Certainly," wrote one editorialist, "the situation is unique in diplomacy where a man who enjoys diplomatic protection defies the Government to which he is accredited. The stubborn stand of Mr. Cummins . . . places the British Government's prestige in Mexico in jeopardy."[10] In Britain, meanwhile, men of business were incensed. One merchant dismissed the break in relations as a simple "departmental misunderstanding. . . . Old style diplomacy here is losing ground and naturally hangs on to its position as strongly as possible. . . . [But] it is become more and more apparent that the real bonds which bind nations together are those honest personal contacts which result from mutual business interests."[11]

This sort of thinking was the type that most infuriated Mrs. Evans, who yielded nothing to the Bolsheviks in denouncing the injury inflicted by "a few capitalists for private ends." Narrow, selfish, and cynical, the capitalists were guilty of nothing less than confounding the profane with the sacred. Mrs. Evans was clearly swimming against the tide here, for at the moment U.S. policymakers — and, increasingly, their British counterparts — were embracing an almost mystical faith in the ability of well-handled private capital to open doors, win hearts and minds, and generally get things done.[12] To the likes of Ambassador Warren, an aficionado of dollar diplomacy, Mrs. Evans looked hypocritical. The price she was now demanding for her hacienda was five times its assessed value, close to double what Harry had paid for it originally, and far more than any other landowner in the region had realized. Mrs. Evans was probably sincere, however, in maintaining that she was not in it for the money. The price she set for the estate was merely one more expression of her refusal to budge in any way. She wrote that "San Pedro and I are one."[13] "Lose me," she told her sister in June, "as I lose myself — in the great struggle against barbarism we are consciously and unconsciously being drawn into."[14]

This kind of talk brought some unsentimental sorts around to the opinion of Alberto Pani — who never forgave Mrs. Evans for bringing two large, glaring dogs into his office — that "Mrs. Evans was demented and should be placed in an asylum."[15] Even some otherwise sympathetic souls judged that Mrs. Evans was taking her struggle too far. "By tact and patience, she might have carried her point," wrote one society lady after Mrs. Evans's death, "but she was a woman alone in the world, frantic, and, toward the end of her lone stand against the inevitable, she was undeniably mad."[16]

MILITARY SEMIFEUDALISM

Although it looked to some as if Rosalie Evans herself was coming mentally unhinged, she felt that the madness was always something external to herself. This is not to say, however, that she saw herself surrounded by a kind of social psychosis. The situation that so beset her had, she judged, been deliberately manufactured by a few power mongers and could just as readily be halted. It was an article of faith with her that someone, somewhere, was in absolute control. She reduced the many contending forces in Mexico to a hierarchy of villains, which began with the local agraristas, ran through Montes and Sánchez, and finally ended up at the "Supreme Government in Mexico."[17] In fact, it did not even stop with Obregón. Perhaps the greatest villain of all, in her view, was Ambassador Warren. "If [he] really lifted his little finger," she fumed, "he could stop them, but he does not want to."[18]

What Mrs. Evans could never bring herself to admit was that she was in the midst of a maelstrom: a kind of madness was indeed gripping the countryside of Puebla. In company with their unconditional followers and occasional hangers-on, powerful individuals forged expedient alliances, only to betray them the instant they were no longer useful. Political organizations changed names and adherents with vertiginous speed, as if their leaders were searching frantically for some winning combination. The alliance that Mrs. Evans had reckoned a key to her misery — between Montes and Sánchez — was one of the casualties of the overheated politics of mid-1924.

Like other agrarista caciques in the state, Montes was already dismayed that Sánchez — the self-styled "hero of Ocotlán" — had been remiss in acknowledging his debt for their help in raising campesino contingents to fight the recent rebellion. Governor Alberto Guerrero watered the seeds of dissent in May of 1924 when, hoping to make some order out of chaos, he tried to rein in what he described as "a military semifeudalism" in the state.[19] He began by systematically removing local town councils, claiming that these were either "Delahuertistas" or notoriously unpopular "laborista" elements imposed by Vicente Lombardo Toledano. Although he insisted that he wished to convoke popular plebescites to decide local political issues, he did not hesitate to impose his own choices — or, more accurately, to impose the partisans of José María Sánchez — when such convocation was "not possible."

Sánchez was already serving as federal deputy from the district of Tepeaca — a curious circumstance because technically he was also governor of Puebla. The fact that he held two high-level public offices at the same time was illegal, of course, but also an accurate measure of the power he enjoyed. Ambassador Warren believed that Sánchez had Obregón "mesmerized," but there were also practical matters to consider in their relationship: the presidential elections were set for early July, and Obregón would not risk alienating such an important caudillo by insisting on technicalities.[20] For Sánchez, meanwhile, public office was less a luxury than a necessity. If he lost it, he would also lose his *fuero,* or immunity from prosecution, in which case his enemies would be free to procede against him for the murder of the Moro brothers in 1922.

Imposing local councils and stealing elections was standard operating procedure for Puebla's governors during the 1920s, but that procedure held special hazards in June and July of 1924. Agrarian caciques in the state's various districts were now heavily armed and resolved to assert their power — most by having themselves elected to the national Congress. By imposing local authorities, Guerrero and Sánchez jeopardized the caciques' hold on the electoral machinery. Using the weapons and forces they had acquired during the recent rebellion, the caciques rose up one by one in their separate regions, eventually coalescing into a tenuous but broad-based anti-Sánchez force. As a result, Montes and Sánchez became full-fledged enemies. Adding further to the growing confusion, the agrarian caciques were joined in their opposition to Sánchez by the textile workers of the CROM, which was at that time mounting a decisive push to consolidate its control of the state's industrial labor force.

Obregón viewed this growing assertiveness with a jaundiced eye. Manuel P. Montes must have seen which way the wind was blowing when he wrote to Obregón to remind the president of the sacrifices his campesino contingents had made in the recent rebellion and to ask him for support against a group of enemies. Obregón's reply was cold. He appreciated "the fact that you lent your more-or-less efficient services in combatting the traitors, but we must not forget that we were defending institutions, which we must be the first to respect."[21] At about the same time, Obregón issued the order that all "armed nuclei that, under different names, operate in the state" be disarmed.[22]

Like other caciques, Montes interpreted this order as a grave threat to his local power and to his future political career. He responded violently. In mid-June, he and his followers launched a series of raids aimed at imposing themselves in all of the villages of the district. On June 18, when the Sanchistas tried to take control of the government of the district seat, Huejotzingo, Montes was waiting for them in the central plaza along with about eighty well-armed men. The Sanchistas prudently withdrew,[23] only to return on June 30. This time Montes had three hundred armed men. The Montistas thrashed the would-be authorities, tied them up, and carted them off to the headquarters of the Domingo Arenas Confederation in El Moral,[24] contending that they were merely resisting a gross violation of popular sovereignty.[25] This claim, however, did not stop Obregón from ordering Montes's arrest on a charge of kidnapping. The National Agrarian Party came to Montes's defense, charging that the affair was merely a maneuver by Sánchez to remove a political rival from the district so he could carry out his "cynical imposition."[26] Despite the arrest order, Montes remained at large, active, and unrepentant. On July 9 his men kidnapped the municipal president of San Martín Texmelucan and held him in the municipal palace of that city for several days without food or water.

These episodes earned Montes national notoriety. According to *Excélsior,* he and his fellow agrarian caciques had become "lords of the noose and knife" who had "sown terror" throughout the state.[27] The national press continued to blame everything on José María Sánchez — an understandable error under the circumstances, for it had become nearly impossible for anyone to keep account of the mercurial shifts in animosities and alliances. Indeed, the falling out between Sánchez and Montes wrought havoc within the very ranks of Montes's local agrarista coalition, which witnessed the sudden desertion of many old Montista stalwarts.

The situation was even more complicated than it appeared, however. Governor Guerrero, whose tenure as acting governor had all along been contingent on his alliance with Sánchez, was suddenly emboldened by the groundswell of anti-Sánchez sentiment in Puebla, and with little warning, he forsook Sánchez and threw his office behind the caciques. In response, the Sánchez-controlled state Congress moved to oust him by marshalling an impressive list of charges.[28] They proposed to replace Guerrero with Juan Crisóstomo Bonilla, a lawyer from an old political family. (Ironically, Bonilla had been a vigorous enemy of the revolution in its early days: at one point he was implicated in a plot to assassinate Francisco I. Madero.)[29] It was widely supposed that Bonilla would merely pave the way for the return of Sánchez to active duty as governor.

Amid all of this, President Obregón sent a furious telegram to Puebla's chief of military operations, Juan Andreu Almazán, demanding to know if he had "sufficient control" of his subordinates to make them obey the president's instructions and prevent the "anarchic manifestations" plaguing virtually every district of the state.[30]

An excellent question. At this time, Rosalie Evans noticed that her ongoing efforts to harvest San Pedro's wheat would occasionally be blessed with mysterious periods of tranquillity and reasoned that this "merely show[ed] what perfect control the government had over the people."[31] In fact, it showed exactly the opposite. Had the central government had perfect control over the people, surely it could have done a far more credible job of enforcing its will. It is difficult to see whose interests were served by perpetuating a long, drawn out period of anarchy.

ANOTHER BATTLE FOR EL ROSARIO

While the politicians and diplomats fought, Mrs. Evans and George Camp carried on an increasingly lonely, violent, and poignantly hopeless struggle on San Pedro Coxtocán. Following the dispute of early May that had led to Cummins's expulsion, Mrs. Evans spent some time convalescing from the injuries she had suffered after being thrown from her horse. The agrarians of Tianguismanalco and Tepeyecac used that time to good advantage, plowing over the beans she had planted on El Rosario and putting corn in their place. Camp went daily to issue them warnings, but for now kept his guns holstered.

In late May, when Mrs. Evans was again able to ride, she and Camp ventured out to the fields, intent on forcing a confrontation. The lieutenant in charge of the detachment then guarding San Pedro accompanied them, along with four of his men, but he obviously did not welcome the duty. They found some forty villagers working in the field, and Mrs. Evans ordered them off. Although still made nervous by the presence of the soldiers, the villagers surrounded them, some clutching sticks or stones and standing their ground. "They vilely cursed us," Camp recalled later, "as well as the soldiers for helping. They said they were ordered to work that land by President Obregón and they meant to work it if it cost them their lives." The lieutenant, called upon to adjudicate this conflict, was "visibly in a quandary."[32] (He would have been in even more of a quandary had he known that en route to the field Camp had ridden behind him with a pistol aimed at his back, intending to shoot him if he sided with the agrarians.)[33]

The lieutenant explained that his orders had been to protect Mrs. Evans as long as she remained close to her home and did not try to interfere in agrarian matters. He pleaded with her to return to the house, promising that he would go to Puebla to try to clarify precisely who was the legitimate owner of the disputed field. She and Camp agreed.

The lieutenant left and — wisely — never returned.

Soon enough, a new detachment of soldiers was sent to San Pedro with identical orders — to protect, but not to interfere. Frustrated, Mrs. Evans and Camp were more determined than ever to force a showdown. Accompanied by two jittery peons, they rode out to El Rosario intending to plow up the villagers' corn seedlings once again.

No sooner had they arrived at the field than shots were fired, some from the direction of Coxtocán hill and some from Tianguismanalco. One of the peons took off at a sprint, not wishing to learn the import of this development. Camp then put his own hand to the plow, firing a few answering shots at the same time. A large crowd of villagers, hearing the shots, gathered at the edge of the field. Mrs. Evans waved her guns at them and threatened to shoot if they stepped onto the field.

At this point, the lieutenant of the guard rode out from the direction of Tianguismanalco, telling his subordinates to refrain from interfering in agrarian business. If Mrs. Evans did not return to her house, he warned, he would take his men and leave. According to Camp, she replied that "she was in no need of a nursemaid in the house, that what she needed was protection on her fields from thieves and assassins."[34]

The lieutenant tried valiantly to make peace, but he managed only to further inflame all parties. While he parleyed, a group of men with rifles crouched in a gully, cutting Mrs. Evans and Camp off from the house; so Camp lay on the ground and took aim at them. The lieutenant went pale, sensing serious bloodshed in the offing. This time, however, Camp and Mrs. Evans backed down. Upon realizing that the soldiers had no intention of taking their side in a firefight, they apparently lost faith in the "natural" cowardice or acquiescence of the villagers and allowed the soldiers to escort them back to the house. Mrs. Evans had by now determined that the soldiers were worse than useless, and she ordered them to leave. They obeyed.

Whether or not she was correct about the soldiers' inherent treachery, she would later find it extremely difficult to explain her position. She could no longer complain convincingly that she lacked army protection when she had deliberately sent the soldiers away. When a British investigator later asked the zone commander, General Almazán, about military protection for Mrs. Evans, the general complained that Mrs. Evans had been "a very difficult woman to deal with, since she sent the last detachment away with an impolite note to the effect that she considered its presence an insult." The investigator reluctantly concluded that "her treatment of the authorities has been the reverse of tactful."[35]

Right or wrong, Mrs. Evans was now thrown back on her own resources and those furnished by her sanguinary companion, George Camp. Knowledgeable, proficient, and passionate about firearms, Camp began imparting his knowledge to her in earnest during early May. "He believes I have a mission," she wrote, "and he is training me in what I lack for it. I am being given just the training the boys got in France."[36] He was "armed to the teeth," and Mrs. Evans herself took to packing an army issue Colt .45 pistol and a Winchester .30-.30 rifle.

She confessed, not without a certain pride, that these weapons would enable her to "do some damage." She seemed also to rather enjoy the notoriety the weapons gave her. On one occasion, when she and her entourage braved a trip to San Martín to pick up some provisions, people gathered in the streets and balconies to peer at the famous outlaw hacendada. "But," she recounted, "no one dared arrest me. It was well they did not for we were well-armed and ready for them." She was not entirely invulnerable to arrest and deportation, but she took great pride in broadcasting that she would be sure to make it a messy business. She had made it clear often enough that she would only go out in a blaze of glory.

Camp, for his part, was so eager to provoke a showdown he made even Mrs. Evans nervous. Although she considered him a godsend — "the only man in Mexico who could help me" — she also found him frightening. His taste for violence often horrified her, despite the fact that she had become jingoistic enough in her own right. A lawyer who later became involved with the estate shared her apprehension, speaking of the "queer complex" Camp had developed, presumably as a result of his wartime experience. "His intense hatred of Mexicans," complained the lawyer, "was a source of considerable embarrassment, but he was without doubt a most courageous and daring man."[37] Privately, Camp later confessed that his ideal labor system would be "that used on the prison farms in east Texas where they farm out the negroes: with each gang a guard with a rifle to shoot any one that tries to run and a foreman with a blacksnake whip to make them work."[38]

While Camp — "a gaunt ghost with hollow bloodshot eyes" — stockpiled armaments and spoiled for a fight, Mrs. Evans did some wrestling with her conscience. This new and dangerous stage of the struggle did not accord well with her self-image as the light of civilization and reason in a savage land. "I know they fear him and he protects me," she wrote of Camp, "but he is so alien to the spirit of San Pedro and I wish he would not be so bloodthirsty."[39] The best cast she could give the matter was that her fight was defensive and fought in the

George Camp—"He believes I have a mission." *Credit:* Rosalie Evans Papers (#2895), Special Collections Department, University of Virginia Library.

name of a greater good. She tried to rein in Camp, who advocated firing on the unarmed men who came to plow El Rosario, assassinating Manuel P. Montes, and executing any prisoners they managed to take. "Mind," she said, "I do not say they should not be killed—but in an open fight!"[40]

Toward the end of May, Mrs. Evans hung placards on the trees around the disputed field warning armed men that they trespassed at their own risk, but on May 31 a large group of villagers entered the field just the same and commenced plowing up the earth. When they ignored a warning to leave, Camp took a shot at them, thus beginning a three-hour battle in which one of the agrarians fell, although whether he was killed or merely wounded was never ascertained.

Mrs. Evans and Camp took refuge on the long flat roof of the burned-out hacienda buildings, which had been remade into a fortress. The December fires that had destroyed the roofs of the house's middle rooms now seemed a blessing: a ladder was stationed in a burned-out bedroom, enabling the home's defenders to mount to the roof without exposing themselves to gunfire. Mrs. Evans had ordered her servants to bring adobe blocks onto the roof to build a series of parapets along the outer edges, and she had a mattress brought up as well so she could stand guard in relative comfort, and in the fragrant shade of bougainvillea.

In the ensuing days, Mrs. Evans, Camp, and three servants took shifts standing guard on the roof while agrarista plows invaded El Rosario. A few loyal villagers crossed the hostile lines to bring news. More than a thousand armed men, they said, had the hacienda surrounded. Men with rifles were stationed all along the road to San Martín. Camp and Mrs. Evans heard rumors that they both had been targeted for assassination. Mrs. Evans managed to get a telegram off to Cummins, who at that moment had just received the orders for his own expulsion from the country: "Only orders from Mexico will hold them back. Getting too strong for us. Swarm like ants on 'Rosario.'"[41]

Despite this tense situation, Mrs. Evans managed to harvest some wheat on the land she still held legally and uncontested.[42] Montes tightened his stranglehold, however, by ordering the Domingo Arenas Confederation out on strike and arresting anyone who worked for the hacienda. Mrs. Evans joined the battle for the hearts and minds of the field hands, at one point even promising land to anyone who would work for her as long as they signed a statement that said they would not ask for or accept land from the agrarians.[43] Some took the deal and agreed to break the strike, although it meant being attacked or taken prisoner. "My only chance," she said, "is that these people want to work — don't want to belong to the agrarians, are very hungry and for the first time dare say so!"[44] She also got a threshing machine onto her property, but the agrarians managed repeatedly to sabotage it. While the standoff continued, Camp went to Mexico City to confer with the U.S. and British consuls. In response to his efforts, the British consul-general, Norman King, sent his secretary to investigate at the end of June.

CAPTAIN HOLLOCOMBE

The secretary, Captain Rudolph Hollocombe, was a tall, lanky Englishman who knew Mrs. Evans's reputation well and did not count himself among her admirers. He was especially dismayed, he confessed, by the way she so ostentatiously participated in Mexico City's society life whenever she was in town, which he deemed unbecoming to a woman under siege. Still, he toured the hacienda with an open mind and was obliged to confess that it was undoubtedly a valuable property, even if Mrs. Evans's own assessment was a bit overblown. "She went so far as to say," reported Hollocombe, somewhat mystified, "that she was fighting for a principle, and that, rather than accept less [than five hundred thousand pesos], she would go out penniless." His own attitude was more pragmatic: "It is to be feared," he noted soberly, "that insistence on a principle of absolute justice in this country is rather apt to defeat its own ends."

Mrs. Evans did her best to respond to Hollocombe's other complaints — telling him that she had never received any order confiscating her land, that "any land of hers now worked by the Agrarians has been simply occupied and ploughed up, without any definite demand having preceeded the seizure." These claims, of course, were untrue: she had simply never credited the legitimacy of the orders she had received. She also explained why she had ordered the military detachment off her land, although her reasoning on this score left him unconvinced.[45]

She never got the chance to parry Hollocombe's most cutting criticism, however, for just as he was upbraiding her for her unseemly dalliance with the haut monde, a man charged into the dining room shouting that agraristas had entered the fields and were approaching the house. Hollocombe was aghast at how casually Mrs. Evans grabbed up a pistol and ran out to meet them. He followed just in time to see a band of eight men firing from behind eucalyptus trees. Although their shots were wild and fired from too great a distance to do any damage, Mrs. Evans ordered everyone onto the roof with the authority of a veteran campaigner.

From the roof, they heard the crack of shots echoing from the distant field where Camp had been overseeing the harvest. About a half hour later, Camp rode up, unnerved and breathless, with a harrowing tale to tell. Only seven men had showed up to help with the harvest that morning, he explained, but even before he could put those seven to work, a large crowd appeared from the direction of Tianguismanalco. He ordered the workers to run for their lives, but he himself could not escape before armed villagers surrounded his horse. They tried to arrest him, but he refused to dismount. A villager struck him across the shoulders with a rifle butt, while another tried to grab the horse's bridle. Luckily for Camp, that move spooked the horse and made it buck, scattering the attackers so that he was able to spur the horse and ride furiously toward the house, albeit amid a hail of bullets.

Camp later offered his anecdote as evidence that the villagers were poor marksmen — a colossal understatement if his account is true and unembellished, for he estimated that some three hundred villagers had fired perhaps five hundred shots at him with intent to kill. More villagers had been hidden behind rocks and trees along the road, waiting in ambush, while four men chased him on horseback, firing continually. Yet, not a single shot found its mark.

"And," Camp marveled, "amongst that crowd were their best marksmen."[46]

"THE JESUIT"

During much of July, the hacienda remained eerily quiet. Mrs. Evans took the opportunity to go to Mexico City for another round of talks with Ambassador Warren, whom she had privately nicknamed "the Jesuit."[47] She hoped forlornly that Hollocombe's tale, coupled with the feverish publicity campaign that Daisy had been mounting in the United States, might have softened his attitude toward her.

Her hopes were quickly deflated. Warren began the interview by calling her "an hysterical person" and scolding her for Daisy's publicity campaign. He insisted that she still had military protection and that she had him to thank for it. Captain Hollocombe only made matters worse when, carrying diplomatic protocol to an extreme, he refused to contradict the ambassador on this score.

"[Y]ou want me to ask protection for you against confiscation," Warren lectured, "when many Americans are in the same position and hundreds have been murdered, what would Obregón think of me?" Then, according to Mrs. Evans, he added "a lot of twaddle about the Claims Commission," at which point she brusquely ended the interview. "I think he wanted me to die of hysteria," she concluded. "It was a cowardly attack on one who he knows has been making a desperate defense against great odds. To have one of your own countrymen . . . join with the Mexican Government, (which, by the way, he himself said was largely made up of assassins, robbers, worse than the Russians) and then deliberately try to discredit you by the old time-honored attack 'that she was hysterical!'"[48]

Warren saw her again the next day, this time with a more conciliatory attitude but still unwilling to offer the kind of ironclad assurances she sought. He expressed admiration for her obstinate resistance. "In your place," he boasted ingenuously, "I should act just as you do." He also told her, however, that her resistance was unnecessary because the government planned "to stop the agrarian question, and you without fighting will get your land back. You would have all along." This message was mysterious and clearly contradictory ("I suppose that is the Jesuit's idea of diplomacy," commented Mrs. Evans acridly). Almost with a wink, he hinted that what he had just told her was based on solid inside information. In the light of subsequent history, this hint was in fact a rather stunning revelation, one that Mrs. Evans would not live to appreciate. Incoming president Calles had, it appeared, told the U.S. ambassador that he had grown weary of the agrarian agitation in the country and had a plan to undercut it. Mrs. Evans did not buy that possibility for a second.

"Calles is going to support capital," she wrote derisively. "This was hardly worth a week in town!"

JOHANN STRATHAUS

Prior to her visit to Ambassador Warren, in mid-June Mrs. Evans had received a visit on her hacienda from a young man named Johann Strathaus. Strathaus was not yet twenty years old, a native of Hamburg, Germany, who somehow — no one seems ever to have asked just how — found himself in Mexico in the violent 1920s. He explained that he had heard Mrs. Evans required a "steward," and he carried a splendid recommendation from Father José Rubio Contreras, a priest from Puebla whose opinion apparently carried some weight among the city's conservative elite. Mrs. Evans told Strathaus that her situation was dangerous and that she would need time to consider the matter of his employment. When he came back at the end of June, at the time of Captain Hollocombe's visit, Mrs. Evans promised him a definite answer at the end of July.

While riding back to San Martín after this visit, Strathaus was waylaid by a group of men from El Moral, the headquarters of the Domingo Arenas Confederation. When they asked his business, he inexplicably concocted a provocative lie: he was, he claimed, a salesman from a munitions factory who had just sold Mrs. Evans a heavy gun to use against the agrarians.

The matter of Strathaus's employment was not such a hard decision to make. Mrs. Evans had already determined to send Camp away. Strathaus was a far less volatile character. In fact, he seemed refreshingly innocent, a youthful and bookish-looking sort with thick, round, goggle-like spectacles. She was not anxious to put him in danger, but by the end of July it looked as if the situation had — at least for the moment — changed completely. Through her loyal contacts in the villages, she got word that Manuel Montes was just back from Mexico City with the momentous news that Calles, the president-elect, had promised to back him against his rival, José María Sánchez, who continued to have the support of Obregón. Montes thus advised his followers to cooperate with the obstinate hacendada, for in a short while the agraristas would be enjoying complete hegemony in the Texmelucan Valley — including the full support of the federal army — and they could make their final push. The ominous peace that spread over the valley, like the windless calm between tropical squalls, lent some weight to the rumors. Though by now somewhat innured to these perverse vicissitudes, Mrs. Evans confessed that "these lulls always alarm me."[49]

The tranquillity was not perfect, of course. One of Mrs. Evans's most loyal houseboys, Gabriel Morín, suddenly led an attack against the men who were running the hacienda's threshing machine and the next day hauled them to court on the charge of "slandering" syndicate workers. The police chief of the village strongly endorsed the charges — "one thing I will never permit," he wrote, "is that I be slandered by the bitter enemies of social ideals, lackeys of the hacendados" — and held Mrs. Evans's workers in jail.[50] At the same time, a group of nine women and children filed charges against George Camp for beating them and threatening them with his rifle.[51]

But these incidents seemed trivial compared to previous woes. In fact, things were not so bad just now. Montes's strike had ended, albeit in the same mysterious way that such actions so often did — that is, without winners, losers, or resolution of any kind. What was more, the harvest was being gathered quickly, and each day the threshing machine rattled and hummed. Perhaps hiring Strathaus now would not be such a bad thing. True, the young German was not a refined person — Mrs. Evans would never allow him to dine at the same table with her — but he was adept with electricity and machines, skills which at the moment would be far more useful than Camp's brawn and firepower. Also, by simply returning to Mexico City, Camp could escape the annoyance of local court battles. In fact, Mrs. Evans was rather eager to be rid of the gun-toting Texan whom she suspected of having sinister intentions of his own.[52]

So, good as her word, Mrs. Evans went to Puebla on Tuesday, July 29, and contracted for Johann Strathaus to begin work for her on Thursday. "If he only stays during the threshing," she wrote hopefully, "it will be a great help." At first, all went smoothly. On Wednesday she got her first load of wheat to San Martín for shipment to Puebla. Her broker in San Martín even sent a special car to pick up her shipments, sparing her the expense of renting cars. Ominous though it all was, she was in good spirits. For the first time in weeks she was able to wrest her thoughts from her present woes and think about the future. Perhaps, she thought, she would travel "incog" to the United States after the wheat was in. That had worked for Jesús Bermejillo, her dashing former administrator; once the de la Huerta rebellion had failed, he had slipped out of Mexico with help from Mrs. Evans's family, and he was now trying to make his way as an engineer in the United States. Mrs. Evans thought she might try her hand at writing about her adventures — something that might be both gratifying and lucrative, perhaps a necessity given the relative paucity of the wheat crop, the precariousness of her finances, and the uncertainty of her future. "My ambition," she admitted to her sister, "is to make Great Britain and America hotly claim my birth."[53]

Strathaus, meanwhile, was generally impressed by the efficiency of the farm's operation, though he could not help but notice how the workers "performed their work only reluctantly and sullenly, going from place to place very wretchedly and slowly." He spent Thursday on the hacienda, acquainting himself with the grounds and the books, while Mrs. Evans rode to San Martín with a shipment of wheat. On Friday, he accompanied her for the first time on her ride into town. The wheat broker in Puebla had promised to send his payment to the El Pilar textile mill. Had all gone according to plan, Mrs. Evans and Strathaus would have picked up the money and paid the workers when they showed up for work at four o'clock the next morning, the usual starting time. The money was delayed, however, so Mrs. Evans and Strathaus rode back to the hacienda empty-handed, and the next morning, when Strathaus explained that payday was to be postponed, the workers had one more reason to grumble.

THE LAST RIDE

The late summer storms in the Puebla highlands are normally constant and abundant, heavy at times, but seldom the pelting, pitiless tempests of high tragedy. They tend more to be gray and gentle, welcome spells of steady rain without the drama of thunder and driving winds. The rain that fell in the early afternoon of Saturday, August 2, was harder than usual, a proper tropical downpour, but not so hard as to discourage the planned trip to San Martín. A month ago, the season's plentiful rain had been a blessing, setting African lilies, plumbago, and canterbury bells to bloom in prodigal splendor in the chapel garden, and speeding the ripening of late-planted wheat, boosting the crop beyond wildest expectations. Now, however, it only washed away the over-ripe grain left in the fields and threatened to rot the wheat stacked in carts. There was much harvesting and shipping left to do and no time to waste.

Although she reminded herself constantly that peace was portentous, Mrs. Evans was relaxed enough that afternoon to forget her pistol upon first climbing into the buggy. A man approached to ask something about land, but Mrs. Evans recognized him as one of the agraristas and angrily sent him away. Perhaps that encounter jogged her memory, for she returned to the house for her pistol, which she placed on the seat between herself and Strathaus, who held the reins. Two dachsunds also shared the seat, and a small white dog ran beneath the buggy, while Brunhilda — Mrs. Evans's beloved "police dog" — ran ahead of the mules, barking happily to goad them along. The buggy's canopy was raised against the rain, and its black side curtains were drawn.

At San Martín, Mrs. Evans stowed her pistol under the seat of the buggy so it would not be confiscated by the agrarista soldiers who patrolled the city's streets. She and Strathaus went first to seal a boxcar of wheat for shipment to the Puebla flour mill of her usual broker, the Frenchman Fermin Besnier. The money Besnier had sent in payment for earlier shipments was now waiting at El Pilar — a bag bearing the broker's logo and holding five hundred pesos in silver coins. While Mrs. Evans was occupied with these tasks, Strathaus was approached by several hacienda field hands who complained that, owing to the urgency of the harvest, they had worked many hours beyond what was customary and believed themselves entitled to a small wage increase. Mrs. Evans agreed to that, but refused their request that she give them their wages there and then. Perhaps to ward off robbers, she claimed she had no money with her, but would pay them at six o'clock on the hacienda.

By 4:30 in the afternoon, when Mrs. Evans had finished her business in San Martín, the rain had stopped. Thinking to take advantage of the lull, she decided to set out at once for the hacienda, taking the road leading south toward Huejotzingo, which would pass San Pedro Coxtocán about two and a half miles hence. As they were crossing the small concrete bridge over the Coatzala River, the rain began again. Mrs. Evans took the pistol from its hiding place and set it again on the seat, then she leaned far back in the carriage to avoid the splashing raindrops. Speaking in German to confound the eavesdropping of agrarista

The Road to Huejotzingo. *Credit:* Rosalie Evans Papers (#2895), Special Collections Department, University of Virginia Library.

spies, she told Strathaus of the dangers all around them, of the ever-present threat of attack. As the young man drove the mules, she calmed enough to reminisce about trips she had made to Germany and California. She seemed anxious but cheerful, and Strathaus was impressed by her command of his native tongue.

Perhaps she sensed some skepticism in Strathaus regarding the hidden dangers she spoke of, or perhaps it was just the dreariness of the sky and the sinister shapes of the eucalyptus trees towering above the muddy road that turned her mind toward tragedy. She launched into a recitation, in German, of Goethe's poem "Erlkönig," whose singsong cadence matched the measured gait of the mules as they slogged down the damp lane. It is a harrowing tale of a young boy out riding with his father on a stormy night. The child imagines the sinister yet seductive figure of the evil Erl King lurking in the dark clouds and trees, and despite the father's efforts to calm the boy, the Erl King's power — something primitive, subliminal — overwhelms the power of reason. "Father, father," screams the child, "now he's taking hold of me, he has hurt me!" The terrified father rides faster, holding the groaning child, until at long last he reaches his farm and finds himself holding the child, dead of fright, in his arms.

Mrs. Evans had just spoken the poem's final line — "das Kind war tot" — when a volley of shots ripped through the canopy from the right of the buggy. She grabbed the pistol and leaned out to return the fire,[54] but by the time Strathaus turned to her in terror, her face was already white as chalk, and she had fallen toward him on the seat. He dropped the reins and the whip and was struggling with both arms to bring her upright on the seat when he felt a searing pain in his own shoulder. He let Mrs. Evans's body fall face down to the carriage floor. Her long white hair came loose and twined itself in the spokes of the right front wheel, tearing part of her scalp away. When the shots continued to rain all around the buggy, Strathaus grabbed the pistol with his right hand from the floor where Mrs. Evans had let it fall and emptied it in the general direction of the phantom shapes crouching under the roadside embankment or lurking mistily behind trees and stones and tall stalks of corn. Then he threw the empty pistol on the seat, where one of the dachsunds lay bleeding from a belly wound, and he took up the reins weakly. As he struggled to spur the mules, one of the animals lurched violently sideways and fell to the ground, a bullet in its right thigh. Brunhilda, the police dog, barked furiously and lunged at the mule's rump, forcing it to struggle forward, although it managed no better than a funereal pace.

At some point, Strathaus threw the bag of silver coins out of the buggy, although his accounts of when he did this are imprecise. He also remembered seeing three men on mules and begging them for help, but they only slapped the mules pulling the buggy and told him to keep going, the killers were close behind. Strathaus was weak from the loss of blood, and his different accounts of the event — some delivered while he was delirious from fever and others long after the fact — take on a certain hallucinatory quality. What is certain is that the buggy came to rest at the spot where a road crossed the Texmelucan-Huejotzingo highway. To the left, the road led to the main plaza of San Jerónimo Tianguismanalco; to the right, it led to the main buildings of San Pedro Coxtocán, some three-quarters of a mile distant.

It seemed to Strathaus a very long time before anyone arrived, although it was probably only a matter of minutes before a few villagers of Tianguismanalco began gathering to view the ghastly sight. The police dog had mounted to the buggy's seat and was barking furiously, keeping the onlookers at bay. The young German lay bloody and groaning on the seat, his left shoulder shattered beyond repair. And Mrs. Evans was lying on the carriage floor, her arms dangling outside the buggy and her bejeweled hands caked with dirt and mud. Her hair was so entangled in the hub of the wheel that, once the hacienda servants had calmed the dog, several men had to lift the carriage from the ground and turn the wheel backward to free it before the body could be moved.[55]

In the dreary distance, the church bell of the village began to peal, as if gathering the villagers to one more agrarian junta. Only this time it clanged out the mournful news that the famous widow Evans was dead.

Ten

Harvest the present. Those who prefer pursuit
of after-fame do not reflect that posterity will
be men just like those who gall them now; and
that they too will be but mortal. And after all
what matters to you the rattle of voices, or the
kind of views they entertain about you?
— Marcus Aurelius, *Meditations*

ADMIRERS AND GAWKERS gathered at the Puebla station as Mrs.
Evans's body was taken to the capital in a rude pine box, which
would be exchanged for a fine silver coffin before she was lowered
into the earth next to her husband in Mexico City's old British cemetery. A large
and incongruous crowd of foreign dignitaries and weeping peasants gathered at
the flowery gravesite. The short and elegant ceremony gave no hint of the storm
raging around the dead woman's legacy.

In fact, the murder of Mrs. Evans had already become a potent factor in
Mexican and international politics, a bludgeon to use against enemies of all
stripes. The contending factions played so fast and loose with evidence and
accusation that within days they had ensured that the truth would never come
to light. It was a strenuous fight — a fight without winners.

THE RATTLE OF VOICES

Daisy Caden Pettus set the tone for the fight at the outset. She drowned her
grief in a rage for vengeance and a religious zeal to carry on her sister's crusade,
even composing a small prayer to steel herself for the fight: "That I may ever
bear in mind her memory; . . . that I may always remember the cause for which
she lived and died, and direct my course to the journey's end that she so bravely
sought."[1] She and her husband left for Mexico four days after the murder,
brandishing a list of Montistas who, Rosalie had once predicted in a letter,
would figure among her killers. Such evidence barely qualified as hearsay, but

Daisy was in full fighting feather as she declared that the men on her list were no more than hired help. "The Mexican Government may try to still public opinion in civilized lands by hanging a few Indians," she told the *San Francisco Examiner*. "But I know that the real murderers of my sister are to be found in higher positions. I am going to the ranch in Puebla and I shall stay there until the men who engineered the assassination are brought to justice."[2]

Meanwhile, the men in "higher positions" immediately declared that the murder had no connection to the agrarian movement, but was rather a "common crime."[3] It was regrettable that some ill-intentioned folks might draw connections between this crime and the agrarian movement. President Obregón said that never in his military career had he been so vexed as when told of the awful deed carried out by "the worst enemies of Mexico,"[4] but blaming the agraristas was blaming the victims. "The attitude assumed by the eternal enemies of progress in the unfortunate 'Evans incident,'" Obregón declared, "constitutes one more factor of ignominy that public opinion adds to the already heavy weight which history has placed on the backs [of the rural poor]."[5]

In Great Britain and the United States, the murder reinforced some opinions but altered few. British conservatives, predictably, took the occasion for another attack on Ramsay MacDonald and his foreign policy, which they blamed for making a mighty empire appear a weakling in the eyes of the world. "Thousands of our countrymen are obliged to live in half-civilized communities for the conduct of trade, on which our existence depends," wrote *The Times* of London. "Interest as well as justice forbids that we should allow their property or their lives to be taken with impunity."[6]

Of course, if there were to be any retaliation for the murder, the Monroe Doctrine made it plain that the task would fall to the United States, where jingoistic cries were greeted with the same indifference as Mrs. Evans's own anguished pleas. The right denounced the Mexicans as a horde of common bandits, whereas the left lauded them as a noble, suffering mass, but few reckoned the United States capable either of disciplining or uplifting them. The most pervasive attitude was illustrated by the reception given to Plutarco Elías Calles, the president elect, who by an awkward coincidence was passing through New York at the very moment that news of the murder broke. Clad in a Palm Beach suit, sporting an undersized fedora and a shimmering silk cravat, and flanked by a son and two daughters, Calles cut a striking, if taciturn, figure. He refused to comment on the Evans case, and instead took himself off to Ziegfeld's Follies, where a jovial Will Rogers introduced him approvingly as "a president of Mexico who was elected by votes and not shots." After much cajoling and repeated assurances of the warm and enduring friendship of the American people, Calles took a bow from his balcony seat, hailed by "vociferous applause."[7]

The investigation of the crime proceded vigorously and tendentiously. Puebla's chief of police, a hard-drinking veteran revolutionary named Honorato Teutli, launched a draconian sweep that netted some seventy people and two confessions. Two young men of Tianguismanalco, Alejo García and Francisco Ruiz, said they had been part of an ambush party led by a comrade named Francisco Pérez, who remained at large. Both García and Ruiz were dirt-poor and illiterate, reckoning themselves to be about twenty years old, although neither could assert this fact with authority. Ruiz was married and the father of two.

The authorities proclaimed that they had physical evidence against the suspects; a search of their homes had yielded quantities of ammunition, the bag of silver coins, a silk scarf, and Mrs. Evans's pistol. Some discrepancies cropped up, however: the bag found in Ruiz's home, for example, was said to contain one thousand pesos, whereas Mrs. Evans had been carrying only five hundred. But it was not the shakiness of the evidence that strained credulity so much as the way everything fell so quickly into place, all of it neatly supporting the government's version of events. It looked very much as if the government planned to do precisely what Daisy Pettus had predicted — that is, "still public opinion . . . by hanging a few Indians."

In fact, the federal government mostly likely *did* hope to railroad Ruiz and García, at least if the character of the "investigation" gives any clue. From the start, the chief investigators were more intent on suppressing potentially troublesome contradictions than on finding the real culprits. Among those annoying potential contradictions was young Johann Strathaus, who at that point lay weak and febrile in a Puebla hospital room.

Strathaus, of course, rued the day he had approached the hacienda San Pedro Coxtocán. His suffering had already been immense. After the ambush he had been left bleeding and unattended in the rain for several hours. It was not until well after dark that he had been covered with a blanket, strapped to a board, and carried to San Martín, where he was left to find his own accommodations. He might never have received even rudimentary medical attention had he not first received attention of other sorts: reporters and local authorities flocked around him the next morning, demanding statements. Uncertain and fearful of what he might disclose, the state authorities spirited him away to a Puebla sanitorium and placed armed guards at the door of his room.

Three days after the attack, Chief Teutli visited Strathaus in the hospital, accompanied by a man Strathaus believed to be a Mexico City agent sent to destroy evidence incriminating the agraristas. Teutli sounded Strathaus out carefully. Strathaus speculated that Manuel Montes must have masterminded the attack, but he had no evidence beyond what Mrs. Evans had told him. Teutli nodded philosophically, agreeing that Montes was a likely culprit.

The next day Teutli and the agent came again, this time accompanied by a crowd of "captured Indians," the fruits of Teutli's dragnet. Strathaus looked them over as they were led one by one into his room. He said he positively recognized only one of them—a large, round-faced man from Atlixco named Juan Moreno. When Teutli then brought Francisco Ruiz and Alejo García forward, Strathaus denied ever having seen either of them, at which point Teutli explained flatly that they were the men Strathaus had to identify. Juan Moreno was set free. Ruiz and García were packed off under heavy guard to Puebla's state penitentiary.[8]

A week after the murder, Puebla's state prosecutor, Cosme Zafra, wired Obregón that he had everything in place for a speedy trial—"witnesses, instruments of crime, German Strathaus, people who can identify perpetrators"—all of it tending to prove the exclusive guilt of the "common bandits" Ruiz and García. The judge in the case had orders to control strictly all access to the prisoners, ensuring that their testimony would be predictable.[9] Zafra was perplexed, then, when certain state officials—unconditional supporters of José María Sánchez—told him that Obregón had ordered the arrest of Manuel P. Montes for the murder. Zafra had been under the impression, he told Obregón, that Montes and his agraristas were to be cleared.[10] Obregón set his mind at ease by denying vehemently that he had ordered the arrest of Montes. Obviously, this was a ploy by the Sanchistas to use the Evans murder to exact vegeance on their political enemies.[11]

A VISIT TO STRATHAUS

In the immediate aftermath of the murder, Foreign Minister Sáenz had confidently predicted that before the month was out the entire matter would end with the conviction and execution of the perpetrators. His prediction was wide of the mark indeed. By the end of August the complications were only beginning.

Having parried the Sanchistas' maneuver to pin the blame on Montes, Zafra now turned his prosecutorial attention to the worrisome matter of Johann Strathaus. Although by now it was apparent that Strathaus had no idea who had attacked him and Mrs. Evans, or why, this lack of knowledge had not prevented him from speculating on the issue, so there was always a chance he might drop a bombshell into the proceedings. Specifically, he might be inclined to favor the version of events championed by the foreigners working at the behest of Daisy Pettus and the British consulate.

Accordingly, in company with the judge who was slated to hear the trial,

Zafra visited Strathaus in his hospital room toward the end of August. When the nurse attending Strathaus explained that her patient was running a fever of 104° and in no condition to answer questions, Zafra and the judge paid her no mind. In fact, they made themselves deliberately obnoxious, befouling the air with smoke from enormous cigars and browbeating the ailing Strathaus with accusations. He was, they charged, a Delahuertista and a fugitive from the German police. They claimed he had been bribed by Captain Hollocombe of the British consulate — the same Captain Hollocombe who had investigated Mrs. Evans's situation for the British in July — to slander Mexican authorities, and they tried to make him sign a confession to that effect. If he did not sign, they threatened, they would have him moved to a "military hospital," which would be indistinguishable from prison. On the other hand, if he signed, they would help him sue the Evans estate to win compensation for his injuries and would use their influence to get him additional funds from the Mexican government. Strathaus refused to sign. When Zafra and the judge finally left late that night, they ordered that the guard at the hospital door be reinforced and stationed round the clock.[12]

After the interrogation, Strathaus suffered a serious relapse and remained in a precarious condition for another six weeks. The trial was postponed, and nearly everyone concerned grew more pessimistic about the prospects of seeing their version of justice done. Even Daisy Pettus forgot her defiant resolution to remain at San Pedro until the real killers were punished. She left Mexico in mid-September — having stayed only long enough to see her sister buried and to hire George Camp to run the hacienda — and returned to the relative safety of Santa Barbara, California, to wage war by proxy.

George Camp, who visited Strathaus around this time, told Daisy that the "German boy" was in pitiable shape. The doctors were talking about rebreaking his bones to reset the fracture caused by the bullet's impact, although they seemed certain that he would never regain the use of his left arm. "Have you made any arrangements about him?" inquired Camp. "Are you to pay his hospital bills? If so, why not get the poor boy some competent care? The things they are doing are criminal."[13]

Camp was not the only one who was curious on that point. The German embassy had been fronting Strathaus money for his hospital stay, assuming that Daisy would eventually reimburse those funds. Daisy, however, had very pointedly departed Mexico without paying anybody for anything: by the end of the year she was besieged by claims not only from Strathaus and the German embassy, but also from the man who had embalmed her sister and two lawyers who had earlier involved themselves in the investigation. On the advice of her Santa Barbara attorney, she denied responsibility for these debts because paying them would have undermined her legal position. She held that the attack on her sister was a political act; therefore, the Mexican government was wholly liable. Had it been a bandit attack, as the Mexican government contended, it would have qualified as a work-related accident under the labor law, in which case the employer — or her estate — would have had to pay compensation. Both Daisy and the Mexican government steadfastly maintained that their legal positions could not be compromised, even if innocent people suffered.

AN ATTACK ON SÁNCHEZ

While Johann Strathaus fought his fever, the agrarian reform itself was taking its lumps in the national Congress. The occasion was an August 25 session held to discuss the "credential"[14] of José María Sánchez, who, although not forsaking his fight to retake the governorship of Puebla, also claimed election as a federal deputy.[15]

Luis Morones, the corpulent leader of the Regional Confederation of Mexican Workers (CROM), led the vitriolic attack. An ex-radical whose advocacy of cooperation with capital had grown in tandem with his own personal fortune,[16] he made his attack both personal and sweeping. "With the frankness that is habitual to me," he shouted at Sánchez, "I maintain that you are the cause of all the misfortunes that have occurred in the state of Puebla."

Sánchez sat calmly as Morones accused him of every sort of murder, mayhem, and malfeasance. With his bejeweled fingers, fleet of automobiles, and vast urban real-estate empire, Morones himself was already a legend of Mexican official corruption, and Sánchez did not deny himself the pleasure of accusing him of "living like a prince and eating like a bourgeois," nor did he suppress a grin when the erstwhile radical took him to task for encouraging strikes and factory takeovers. At that, Morones blew up. "Don't you smile!" he yelled. "I know I have my responsibilities in these matters. But nowadays agitators and everyone else has the duty to be responsible for their acts."

At the heart of Morones's tirade, however, was the agrarian question. "You don't understand agrarianism as it should be understood," he charged, "because the only thing you've done is take lands in order to give them to men who cannot work them." Because the state could not presently provide the "means and funds" to make small peasant parcels productive, the agrarian reform should drastically be curtailed.[17]

Morones's diatribe accurately reflected the views of Plutarco Elías Calles, who had won the national presidential election in July and was scheduled to take office in November. It looked as though Calles had meant what he told Ambassador Warren some months earlier; he intended to rein in the agrarian reform and had a plan to accomplish this objective. Morones's speech hinted at the nature of that plan: Calles would use the CROM to spearhead an attack on organized agrarismo. The import of Morones's speech was therefore unmistakable, coming as it did so soon after the killing of Mrs. Evans and in an attack on Puebla's leading radical politician.

THE TRIAL BEGINS

Precisely at this time the state made its first attempt to try the alleged killers of Rosalie Evans, but no one seemed eager to cooperate. The court was still awaiting promised affidavits from Strathaus and his doctors, as well as from the various municipal authorities interested in the case.[18] The most serious setback occurred on the very eve of the trial's opening, when the defendants suddenly retracted their confessions and claimed they had not been present at the scene of the crime. Prosecutor Cosme Zafra, seeing his entire case go up in smoke, responded with a serious charge: Captain Hollocombe of the British consulate had suborned Alejo García and Francisco Ruiz.

According to statements given by the two prisoners, Hollocombe had cornered them in an isolated part of their prison yard and told them they had been duped by government officials. Through bribes and threats, those officials had induced them to confess with the clear understanding that they were straw men who would quietly be released once the publicity blew over. Hollocombe, however, allegedly delivered the sobering news that the government really *did* plan to execute them because it was the only way to placate both national and international opinion. Their only hope, then, was to revise their confessions to implicate Manuel Montes and the "agrarian elements," in which case they would have the support of the foreigners who would see to it that they were freed. Hollocombe had also, Zafra maintained, implied that the prisoners would come in for some unspecified financial reward if they withdrew their confessions.[19]

Upon hearing these allegations against Hollocombe, Mexican officials made much of their outrage. Zafra threatened to prosecute a Mexican lawyer for treason merely because he had gone with Hollocombe to the prison. The Mexican government also retaliated by recalling all of its vice-consuls stationed in cities throughout the United Kingdom, thereby making the break in diplomatic relations complete.

The Hollocombe episode was only the beginning of Cosme Zafra's headaches. While his chief suspects were retracting their confessions, rumors were rife that his enemy, José María Sánchez, would soon return to take the Puebla state government by force. As it turned out, the rumors were true, except that there was no need for force. Obregón's legal adviser had studied the constitutional issues and declared that "the State of Puebla has returned to the constitutional order," and so "General José María Sánchez, as Constitutional Governor of the State, may legitimately take charge of Executive Power when he deems it convenient."[20]

Sánchez deemed it convenient on November 2, the Mexican "Day of the Dead." His decision was greeted with noisy outrage. Merchants declared they would withhold taxes, students planned massive anti-Sánchez rallies, and local caciques—including Montes—issued threats of some unspecified but horrible retaliation. Fearing bloodshed, the federal zone commander banned anti-Sánchez rallies, and the streets remained perfectly deserted. A reporter, making the most of the coincidence of dates, wrote that "everyone says that the day of the dead and the gust of frozen wind that blows furiously foretell tragedy and misfortune for Puebla."[21]

The outcome of Sánchez's return was not so dramatic, but it nevertheless did indeed involve some misfortune for prosecutor Zafra, who had been Sánchez's bitter enemy at least since August, when he had accused the governor of trying to interfere in his trial. One of Sánchez's first acts upon declaring himself governor was to fire Zafra as chief prosecutor. After that, he surprised everyone by suddenly resigning as governor and announcing that he would resume his seat in the chamber of deputies.[22] It was not so tremendous a sacrifice, for Sánchez's partisans continued to hold sway in both the state Congress and the city council of Puebla.[23] Back in Mexico City, Sánchez lost little time in exacting his revenge on Luis Morones. On November 12, a shouting match between the two men in the chamber of deputies degenerated into a wild gun battle that sent deputies diving frantically for cover behind marble pillars and wooden desks. Morones took a bullet in the chest—an injury from which he recovered with impressive speed and thoroughness.[24]

Despite such embarrassments as bribe charges, withdrawn confessions, and the dismissal of the state prosecutor, the court found Ruiz and García guilty and sentenced them to death in mid-November. After the verdict was announced, Cosme Zafra—who had just spent three months fighting tenaciously for that very outcome—surprisingly declared that the entire trial, including the verdict, was invalid. His dismissal by Sánchez, he argued, violated the state constitution. Meanwhile, the three attorneys who had defended Ruiz and García also charged irregularity in the proceedings. At the outset of the trial they had requested an extension so they would have more time to familiarize themselves with the details of the case, but the extension had not been granted, so they had done an admittedly poor job of defending their clients.

Now, they claimed, they had new evidence and a new theory: due to the angle of the bullet wound, Mrs. Evans could not possibly have been shot by attackers outside of the buggy. She must have been shot by Johann Strathaus![25]

The hapless Strathaus finally emerged from the hospital on January 31, 1925, nearly six months after the attack. At this same time, Cosme Zafra and the defense lawyers were still demanding a retrial, and they had received a major boost in late December when President Calles himself endorsed their demand.[26] Even so, justice — like Strathaus himself — faced a most uncertain future.

"My position," Strathaus later recalled with some understatement, "was grievous." The money that had been reluctantly advanced him by the German embassy had not been enough to pay for procedures that might conceivably have restored at least partial use of his left arm. The doctors told him that he would be unable to work for another two or three months, and even then he would be limited by his disability. German embassy officials backed the Mexicans in advising Strathaus to seek compensation from the estate of Rosalie Evans, insisting that Daisy Pettus had a moral obligation to help a man whose health had been permanently damaged while he was employed by her sister. The new U.S. consul general, meanwhile, gingerly suggested that Daisy give Strathaus a little something "by way of grace, and not as an admission of any legal obligation."[27] She simply ignored all entreaties for the time being, however, and insisted that she was "neither legally nor morally responsible for [Strathaus's] injuries."[28]

So Strathaus, making the most of his few and unattractive options, filed a claim against the Evans estate in Puebla's labor court. To maximize his chances there, he looked for promising political alliances — not an easy task at the moment because in January three governors and three legislatures had all claimed victory in December's election. By the time Strathaus left the hospital, however, the smoke had cleared somewhat, and Professor Claudio N. Tirado had become Puebla's new governor — the eleventh since 1920, but the first since Sánchez to take office as the result of an election. Although Manuel P. Montes had little in common with the new governor, he was a kingpin in the anti-Sánchez coalition that had brought Tirado to power, and as such he was considerably strengthened not only as a key power broker, but also formally as president of the state legislature.

It was to none other than Manuel P. Montes that Strathaus turned for help in his predicament. Montes responded eagerly to his queries, even though Strathaus sensed at first that Montes "felt very insecure and could not quite look me in the eyes." Both were tense as they set out by car from Puebla toward San Martín Texmelucan, where Montes was to help track down witnesses Strathaus would need to make his claim. The late Mrs. Evans seemed to stand between them like an embarrassing disfigurement that both were too polite to mention, but that neither could ignore. They probed cautiously, each trying to gauge the other's motives.

Strathaus helped break the ice by declaring that he had never for a moment believed Montes was involved in the attack. At that, Montes began to breathe more easily. It was well, he said, that Strathaus should think him innocent, for the newspapers were constantly maligning him. He spoke proudly of his revolutionary career. The two travelers could look out the windows of the automobile and see the fertile plains stretching out on either side of the highway, once again green with ripening wheat. Montes claimed that he had seized those fields from the rich and given them to the poor. It was not gentle work, he admitted, and the burned-out, ruined hacienda buildings bore mute witness to that. He was prepared to "use radical means" with anyone who stood in his way.

As for Mrs. Evans, however, no, he had had no part in that business. It was true that there was no love lost between himself and the stubborn hacendada, but, he assured Strathaus, he had often admonished his people not to harm her, for he knew full well that he would be blamed. Strathaus listened attentively, occasionally adding a sympathetic word or two about exploited Indians having a right to the land, which, said Strathaus, "called forth his entire satisfaction."[29]

If Montes did not order the murder, Strathaus respectfully inquired, then who did? Montes replied that he supposed José María Sánchez had ordered Mrs. Evans killed in order to embarrass, discredit, and undercut his rival. The political battlefield, he implied, was strewn with both the literal and figurative corpses of those who had tried to expose the wicked deeds of Sánchez.

By the time Montes and Strathaus reached this crucial juncture in their conversation, they must very nearly have reached the tree-shaded lane that ran from San Pedro to San Martín — the scene of the crime in question. They had reached an understanding. Montes would help Strathaus guide his claim against the Evans estate through the labor court, and in return Strathaus would revise his account of the murder to pin the blame on the Sanchistas.

The battle for the soul of Johann Strathaus was now fully joined. Strathaus was a tempting pawn for intriguers because he clearly knew very little and yet was willing to testify to just about anything that promised him a way out of his misery. After all, Montes's version of events made as much sense as any other, and Montes had the power to make things happen. He accompanied Strathaus to the labor court in April, helped him file a claim, then took him to meet Governor Tirado, who gave him a hundred pesos and arranged for a special railroad car to take him to Mexico City, where he was supposed to present a letter — an account of the murder composed by Montes — to President Calles himself. Calles refused to see Strathaus, but Gilberto Valenzuela, the interior secretary, told him to write up a detailed statement of his own. Meanwhile, George Camp had got wind of Strathaus's maneuvering and tried to head it off by offering him three pesos for the three days he had actually been employed by Mrs. Evans, plus an additional sum of around 150 pesos—one for each day of his hospitalization—as a "gift." Camp hoped that for about 153 pesos he could induce Strathaus to sign away any further claims against the estate.[30]

Artless though he may have been, Strathaus was not *that* simple. He claimed Mrs. Evans had hired him at a wage of three hundred pesos per month. Because their contract had been verbal and witnessed by no one but Strathaus and the deceased, this assertion was difficult to prove or disprove. Moreover, he claimed the Evans estate owed him 7,550 pesos in wages, medical and legal expenses, and miscellaneous costs. Apparently, however, he had little faith in the Mexican courts, despite sponsorship from such a powerful personage as Montes. While his claim began its circuitous route through the legal system, he approached Francis Price, Daisy Pettus's lawyer, who was visiting Mexico at that moment. Price strongly denied that the estate had any obligation to Strathaus, but he hinted that Daisy might be willing to help him out if he withdrew his claim and promised not to sign anything that could damage her interests. Perhaps Price was persuasive, or perhaps he only seemed a somewhat better bet than the labyrinthine labor courts, but in any case, Strathaus withdrew his suit against the Evans estate and entrusted his fate to Daisy Pettus and her lawyers.

BOLSHEVIKS

Several weeks passed, and nothing much happened. Strathaus, desperate for money, found work in the home of the Dutch ambassador in Mexico City, doing whatever menial chores his disability would permit. Then, in mid-June he suddenly received a jovial note from the governor of Puebla inviting him to come to the government palace for an interview.

When Strathaus obediently arrived in Puebla, he was informed that his signature was required on yet another statement upholding the government's version of the attack. This version portrayed Francisco Ruiz and Alejo García as bumbling robbers who were astounded when they approached the buggy to steal whatever valuables it might contain and discovered that they had killed the famous Señora Evans. The statement had a loud ring of inauthenticity: it also maintained that, just prior to her death, Mrs. Evans had undergone a major change of heart and had determined that "treating the agraristas well was the only way she would be able to work in peace." She was dissuaded from this laudable attitude by George Camp, who urged her to bellicosity and who also, according to the statement, visited Strathaus in the hospital and tried to pressure him to sign several false statements implicating Manuel Montes and the agraristas.

Of course Strathaus signed the statement. At this point, it looked like he had very little to lose, for two months had passed, and he had heard no offers from Daisy Pettus and her lawyers. There was also the more compelling argument that the government officials who offered the statement for his signature seemed really to mean business. "Had I refused to sign this," Strathaus later attested, "then surely had come to me the same end as to Mrs. Evans."[31]

Although Daisy Pettus would never forgive Strathaus for this episode, it is nevertheless true that she and her minions were not altogether innocent victims. Her reluctance to help Strathaus in his hour of need was beginning to inspire disapproving whispers even among the Mexico City social set. There was also the matter of George Camp, who was still on San Pedro and still spoiling for a fight. The flood of complaints from the surrounding villagers had inspired government officials to gather evidence they could use to deport him, which explains why he figured as chief villain in the Strathaus statement.

The main reason why Strathaus was compelled to sign an obviously false statement at this time, however, had to do with the rapid deterioration of U.S.-Mexican relations. Daisy Pettus and her lawyers could claim at least a small share of the credit for that too. In October of 1924, Charles Warren had been replaced by James Sheffield as U.S. ambassador to Mexico, and in Washington Frank Kellogg replaced Charles Evans Hughes as secretary of state. With these changes, the tone of U.S.-Mexican relations quickly changed for the worse. James Sheffield was the sort of man Rosalie Evans had always wanted Warren to be—a Yale man, a corporate lawyer, and a hardliner with a terror of Bolshevik contagion. He was also a virulent racist, whose distaste for Calles's cabinet had much to do with its unfortunate lack of white blood and its overabundance of Indian, Jewish, and Armenian strains (it even included, he noted with horror, an amateur bullfighter).[32] Upon assuming his office, he knew no Spanish and almost nothing of Mexico beyond his own prejudices.[32] Not surprisingly, he proved very receptive to the efforts of Daisy Pettus and her lawyer, Francis Price, to educate him about that southern republic.

The lessons Francis Price imparted did not flatter the Mexicans. Not even the acquisition of land, capital, and modern equipment, he asserted, could make a decent farmer out of the Mexican peon, so lacking was he in "intelligence and enterprise." This very lack of intelligence made the peon susceptible to "radical theories emanating from Russia in the throes of the Third International." Price even claimed to have a secret source inside the Third International (the organization founded in Moscow in 1919 to promote international revolution) who informed him that Communism "was tried out in Mexico before it was introduced in Russia, just as a new play is tried out in a rural district before it is presented in the city." Of course, in Price's view most Mexicans were too dim to understand radical theories, but just the same they "have readily accepted [Communism] as an excuse for the destruction of the remnants of the European civilization in Mexico and as license for indulgence in the primitive passions of the Indian race, concealed but not controlled by the veneer of European culture imposed by the Conquest." The United States should feel free to make its demands, for U.S. support was the Mexican government's only antidote to anarchy.[33]

These views fit well with those of Ambassador Sheffield, who had steeped himself in anti-Mexican propaganda. "The Mexican situation," his reading material had persuaded him, "is an abscess which cries for a lancet."[34] He was convinced that a showdown was approaching—that the Mexicans were plotting a wholesale confiscation of foreign property and that only forceful action could save the situation. Armed with these convictions, he went to work on the secretary of state, Frank B. Kellogg. In June of 1925, his efforts paid off when Kellogg issued a statement to the press that concluded with a dire warning: "The government of Mexico is now on trial before the world."[35] This highhanded sentiment provoked strong reactions in Mexico,[36] and U.S.-Mexican relations would worsen steadily until 1927, when Mexico aired well-founded fears of U.S. military intervention. The two countries then made what one journalist called an "unnecessary, Dantesque pilgrimage along the brink of war."[37]

In June of 1925, some Mexican officials apparently reasoned that if they were on trial before the world, their best defense would be a good offense, so their thoughts turned to young Strathaus. A well-tailored and well-publicized— albeit false—statement might undo a bit of the damage done to Mexico by the Evans murder. As it turned out, however, this statement was never made widely public, partly owing to the very lack of political coordination that had made Puebla ungovernable for so long and partly because Daisy Pettus and Francis Price were suddenly spurred to action. The bogus Strathaus statement had caused Daisy's lawyers to fear that the German boy "might be used as a pretext to delay and obstruct the negotiations for the settlement of [Daisy Pettus's] property rights." Still fearful that any aid to Strathaus could compromise their legal claims, they suggested that Price, "through some discreet channel, might be able to have him come to the United States and furnish him the means of proceeding to Germany without disclosing the benefactor."

STRATHAUS GOES TO CALIFORNIA

At roughly the same time, the Baroness Alsbeck, wife of the Dutch ambassador, mentioned Strathaus to her friend Zelia Nuttall, expressing "surprise and disapprobation" that Daisy had done "nothing at all" to help the boy. Young Strathaus could hardly have wished for a better advocate than Zelia Nuttall. The heiress of a vast California fortune, ex-wife of a famous French explorer, and a noted archaeologist and ethnologist in her own right, Mrs. Nuttall was practically a legend in Mexico City society. She lived in a mansion that had been built for the famous conquistador, Pedro de Alvarado, and that was now renowned for its lavish garden and bougainvillea-laced bulwarks, as well as its elegant antique furnishings, artworks, and pre-Columbian artifacts. Above all, it was a gathering place for Mexico City's upper crust.[38] Rosalie Evans herself, a frequent teatime guest at Mrs. Nuttall's, had been impressed that even the cream of society would "take any slight from Mrs. Nuttall and call and call again! . . . Bow before her power!"[39]

In July of 1925, the powerful Zelia Nuttall wrote to scold Daisy for her insensitivity, pointing out how cruelly fate had treated Strathaus. He had suffered a long and painful hospital stay, lost the use of his left arm, endured indignities at the hands of Mexican officials, and been forced to compromise his integrity by bearing false witness and filing suit against the estate of Rosalie Evans, a woman he claimed greatly to admire. Now, said Mrs. Nuttall, he wanted only to return to Germany to live with his family while pursuing a degree in engineering. If only Daisy would send him a thousand dollars, he would leave Mexico immediately. His suit against the estate was for a much larger figure, but he would rather get the smaller sum in an honest and honorable way than to associate with "those whose principles he despises and who wish to make use of him to make serious trouble for you." Strathaus also promised that, once safely out of Mexico, he would give testimony that Daisy would find helpful to her cause.[40]

Daisy was no doubt humiliated and deeply resentful of Strathaus's very existence. In a letter to William E. Borah, chairman of the Senate Foreign Affairs Committee, she complained that the Mexicans were "stimulating Strathaus to harass me" by forcing her to choose between a lawsuit and a legally damaging admission.[41] By August, however, the false statement combined with Zelia Nuttall's advocacy had finally persuaded Daisy that the Strathaus issue would simply not go away, so she sent Strathaus some money with the proviso that he come directly to Santa Barbara, California, and make a detailed statement before traveling on to Germany.

This new statement would be no problem, for by now Strathaus was becoming quite the raconteur, eager to spin his yarn for just about anyone who crossed his path. In fact, on the train from Mexico City to El Paso he unburdened himself to his seatmate, one Alberto Gayou, who promptly reported the entire conversation to President Calles, noting at the same time that Strathaus seemed to be engaged in some sort of intrigue with the U.S. consul who greeted him at El Paso.[42] Later, while working as a busboy at a hotel restaurant, Strathaus would regale his fellow workers with such exotic tales that his boss felt compelled to write Francis Price for verification, "as the man in question is rather young and might be carried away with juvenile emotions to make himself a hero."[43] Regarding his formal testimony — which dutifully blamed Mrs. Evans's death on Obregón and Montes — Daisy, her lawyers, and the officials at the British consulate all pronounced themselves well pleased, for they "considered it most important in spite of the contemptible character of the witness."[44]

By the time Strathaus got to California, however, he unfortunately had little more than stories. The German embassy claimed a share of the settlement to compensate the money they had advanced him while in the hospital. Father Rubio Contreras of Puebla, who apparently had staked Strathaus some funds during his recovery, also came in for a cut. Strathaus had to use his settlement money to pay his way to California and his room and board while there, and he spent a bit more on new clothes and other odds and ends, so the ink was barely dry on his new testimony — and on the writ releasing the Evans estate from further claims — when he noticed that his nest egg was almost gone and that he lacked the funds to continue on to Germany.

Despite the release he had signed, Strathaus was soon back on Daisy's doorstep with his hand out, insisting that Daisy was obliged to pay the cost of his transportation to California.[45] Daisy assured him that travel expenses were included in the settlement already paid. She told Mrs. Nuttall that Strathaus was a "spendthrift" who was making himself so objectionable that she and her husband had banned him from entering the hospital grounds where they lived.[46] Strathaus was reduced to taking work as a busboy in a San Francisco hotel and occasionally writing to Daisy, threatening to change his testimony if she did not come through with more money. By December, he had found work as an apprentice repairman for the Wurlitzer Organ and Piano Company. He wrote to Mrs. Nuttall, who had come to believe Daisy's stories about him, and asked her to use her influence to get Daisy to help him get an extension on his passport. "Hoping that all will end well," he wrote in his characteristically tortured syntax, "I ask you again to trust me, because so much has happened to me against my will, and more, because people are prejudiced, but I am always anxious to make good."[47]

Around this time, he also changed his name to John Berger and apparently determined to make his way as an American. Whether he succeeded we will never know, for it is at this point that he disappears from the historical record.

THE PROBLEM WITH CAMP

George Camp, who had done so much to encourage Mrs. Evans in her defiance and paranoia, seemed determined to follow her example. He remained on San Pedro, making few friends and a host of enemies.

In November 1924, when the agraristas of Tianguismanalco tried to take water from the irrigation tunnel they had been granted in July, Camp responded by destroying their dam and sluice gate, flooding the village's ejidal fields and provoking the villagers to complain that he was "even more aggressive than Mrs. Evans herself."[48] In May, as the harvest drew near and Manuel Montes decreed another labor strike, Camp refused to hire unionized workers and drove the union men off at gunpoint.[49] In July, a villager of Tianguismanalco accused him of stealing two cows that had wandered onto hacienda land and selling them to a slaughterhouse in San Martín, but he evaded prosecution for the deed by simply ignoring repeated summons to court.[50] Even Ambassador Sheffield, a great admirer of assertiveness, was obliged to warn him against "indiscreet or ill-considered action."[51] If issues were to be forced, U.S. officials preferred to force them on their own terms rather than have a crisis foisted on them by the irascible Camp. The Mexicans too feared Camp's audacity. "He is a very nervous man," Foreign Minister Sáenz told Ambassador Sheffield, "to say the least."[52]

Unfortunately for Camp, the villagers were not the only ones working against him. Like Mrs. Evans, he wanted to hold the hacienda to the bitter end, whereas Daisy and her lawyers were busy negotiating a sale. Her price was a whopping one million pesos in untaxed gold — fully twice Rosalie Evans's supposed minimum figure. Unlike her sister, however, Daisy was actually anxious to sell. In fact, the hacienda had become an insufferable nuisance. Mexican authorities tried to exhaust both her means and her patience by, for instance, demanding an exhorbitant inheritance tax and supporting Johann Strathaus in his claims. At the same time, lawyers for Harry Evans's brother appeared with a claim for repayment of a loan made to Harry back in 1914, plus interest. Daisy hoped to do justice to her sister's legacy, but petty irritations were taking their toll.

Camp was the greatest irritation of all. Far from the chivalrous, swashbuckling hero of her sister's letters, the real George Camp struck Daisy as devious and self-interested. In fact, according to Francis Price, he was "the greatest burden of the whole matter. He has practically assumed the attitude of one who has salvaged an abandoned ship, not realizing that without your protection he would never have been permitted to live, let alone operate the hacienda." Moreover, he was "a most persistent and forceful man and the most difficult person to handle that I have ever met."[53]

Camp obstinately refused to cooperate with the lawyers. During 1925, Price began to suspect that he had sinister intentions. That spring, a newspaper man named Colonel Robert Murray, a well-known propagandist for the Calles government,[54] appeared in the office of Ambassador Sheffield with a plan to purchase San Pedro Coxtocán. Sheffield and Francis Price were suspicious of Murray from the start, however, even going so far as to charge privately that he was a hit man detailed by Calles to assassinate Price. When Camp urged Daisy to consider Murray's offer, her lawyers concluded he must be either a dupe or a co-conspirator in Murray's nefarious plot to get the hacienda.[55]

Camp became a further liability when Price hit upon a new legal strategy that would demand at least some measure of Mexican official goodwill. The new strategy harkened back to Obregón's mysterious decree of July 1923 in which he had declared that San Pedro Coxtocán was to be expropriated in order to found a "military-agricultural colony." Both before and after that decree, other piece-meal grants had been made of hacienda lands to the villages. Clearly, the various decrees could not legally or logically be reconciled. Price now argued that the July 1923 decree took precedence and that Mrs. Evans and her sister had actually been working in the government's interest by fending off villagers who sought to occupy the lands they had been granted, thereby keeping the estate intact.[56] The plan, then, was to remind the Mexican government of the favors Rosalie Evans and her heir had done them, exploit the growing differences between the government and the agrarians, and talk in terms of a single, rather large, lump sum. In return, Daisy would drop her pending three hundred thousand peso claim for indemnity for her sister's death.[57]

George Camp was not privy to any of this because Daisy was convinced he would "take advantage of our frankness and [try] to frustrate our plans."[58] She and her lawyers repeatedly scolded Camp for his violent temperament, which they feared would alienate key government officials and scotch their best deal. Camp reacted angrily: "Please tell Mrs. Pettus," he told Price at one point, "that if she wants to run this hacienda please come down and do it."[59] Otherwise, he insisted that the only way to make the hacienda profitable would be for Daisy to send him enough money to buy a tractor because it was impossible to find willing workers.

Daisy never sent the money. Instead, she summarily ordered Camp off the property. Administration of the hacienda was now placed in the hands of the only hacendado left in the area, Ignacio Ovando of the neighboring Mendocinas hacienda. Camp went to Mexico City, where he laid low for several months to evade arrest. Eventually he found work supervising the drilling of a dam for the Mexico Light and Power Company in western Mexico. Later he lived at the University Club in Mexico City and made a meager living as a "consulting engineer" until his death in 1984.

The intervening years did little to mellow Camp. In 1963, the writer Ross Parmenter tracked him down and interviewed him at the Harvard Club. Camp's charges were freewheeling indeed. He maintained that Ambassador Charles Warren had actively collaborated with the Mexican government to have Rosalie Evans murdered. Because it would be difficult to kill Mrs. Evans as long as her protector (Camp) remained with her, Warren had summoned him to the em-

George Camp in 1963. *Credit:* Photo by Ross
Parmenter, used by permission.

bassy on the pretext of having him construct a building for the embassy garden. While he was at the embassy and unable to protect Mrs. Evans, the assassination was carried out.[60]

Warren, however, was not the only treacherous American in Camp's tale. Camp charged that Daisy and her lawyers were also in league with the agrarians and that they had conspired to get him "out of the way" by any means possible, even sending soldiers to San Pedro to kill him. To the end of his life, he was convinced that the U.S. government had conspired with Mexico's agrarians to kill Mrs. Evans, that they had hoped to kill him as well, and that the true story would never be told.[61]

THE BOOK

The dismissal of Camp did not have quite the salutary effect on the negotiations for the hacienda that Daisy and her lawyers had hoped for. Just when it seemed that the Mexican government intended to meet Daisy's price, the official in charge of the negotiations suddenly adopted a cool attitude — sitting in silence, smoking a cigar, and ignoring Price's overtures. It seemed that they were back to square one.

All the while, Daisy explored other ways of bringing pressure to bear on the Mexicans — and on U.S. officials who might be persuaded to take a hard line toward Mexico. Her most important strategy was to produce "the book," a project she had discussed with Rosalie just before her death. Rosalie had talked of writing a book based on her adventures, but failing that she hoped Daisy would polish her letters a bit and publish them.

Daisy began this crusade shortly after her sister's death, when she paid a call on the popular California novelist Gertrude Atherton. Atherton, whose own novels were filled with intelligent, indomitable women, quickly concluded that Rosalie Evans had been "one of the most remarkable and complex women that ever lived."[62] She sent the letters immediately to the Bobbs-Merrill publishing house in Indianapolis.

Bobbs-Merrill — whose catalog already included a few works with titles such as *Is Mexico Worth Saving?* — jumped at the opportunity to publish the letters. "We feel," editor H. H. Howlin wrote Daisy, "there is something more here than merely another book to manufacture and sell. You have laid at our door an obligation and an opportunity, neither of which we should, or would, shirk."[63] The editors were always conscious of the book's timeliness, and their awareness was heightened when Secretary of State Kellogg declared Mexico to be "on trial before the world" (more than one critic would treat the book as a bit of damning evidence in Mexico's trial "at the bar of world opinion").[64] W. C. Bobbs himself observed that "any straining in our relations with Mexico might have an exceedingly important effect on the publicity connected with the book."[65]

The objective of the book was to paint Mexico in the blackest possible hues, and the editors were not subtle about it. A foreword — credited to Daisy Pettus, but in fact supplied by Francis Price[66] — anticipates readers whose admiration for Mrs. Evans might have been mitigated by the perception that she had violently defied the laws of a foreign country. "Mrs. Evans," responds Price, "in the use of force, was not resisting the Mexican laws but was seeking the protection and rights afforded her under those very laws." In addition to a thumbnail sketch of corrupt courts and arbitrary officials, Price puts forth a picture of formerly content peons who neither needed nor wanted land. "The peon," he claims, "as a result of the abuses against which Mrs. Evans fought, finds himself in the richest land in the world at the point of starvation."[67] The entire text of the book is peppered with tendentious explanatory comments (e.g., "If all the other haciendados [sic] had joined with Mrs. Evans and resisted illegal land confiscation, Mexico would not be in the state it is in to-day").[68] The publisher also splashed the dust jacket with quotations denouncing several Mexican officials by name and characterizing the Mexican people in general as a "monkey-minded race" — an unfortunate turn of phrase Mrs. Evans had used in a moment of great distress. The jacket even implies that Harry Evans's death had been "sudden and suspicious," something not even Mrs. Evans — who had never shirked from bending the truth — had suggested. Francis Price had somehow conceived the idea that it was "generally believed that [Harry Evans] was poisoned,"[69] and this sensational suggestion was now conveyed to the reading public. Daisy also urged Price to plant an anonymous review that would bring out some "key points other reviewers might miss."[70]

The publisher also aimed the book at groups that already had cause for anti-Mexican feeling — conservatives, property-owners, and Catholics angered at the Mexican government's anticlerical policies. A special Knights of Columbus edition was printed, and copies of the book were mailed to such groups as the Daughters of the American Rvolution and clergy of the Episcopal Church.[71] Most importantly, the publishers saw to it that a copy found its way into the hands of Ambassador James Sheffield, who reacted with unqualified enthusiasm. An agent for the publisher reported that Sheffield considered the book "virtually a textbook, giving a trustworthy account of Mexican affairs, showing great insight into the Mexican character." Sheffield ordered as many copies as he could obtain and handed them out to visiting Americans and Englishmen for their edification. He kept his personal copy displayed prominently on his desktop and locked it up each night for safekeeping.[72]

Critics generally received the book warmly. Even the harshest found Mrs. Evans to be a fascinating and admirable figure. "Her violence and intrepidity," wrote the left-wing journalist Carleton Beals, "make her the twin-sister of my old-time neighbor and godmother, Carrie Nation."[73] And few could resist the tale of "high adventure in the midst of revolution."[74] The fledgling *New Yorker,* which could seldom spare more than a scant paragraph for the latest literary productions, devoted its entire "New Books" column to *The Rosalie Evans Letters from Mexico,* pronouncing it "the book of the spring." The *New Yorker* critic was captivated by the drama in which a "gentlewoman" of "recessive" character goes through inhuman trials and "finishe[s] as a sort of feminine, thoroughly feminine, John Brown."[75] Gertrude Atherton was the most effusive on the book's literary merits: "Only a Dumas," she wrote, "could conceive fiction that equaled it; no modern spinner of adventure stories has ever approached it in thrills."[76]

Among the book's "characters," Ambassador Charles Warren took the worst battering from reviewers. Atherton predicted that Warren, despite his ambitions for a European appointment, would "probably spend the rest of his life in retirement." Indeed, his résumé is notably thin in the years from 1924 to his death in 1936.[77] According to *Catholic World,* he was an affront to his gender. "One is thankful," wrote this critic, "that there is a Dashiel [the book's pseudonym for Camp], a Cummins . . . and a Don Iago [Jesús Bermejillo], to offset the picture and restore one's faith in masculine character."[78] Only a few critics sprung tepidly to Warren's defense: "There is internal evidence in these letters," the historian Charles Beard noted, "to the effect that Mrs. Evans presented knotty problems for Mr. Warren to solve and thrust upon him perplexities that must have tried his soul. One need not be lacking in respect for her intrepidity if one feels that the latter is entitled to a large measure of public sympathy."[79]

On the more trenchant issue of agrarian reform, critics parted company depending largely upon how they viewed the liberal notion of progress — the vision of a world driven by ever-increasing cycles of consumption and production — and upon their evaluation of the Mexican peasant's capacity to adapt to such a world. Critics of all persuasions homed in on Mrs. Evans's account of a trip through a part of southern Tlaxcala: "[T]he country has returned to savagery," she wrote, "not always fierce — just cultivating land enough for their simple wants. Then they lie in the sun, in front of their mud huts."[80] It was her vision of what Mexico might be like if she were to give up the good fight, and she was not alone in finding it abhorrent. "The issue seems not to be the simple one of 'The Land to the Peasants,'" wrote the *New York Times* critic in an effort to account for Mrs. Evans's apparent indifference to the plight of the poor. "If it were, the sympathy of the world [for Mrs. Evans] would not be so strongly enlisted. According to Mrs. Evans and her sister, the land confiscated falls into neglect and ruin."[81]

To others, however, attending to simple wants and lying in the sun did not sound like an altogether bad thing. Carleton Beals, a veteran Mexico watcher and the bane of conservatives,[82] noted that Tlaxcala "has never suffered the violences that have occurred in Puebla; few Mexican states are so peaceful and prosperous." Mrs. Evans, he wrote, "was utterly unconscious that a great social movement has been sweeping over Mexico."[83]

By far the harshest words came from the pen of Katherine Anne Porter, at the time a struggling journalist who had yet to make her mark in literature. She, like Rosalie Evans, hailed from southern Texas and had a long acquaintance with Mexico. Any similarity ended there, however. Porter's experience of Mexico involved a measure of active collaboration with the revolution (e.g., carrying "messages to people living in dark alleys," as she put it).[84] In 1926 she had a rather uncritical admiration for revolutionaries, and it was in this spirit that she read Mrs. Evans's letters. "The demon that possessed her," wrote Porter, "was by no means of so spiritual a nature as she fancied: she was ruled by a single-minded love of money and power." Porter did profess some admiration for Mrs. Evans as a "personality" — "beautiful, daring and attractive" — but as a "human being" she considered her to be "avaricious, with an extraordinary hardness of heart and ruthlessness of will; and she died in a grotesque cause."[85]

Daisy's friends were quick to close ranks in the face of such barbs. "The article of Katherine Anne Porter is simply disgusting," wrote a certain Henri Ovier of Switzerland, who could not bring himself even to credit Porter with so noble a motivation as political subversion. "One can guess [Porter's review] is written by a jealous little woman who must be plain and does not move in the fine sets. One breathes the mean jealousy that inspired those heartless sentences."[86] Daisy's friends also urged her to carry her crusade to new heights, with more than one correspondent suggesting that she seek funding — perhaps from "some influential Catholic" — to have the story made into a motion picture.[87] Yet another friend found heroic words to bolster Daisy in her faith: "Why," she exclaimed, "I wish to rush down into the benighted country and personally strangle the perpetrators of such incredible, such unparalleled outrage."[88]

The alleged perpetrators of the outrage did not take all of this adverse publicity with complete equanimity. *The Rosalie Evans Letters from Mexico* was banned in Mexico (which is why Sheffield felt it necessary to lock up his copy in a safe at night), and at least one scurrilous rumor regarding the Evanses and their hacienda became current. The book's publication coincided with a renewed official attack on the Catholic Church, which met with armed resistance from many of the nation's Catholics. According to one tale, Mrs. Evans had had a younger sister who dwelt in a convent in Mexico City. When the government, as part of its anticlerical campaign, expelled all foreign members of religious orders, the younger sister's affairs came under scrutiny, whereupon it was discovered that the hacienda San Pedro Coxtocán had never belonged to Rosalie Evans at all. It belonged to the Catholic Church![89]

MONTES BECOMES GOVERNOR

In November of 1926, just as Rosalie Evans's book hit the stands, her old arch-foe Manuel P. Montes became governor of the state of Puebla. George Camp, predictably enough, charged that his ascendance was the result of intrigue. In Camp's version, Montes possessed written orders, presumably from President Obregón, to kill Mrs. Evans, which he threatened to make public unless Obregón made him state governor.[90]

Of course, Camp's story can neither be proved nor disproved, though it seems highly improbable that Obregón would have been foolish enough to commit such an order to paper. The more likely explanation is at once more mundane and more complex. During the latter half of the 1920s, President Calles began making good on the promise he had made to Ambassador Warren in 1924 to slow the pace of agrarian reform. His vehicles for accomplishing this task were to be the CROM, which had expanded dramatically in size and influence during his administration, and the union's political arm, the National Laborista Party (PLN). His aim was to perfect a system similar to the one Obregón had preached to the agrarista convention of 1923; society was to be considered a single organism, its vertebrae running from the president of the republic down to the humblest wage earner. At the moment, strong military men and many local caudillos were living more or less as parasites on that organism, and surrounding it were various smaller organizations that provided a sometimes useful counterweight to the CROM/PLN and military caudillismo.[91]

The CROM had earlier provided strong backing for José María Sánchez, and its representatives had helped Manuel P. Montes found his Domingo Arenas Confederation, but in the wake of the de la Huerta rebellion, that unity had disintegrated. President Calles used his power to impose a frankly anti-agrarista governor in neighboring Tlaxcala, who brought down a wave of repression against the agraristas of the valley.[92] Forced onto the defensive, Montes joined with other nationally prominent agrarian leaders in forming the radical National Peasant League in 1926. At the same time he embraced the General Confederation of Workers (CGT), a union that had been founded in 1921 with help from the Mexican Communist Party. From the time of its founding, the union's express purpose had been to compete with the CROM for control of the Mexican working class, a task that became more difficult in the face of official sympathy for the CROM.

Intent on cementing its hegemony nationwide, the CROM focused considerable energy on the heavily industrialized Puebla-Tlaxcala Valley. Among its targets was Claudio Tirado, the current Puebla governor who had ridden to power with the support of the so-called "Federation of Regional Revolutionary Parties." The main purpose of that federation had been to unite the enemies of José María Sánchez, and as such it enjoyed the strong backing of Manuel P. Montes. Unfortunately, Montes had considered Tirado, a relative moderate, as merely a candidate of convenience, so when Tirado opposed the CROM's efforts to take control of Puebla's labor movement—and especially when he tried to impede the congressional campaign of CROM heavyweight Vicente Lombardo Toledano—he became a target. Cromista legislators charged Tirado with racketeering and political corruption, at which point the beleaguered governor found he lacked even the tepid support of his erstwhile allies. Montes had his own reason for failing to spring to Tirado's defense: as president of the state legislature, he was next in line to succeed to the governorship. On November 24, 1926, when Tirado followed the well-worn trail into an ignominious early retirement, Montes became Puebla's interim governor.

Montes's ascension to executive power brought on Puebla's last great political battle of the 1920s, one in which nearly every level of Poblano society joined. Montes's violent and autocratic methods had earned him much enmity among large numbers of villagers, and those villagers did not hesitate now to style themselves *laboristas* or to use the national political conflicts to settle local scores. The divisions within some villages were extreme. In Santa Ana Xalmimilulco—a relatively large village of roughly two thousand inhabitants, located perhaps five miles due south of San Martín—the agraristas (or "Montistas") went so far as to secede from the village to found their own "colony." The fight between the colony "La Victoria" and the rest of the village raged for years, with sporadic sniping, arson, and occasional gun battles.

In November of 1926, Montes sought to use his position as governor to deal decisively with the laboristas. Within days of taking office, he called elections for a new legislature, then personally led mounted police into Huejotzingo to impose his men in office—sparking riots that left three laboristas dead. In some villages, Montistas rounded up laboristas and jailed them to prevent them from voting. Despite Montes's efforts, the elections ended with three legislatures all claiming victory and setting themselves up to run the state and name a new governor. The federal government declared all three legislatures illegitimate, thus leaving Montes's power unchecked from below.

To the conservative press, the idea of Montes in the governor's chair was one of the crowning absurdities of an absurd era, and they were quick to recall Montes's alleged complicity in the murder of Mrs. Evans. According to *Excélsior,* he was a "caveman" and a "red communist." "But what can we do?" asked the editorialist incredulously. "General Montes is a famous distributor of ejidos, a veritable Nimrod in the hunt for foreign landowners; he carries the red-and-black in his blood, can barely read or write, and this qualifies him to govern a state of over a million inhabitants!"[93] An editorial of February 3, titled "Mrs. Rosalie Evans and General Montes," explicitly accused Montes of the murder, citing Mrs. Evans's own letters as evidence. The longer he held office, the more lurid became the newspaper denunciations—one even conjuring the fear of a primordial savagery that some supposed to be latent in Mexican character and society. The agrarian reform, said *Excélsior,* was nothing but robbery and murder, and Montes "might as well be clad in a loin-cloth, with rings through his lips and painted with pitch, with cactus leaves clinging to his long mane, armed with a butcher's knife and leaning over his victims on the sacrifical stone so as to rip out their hearts and offer them steaming before a statue of Huitzilopochtli seated on his blue *icpalli* [throne]."[94]

The CROM, although less colorful in its rhetoric, also found much cause for complaint. It claimed that Montes had used his executive power in an attempt to fill the region's factories with members of the communist CGT. His campaign to pack the factories focused on the few textile mills in San Martín Texmelucan and primarily involved pressuring factory owners to hire "reds" (CGT workers) while at the same time kidnapping, beating, and otherwise intimidating "yellows" (CROM workers). Cromistas charged that he brought in outside agitators to preach communism in the unions.[95] Montes's only real success, however, came when the CGT managed to take over El Pilar, the textile mill that had once been something of a second home to Rosalie Evans. The struggle devolved into a local feud between El Pilar and the larger Cromista factory, El Carmen.[96] Moreover, in the storm of accusatory telegrams the Cromistas sent to Calles, they seldom neglected to remind the president that Montes remained the chief suspect in the killing of Mrs. Evans.[97]

In the national Congress, Vicente Lombardo Toledano—ex-governor of Puebla and now education secretary for the CROM—led the fight against Montes as he had against Tirado. He recommended that the Permanent Commission of the Senate declare powers in Puebla to be defunct ("disappeared") and then name a replacement for Montes.[98] Trying to salvage his political fortunes, Montes threw all of his political weight behind Alvaro Obregón, who was making a bid for a second term as president. He spent vast sums from the state treasury in order to throw an elaborate banquet for Obregón on June 25, but it was not enough. Four days later, his enemies in Congress deposed him and replaced him with a CROM stalwart, General Donato Bravo Izquierdo.[99] A stern-looking ex-textile worker with a stiffly upturned mustache, Bravo Izquierdo made a series of pronouncements against "the exploiters of agrarismo: the false apostles who flourish under the impunity of land division, the leeches of the agricultural class."[100] There was, he explained, no longer any room for "politics." From now on, the state government would take its marching orders from the central government. Even José María Sánchez, who offered his political savvy to the new governor, was frozen out of the system.[101]

THE DEATH OF MONTES

When Montes returned to private life on a newly acquired hacienda, San Miguel Lardizábal, on the outskirts of San Martín Texmelucan, the press, with the apparent connivance of Governor Bravo Izquierdo, charged that his acquisition of the hacienda was enabled by his monstrous corruption. They said he had bought the hacienda at an artificially low price with money looted from the state's coffers. Moreover, intent on restoring the hacienda to its old opulence, he had ordered all ejidatarios summarily ejected from former hacienda lands, and those who had resisted had been tamed by a series of "exemplary executions." When Montes parried the wild charges and proclaimed himself a loyal defender of the poor and downtrodden, he seemed a voice in the wilderness.[102] He also sounded a curious and ironic echo of Rosalie Evans when he asked for official protection, for he had cause to fear that his life was in danger.[103]

All the while, the fight for control of the local textile industry had grown more heated. In mid-August, when the general secretary of the CROM union in El Carmen was found dead in San Rafael Tlanalapan, the crime was immediately and plausibly charged to Montes and his agents. The streets of San Martín Texmelucan turned vicious and unsafe, as workers from El Pilar and El Carmen carried on their armed feud. The state was set for a showdown on Tuesday, August 30, when Montes called a major rally in San Martín to commemorate the twelfth anniversary of the death of Domingo Arenas.

Montes arrived a little after noon to find his agraristas already gathered around the kiosk in the city's main square, listening to a series of impassioned orators. There were a few ominous signs: someone shouted "Death to Obregón" and was roughed up by the agraristas; an anonymous policeman fired a shot and fled before the agraristas could catch him. The scene was relatively quiet at 2 p.m., however, when the agraristas began their march through the streets, chanting "long life to Obregón and the agrarian revolution." As they passed in front of the municipal palace, a volley of shots rang out from the roof of a general store owned by a well-known supporter of the El Carmen faction, and two Montistas fell dead. The orderly procession dissolved in panic. Unable to catch the snipers, the marchers sacked the store, leaving glass and crockery shattered, dry goods scattered, and bullet holes in the adobe walls and wooden counters.

Despite the violence, Montes went ahead with a banquet he had planned for several visiting dignitaries, including Sonoran deputy Ricardo Topete, a leading campaign strategist for Obregón, and Ursulo Galván, an important agrarian leader from Veracruz. They gathered in the dining hall of Montes's new hacienda to discuss ways to promote their candidate, while a band of musicians played in the background. At one point the dinner was interrupted when a squad of federal soldiers showed up, claiming they had orders to search the place for weapons. Finding nothing untoward, they departed, followed shortly thereafter by the dignitaries.

At about 6 p.m., Montes and two assistants mounted their horses and headed for El Moral, where they planned to oversee the closing ceremonies of their agrarista congress. One of Montes's assistants barely had time to notice a group of some twenty men, apparently wearing federal army uniforms, crouched in the undergrowth some three hundred yards distant. The assistant ran off through the cornfields and was not pursued. Montes made a dash for his house in hopes of escaping through the back, but another group of attackers — dressed as workmen — waited on the other side. The shots rained in from every direction, and though Montes managed a few shots from his pistol, there was no escape. Hit in the neck and the left side, he toppled from his horse and was probably dead before he landed in the dirt of his own field — muddy from the recent rains, furrowed and sown with yet another season's planting.[104]

Epilogue

OR SEVERAL DAYS after the killing of Manuel P. Montes, San Martín Texmelucan lay under something like a state of siege. Merchants closed their doors for fear of agrarista reprisals, and citizens remained nervously indoors, leaving the streets, plaza, and marketplace deserted.

Some three thousand mourners attended Montes's funeral in El Moral. Three bands played, and a series of orators urged the people to carry their agrarian struggle forward and to exact a fitting revenge against their leader's killers. When Montes's coffin was lowered into the earth, agraristas gathered around and extended their right arms over the open grave, swearing solemnly to maintain their ideals until they triumphed.[1]

Leaders of the National Agrarian Party pondered the problem of succession to the leadership of the Domingo Arenas Confederation (which in 1926 had become the State Peasant League, linked with the Communist National Peasant League). They wanted a reliable representative in the vital Texmelucan region, but they no doubt were leery of another Manuel Montes — charismatic, but also ruthless, ambitious, and not readily controlled. In the end, the national leaders, represented by the Veracruzano Ursulo Galván, gave the nod to General Montes's sixteen-year-old son, Antonio. "Compañero," they told him, "we have confidence in you. Never betray us."[2]

Now well-advanced in years, Antonio Montes is still the key figure in agrarian politics in the region, a loyal — if occasionally irascible — representative of Mexico's longtime ruling Institutional Revolutionary Party.

Octavio Paz (father of the poet) was sent by the National Agrarian Party to investigate the killing of Montes. The general opinion, Paz reported, was that the deed had been ordered by the new governor, Donato Bravo Izquierdo. Paz found that plausible enough, for Bravo Izquierdo was renowned for brutality. Paz himself claimed to have seen him order the executions of some forty young people in the main square of Ixtapa de Sal, Chiapas, some years earlier.[3] Bravo Izquierdo became an even more plausible suspect when, in the following days, his government publicized some very convenient evidence discrediting Montes, including signed affidavits from local villagers declaring that Montes had planned to rally his forces for a march on Puebla, where he would retake the state government by force.[4] Bravo Izquierdo floated several tentative versions of the events before settling on the one that would become official — a version that described a simple feud, something beneath politics. At the banquet on the hacienda San Miguel Lardizábal, he claimed, Montes and his partisans had imbibed enough pulque to impair their judgment and impel them to reckless action. The hacienda, as it happened, was located only a short distance from the El Carmen textile plant, and Montes and his companions, recalling their rivalry with the workers of that plant, decided the time was ripe for revenge. They attacked a group of workers; federal troops intervened; Montes was hit in the crossfire.[5]

The Mexican Communist Party, which had backed Montes in his bid to take over the local textile industry, located responsibility for the murder higher up, however. "The assassination of Montes," they charged, "is an act premeditated and plotted among reactionary and laborista elements, in connivance with federal forces. The Communist Party blames the death of Montes on the divisive policy of Luis N. Morones, who has made possible the reestablishment of the reaction in Puebla, where currently revolutionary campesinos who struggle for land and social emancipation are being assassinated."[6]

Montes's daughter, who still lives in San Martín Texmelucan, places the blame higher still, claiming that the assassination was ordered by President Calles himself in reprisal for Montes's work on behalf of Calles's rival, Alvaro Obregón.[7]

In the end, it matters little who gave the order. The fact remains that Montes was a leader who had outlived his time. Calles had no use for mavericks: he wanted organization men, the kind whose ambitions could be contained within an institutional structure, not those who were prepared to smash every cog in the political machinery in order to realize their ideals or for personal aggrandizement. When Obregón himself (once again president elect) fell to an assassin's bullet in the summer of 1928, Calles declared that he was to be the "last caudillo": these caudillos — personalist leaders — had long obstructed the "peaceful, evolutionary development of Mexico as a country of institutions, [one] in which men are mere accidents . . . of no real importance next to the perpetual and august serenity of institutions and laws."[8]

General Donato Bravo Izquierdo. *Credit:* Gustavo
Casasola, *Historia gráfica de la Revolución Mexicana,*
1900–1970, 2d ed. (Mexico City: Editorial Trillas, S.A.
de C.V., 1973).

Even José María Sánchez grew tame in the wake of the assassination of Obregón, his longtime *compadre*. He was among those who pleaded with Calles not to retire to private life, which, he warned, would leave Mexico without "an able pilot with a virile hand and sure control of the ship."[9] In October of 1929, he bought the hacienda Santo Domingo Ciénega Honda, in the jurisdiction of Huejotzingo, from the heirs of Marcelino Presno. Soon enough, tensions arose between himself and the villagers he had once claimed to represent. He complained to the state and national agrarian commissions that villagers were trespassing on his property, and the villagers, in turn, accused him of abusing his field hands and generally behaving very much like any hacendado of the old school.[10] He died in 1959.

The trial of the suspects in the murder of Rosalie Evans moved along in a desultory way. The defense lawyers' appeal at the end of 1924, which maintained that they had not had adequate time to prepare their case, was denied by the state supreme court but granted by a federal court. The case eventually found its way to the federal Supreme Court, whose decision was still pending in the spring of 1926 according to the last available word on the subject. "You will see, therefore," wrote U.S. vice-consul William O. Jenkins to the U.S. consul general, "that this case may be drawn out for an almost indefinite time."[11]

Jenkins was prophetic, for if the case was ever concluded there appears to be no record of it. When asked whatever became of the defendants, the villagers of the region maintain that they were taken from their jail cells and executed by the Montistas, apparently acting on their own account. "They killed them like dogs," said a villager from San Jerónimo Tianguismanalco.[12]

This story is probably true. In 1927, the national newspaper *Excélsior* claimed that Francisco Ruiz and Alejo García, two key suspects and the defendants in the trials, had been executed only a few days after the crime. Although that information was obviously inexact, it appears nevertheless to be true that by 1927 Ruiz and García were no longer among the quick, and no one seemed to know quite what had become of them. The third individual accused of the Evans murder, Francisco Pérez, had remained at large for many months. From time to time, the papers would report that Pérez had been captured, only later to retract the information. "Francisco Pérez" is hardly an exotic appellation in the region, and most of the men captured would later be revealed as innocent parties who just happened to have the same name. Then, in August of 1927, a corpse was found very near the spot where Manuel Montes had just been killed, and the dead man was identified as the very Francisco Pérez who had been implicated in the death of Rosalie Evans. According to *Excélsior*, Pérez had been mysteriously taken from the state penitentiary and killed execution style, although the report did not explain how he came to be in the penitentiary in the first place. The report added extra layers to the mystery by claiming that an unnamed lawyer—according to the newspaper, the only who had known the real secret of the Rosalie Evans murder apart from Pérez—had disappeared some months earlier without a trace.[13] Although the report, of course, may well be the newspaper's attempt to mold melodrama out of chaos, it was accurate enough in implying that any dark secrets would never come to light. María Alba Pastor, now a professor at Mexico's National University, interviewed one of the men whose names appeared on Rosalie Evans's list of likely assassins. The man denied any knowledge of the murder, although Professor Pastor remarked that he seemed rather uncomfortable and evasive on the topic.[14]

In subsequent years, the cynics and naysayers who said that the ejidos were doomed to fail found ample evidence to bear out their predictions. The Mexican countryside is still filled with frustration, repression, and violence. The presumed purpose of the agrarian reform—to transform a majority of the population from a socially and economically marginalized sector into a full participant in society's wealth and power—was, by almost any standard, not realized.[15] The centuries-old debate on the proper attitude toward indigenous people—benign neglect, special protection, full assimilation—remains unresolved nearly five centuries after the conquest.

The failure of the reform, of course, was not caused by any inherent ineptitude of the indigenous peoples. The more conservative critics of the agrarian reform were apt to forget that the prerevolutionary agricultural economy in central Mexico was itself badly distorted. They tended to essentialize the land, thus joining with the agrarian propagandist in reducing it to the sort of panacea it plainly could never be. Nor have more recent analysts of agrarian reform abandoned the notion that land is everything. For example, one recent writer maintains that "in an agrarian society, land reform is a revolutionary act because it redistributes the major source of wealth, social standing, and political power."[16] However valid this argument may be as a general proposition, the case of the Puebla-Tlaxcala Valley may present an important exception: an essentially agrarian society in which land was *not* the major source of wealth, social standing, and political power. For this valley, in fact, the writer's argument should be inverted: wealth, social standing, and political power were what made participation in agriculture possible and profitable. Structural and ecological factors forced Mexican wheat growers to rely on protective tariffs, generous tax breaks, and above all cheap labor, for their economic survival. In order to obtain such benefits, they needed to have considerable clout from the outset.

Distribution of the land did nothing at all to address the problems inherent in Mexican wheat agriculture. Indeed, during the 1920s the structural difficulties merely worsened with the worldwide wheat glut that foreshadowed the Great

Depression. Distributing land meant redistributing the problems it entailed, but without major restructuring, it did little to set right the power imbalance. From the outset, the villagers of the Texmelucan Valley who had received hacienda lands discovered that they had also inherited the headaches that had plagued the valley's older hacendados: lack of credit and technology, lack of competitive advantage in basic grain production, and an underdeveloped market.

To be sure, there is ample reason to believe that the rural folk of the Puebla-Tlaxcala Valley were well aware that land reform would be no panacea, which was one of the reasons for the bitter factionalism of the postrevolutionary years. To be sure, this valley was among the Mexican regions where the agrarian problem was most severe. Alan Knight has categorized it as a region of "primary" agrarian reform—that is, one where popular demand for land was genuinely "bottom up"—as opposed to "secondary," where demand for land was minimal and where land reform was more or less foisted upon a recalcitrant peasantry for political purposes.[17] The distinction is useful, but it should not be overdrawn. Even in primary regions, seamless solidarity was hardly the order of the day. The agrarian reform was a trauma that left lasting scars. Many villagers opposed the agrarian reform quite strenuously for many reasons, not all of which hinged on entirely rational calculations. The psychological effects of generations of marginalization, abuse, and degradation on the village populations practically ensured that agrarian reform would be a bitter affair. Some villagers, unable to overcome the fears and suspicions acquired during long years as hacienda peons and preferring a secure if exiguous paycheck to uncertain promises, rejected the agrarian reform in favor of the safe posture of patient fatalism. Others, in common with their fellows in other parts of Mexico, held a jaundiced view of nearly anything the federal government promised to do for them.[18] For still others, agrarian reform seemed to hold out great promise of sudden wealth and power, a promise that sparked a brutal struggle wherein the more sheepish society members were seen either as a force to be harnessed or an obstacle to be crushed. In these circumstances, neutrality could be difficult, dangerous, and perhaps impossible. The agrarian reform also accentuated existing class antagonisms in village society—between jornaleros, *medieros* (sharecroppers), fraccionistas, factory workers, and merchants. Motivation for collaborating with or resisting the agrarian reform were complex, but once under way feuds could be durable and self-perpetuating.

The intense factionalism of the early agrarian reform was not eliminated by institutionalization, either. Rather, it was channeled into a byzantine agrarian bureaucracy that linked community, municipality, region, state, and nation into a single complex organism within the larger organism of the official ruling party. The ejidal bureaucracy became a breeding ground for ambition, greed, corruption, and ongoing factionalism. Ejidal leaders were often less interested in serving the interests of their constituents than in jockeying for position within the bureaucracy. Success in that bureaucracy entailed advocacy not of agrarian interests as a whole, but of the interests of a particular agrarian faction against all other factions. Solidarity within the ejidal sector would have been a minimum prerequisite for success in the unforgiving world of postrevolutionary Mexican agriculture, but solidarity was a pipe dream.[19]

The agrarian reform was damaged from the outset by the fact that it was undertaken by a national state that had yet to stabilize itself, one that had neither the will nor the means to do a creditable job of it. The Sonorans who took up the reins of national government in the wake of the revolution were ambiguous in their attitudes toward agrarian reform. Generally, they would have preferred hardy individuals with ready capital who could make the deserts bloom with enough produce to feed an urban, industrial, and thoroughly modern population. Agrarian reform was thus an expedient that they undertook without conviction, its only real purposes being to placate wrought up passions and to cultivate the gratitude and dependence of the beneficiaries. Ironically, most of what Rosalie Evans saw as evidence of the virtual omnipotence of the central government was, in fact, evidence of precisely the opposite. The debility of the central government obliged it to constitute itself as a faction among factions and to play the intricate game of undercutting rivals and bolstering friends with a view to asserting its own dominance. It was a difficult game to play: it involved placating foreigners, taming a fractious military, combating centripetal forces in the states even while appearing to respect state sovereignty, and all the while attempting to satisfy at least some of the vaunted promises of the revolution. It appeared to Rosalie Evans that President Obregón had a hand in nearly everything precisely because he *did* have a hand in nearly everything. It was not, however, the deft hand of a puppet master in perfect control, but rather the hand of a skilled machinator who was prepared to do whatever it might take — from issuing imperious decrees to engaging in the basest subterfuge — to assert some measure of control. If Obregón had possessed the sort of power Mrs. Evans imagined, he would have had no need to interfere personally in so many local struggles. A successful agrarian reform would have demanded a central government with a strong commitment and the effective tools — particularly an obedient military and an independent judiciary — to carry it out. The Mexican agrarian reform lacked these ingredients.

The agrarian reform also suffered from the opposition of foreigners. In the United States and Great Britain, the dominant players in the 1920s gave short shrift to agriculture, preferring more glamorous sectors such as petroleum, industry, communications, and infrastructure. A vociferous political subcurrent, however, took violent exception to any compromise of individual private property and figured always as at least a potential threat. Mexico's real economic importance to Great Britain was minimal, but for some it became a kind of test case: if British property rights could be violated in Mexico, it would set a dangerous precedent for radicals in more vital regions. It was, in short, a place to assert British prestige and, with luck, send a message to the rest of the world that Britain was not to be trifled with. In the wake of the First World War, Great Britain had little power to act autonomously in the Western Hemisphere, but British hardliners did not merely resign themselves to a feckless role. Rather, they fashioned the case of Mrs. Evans into a bit of theater designed to pressure the United States to act decisively. Their attitude gave Mexico's leaders one more reason for approaching the agrarian issue with trepidation.

Finally, the agrarian reform was undone by the shift in the global equation that came with the Second World War. The Mexican governing elite — which had long concurred with the dictum that "a central distinguishing characteristic of economic backwardness is an unresolved agrarian question"[20] — conceived the idea that the best solution to the agrarian question would be to leap right over the top of it and into industrial prosperity. With the United States distracted and the world economy stimulated by the war, Mexican leaders saw an opening and began to retool for an industrial future.

Few areas felt the impact of that shift more profoundly than the Texmelucan Valley of Puebla, for the region nearly fulfilled the planners' every wish: it had a relatively abundant water supply, ready access to two major urban centers, and an ample surplus population. The only thing lacking was a modern transportation and communication system, a project tackled during the 1940s with the construction of an airfield and during the 1950s with the construction of the Mexico City–Puebla superhighway. Lands that had been won at considerable cost by the villagers were now reexpropriated by the government on the grounds of "public utility." A paper factory was built, then a methanol plant, then an electric generator. In 1971, the federal government decreed the expropriation of two kilometers on either side of the highway from San Martín to Puebla for the purpose of forming an "industrial corridor." President Luis Echeverría tried to calm the howls of protest that arose in response: "The agrarian communities," he assured them, "must not be victims of our urban development." On the contrary, he promised that the local people would receive "adequate and opportune" indemnization and full protection of their rights as citizens. More importantly, he predicted that the villagers — especially women and young people — would find employment in the new industries.

Echeverría's promises and predictions offered small comfort to many who had lost lands to the superhighway and earlier industries without receiving either work or indemnities. The most compelling argument the federal government had to offer the campesinos, however, was simply that there was no other alternative. Mexico City had seen an unprecedented and unparalleled demographic explosion, as people fled the grinding poverty of the countryside for the brighter promise of the big city, which was fast becoming all but unmanageable. Decentralizing industry by focusing on regions like the San Martín Valley might take some of the pressure off of the capital.

Water — once among the Texmelucan Valley's most attractive assets — grew scarce. As thirsty factories and thirstier cities vied for the prized resource, the needs of agriculture were practically forgotten.[21] Industrial pollutants found their way into the dwindling supply of water, poisoning the once fertile fields. Farmers, for want of resources and markets, left off growing wheat, reduced their plantings of corn, and took to growing whatever they could sell — alfalfa for fodder, artichokes and parsley for foreign dinner tables, flowers for decorating on the Day of the Dead. Response to the wave of official expropriations once again divided communities, and organized resistance was notably unsuccessful.[22] During the 1980s, federal investment in agricultural development fell by 70 percent, and at the end of 1991 President Carlos Salinas de Gortari proposed a controversial bill — subsequently approved — that effectively ended Mexico's long, dramatic experiment in agrarian reform.[23]

The campesinos no longer wear the little breeches and wide-brimmed hats that they wore in Rosalie Evans's day. They do, however, still wear their huaraches — crude sandals with leather straps, though these days they are soled with rubber from old automobile tires. Their feet and hands and faces are still leathery and dried from a long and intimate acquaintance with the elements. Many still affix thumbprints in place of signatures on documents of protest, and many still seem to waver between abject fatalism and explosive anger. Their villages are still composed of squat adobe or cement-block huts, unpaved streets marred by rocks and craters and waste, and a homely little church at the center. Were she alive today, Rosalie Evans would see much that was familiar and little to admire.

The changes for the campesinsos were subtle, but important. The experience of the revolution gave them a measure of pride and self-reliance they had not previously had. "Our ancestors," said one elderly campesino in 1992, "were more martyrs than we are [eran más mártires que nosotros]."[24] In a makeshift newspaper called *El Campesino en Acción* ("The Peasant in Action"), militant villagers in the 1970s protested the "industrial corridor" with a long look back at history: "At the start of the Colony," they claimed,

> the powerful told the civilized world that [in America] there were creatures who looked like men, but they did not deserve respect; but they were answered that these creatures were indeed men, and they did deserve respect. So say the historians and the story books.

At the height of European domination, the *encomenderos* promised to care for the souls of the natives in exchange for the LAND and other things of the sort. A little later they said to the Mexicans born in these lands: YOU WERE BORN TO WORK AND TO OBEY. So say the historians, and we are the inheritors of this abjection.

But all this has now passed. It was for this reason that we made our Revolution of Independence, [declaring] that RESPECT FOR THE RIGHTS OF OTHERS IS PEACE, and [taking up] the slogan LAND AND LIBERTY of General Zapata and the Madero Revolution.[25]

Like a litany, the document repeated the assertion that the days of misery and abjection were supposed to be over. Now more than ever, the villagers seemed to say, their government stood in dire need of a reminder.

The haciendas of the region are now largely in ruins, and most of the few exceptions serve as resorts for the well-to-do. San Pedro Coxtocán is among the exceptions. Daisy Pettus struggled for years to sell the hacienda for a price that would stand as a "monument to my sister's efforts."[26] That struggle cost her dearly: she spent at least $10,000 merely to finance her lawyer's several trips to Mexico and thousands more on taxes and miscellaneous expenses. "Curiously enough," she recalled years later, "I do not regret it. I was so angry at the time, I had to exhaust every effort to get justice."[27] She never did get "justice," at least not of any tangible sort. Sometime during the 1930s, she was obliged to turn the matter of the hacienda's expropriated lands over the the Mexican-American Mixed Claims Commission — the very course Ambassador Warren had suggested to Rosalie Evans back in 1924. In 1945, the claims commission set the value of the seized lands at $46,988. Daisy Pettus never saw any of the money: the first installment arrived on December 17, 1945, ten months after her death. The government sold what remained of the "ex-hacienda" San Pedro Coxtocán — its buildings and a little land — for $65,000 in 1947. Daisy's heir, her husband Jerdone, died that same year at the age of 85.[28]

After that, the ex-hacienda passed from hand to hand until 1956, when it was bought by Justo Fernández, a wealthy coffee planter who at considerable cost restored the ruined buildings and gardens to their former opulence. Thoroughbred racehorses now graze on what is left of the estate's land.[29]

In the light of all these developments, some might be tempted to dismiss Rosalie Evans's passionate struggle as essentially irrelevant. She routinely contrasted her difficulties to a presumed golden age, the Porfiriato, when the farms were bountiful and society glamorous. That roseate vision was belied by the Porfirian hacendados themselves, who complained incessantly of bad workers and meager markets, and of how such blessings as capital and technology were monopolized by a fortunate few. It was undercut even more by the harrowing images of gaunt and weary workers who gathered in the predawn hours to sing the "Alabada," then worked till dusk with little nourishment or remuneration. Only one with blinders securely in place could claim this situation was idyllic, just as only the most zealous apologist or ideologue could maintain that the agrarian reform was a smashing success.

At first glance, then, it appears that Katherine Anne Porter was right: Rosalie Evans's tenacious struggle was aimed at preserving her place of privilege in a grotesquely unjust order; all her rantings about civilization and fairness served to mask a naked struggle for power and money. This view needs at least to be qualified, however. In a draft of her introduction to *The Rosalie Evans Letters,* Daisy Pettus belabored an oddly apt analogy. To those who said Rosalie Evans should have saved herself trouble by taking what she could and getting out, Daisy replied: "So could the United States have avoided trouble with Germany by not resenting the sinking of the Lusitania nor the submarine warfare. So could France have avoided trouble by not defending herself after the violation of Belgium. It was not in my sister's nature to run away from injustice and danger, but to meet conditions as they arose, valiantly, face to face."[30]

These observations never appeared in the book, most likely because they smacked too much of preaching to the converted: readers who viewed Mrs. Evans unsympathetically were likely the same ones who blamed World War I on a conspiracy of Wall Street bankers and munitions makers. Daisy's point is worth considering, however, for Rosalie Evans was a creature out of her time. Her sentiments were molded in a prewar world where privilege and virtue seemed indistinguishable and where humanity had not yet gained, in Barbara Tuchman's words, such "a painful view of its own limitations."[31] Her struggle, then, was by no means simply for power and money. Had they been her main interest, she might well have followed the lead of men like William O. Jenkins, an American of acute intuition and few scruples who quietly emerged from the Mexican revolution with vastly increased wealth and power. Money alone could hardly have roused Rosalie Evans to extremes of ruthlessness and pertinacity. To many bemused observers, her behavior seemed as odd as Mexico itself, a land where categories were fluid enough to turn a gentlewoman into an outlaw. She found her meaning in the symbolism of Manichaean struggle, admitting no compromise or hypocrisy. In a review of her letters, Carleton Beals observed that "given a different background and training," she might even have been another Manuel Montes, her equally determined and intransigent antagonist.[32] Much as Mrs. Evans would have objected, the comparison is apt. They both aimed, as she put it, to "strike a blow for San Pedro and all the world holds worth having."[33]

Appendix 1

The Partitioning of San Pedro Coxtocán

The 1,085 hectares of the hacienda San Pedro Coxtocán were divided among four villages in differing quantities and at different times. Information from the following tables, it should be noted, is not entirely reliable. The population figures are taken from agrarian inspections carried out at the start of the agrarian reform. Investigators were sent out with instructions to find out the occupational distribution of the villagers, but were seldom precise in doing so—almost invariably declaring that "all" or "nearly all" of the villagers worked in agriculture, that only a handful of villagers had land of their own, and that the remainder worked as *jornaleros, medieros* (sharecroppers), or *aparceros* (tenant farmers). These "findings" were a matter of heated dispute, for the hacendados repeatedly claimed that agriculturalists were a minority of the inhabitants of any given village. For example, Ricardo García, the inspector who visited Santa María Moyotzingo in January of 1918, declared categorically that all of the villagers were farmers, "serving for the most part as *jornaleros* on the nearby haciendas." The hacendado Marcelino Presno insisted that fully one-third of the villagers worked as muleteers and merchants or had other nonagricultural occupations. Mrs. Evans's lawyer, Salvador Cancino, claimed an even higher percentage. The hacendados and their lawyers also hotly disputed the inspectors' figures regarding the amount of land already owned by the villages, insisting (usually vaguely) that they had more than enough land for their needs. In any case, the following figures are taken from inspectors' reports and presidential resolutions, and should be treated with some caution.

San Jerónimo Tianguismanalco

Population, c. 1917:	616 (158 families), nearly all in agriculture
Amount of land owned, 1917:	17 hectares
Original petition:	April 2, 1917
Governor's approval:	January 10, 1918
Presidential resolution:	November 9, 1922
Published in *Diario Oficial*:	January 22, 1923
Land granted from San Pedro:	44.3 hectares (approx. 109.5 acres)
Total land grant:	237 hectares
Other haciendas affected:	San Jerónimo Tepoxtla, San Francisco Coxtocán, Mendocinas

San Francisco Tepeyecac

Population, c. 1917:	111 families, nearly all in agriculture
Amount of land owned, 1917:	4.5 hectares, by several villagers
Original petition:	May 7, 1917
Governor's approval:	June 25, 1920
Presidential resolution:	November 9, 1922
Published in *Diario Oficial*:	January 22, 1923
Land granted from San Pedro:	100.4 hectares (approx. 248 acres)
Total land grant:	166.5
Other haciendas affected:	San Francisco Coxtocán

Santa María Moyotzingo

Population, c. 1917:	1,825 (470 families), all in agriculture
Amount of land owned, 1917:	222 hectares "owned by only a few villagers"
Original petition:	May 28, 1917
Governor's approval:	April 14, 1920
Presidential resolution:	November 27, 1920
Published in *Diario Oficial*:	January 14, 1921
Land granted from San Pedro:	641.67 hectares (approx. 1,585.5 acres)
Total land granted:	1,658 hectares
Other haciendas affected:	San Bartolo Granillo, San Jerónimo Tepoxtla

San Mateo Capultitlán

Population, c. 1917:	433 (134 families), all in agriculture
Amount of land owned, 1917:	"a few small properties"

Original petition: February 4, 1915
Governor's approval: August 31, 1923
Presidential resolution: February 29, 1929
Published in *Diario Oficial*:   April 20, 1929
Land granted from San Pedro: 174.7 hectares (approx. 431.6 acres)
Total land granted: 268 hectares
Other haciendas affected: San Mateo Xopanac

Appendix 2

The Revolutionary Governors of Puebla, to 1930

1911   Lic. Nicolas Meléndez
       Lic. Rafael Isunza
       Lic. Rafael P. Cañete

1913   General Joaquin Mass
       Lic. Juan B. Carrasco

1914   General Juan Hernández
       General Rafael Espinoza
       General Francisco Coss

1915   Dr. Luis G. Cervantes

1916   General Cesareo Castro

1917   Dr. Alfonso Cabrera

1920   General Rafael Rojas
       Lic. Luis Sánchez Pontón

1921   Lic. Claudio N. Tirado
       Roberto Labastida
       General José María Sánchez

1922   Prof. Froylán C. Manjarrez

1923   Vicente Lombardo Toledano
       Francisco Espinosa Fleury

1924   General Alberto Guerrero

1925   Lic. Arturo Osorio
       Lic. Wenceslao Macip

1926   General Manuel P. Montes

1927   General Donato Bravo Izquierdo

1929   Dr. Leonides Andreu Almazán

Notes

INTRODUCTION

Unless otherwise noted English translations of Spanish quotes are my own.

1 Quoted in John Duncan Powell, *Political Mobilization of the Venezuelan Peasant* (Cambridge: Harvard University Press, 1971), 2.

2 See, for example, the profiles of Zapatista leaders in Aquiles Chiu, "Peones y campesinos Zapatistas," in *Emiliano Zapata y el movimiento zapatista* (Mexico City: INAH, 1980): 119–153.

3 Cf. Sidney Mintz, "The Rural Proletariat and the Problem of Rural Proletarian Consciousness," *Journal of Peasant Studies* 1.3 (April 1974): 293.

4 Mariano Azuela, *The Underdogs: A Novel of the Mexican Revolution,* trans. E. Munguía Jr. (New York: New American Library, 1963), 31.

PROLOGUE

1 Trans. Walter Kaufman (New York: Anchor, 1963).

2 The dream is described in Rosalie Evans to Daisy Pettus, Mar. 28, 1917, and Rosalie to Harry Evans, n.d. (Mar.? 1917), Rosalie Evans Papers (REP), Alderman Library, University of Virginia, box 1, "Correspondence" folder. This collection has been extensively rearranged since I did my research in the early 1990s. Future researchers can consult an excellent new finding aid there should they wish to see any REP item referenced in this book.

3 Rosalie to Harry Evans, n.d.; Rosalie Evans to Daisy Pettus, Mar. 28, 1917; Harry to Rosalie, Oct. 11, 1917; Rosalie to Harry, n.d.; Rosalie to Harry, Nov. 22, 1917. All in REP, box 1,"Correspondence" folder.

4 Sir Oliver Lodge, *Raymond, or, Life and Death* (London: Metheun, 1916).

5 Preceding quotations from Rosalie Evans diary, Dec. 4, 1917–Jan. 7, 1918, entries for Dec. 4, 9, 14, 1917, REP, box 3.

1 Rosalie Evans, *The Rosalie Evans Letters from Mexico* (Indianapolis: Bobbs-Merrill, 1926), 30–31.

2 Henry Evans is listed as superintendant of locomotives for that railway in the *Memoria de la Secretaría de Fomento, Industria y Comercio de la República Mexicana,* vol. 3 (Mexico City: Oficina Tipográfica de la Secretaría de Fomento, 1885), 365.

3 Evans's certificate of apprenticeship to Thomas Francis of Bristol, Manchester, and General Warehouseman, 1885. Evans completed his term in March 1890 "with credit to himself and with every satisfaction to us." REP, box 2.

4 The circumstances of Rosalie Caden's birth are obscure. In a will she drew up in Mexico in 1918 she claimed to have been born in Brownsville, Texas, in 1882. This information conflicts with every other estimate and is quite unlikely in view of the child's diaries Rosalie kept, which would have her reading the likes of Chateaubriand and Goethe at age four. Her sister claimed she was "about nineteen" when she met Harry Evans in 1896, giving her a birth year of 1877. Some authors have suggested 1875, but do not say where they came by this information. The birthdate of January 6 can be surmised from Evans, *Letters,* 272, in which she refers to January 6 as "my awful natal day."

5 Ray Miller, *Ray Miller's Galveston* (Austin, Tex.: Cordovan, 1983), 108.

6 Evans, *Letters,* 397.

7 Miller, *Ray Miller's Galveston,* 108–141; Gary Cartwright, *Galveston: A History of the Island* (New York: Atheneum, 1991), 144–145.

8 Among such efforts are "To the Great Tree near Atlixco, the River San Baltazar," in REP, box 1; and another inspired by a lunar eclipse of 1900, in Rosalie Evans diary, box 3.

9 Rosalie Evans diary entry, May 11, 1902, REP, box 3.

10 Frisbie's comments are found in the *Texas Journal of Commerce,* Mar. 13, 1880; Grant is quoted in ibid., July 10, 1880. Frisbie's annexationist sentiments are mentioned in David M. Pletcher, *Rails, Mines, and Progress: Seven American Promoters in Mexico, 1867–1911* (Ithaca, N.Y.: Cornell University Press, 1958), 163.

11 On the trade in hides, see Oct. 4, 1885, entry in *Memoria de la Secretaría de Fomento,* 3: 56–58.

12 Florence Caden to Rosalie Caden, June 25 and June 29, 1896. REP, box 1, "Correspondence, 1895" folder.

13 Florence Caden to Charlotte Brookes Caden, Aug. 7, 1893, REP, box 1, "Correspondence 1893" folder.

14 Florence Caden to Rosalie Caden, Oct. 6, 1895, REP, box 1; Florence to Rosalie, n.d., REP, box 2, "Misc" folder.

15 Fairfax Harrison to Hetty C. Harrison, July 20, 1896, Fairfax Harrison Papers, Virginia Historical Society. Harrison was a lawyer for the Southern Railway.

16 Harry's promotion is mentioned in J. R. Southworth, *El Estado de Puebla* (Puebla: n.p., 1901), 58. Details on the move to Puebla and on the wedding are mentioned in Rosalie Evans diary, May 16, 1902, REP, box 3.

17 Harry's geological interests are mentioned in Juan Enrique Palacios, *Puebla: su territorio y sus habitantes,* vol. 1 (Puebla: Junta de Mejoramiento Moral, Cívico y Material del Municipio de Puebla, 1982; originally published 1917), 49.

18 Diary of European trip, entry for Nov. 7, 1911, REP, box 1.

19 Rosalie to Harry Evans, Nov. 23, 1917, REP, box 1.

20 "Henri" to Florence Caden, Oct. 6, 1898, REP, box 1.

21 Rosalie Evans diary entry, Feb. 2, 1901, REP, box 3.

22 Rosalie to Harry Evans, Oct. 4, 1903, REP, box 1.

23 Related in Harry to Rosalie Evans, Nov. 7, 1904, REP, box 1.

24 Notes made by Rosalie Evans, July 16, 1918, on a letter from Florence Caden to Rosalie Caden, Oct. 6, 1895, REP, box 1.

25 Rosalie to Harry Evans, Jan. 4, 1904, REP, box 1.

26 Harry to Rosalie Evans, Nov. 7, 1904, REP, box 1.

27 Harry to Rosalie Evans, Nov. 8, 1904, REP, box 1.

28 Rosalie to Harry Evans, Jan. 25, 1905, REP, box 1.

29 George Camp to Ambassador James Sheffield, Mar. 5, 1925, REP, box 6.

30 Evans, *Letters,* 77.

31 Percy F. Martin, *Mexico of the Twentieth Century,* 2 vols. (New York: Dodd, Mead, 1908), 1:13–14.

32 Description based on Luis Vargas Piñeiro, article in *Excélsior,* Aug. 6, 1939, reprinted as a prologue in Porfirio del Castillo, *Puebla y Tlaxcala en los días de la Revolución* (Mexico City: n.p., 1953).

33 Francisco Bulnes, quoted in Ramón Eduardo Ruiz, *The Great Rebellion, 1905–1924* (New York: W. W. Norton, 1980), 27.

34 "Entrevista con el Gral. Brigadier Tiburcio Cuellar Montalvo, realizada por Eugenia Meyer, el día 8 de mayo de 1973, en la Ciudad de México," Archivo de la Palabra/Instituto de Investigaciones Dr. José María Luis Mora, Mexico City, Proyecto de Historia Oral (PHO)/1/45.

35 Quoted in David G. LaFrance, *The Mexican Revolution in Puebla, 1908–1913: The Maderista Movement and the Failure of Liberal Reform* (Wilmington, Del.: Scholarly Resources, 1989), xxxii–xxxiv. See also "Entrevista con Sr. Luis Sánchez Pontón, realizada por Daniel Cazes, en abril de 1961 en la Ciudad de México," Archivo de la Palabra/Instituto de Investigaciones Dr. José María Luis Mora, Mexico City, PHO/1/20.

36 "Entrevista al Sr. Máximo Flores, realizada por María Alba Pastor, el día 14 de junio de 1974, en San Martín Texmelucan," Estado de Puebla Archivo de la Palabra/Instituto de Investigaciones Dr. José María Luis Mora, Mexico City, PHO/1/140.

37 On the Santa Fé rebellion, see Arturo Obregón, *Alberto Santa Fé y la Ley del Pueblo, 1878–1879* (Mexico City: Centro de Estudios Históricos del Movimiento Obrero Mexicano, 1980), and Leticia Reina, *Las rebeliones campesinas en México (1819–1906)* (Mexico City: Siglo XXI, 1980). Santa Fé's own account of the repression following his rebellion can be found in "Carta abierta del socialista Alberto Santa Fé," reprinted in L. Chávez Orozco, *Documentos para la historia económica de México,* vol. 10: *Orígenes del agrarismo en México* (Mexico City: Secretaría de la Economía Nacional, 1936), 39–42. On Serdán Guanes, see Manuel Frías Olvera, *Historia de la Revolución Mexicana en el Estado de Puebla* (Mexico City: Instituto Nacional de Estudios Históricos de la Revolución Mexicana, 1980), 62. On Aquiles Serdán — his antecedents and ideology — see LaFrance, *Mexican Revolution in Puebla,* 5–8.

38. Del Castillo, *Puebla y Tlaxcala,* 38.

CHAPTER TWO

1 Manuel de la Peña, "El rendimiento económico del trabajo del peón," *Boletín de la Sociedad Agrícola Mexicana (BSAM)* 30.37 (Oct. 1, 1906): 727–728.

2 Harry Evans to Rosalie Caden, Sept. 5, 1898, REP, box 2.

3 "A Vision of Mitla," REP, box 2.

4 J. J. Aubertin, *A Flight to Mexico* (London: Kegan Paul, Trench, and Co., 1892), 182.

5 "The White Man's Burden-Bearer," in *Mexico: The Wonderland of the South* (New York: MacMillan, 1909), 184–197.

6 Some venerable statements on the Latin American peasant include those made by George M. Foster, "Peasant Society and the Image of Limited Good," *American Anthropologia* 67.2 (Apr. 1964): 293–315; and his *Tzintzuntzan: Mexican Peasants in a Changing World* (Boston: Little, Brown, 1967); Andrew Pearse, *The Latin American Peasant* (Pall Mall, 1970); Gerrit Huizer, *The Revolutionary Potential of Peasants in Latin America* (Lexington, Mass.: Lexington Books, 1972), esp. 7–69; Peter Singelmann, *Structures of Domination and Peasant Movements in Latin America* (Columbia: University of Missouri Press, 1981); and Paul Friedrich, *Agrarian Revolt in a Mexican Village* (Chicago: University of Chicago Press, 1977) and his *The Princes of Naranja: An Essay in Anthrohistorical Method* (Austin: University of Texas Press, 1986). For more recent commentary, see Florencia E. Mallon, *Peasant and Nation: The Making of Postcolonial Mexico and Peru* (Berkeley and Los Angeles: University of California Press, 1995).

7 *The Eighteenth Brumaire of Louis Bonaparte,* ed. C. P. Dutt (New York: International Publishers, 1963), 15.

8 See, for example, Mario Ramírez Rancaño, "Despojo de tierras, colonias agrícolas y reforma agraria en Tlaxcala," in *México en los años 20: procesos políticos y reconstrucción económica,* ed. Mario Cerutti (Nuevo León: Universidad Autónoma de Nuevo León, 1993), 305. This study of land tenure in southern Tlaxcala indicates that of 125 petitions for land submitted during the agrarian reform, thirty-seven claimed *despojo,* or despoilment, by the haciendas. However, all but four of these cases took place during the sixteenth or seventeenth centuries.

9 Sonya Lipsett-Rivera, "Indigenous Communities and Water Rights in Colonial Puebla: Patterns of Resistance," *Americas* 47.4 (Apr. 1992), 463–483; Hanns J. Prem, "El Río Cotzala: estudio histórico de un sistema de riego," *Comunicaciones* 11 (1974): 53–76, and his "Los afluentes del Río Xopanac," *Comunicaciones* 12 (1975): 27–46.

10 See, for example, James Lockhart and Enrique Otte, *Letters and Peoples of the Spanish Indies: Sixteenth Century* (Cambridge: Cambridge University Press, 1976), 138–143.

11 On population decline, see Günter Vollmer, "El perfil demográfico de Huejotzingo: realidades de la base documental e imponderables de la reconstrucción," *Comunicaciones* 16 (1979): 191–198. On the founding of San Jerónimo Tianguismanalco, see "Testimonio de los autos de composición de tierras de San Jerónimo Tianguismanalco, Nov. 3, 1752," Archivo General de la Nación (AGN) —Tierras, vol. 2693, exp. 2, f. 4.

12 Julia Hirschberg, "Social Experiment in New Spain: A Prosopographical Study of the Early Settlement at Puebla de los Angeles, 1531–1534," *Hispanic American Historical Review* 59.1 (1979): 1–33; Guy P. C. Thomson, *Puebla de los Angeles: Industry and Society in a Mexican City, 1700–1850* (Boulder, Colo.: Westview, 1989), 4–5; François Chevalier, *Land and Society in Colonial Mexico: The Great Hacienda* (Berkeley and Los Angeles:

University of California Press, 1970), 139; Hanns J. Prem, "Early Spanish Colonization and Indians in the Valley of Atlixco, Puebla," in *Explorations in Ethnohistory: Indians of Central Mexico in the Sixteenth Century,* ed. H. R. Harvey and H. J. Prem (Albuquerque: University of New Mexico Press, 1984), 205–228.

13 Hanns J. Prem, *Milpa y hacienda: tenencia de la tierra indígena y española en la cuenca del Alto Atoyac, Puebla, México (1520–1650)* (Mexico City: Fondo de Cultura Económica, 1988), 204–205. Dates on the formation and resale of San Pedro Coxtocán are found in Prem volume, appendix 1, 280.

14 In order to maximize their profits, the sellers set prices by the square yard. The usual price for small lots in 1885 was one to three centavos per square yard. At that rate, one hectare of good quality land would have cost 418 pesos, and an estate the size of San Pedro Coxtocán (1,085 hectares) would have fetched more than 450,000 pesos. That price was high indeed. Harry Evans paid only $200,000 for it in 1906, even though property values in the region had more than doubled since 1885. On the prices of a square yard or square vara, see *Memoria de la Secretaría de Fomento Industria y Comercio de la República* (Mexico City: Oficina Tipográfica de la Secretaría de Fomento), vol. 3, no. 2 (Aug. 1885), 183; vol. 3.8, no. 4 (Oct. 1885), give the average selling price for a *caballería* (42.5 hectares) at $1,500, and the price for irrigated lands from three thousand dollars per caballería to two centavos per vara. On the rise in property values in the region, see Puebla, *Memoria instructiva y documentada del Departamento Ejecutivo del Estado, presentada al XX Congreso Constitucional* (Puebla: n.p., 1909), 125, and Arthur Schmidt, *The Social and Economic Effects of the Railroad in Puebla and Veracruz Mexico, 1867–1911* (New York: Garland, 1987), 79.

15 "Entrevista con el Sr. Bonifacio Reyes Sebastián, realizada por María Alba Pastor, el día 8 de junio de 1974, en San Jerónimo Tianguismanalco, Edo. de Puebla," Mexico City: Archivo de la Palabra/Instituto de Investigaciones Dr. José María Luis Mora, Mexico City, PHO/1/138.

16 See, for example, the comments of Francisco Fernández Ibarra, July 3, 1885, in *Memoria de la Secretaría de Fomento,* 3.1: 104.

17 Mario Ramírez Rancaño, "Un frente patronal a principios del Siglo XX: El Central Industrial Mexicano de Puebla," in *Clases dominantes y estado en México,* ed. Salvador Cordero H. and Ricardo Tirado (Mexico City: UNAM, 1984), 19–45.

18 "Entrevista con el Sr. Bonfacio Reyes Sebastián," p. 4.

19 "Entrevista con el Sr. Luis Sánchez Pontón, realizada por Daniel Cazes, en abril de 1961 en la Ciudad de México," Archivo de la Palabra/Instituto de Investigaciones Dr. José María Luis, Mexico City, PHO/1/20, p. 12.

20 Schmidt, *Social and Economic Effects of the Railroad,* 188–189.

21 "Entrevista con el Sr. Bonifacio Reyes Sebastián"; interview with Ignacio Téllez Escalona, Santa Ana Xalmimilulco, Puebla, Mar. 30, 1992 (T. Henderson).

22 *BSAM* 9.14 (Dec. 16, 1885): 212.

23 Luis Pombó, *México: 1876–1892* (Mexico City: Imprenta de "El Siglo Diez y Nueve," 1893), 136.

24 See figures in Archivo Municipal de San Martín Texmelucan (AMSMT), caja "Documentos del Siglo XIX," leg. "Educación"; and "Entrevista con el Señor Bonifacio Reyes Sebastián," pp. 2, 5.

25 "Entrevista al Sr. Máximo Flores realizada por María Alba Pastor, el día 14 de junio de

1974, en San Martín Texmelucan, Estado de Puebla," Archivo de la Palabra/Instituto de Investigaciones Dr. José María Luis Mora, Mexico City, PHO/1/140, p. 10.

26   Luis Cabrera, "La reconstitución de los ejidos de los pueblos como medio de suprimir la esclavitud del jornalero mexicano," in *Problemas Agrícolas e Industriales de Mexico* 4.2 (Apr.–June 1952), 192–203.

27   For descriptions at midcentury, see especially Alberto Santa Fé, "El fondo de la cuestión: origen de la miseria del pueblo. — El feudalismo. — Los peones," *El Hijo de Trabajo* 3.106 (Aug. 4, 1879). For a good sampling of editorials from the socialist press on the agrarian question, see Luis Chávez Orozco, *Documentos para la historia económica de México,* vol. 10: *Orígenes del agrarismo en México* (Mexico City: Secretaría de la Economía Nacional, 1936).

Much of the information in the chapter paragraphs that follow comes from a series of articles by the progressive hacendado Manuel de la Peña of Querétaro. These are lectures de la Peña delivered at the convention of the Mexican Agricultural Society in 1906, printed in the *BSAM*. The intent of the articles was not so much to rend hearts, as had been the case with the earlier socialist writers, but to explain why the labor of Mexican peons was so unproductive. See de la Peña, "Nuestra agricultura: la despoblación de los campos, 1a parte," *BSAM* 30.30 (Sept. 1, 1906); "2a parte," *BSAM* 30.35 (Sept. 9, 1906), and "3a parte," *BSAM* 30.36 (Sept. 17, 1906); and "El rendimiento económico del trabajo del peón," *BSAM* 30.37 (Oct. 1, 1906).

28   Moisés González Navarro, ed., *Estadísticas económicas del porfiriato: fuerza de trabajo y actividad económica por sectores* (Mexico City: El Colegio de México, 1965), 183.

29   Alberto Paní, cited in Fernando González Roa, *El aspecto agrario de la Revolución Mexicana* (Mexico City: Liga de Economistas Revolucionarios, 1975; originally published 1919), 129.

30   Lic. Martínez Sobral, quoted in ibid., 222.

31   Presidente auxiliar de Atoyatenco to presidente municipal de San Martín Texmelucan, AMSMT, Documentos del Siglo XIX, Ayuntamientos 1909.

32   De la Peña, "El rendimiento económico del trabajo del peón," 725.

33   On this theme, see especially James C. Scott, *Weapons of the Weak: Everyday Forms of Peasant Resistance* (New Haven, Conn.: Yale University Press, 1985), and his *Domination and the Arts of Resistance* (New Haven, Conn.: Yale University Press, 1990).

34   Violent uprisings in the region, although relatively rare, were frequent enough that it would be no exaggeration to say that there was a tradition of resistance. For the later nineteenth century, see the literature on the Santa Fé rebellion, cited in chapter 1. On rebellions during the independence period, see Brian R. Hamnett, *Roots of Insurgency: Mexican Regions, 1750–1824* (Cambridge: Cambridge University Press, 1986).

35   John Hatfield to Ramsay MacDonald, June 24, 1924, Great Britain, Public Records Office, Foreign Office (FO) 371/9565, A3891.

36   Ciro F. S. Cardoso, "La agricultura en la economía mexicana del siglo XIX," *Boletín de Estudios Latinoamericanos y del Caribe* 58 (June 1981): 49–86.

37   Donald J. Fraser, "La política de desamortización en las comunidades indígenas, 1856–1872," *Historia Mexicana* 21.4 (Apr.–June 1972): 631; and T. G. Powell, "Los Liberales, el campesinado indígena y los problemas agrarios durante la Reforma," ibid., 653–675.

38   Quoted in Luis González y González, "El agrarismo liberal," *Historia Mexicana* 7 (July 1957–June 1958): 482.

39 Sir Francis Denys, "The Railways of Mexico," *The Mexican Financier* 14.7 (May 11, 1889).

40 Schmidt, *The Social and Economic Effects,* 165–166.

41 Alfred Tischendorf, *Great Britain and Mexico in the Era of Porfirio Díaz* (Durham, N.C.: Duke University Press, 1961), 42–43.

42 González Roa, *El aspecto agrario,* 246.

43 Puebla, *Memoria instructiva y documentada,* 125; Schmidt, *The Social and Economic Effects,* 79.

44 On the mania to export, see *Informe de la Secretaría de Fomento* núm. 5 (Nov. 1885): 245–246, and González y González, "El agrarismo liberal," 471.

45 González Navarro, *Estadísticas económicas,* 63; Cardoso, "La agricultura," 60, 72.

46 Simon Miller, "Mexican Junkers and Capitalist Haciendas, 1818–1910: The Arable Estate and the Transition to Capitalism between the Insurgency and the Revolution," *Journal of Latin American Studies* 22 (May 1990): 229–263.

47 The *chahuixtle* (or *chahuistle*) was a frequent topic among the farmers of the Mexican Agricultural Society. See especially *BSAM* 13.9 (May 31, 1889): 129–131.

48 Karl Kaerger, *Agricultura y colonización en México en 1900,* trans. Pedro Lewin and Gudrun Dohrman from the German edition of 1907 (Mexico City: Universidad Autónoma Chapingo, 1986): 236–239.

49 On ecological issues, including deforestation, see ibid., 223, 236–239; *Memoria de la Secretaría de Fomento,* vol. 3, no. 2 (Aug. 1885): 158, and vol. 3, no. 4 (Oct. 1885): 182; and *BSAM* 16.13 (Apr. 8, 1892): 193.

50 Kaerger, *Agricultura y colonización.*

51 Their complaint was rather ironic given the fact that Mexico was among the world's leading producers of the fiber used to make binder twine. See Gilbert Joseph and Allen Wells, "Corporate Control of a Monocrop Economy: International Harvester and Yucatán's Henequen Industry during the Porfiriato," *Latin American Research Review* 17.1 (Spring 1982): 69–99, and Allen Wells, *Yucatán's Guilded Age: Haciendas, Henequen, and International Harvester, 1860–1915* (Albuquerque: University of New Mexico Press, 1985).

52 See statistics in *BSAM* 19.38 (June 16, 1886): 593–595, and 11.28 (Jan. 16, 1888): 442–443.

53 Much of the preceding discussion is based on Eulogio Gillow, "Sobre el cultivo de los cereales por medio de maquinaria agrícola Norte Americana," *BSAM* 1.23 (June 12, 1880): 352–358.

54 *BSAM* 25.3 (Jan. 17, 1901): 42–43, and 29.35 (Sept. 17, 1905): 682–683.

55 On the population of Mexico, see Cardoso, "La agricultura," 51. For the population of Puebla, see *Censo general de la República Mexicana: Estado de Puebla* (Mexico City: Secretaría de Fomento, 1902), and Herbert J. Nickel, *Morfología social de la hacienda mexicana,* 234–235. On prices of wheat and other commodities, see González Navarro, *Estadísticas económicas,* 69–70. On the relative cost of these commodities to consumers, see González Roa, *El aspecto agrario,* 201.

56 González Roa, *El aspecto agrario,* 119–123.

57 *BSAM* 8.42 (Aug. 28, 1885). See also *BSAM* 17.29 (Aug. 8, 1893): 451.

58 For debate on this point, see John Coatsworth, "Anotaciones sobre la producción de alimentos durante el Porfiriato," *Historia Mexicana* 26.2 (Oct.–Dec. 1976): 167–187: Herbert Nickel, "The Food Supply of Hacienda Labourers in Puebla-Tlaxcala during the

Porfiriato: A First Approximation," in *Haciendas in Central Mexico from Late Colonial Times to the Revolution,* ed. Raymond Buve (Amsterdam: Centre for Latin American Research and Documentation, 1984); and Cardoso, "La agricultura," 60.

59 González Roa, *El aspecto agrario,* 242–244.

60 Abdiel Oñate, "Banca y agricultura en México: la crísis de 1907–1908 y la fundación del primer banco agrícola," in *Banca y poder en México, 1800–1925,* ed. Leonor Ludlow and Carlos Marchal (México: enlace/historia grijalbo, 1986), 355; Walter Flavius McCaleb, *Present and Past Banking in Mexico* (New York: Harper and Bros., 1920), 155; González Roa, *El aspecto agrario,* 135; Cardoso, "La agricultura," 82.

61 Report by the Duque de Amalfi, May 13, 1919, Archivo Histórico de la Embajada de España (AHEE), microfilm roll 52.

62 Nickel, *Morfología,* 255, 262.

CHAPTER THREE

1 Rosalie to Harry Evans, Mar. 15, 1911, REP, box 1.

2 Porfirio del Castillo, *Puebla y Tlaxcala en los días de la Revolución* (Mexico City: n.p., 1953), 44–45; "Entrevista con el Sr. Luis Sánchez Pontón, realizada por Daniel Cazes, en abril de 1961 en la Ciudad de México," Archivo de la Palabra/Instituto de Investigaciones Dr. José María Luis Mora, Mexico City, PHO/1/20/, 5.

3 David G. LaFrance, *The Mexican Revolution in Puebla, 1908–1913: The Maderista Movement and the Failure of Liberal Reform* (Wilmington, Del.: Scholarly Resources, 1989), 46.

4 John Womack, *Zapata and the Mexican Revolution* (New York: Vintage, 1968), 69.

5 Interview with Ignacio Téllez Escalona, Santa Ana Xalmimilulco, Mar. 30, 1992.

6 Del Castillo, *Puebla y Tlaxcala,* 51.

7 Thomas Hohler to Francisco de la Barra, May 24, 1911, and subsecretary V. Salado Alvarez to Hohler, May 27, 1911, 12:30:42, both in Archivo Histórico Genaro Estrada — Secretaría de Relaciones Exteriors (AHSRE), notebook no. 5.

8 Charles Cumberland, *Mexican Revolution: Genesis under Madero* (Austin: University of Texas Press, 1952), 151.

9 Despacho núm. 34, Feb. 28, 1911, AHEE, microfilm roll 45, 281:1:1.

10 Womack, *Zapata and the Mexican Revolution,* 90.

11 LaFrance, *Mexican Revolution in Puebla,* 101–104, 113.

12 Various letters and memos, Archivo General del Estado de Tlaxcala, Fondo Revolución Obregonista (AGET), Hacienda y Guerra, caja 6, exp. 57.

13 Del Castillo, *Puebla y Tlaxcala,* 83.

14 David LaFrance, "Germany, Revolutionary Nationalism, and the Downfall of President Francisco I. Madero: The Covadonga Killings," *Mexican Studies/Estudios Mexicanos* 2.1 (winter 1986): 59–82.

15 Despacho núm. 126, Aug. 3, 1911, AHEE, roll 45, 281:1:40.

16 José María Lozano, quoted in Antonio Díaz Soto y Gama, *La Revolución agraria del sur y Emiliano Zapata, su caudillo* (Mexico City: El Caballito, 1976), 102.

17 See Peter Singelmann, "The Closing Triangle: Critical Notes on a Model for Peasant Mobilization in Latin America," *Comparative Studies in Society and History* 17.4 (Oct. 1975): 389–409.

18 For a recent work that emphasizes Zapata's leadership skills and ability to overcome — at

least to an extent—the antagonisms within the ranks of his followers, see Samuel Brunk, *Emiliano Zapata: Revolution and Betrayal in Mexico* (Albuquerque: University of New Mexico Press, 1995).

19 The Plan of Ayala is translated and reproduced in Womack, 395–404.

20 Diary of European trip, entries for Oct. 10 and Oct. 27, 1911, REP, box 1.

21 Francis Stronge to Secretaría de Gobernación Manuel Calero, Dec. 27, 1911, 12:30:43, AHSRE, vol. 5, p. 91.

22 Francis Stronge to Harry Evans, Jan. 31, 1912, and British legation to Harry Evans, Feb. 19, 1912, REP, box 1.

23 Henry Lane Wilson to secretary of state, Mar. 21, 1912, in Gene Z. Hanrahan, ed., *Documents on the Mexican Revolution*, vol. 8: *The Rebellion of Félix Díaz* (Salisbury, N.C.: Documentary Publications, 1983), 26.

24 Javier Garciadiego, "Higinio Aguilar: Milicia, rebelión y corrupción como modus vivendi," *Historia Mexicana* 41.3 (Jan.–Mar. 1992): 446–449.

25 Factory owners of Puebla to foreign ministers of France and Spain, Sept. 29, 1912, AHEE, roll 46, 289:1:1.

26 Despacho núm. 40, Mar. 29, 1912, AHEE, roll 46, 206:4:17.

27 Leone B. Moats, *Thunder in Their Veins: A Memoir of Mexico* (New York: Century, 1932), 76.

28 Cumberland, *Mexican Revolution: Genesis Under Madero*, 166–170, 186–190.

29 Manuscript in REP, box 2, "Miscellaneous" folder. The account was apparently written by the wife of a diplomat referred to only as "Guillermo."

30 Alan Kight, *The Mexican Revolution* (Cambridge: Cambridge University Press, 1986), 1:488.

31 Ramírez Rancaño, *Domingo y Cirilo Arenas en la Revolución Mexicana* (Mexico City: Centro de Estudios Históricos del Agrarismo en México, 1991), 18.

32 Mark T. Gilderhus, *Pan American Visions: Woodrow Wilson in the Western Hemisphere, 1913–1921* (Tucson: University of Arizona Press, 1986), 30.

33 Peter Calvert, *The Mexican Revolution 1910–1914: The Diplomacy of Anglo-American Conflict* (Cambridge: Cambridge University Press, 1968); Howard Cline, *The United States and Mexico* (New York: Atheneum, 1963), 139–162; Robert E. Quirk, *An Affair of Honor: Woodrow Wilson and the Occupation of Veracruz* (New York: Norton, 1962).

34 Rosalie Evans diary for 1914, REP, box 5.

35 Francisco de Velasco, *Autobiografía* (Puebla: n.p. 1946), 60.

36 Despacho núm. 223, AHEE, roll 48, 298:2:4. On the looting of the haciendas, see Eulogio Gillow, *Reminiscencias de Ilmo. y Rmo. Sr. Dr. Eulogio Gillow y Zavalza, arzobispo de Antequera*, ed. José A. Rivera G. (Los Angeles: El Heraldo de México, 1920).

37 Zapata to Luis Cabrera, Sept. 19, 1914, Archivo Gildardo Magaña, Biblioteca Nacional de México (AGM-BN), 27:12:217; Cabrera to Zapata, Sept. 23, 1914, AGM-BN, 27:12:226. Womack, *Zapata and the Mexican Revolution*, 203–209. Quotations from Friedrich Katz, *The Secret War in Mexico: Europe, the United States, and the Mexican Revolution* (Chicago: University of Chicago Press, 1981), 260.

38 Díaz Soto y Gama, *La Revolución agraria del sur*, 203–204.

39 William O. Jenkins, American consul at Puebla, to Arnold Shanklin, American consul general, Nov. 18, 1914, U.S. State Department Archives, Record Group 59 (SD), 812.00/14073.

40 For a vivid description of the battle, see Jenkins to Shanklin, Jan. 6, 1915, SD, 812.00/14285.

41 Villa to Zapata, Nov. 10, 1914, AGM-BN, 30:7:130; Womack, *Zapata and the Mexican Revolution*, 222; Jenkins to Shanklin, Jan. 6, 1915, SD, 812.00/14285.

42 Moisés González Navarro, *Estadísticas económicas del Porfiriato: fuerza de trabajo y actividad económica por sectores* (Mexico City: El Colegio de México, 1965), 105–124.

43 Claudio Lomnitz-Adler, *Exits from the Labyrinth: Culture and Ideology in the Mexican National Space* (Berkeley and Los Angeles: University of California Press, 1992), esp. chap. 3.

44 On the makeup of the Zapatista movement of Morelos and the diversity of its leadership, see Aquiles Chiu, "Peones y campesinos zapatistas," in *Emiliano Zapata y el movimiento zapatista: cinco ensayos* (Mexico City: INAH, 1980), 100–178.

45 For examples, see the oral histories recorded in Franciro Javier Gómez Carpintero, ed. *Los días eran nuestros . . . vida y trabajo entre los obreros textiles de Atlixco* (Pueblo: Dirección General de Culturas Populares, 1988).

46 Alberto Leduc, Luis Lara y Parod, and Carlos Roumagnac, *Diccionario de geografía y biografía mexicana* (Paris and Mexico City: Liberería de la Vda. de C. Bouret, 1910), 1080.

47 Ramírez Rancaño, *Domingo y Cirilo Arenas,* 14.

48 Del Castillo, *Puebla y Tlaxcala,* 137–155; Ramírez Rancaño, *Domingo y Cirilo Arenas,* 19–21; Raymond Th. J. Buve, "Peasant Movements, Caudillos and Landreform during the Revolution (1910–1917) in Tlaxcala, Mexico," *Boletín de Estudios Latinoamericanos y del Caribe* 18 (June 1975): 112–152.

49 Arenas to Zapata, Oct. 28, 1914, AGM-BN, 27:7:146.

50 Gildardo Magaña, *Emiliano Zapata y el agrarismo en México* (Mexico City: Liga de Economistas Revolucionarios de la República, 1975), 312–314.

51 British legation to Harry Evans, Dec. 14, 1914, REP, box 1.

52 See, for example, Col. Rafael Huerta to Zapata, Jan. 13, 1915, Archivo General de la Nación, Fondo Zapata (AGN-FZ), 4:1:56; vecinos of San Martín Zacatempa to Zapata, Apr. 20, 1915, AGN-FZ, 7:5:85–86.

53 Gral. Ricardo Reyes Márquez to Zapata, May 3, 1915, AGN-FZ, 8:1:59; Col. Sánchez Peña to Zapata, July 26, 1915, AGN-FZ, 9:3:25; interview with Miguel Juárez César and Hermelinda Espinosa Maro, Santa Ana Xalmimilulco, Apr. 2, 1992.

54 Despacho dated May 27, 1915, AHEE, roll 48, 311:29.

55 British legation to Harry Evans, May 26, 1915, REP, box 1.

56 William Blowser, U.S. vice-consul at Piedras Negras, Coahuila, to secretary of state, Sept. 25, 1915; SD, 812.00/16328.

57 Spanish grocers of the Junta de Abarroteros to Spanish embassy, June 10, 1915, AHEE, roll 48, 311:29; *Periódico Oficial de Puebla,* Sept. 2, 1914.

58 *The Eagle and the Serpent,* trans. Harriet de Onis (New York: Doubleday, 1965), 73.

59 Eugenia Meyer, *Luis Cabrera: teórico y crítico de la Revolución* (Mexico City: SepSetentas, 1972); Gabrella de Beer, *Luis Cabrera: un intelectual de la Revolución Mexicana,* trans. Ismael Pizarro and Mercedes Pizaro (Mexico City: Fondo de Cultura Económica, 1984). De Beer discusses Cabrera's contribution to the Law of January 6 on p. 97.

60 Gibert Joseph, *Revolution from Without: Yucatán, Mexico, and the United States, 1880–1924* (Durham, N.C.: Duke University Press, 1988), 122.

61 In 1991, President Carlos Salinas de Gortari cited this ambiguity as one of the reasons for his proposed reform of Article 27 of the Constitution: "Few knew to whom the ejidos and communities belonged: some thought they belonged to the government, others that they belonged to the ejidatarios and comuneros. In reality they belong to the Nation, though the Constitution does not clearly define the relations of property." *La Jornada,* Nov. 15, 1991.

62 "Entrevista con el Sr. Luis Sánchez Pontón realizada por Daniel Cazes, en abril de 1961 en la Ciudad de México," Archivo de la Palabra / Instituto de Investigaciones Dr. José María Luis Mora, Mexico City, PHO / 1 / 20.

63 Eyler N. Simpson, *The Ejido: Mexico's Way Out* (Chapel Hill: University of North Carolina Press, 1937), 78.

64 Del Castillo, *Puebla y Tlaxcala,* 214, 254.

65 Robert E. Quirk, *The Mexican Revolution: the Conventions of Aguascalientes* (Bloomington, Ind.: Indiana University Press, 1960), 221–227.

66 Ramírez Rancaño, *Domingo y Cirilo Arenas,* 37; Ayaquica to Zapata, Dec. 26, 1915, AGM-BN, 29:15:757; Arenas to Zapata, Jan. 7, 1916, AGM-BN, 30:11:219.

67 William Canada, U.S. consul at Veracruz, to secretary of state, Sept. 24, 1915, SD, 812.00 / 16381.

68 Arenas to Zapata, Jan. 21, 1916, AGM-BN, 30:11:224.

69 Arenas to Zapata, Sept. 15, 1916, AGM-BN, 28:2:50.

70 Arenas to Zapata, Dec. 7, 1916, AGM-BN, 28:2:86; Arenas to Zapata, Dec. 21, 1916, AGM-BN, 28:2:87; Arenista agent J. Espinosa Barreda to Arenas, Mar. 7, 1917, AGM-BN, 28:1:6.

71 Quoted in del Castillo, *Puebla y Tlaxcala,* 160.

72 Parroquía de San Martín Texmelucan, Libro de Gobierno, 3a parte, entries for Dec. 7 and Dec. 14, 1916, AMSMT.

73 Arenas to juez de la 1a instancia y de los criminales de Puebla, May 25, 1917, and Teodor Sánchez, juez de paz de San Juan Tetla, to Arenas, May 22, 1917, both in Archivo de Poder Judicial del Estado de Puebla (APJP), Huejotzingo.

74 Knight, *The Mexican Revolution,* 2:468–469.

75 Sindicato de Terratenientes to Finance Minister Adolfo de la Huerta, n.d., AGN — Fondo Obregón-Calles (AGN-OC), 818:P:38.

76 "Entrevista con el Sr. Pedro L. Romero, Cortés, realizada por María Alba Pastor del día 8 de junio de 1974 en San Martín Texmelucan," Archivo de la Palabra / Instituto de Investigaciones Dr. José María Luis Mora, Mexico City, PHO / 1 / 139, 12.

77 Del Castillo, *Puebla y Tlaxcala,* 251.

78 Exp. núm. 120, "Dotación de San Mateo Capultitlán," Aug. 12, 1916, Departamento de Asuntos Agrarios y de Colonización de Puebla (DAACP).

79 "Entrevista con el Sr. Pedro L. Romero," 19.

80 Gral. V. Rojas and Cirilo Arenas to Col. Andrés Rufino, June 10, 1917, AGM-BN, 29:13:607.

81 Buve, "Peasant Movements," 145; Ramírez Rancaño, *Domingo y Cirilo Arenas,* 42.

82 Del Castillo, *Puebla y Tlaxcala,* 158.

83 Buve, "Peasant Movements," 147.

84 Marcelino Presno to Comisión Local Agraria de Puebla, July 3, 1917, exp. núm. 103, "Dotación de Ejidos de Santa Ana Xalmimilulco," DAACP.

85 Zapatista versions can be gleaned from Ayaquica to Francisco Mendoza, Sept. 1, 1917,

AGM-BN, 29:13:641, and Ramírez Rancaño, *Domingo y Cirilo Arenas*, 48–49. A somewhat different, though clearly Zapatista, version can be found in Womack, *Zapata and the Mexican Revolution,* 293. Other variations are compiled in Ramírez Rancaño, *Domingo y Cirilo Arenas,* 45–48. Zapatista Gral. Fortino Ayaquica's version, originally printed in *El Hombre Libre,* Nov. 3 and 8, and Dec. 3, 1937, is reprinted in Miguel León-Portilla, *Los manifiestos en Náhuatl de Emiliano Zapata* (Mexico City: UNAM), 31–38.

86 "A los jefes, oficiales y soldados que hayan militado bajo las órdenes de Domingo Arenas," Sept. 27, 1917, AGM-BN, 29:13:650; Ayaquica to Francisco Mendoza, n.d., AGM-BN, 29:13:679.

87 *La Prensa,* Dec. 12, 1917.

88 David G. LaFrance, "Carrancismo and the State Governorship in Puebla, 1917–1920," paper presented at the Rocky Mountain Council for Latin American Studies, El Paso, Texas, Feb. 1992. My thanks go to Prof. LaFrance and Prof. Marco Velázquez Alba for the use of this paper.

89 *La Prensa,* Dec. 2, 1917.

CHAPTER FOUR

1 Rosalie Evans diary entry, Jan. 9, 1918, REP, box 3.

2 Ibid.

3 Rosalie to Harry Evans, Jan. 30, 1918, REP box 2, "Miscellaneous Correspondence" folder; Rosalie Evans diary entry, Jan. 19, 1918, REP, box 3.

4 Robert Graves and Alan Hodge, *The Long Week-End: A Social History of Great Britain, 1918–1939* (New York: W. W. Norton, 1940), 11–35; Geoffrey K. Nelson, *Spiritualism and Society* (New York: Schocken Books, 1969), 155–162.

5 Rosalie Evans diary entry, Jan. 17, 1918, REP, box 3.

6 Rosalie Evans, *The Rosalie Evans Letters from Mexico* (Indianapolis: Bobbs-Merrill, 1926), 37–38.

7 Ibid., 95.

8 Ibid., 92.

9 Interview with Miguel Juárez César and Hermelinda Espinosa Maro, Santa Ana Xalmimilulco, Apr. 2, 1992.

10 Comisión Nacional Agraria (CNA), Resoluciones Presidenciales, vol. 7, San Lucas Atoyatenco, Apr. 22, 1920, AGN-CNA "Información testimonial rendida por los CC. Valeriano Cortéz y Trinidad Pérez, representates del pueblo de San Lucas Atoyatenco del municipio de San Martín Texmelucan, para justificar el despojo de tierra y aguas que poseía dicho pueblo," Sept. 10, 1917, APJP.

11 CNA, Resoluciones Presidenciales, vol. 12, pp. 65–67, San Jerónimo Tianguismanalco, Nov. 9, 1922, AGN-CNA; exp. núm. 87, Santa María Moyotzingo, Moyotzingo to (CLA), Mar. 28, 1917, DAACP.

12 Vicente Pérez to Comisión Local Agraria de Puebla (CLAP), Aug. 27, 1917; Mariano Pérez to CLAP, Sept. 4, 1917, dotación núm. 87, Santa María Moyotzingo, DAACP.

13 Informe de Ing. Ricardo García, Apr. 5, 1918, dotación núm. 103, Santa Ana Xalmimilulco, DAACP.

14 San Francisco Tepeyecac to CLAP, Oct. 26, 1917, dotación núm. 117, DAACP.

15 Ramírez Rancaño, *Domingo y Cirilo Arenas en la Revolución Mexicana* (Mexico City:

Centro de Estudios Históricos del Agrarismo en México, 1991), 49–51; Buve, "'Neither Carranza nor Zapata!': The Rise and Fall of a Peasant Movement That Tried to Challenge Both, Tlaxcala, 1910–19," in *Riot, Rebellion, and Revolution: Rural Social Conflict in Mexico,* ed. F. Katz (Princeton, N.J.: Princeton University Press, 1988).

16 *Boletín del servicio informativo del Ejército Libertador,* núm. 1, Apr. 28, 1918, AGM-BN, 29:3:243.

17 Testimony of William O. Jenkins, *Investigation of Mexican Affairs. Doc. no. 285. Pursuant to S. Res. 106* (Washington, GPO, 1920), 3191–3196.

18 Zapata to Gral. Francisco Mendoza, Apr. 29, 1918, AGM-BN, 29:3:244. On the unification of the Arenista and Zapatista forces of May 13, 1918, see P. Cabañas to Gral. Everardo González, May 15, 1918, AGM-BN, 27:15:316; *Boletín del servicio informativo del Ejército Libertador,* núm. 3, May 18, 1918, AGM-BN, 27:15:331, and núm. 4 May 25, 1918, AGM-BN, 27:15:348.

19 Magaña to Zapata, May 3, 1918, AGM-BN, 28:15:277; "A los pueblos comprendidos en la zona de la División Arenas," manifesto issued from Zapatista headquarters at Tlaltizapan, Morelos, June 1, 1918, AGM-BN, 30:17:284.

20 A reference to a year she spent attending school in New York, which she recalled as one of the few happy times in her childhood.

21 Rosalie Evans to Daisy Pettus, Jan. 23, 1918, REP, box 3. This letter appears in Evans, *Letters,* dated Jan. 11, slightly edited and altered.

22 Rosalie Evans diary entry, May 26, 1918, REP, box 3.

23 Ibid., May 7, 1918.

24 Ibid., April 29, 1918.

25 Evans, *Letters,* 37.

26 Ibid., 40.

27 Ibid., 220. The Irving quotations are from *Life and Voyages of Christopher Columbus* (New York: Lovell Coryell, n.d.), 152.

28 Nevin O. Winter, *Mexico and Her People To-Day* (Boston: L. C. Page and Co., 1907), 186.

29 James Scott makes note of experimental data indicating that "whenever subjects find themselves unjustly treated but unable, except at considerable cost, to respond in kind, they can be expected to show signs of aggressive behavior as soon as the opportunity presents itself." The experiments referred to — mostly with school-aged children — are recorded in Leonard Berkowitz, *Aggression* (New York: McGraw Hill, 1962), 87, and mentioned in Scott, *Domination and the Arts of Resistance: Hidden Transcripts* (New Haven, Conn.: Yale University Press, 1990), 213.

30 Evans, *Letters,* 40.

31 Alan Knight, *The Mexican Revolution,* 2 vols. (Cambridge: Cambridge University Press, 1986), 2:454, 482.

32 "Decreto reformando los arts. 7, 8 y 9 de la ley de 6 de enero de 1915," in Manuel Fábila, *Cinco siglos de legislación agraria en méxico 1493–1940* (Mexico City: Seretaría de la Reforma Agraria and CEHAM, 1981), 296–297.

33 "Circular no. 32 bis., Previniendo que en casos de posesiones provisionales, o cuando se hayan dado tierras para evitar que permanecieran improductivas, los frutos son de quienes hubiesen sembrado y cultivado las tierras," in Fábila, *Cinco siglos,* 334–335. The handbill circulated by Cirilo Arenas was shown to me by Jesús Contreras Hernández, *cronista oficial* (official chronicler) of San Martín Texmelucan. It is dated Nov. 8, 1917. See also Mar-

celino Presno to Gov. Cabrera, Nov. 29, 1917, and Pastor Rouaix to Presno, Nov. 17, 1917, both in AMSMT, "Hojas Sueltas."

34 Marcelino Presno to CLAP, July 3, 1917, exp. núm. 103, "Dotación de ejidos de Santa María Xalmimilulco," DAACP.

35 Evans, *Letters,* 41.

36 Evans, *Letters,* 42–43.

37 This account of Mrs. Evans's dealings with Laveaga is based on ibid., 39–45.

38 Evans to Pettus, June 1, 1918, REP, box 2.

39 Evans, *Letters,* 49.

40 David LaFrance, "Carrancismo and the State Governorship in Puebla, 1917–1920," paper presented at the Rocky Mountain Council for Latin American Studies, El Paso, Texas, Feb. 1992; Gustavo Abel Hernández Enríquez, *Historia moderna de Puebla,* vol. 1: *1917–1920. Gobierno del Doctor Alfonso Cabrera Lobato* (Puebla: n.p., 1986), 264–275, 278–286.

41 Alvaro Obregón, *The Agrarian Problem: Short-Hand Notes of the Impressions Exchanged between the President Elect and a Numerous Group of Congressmen, October 1920* (Mexico City: Imprenta de la Secretaría de Relaciones Exteriores, 1924), 7.

42 This scene was edited from the published letters. Rosalie Evans to Daisy Pettus, June 16, 1918, REP, box 2.

43 Rosalie Evans to Daisy Pettus, June 10, 1918, REP, box 1.

44 Evans, *Letters,* 69.

45 Ibid., 68–69.

46 Ibid., 71–72. Guerrero may have been too corrupt for Mrs. Evans, but apparently he was tolerable for the man who had recommended him to her in the first place, Ignacio Ovando, who soon rehired him. "En averiguación de los que resulten culpables, como trastornadores de l órden público cometido en el pueblo de Tacaltcingo," Sept. 26, 1921, exp. 70, APJP. This document accuses the henchmen of Ovando and Guerrero of inciting a rebellion in the village.

47 Notes on an interview with C. Edmonds Allen, grandnephew of Daisy Pettus, by Ross Parmenter, New York City, June 12, 1963.

48 Evans, *Letters,* 60.

49 Ibid., 66.

50 Resoluciones Presidenciales, vol. 12, San Jerónimo Tianguismanalco, Nov. 9, 1922, AGN-CNA.

51 Interview with Paula Romero vda. de Montes, San Buenaventura Tecaltzingo, Feb. 22, 1992 (T. Henderson and Robert Bell).

52 Evans, *Letters,* 82.

53 Ibid., 86.

54 Ibid., 90–91.

55 Ibid., 50.

56 Mariano Pérez to CLAP, Apr. 15, 1919, exp. núm. 87, "Dotación de ejidos a Moyotzingo," DAACP.

57 Sindicato de Agricultores de Puebla, n.d., AGN-OC, 818:P:38, anexo 1.

58 "Información ad perpetuam, Ramón García y socios," May 7, 1928, APJP, "Civil."

59 Alberto Reyes Gil, government investigator, to Puebla governor Bravo Izquierda, Nov. 23, 1927, AGN-OC, 818:X:21.

60 Presno to CLAP, Apr. 1, 1921, exp. núm. 103, Xalmimilulco, DAACP.

61 Vecinos of Santa María Moyotzingo to CLAP, Sept. 12, 1919, dotación núm. 87, Moyotzingo, DAACP.

62 "Entrevista con el Sr. Pedro L. Romero Cortés, realizada por María Alba Pastor el día 8 de junio de 1974 en San Martín Texmelucan," Archivo de la Palabra / Instituto de Investigaciones Dr. José María Luis Mora, Mexico City, PHO / 1 / 139.

63 Rosalie Evans to Daisy Pettus, July 6, 1918, REP, box 1. This letter appears in the published *Letters* with the paragraph just cited edited out.

64 Evans to Pettus, Mar. 30, 1918, REP, box 1.

65 Jenkins to Arnold Shanklin, U.S. consul general, Jan. 7, 1915, SD, 812.00/14285.

66 "Meet Mr. Jenkins," *Time,* Dec. 26, 1960, 25–26; Charles C. Cumberland, "The Jenkins Case and Mexican-American Relations," *Hispanic American Historical Review (HAHR)* 31.4 (Nov. 1951): 586–607; David Ronfeldt, *Atencingo: The Politics of Agrarian Struggle in a Mexican Ejido* (Stanford, Calif.: Stanford University Press, 1973); various letters regarding Jenkins and his properties in AGN-OC, 818:J:4; memoir from Fernando Guzmán to Manuel Covarrubias, sec. de relaciones exteriores, July 14, 1920, AHSRE, 42:26:95, notebook no. 5, 149–152.

67 Vecinos (residents) of Moyotzingo to CLAP, Oct. 30, 1919, dotación núm. 87, Moyotzingo, DAACP.

68 Hernández Enríquez, *Historia moderna de Puebla,* 1:82, 340.

69 Marcelo Caraveo to Zapata, Aug. 9, 1918, AGM, 29:12:602.

70 Oct. 13, 1919, U.S. Military Intelligence Reports (USMIR) no. 1296, reports on the Arenista dynamiting of a train of the Interoceanic Railroad near the Santa Clara station.

71 *La Prensa,* Oct. 1, 1919, and June 14, 1919.

72 Evans, *Letters,* 120.

73 Ramírez Rancaño, *Domingo y Cirilo Arenas,* 54.

74 *Excélsior,* Apr. 4, 1920.

75 Porfirio del Castillo, *Puebla y Tlaxcala en los días de la Revolución* (Mexico City: n.p., 1953), 264.

76 Rosalie Evans diary entry, Mar. 30, 1919, REP, box 5.

77 Evans, *Letters,* 112.

78 Ibid., 115.

CHAPTER FIVE

1 On Carranza's eleventh-hour efforts, see Rosalie Evans, *The Rosalie Evans Letters from Mexico* (Indianapolis: Bobbs-Merrill, 1926), 121; informe by Ing. Agustín Villalobos, Dec. 19, 1919, Oficina de la Reforma Agraria de Puebla (ORAP), dotación núm. 87, Santa María Moyotzingo; and governor's resolution, Mar. 4, 1920, ORAP, dotación núm. 87. The quotation is from Evans, *Letters,* 125.

2 Evans, *Letters,* 125.

3 On the symbolism of sacrifice in protestations of patriotism, see the provocative discussion in Claudio Lomnitz-Adler, *Exits from the Labyrinth: Culture and Ideology in the Mexican National State* (Berkeley and Los Angeles: University of California Press, 1992), 290–291.

4 Linda B. Hall, "Alvaro Obregón and the Politics of Mexican Land Reform, 1920–1924," *Hispanic American Historical Review* 60.2 (May 1980): 214.

5   Alvaro Obregón, *The Agrarian Problem: Short-Hand Notes of the Impressions Exchanged between the President Elect and a Numerous Group of Congressmen, October 1920* (Mexico City: Imprenta de la Secretaría de Relaciones Exteriores, 1924).

6   "El Agrarismo será el hambre del pueblo," *Excelsior,* Apr. 5, 1921.

7   Rosalie Evans to Obregón, Jan. 21, 1921, AGN-OC, 811:E:10.

8   The foregoing is based primarily on Obregón, *The Agrarian Problem*. The quotes are not direct, for the English translation of this pamphlet is inept. I have changed the diction to make them read more smoothly.

9   Manuel Fábila, *Cinco siglos de legislación agraria en México, 1993–1940* (Mexico City: Secretaría de la Reforma Agraria and CEHAM, 1981), 346–361.

10 Alberto Bremauntz, *Setenta años de mi vida: memorias y anécdotas* (Mexico City: n.p., 1968), 113. The deputy referred to is Alberto Coria Cano of Michoacán.

11 Nov. 18, 1921, USMIR, 2711.

12 *Excélsior,* Nov. 6, 1924.

13 José María Sánchez, *La reivindicación del obrero* (Mexico City: n.p., 1923), vii.

14 Del Castillo, *Puebla y Tlaxcala,* 288.

15 *El Monitor,* Aug. 18, 1920; *La Crónica,* Oct. 29, 1920.

16 The foregoing discussion of the political conflict in Puebla is based on the following sources: Gustavo Abel Hernández Enríquez, *Historia moderna de Puebla,* vol. 2: *1920–1924. El Período de la anarquía constitucional* (Puebla: n.p., 1988), 35–64; Del Castillo, *Puebla y Tlaxcala,* 284–286; and "Informe que rinde la Comisión Especial nombrada por el gobernador provisional, C. Claudio N. Tirado, acerca del examen de los documentos relativos al conflicto electoral de poderes del Estado de Puebla, 12 de junio de 1921," "Puebla, conflicto de elecciones 1921 — informe producido por el Lic. Benjamín Aguillón Guzmán, oficial mayor de la Cámara Legislativa," June 12, 1921, and "Informe comprabado que el C. Diputado Claudio N. Tirado rinde a la H. Cámara de Senadores del Congreso de la Unión, con motivo del conflicto electoral del Estado de Puebla, 20 de junio de 1921," all in Fideicomiso Archivo Plutarco Elías Calles y Fernando Torreblanco, gaveta 61, núm. 79.

17 Evans, *Letters,* 145–146.

18 "En averiguación de los que resulten responsables del homicidio perpetrado en la persona de Rosendo Sánchez," May 12, 1921, APJP, proceso núm. 30.

19 Evans, *Letters,* 149–150.

20 See comments to this effect in Hans-Werner Tobler, "Las paradojas del ejército revolucionario: su papel social en la reforma agraria mexicana, 1920–1935," *Historia Mexicana* 21.1 (July–Sept. 1971): 56.

21 Evans, *Letters,* 130, describes how she fed some Obregonista soldiers in May 1920, thereby winning the gratitude of the soldiers and respect of the "natives." In her letter of May 5, 1921, she mentions that "As a precaution, I have a few soldiers — these I get from any officer in command at San Martín — it saves them the keep of the soldiers." Ibid., 144.

22 Ibid., 135, 140.

23 Ibid., 142.

24 Paul Friedrich, *The Princes of Naranja: An Essay in Anthropological Method* (Austin: University of Texas Press, 1986), 181–184. See also Friedrich's classic account of caciquismo in the village of Naranja, Michoacán, *Agrarian Revolt in a Mexican Village* (Chicago: University of Chicago Press, 1977).

25 This description is based on his autopsy report. "Instruido en contra del que o los que

resulten responsables del delito de homicidio del que en vida respondió al nombre de Manuel P. Montes, hecho que tuvo lugar en el pueblo de San Martín Texmelucan, el 30 de agosto próximo pasado," APJP, leg. 637, núm. 78, Sept. 29, 1927.

26 Manuel Montes to Vicente Alvarado, secretaría del ayuntamiento de San Martín Texmelucan, Dec. 29, 1909, AMSMT caja "Documentos del Siglo XIX"; Montes to presidente municipal de San Martín Texmelucan, Jan. 9, 1909, ibid.; various loose papers, AMSMT, caja 15, "Justicia, 1907–1909"; *Manuel P. Montes: su vida revolucionaria, su actuación política* (Puebla: n.p., 1927; reissue 1976).

27 Porfirio del Castillo, *Puebla y Tlaxcala en los días de la Revolución* (Mexico City: n.p., 1953), 157.

28 *Manuel P. Montes,* 22–23.

29 "Entrevista con el Sr. Pedro L. Romero Cortés, realizada por María Alba Pastor el día 8 de junio de 1974 en San Martín Texmelucan," Archivo de la Palabra / Instituto de Investigaciones Dr. José María Luis Mora, Mexico City, PHO / 1 / 139.

30 See, for example, juez correcional de Huejotzingo to juez de la primera instancia de Huejotzingo, Nov. 30, 1917, APJP. A Spaniard named Antonio Concepción complained that Montes had despoiled him of the Rancho de la Luz, which he was renting. Montes maintained it had been seized by Arenas in 1915 and that he (Montes) had already divided it among the villages. Concepción claimed the Rancho was a small property and thus protected according to Article 27.

31 "Entrevista con el Sr. Pedro L. Romero Cortés," 40.

32 Interview with Diputado Antonio Montes (son of Manuel P. Montes), Mar. 21, 1992, El Moral (T. Henderson); Facundo Arias González, "Historia de la relaciones del movimiento obrero con el campesino. El caso de la CROM y la Confederación Social Campesina Domingo Arenas, 1921–1929," in *Historia y sociedad en Tlaxcala: memorias del Primer Simposio Internacional de Investigaciones Socio-hisotóricas sobre Tlaxcala* (Tlaxcala, Tlax.: Universidad Autónoma de Tlaxcala, 1985; Mexico City: Universidad Iberoamericana, 1986), 152.

33 Correspondence between Alvarez and Obregón, Dec. 24, 1920–Oct. 7, 1921; other correspondence between Serafín Monterde, Ignacio Figueroa, Claudio N. Tirado, Eulalio Ramírez, José María Sánchez, Vecinos of El Moral, Partido Nacional Agrarista, Antonio Díaz Soto y Gama, Fernando Torreblanca, Fortunato Maycotte, and Alvaro Obregón, May–Oct. 1921, all in AGN-OC, 818:N:1. Also "Acta de Policía Judicial," Oct. 9, 1921, AMSMT, caja 20, "Justicia, 1919–1921"; and "En averiguación del delito de lesiones que sufrió José Pérez Segundo o Hernández, contra los que resulten responsables," APJP, proceso núm. 77, Oct. 31, 1921. On Maycotte's opposition to agrarian reform, see Tobler, "Las paradojas de ejército revolucionario: su papel social en la reforma agraria mexicana, 1920–1935," 64.

34 Correspondence between Alvarez, Obregón, Lorenzo Meza, José María Sánchez, Cosme Zafra, Marcelino Presno, Pedro Romero, Froylán Manjarrez, dated variously from Nov. 11, 1921 to Apr. 6, 1922, all in AGN-OC, 818:N:1; correspondence between Obregón and vecinos of Teculcingo, Tianguistenco, San Pedro Matamoros, San Lucas, Nov. 30, 1921–Dec. 22, 1921; correspondence between Aarón Sáenz, Pedro Romero, Andrés Martínez, and Obregón, Jan. 3, 1922–Nov. 28, 1922, in AGN-OC, 818:S:125. Also see correspondence contained in AGN-OC, 818:N:1:30, 818:P:5, 818:P:38, leg. 10; "Contra los que resulten responsables de los delitos de allanamiento de morada, lesiones y violaciones de

garantías individuales de que se queja el administrador de la hacienda de Polaxtla," Nov. 26, 1921, APJP, proceso núm. 92. See, as well, Lorenzo Meza to presidente municipal de San Martín Texmelucan, Dec. 5. 1921; Spanish legation to pres. mpl. de SMT, Jan. 2, 1922; and pres. mpl. de SMT to presidente interino del CLA, Jan. 12, 1922, all three in AMSMT, caja "Gobernación, 1922." The *corrido* referred to was graciously lent me by Jesús Contreras Hernández, cronista oficial of San Martín Texmelucan.

35 *Periódico Oficial de Puebla,* 107.4 (July 26, 1921).

36 Nov. 18, 1921, USMIR no. 2711.

37 *New York Tribune,* Dec. 22, 1921.

38 Hernández Enrique, *Historia moderna de Puebla,* 2:64–74; del Castillo, *Puebla y Tlaxcala,* 289–295.

39 *La Crónica,* Mar. 24, 1922.

40 Obregón to Manjarrez, Mar. 6 and Mar. 14, 1922, AGN-OC, 818:P:38, leg. 10.

41 Trinidad García to presidente municipal de San Martín Texmelucan, Feb. 11, 1922, AMSMT, caja 22, "Justicia."

42 See, for example, the complains of Valentín Silva, president of Moyotzingo, regarding intrusions into the village by soldiers of the *destacamento* (military detachment) of the hacienda San Bartolo Granillo. These soldiers, Silva claimed, had sought out the homes of the *regionales,* beaten them, and taken their weapons. Silva to jefe del destacamento de San Bartolo Granillo, Feb. 3, 1922, AMSMT, caja 22, "Justicia."

43 "Contra los que resulten responsables de los delitos de allanamiento de morada y lesiones de que se queja Daniel Rodríguez," 1922, APJP.

44 "Contra el juez de paz, presidente auxiliar, presidente del Comité Particular Administrativo y el individuo Genaro Solís por los delitos de daños en propiedad ajena, despojo de casa inmueble, abuso de autoridad y violación de garantías individuales, de que los acusa el Sr. Serapio Pérez, vecino de Xalmimilulco, de donde son también los presuntos responsables," Apr. 26, 1922, APJP, proceso núm. 21; "Incidente de caución de no ofender, correspondiente a la causa #14 instruida contra Genaro Solís, por los delitos de amenazas, amargos, injurias y difusión contra el Sr. Serapio Pérez," July 1, 1922, APJP, proceso núm. 14; "Diligencias varias," Nov. 13, 1924, APJP, proceso núm. 6; DAACP, exp. 103, 'Dotación de Santa Ana Xalmimilulco.'

45 "En averiguación del delito de lesiones de que se queja el C. Epigmenio Fortís," Feb. 9, 1922, APJP, proceso núm. 3.

46 Cirilo Arenas to Zapata, Oct. 11, 1918, BN-AGM, 30:25:445. On Zapata's search for allies, see John Womack, *Zapata and the Mexican Revolution* (New York: Vintage, 1968), 309–310.

47 Gumaro García to presidente municipal de San Martín Texmelucan, Feb. 18, 1922, AMSMT, caja "Gobernación, 1922." For an example of the doubts aroused by Montes's claim, see Cruz Juárez et al. to Calles, June 15, 1925, AGN-OC, 818:P:5.

48 Presidente municipal de San Martín Texmelucan to Gumaro García, Aug. 29, 1922, AMSMT, caja "Gobernación, 1922."

49 "En averiguación de los que resulten responsables de los delitos de robos y destrucción en propiedad agena perpetrados en terrenos de la hacienda de Polaxtla, promovido por el empleado Rodolfo Rendón," May 18, 1922, APJP, proceso núm. 26; *La Crónica,* May 18, 1922; Alvarez to Obregón, May 17, 1922, AGN-OC, 818:N:1.

50 "En averiguación de los que resulten responsables de los delitos de golpes y otras viola-ciones físicas," May 18, 1922, APJP, proceso núm. 29.

51 "Contra el president auxiliar de Tianguismanalco y Crescencio Reyes, por delitos contra las elecciones populares y violación de la Ley Electoral de Poderes Federales, vigente," July 7, 1922, APJP, proceso núm. 41; "Contra Jacinto Aguilar y socios por delitos contra las elecciones populares y violación de la Ley Electoral de Poderes Judiciales, vigente," July 6, 1922, APJP, proceso núm. 40; Roberto Casas Alatriste to presidente municipal de San Martín Texmelucan, July 3, 1922; pres. mpl. to Col. Pascual Cornejo, jefe del sector de Texmelucan, July 4, 1922, AMSMT, caja "Gobernación, 1922"; *La Crónica,* July 3, 1922. According to official tallies, Casas Alatriste got more than twice as many votes as Montes; the final count was 5,795 to 2,845.

52 Pres. mpl. de SMT to Col. Cornejo, July 10, 1922, AMSMT, caja "Gobernación, 1922."

53 "Contra los que resulten culpables de los delitos de tumulto, lesiones y otros cometidos por soldados federales en ele pueblo de 'El Moral' y en la casa del C. Manuel Montes," Sept. 21, 1922, APJP, proceso núm. 54.

54 *La Crónica,* Mar. 24, 1922.

55 *La Crónica,* Nov. 23, 1922; Hernández Enrique, *Historia moderna de Puebla,* 2:75–83.

56 Eduardo Guerrero, the corrupt administrator whom Mrs. Evans had accused of theft and dismissed, was still working for Ignacio Ovando as of mid-1921.

57 Confederación Social Campesina "Domingo Arenas" to presidente municipal de San Martín Texmelucan, July 23, 1921, AMSMT, caja "Gobernación."

58 "En averiguación de violación de garantías individuales de que se queja Francisco Palacios y socios, vecinos del pueblo de Zacalácoayan," June 20, 1921, APJP, proceso núm. 45.

59 "En averiguación de los que resulten culpables, como trastornadores del órden público cometido en el pueblo de Tecaltzingo," Sept. 26, 1921, APJP, proceso núm. 70; Pascual García to presidente municipal de San Martín Texmelucan, Sept. 30, 1921, AMSMT, "Gobernación."

60 Presidente municipal de San Martín Texmelucan, to Celerino Cano, secretario general de gobierno de Puebla, Nov. 16, 1922, AMSMT, caja 23, "Justicia"; "En averiguación de los que resulten responsables del delito de homicidio perpetrado en la persona de Dionisio García y contra José de Jesús García," Nov. 17, 1922, APJP, proceso núm. 88.

61 Evans, *Letters,* 158.

62 Ibid., 180–181.

63 Ibid., 182–183.

64 Ibid., 183.

CHAPTER SIX

1 Rosalie Evans, *The Rosalie Evans Letters from Mexico* (Indianapolis: Bobbs-Merrill, 1926), 185–186.

2 Biographical notes by Ross Parmenter, kindly lent to author.

3 Evans, *Letters,* 160–161, 167.

4 Ibid., 131.

5 *Japan Chronicle,* Aug. 8, 1924, in AHSRE, 6:10:227(I).

6 Evans, *Letters,* 174. The following six in-text cites are also to this work.

7　On British law regarding nationality, see Ann Dummett and Andrew Nicol, *Subjects, Citizens, Aliens and Others: Nationality and Immigration Law* (London: Weidenfeld and Nicolson, 1990), 87–89, 126.

8　*La Prensa* (Lima), June 16, 1924, clipping in AHSRE 6-10-227(IV).

9　Evans, *Letters,* 154.

10　Statement of the secretaría de relaciones exteriores, 1924, AHSRE 6:10:227 (IV).

11　Friedrich Katz, *The Secret War in Mexico: Europe, the United States, and the Mexican Revolution* (Chicago: University of Chicago Press, 1981), 469.

12　Ross Parmenter, chap. 24 of unpublished manuscript, "Zelia Nuttall and the Recovery of Mexico's Past," n.d., 13.

13　Lorenzo Meyer, *Su Majestad Británica contra la Revolución Mexicana, 1900–1950: el fin de un imperio informal* (Mexico City: El Colegio de México, 1991), 362.

14　Cummins to Lord Curzon, Dec. 18, 1923, Great Britain, Public Records Office — Foreign Office (FO), 371/8468, A7399/187/26.

15　See, for instance, his comments on the Madero government quoted in William K. Meyers, "Second Division of the North: Formation and Fragmentation of the Laguna's Popular Movement, 1910–11," in *Riot, Rebellion, and Revolution: Rural Social Conflict in Mexico,* ed. Freidrich Katz, (Princeton, N.J.: Princeton University Press, 1988), 485.

16　Quote from Katz, *Secret War,* 466. See aslo Emily S. Rosenberg, "Economic Pressures in Anglo-American Diplomacy in Mexico, 1917–1918," *Journal of Interamerican Studies and World Affairs* 17.2 (May 1975): 123–152.

17　Dispatch no. 1229, Aug. 1919, USMIR; Meyer, *Su Majestad,* 303–304, 323.

18　*Japan Chronicle,* Aug. 8, 1924.

19　Cummins to Curzon, Feb. 22, 1923, FO, 371/8467, A1699/215/26.

20　In fact, although wheat production was somewhat below its prewar levels, the Mexican population had declined also, and much of the drop in production could no doubt be accounted for by the destruction of the war. According to notoriously unreliable statistics, wheat production in the 1920s was rapidly returning to prewar levels and would in fact shortly surpass those levels. See *Estadísticas históricas de México,* vol. 1 (Mexico City: Instituto Nacional de Estadística, Geografía e Informática, 1986), 409–410.

21　D. R. Thorpe, *The Uncrowned Prime Ministers* (London: Darkhorse Publishing, 1980).

22　Martin Pugh, *State and Society: British Political and Social History, 1870–1992* (London: Edward Arnold, 1994), 178; Maurice Cowling, *The Impact of Labour, 1920–1924: The Beginning of Modern British Politics* (Cambridge: Cambridge University Press, 1921); Alfred F. Havighurst, *Britain in Transition: The Twentieth Century* (Chicago: University of Chicago Press, 1962), 145–186.

23　The figures for 1922 were as follows: total imports from Mexico: United Kingdom = £8,604,000; United States = £30,147,000. Total exports to Mexico: United Kingdom = £2,301,000; United States = £24,812,000. These are figures introduced into the House of Commons, Mar. 6, 1923; they are contained in an anonymous memo of the foreign office, FO, 371-9555. On the history of the U.S.-British economic rivalry in Mexico, see especially Paulo Riguzzi, "México, Estados Unidos y Gran Bretaña, 1867–1910: una difícil relación triangular," *Historia Mexicana* 41.3 (1992): 365–436.

24　N. Stephen Kane, "Bankers and Diplomats: The Diplomacy of the Dollar in Mexico, 1921–1924," *Business History Review* 47.3 (autumn 1973): 335–352.

25 Meyer, *Su Majestad*, 330.

26 On the so-called Lamont–de la Huerta negotiations for repayment of the debt, see Linda B. Hall, "Banks, Oil, and the Reinstitutionalization of the Mexican State, 1920–1924," in *The Revolutionary Process in Mexico: Essays on Political and Social Change, 1880–1940*, ed. Jaime E. Rodríguez O. (Los Angeles: University of California, Los Angeles, Latin American Center Publications, 1990), 189–211; Robert Freeman Smith, *The United States and Revolutionary Nationalism in Mexico, 1916–1932* (Chicago: University of Chicago Press, 1972), 208–211; and John W. F. Dulles, *Yesterday in Mexico: A Chronicle of the Revolution, 1919–1936* (Austin: University of Texas Press, 1961), 145–157.

27 *Literary Digest,* July 1, 1922, and Aug. 19, 1922. *Flivver* was contemporary slang referring to a small, inexpensive automobile.

28 T. M. Fairbairn to H. A. Vernet, Dec. 9, 1922, FO, 371/8466 A106/106/26; Cummins to Curzon, Dec. 11, 1922, FO, 371/8466 A185/106/26; Cummins to Curzon, Feb. 22, 1923, FO, 371/8469 A1699/215/26.

29 These particular phrases are from a letter to Mexican foreign minister Pani, Dec. 27, 1922, FO, 371/8468, A592/592/26.

30 Evans to U.S. commissioners Payne and Warren, July 17, 1923, FO, 371/8469, A5632/592/26.

31 Cummins to Curzon, Jan. 18, 1923, FO, 371/8468, A879/592/26.

32 Evans, *Letters,* 179. Letter dated Jan. 25, 1923.

33 Cummins to Curzon, Feb. 22, 1923, FO, 371/8467, A1699/215/26.

34 Evans, *Letters,* 190.

35 Ibid., 189.

36 Ibid., 387.

37 *New York Tribune,* Aug. 7, 1924.

38 Evans, *Letters,* 190–191.

39 Ibid., 194–195; Vicente García, president of the Comité Particular Ejecutivo of San Francisco Tepeyecac, to Rosalie Evans, Feb. 26, 1923, and Mar. 1, 1923, warning of the impending *deslinde* (measurement), ORAP, dotación núm. 117, San Francisco Tepeyecac.

40 Evans, *Letters,* 196–197.

41 Charles Dodd, comments on memo of Mar. 23, 1923, FO, 371/8468, A1694/592/26.

42 Comments of E. R. Warner on memo of Apr. 12, 1923, FO, 371/8466, A2130/592/26.

43 Evans, *Letters,* 198.

44 *La Crónica,* Mar. 9, 1923; clipping found in AGN-OC, 818-E-23.

45 George Summerlin, U.S. ambassador, to secretary of state, Jan. 1923, SD, 812.00/267.

46 *Letters,* 202–203.

47 Ibid., 206.

48 David Manjarrez to Obregón, n.d., refuting a report in *El Heraldo* to the effect that the Manjarrez regime was unsympathetic to agrarismo. AGN-OC, 818-T-41. Froylán Manjarrez defended his regime to Obregón in a letter of Apr. 25, 1923, AGN, 818-M-9.

49 On the postrevolutionary Mexican judicial system, see Ernest Gruening, *Mexico and Its Heritage* (New York: Century, 1928), 497–512, esp. 506–508.

50 The memorial of the congress can be found in Jesús Silva Herzog, *El agrarismo mexicano y la reforma agraria: exposición y crítica* (Mexico City: Fondo de Cultura Económica, 1964), 305–309, and Alvaro Obregón, *Discursos del General Alvaro Obregón* (Mexico City: Biblioteca de la Dirección General de Educación Militar, 1932), 381–385.

CHAPTER SEVEN

1 Report by Ben Muse, third secretary of the U.S. embassy, May 17, 1923, in FO, 371/8469, A4115/592/26.
2 Rosalie Evans, *The Rosalie Evans Letters from Mexico* (Indianapolis: Bobbs-Merrill, 1926), 212–214.
3 Evans to Obregón, May 12, 1923, ORAP, dotación núm. 87, Santa María Moyotzingo.
4 Evans to Cummins, FO, 371/8469, A3310/592/26.
5 Muse, "Aspects of the Agrarian Situation in the Valley of San Martín," May 17, 1923, in FO, 371/8469 A4115/592/26; "Visit to Investigate Danger Surrounding Mrs. Morgan," May 16, 1923, REP, box 2, "Correspondence, 1923, January to May."
6 Evans, *Letters,* 218.
7 Ibid., 220.
8 Pani to Summerlin, March 31, 1923, 68th U.S. Congress, *Papers Relating to the Foreign Relations of the United States, 1923* (Washington: GPO, 1938), 2:530.
9 "Memorandum Handed to the United States Commissioners by Mrs. H.E.R. Evans, on July 17, 1923," FO, 371/8469 A5843/592/26; Evans, *Letters,* 219.
10 The decree appears in the *Diario Oficial,* July 19, 1923, and in FO, 371/8466, A5843.
11 Manuel P. Montes and Gumaro García to Obregón, Aug. 28, 1923, AGN-OC, 818-T-104; Montes to Calles, Aug. 28, 1923, Fideicomiso Archivo Plutarco Elías Calles, gaveta 46, núm. 5.
12 Notes on Cummins's memo, July 21, 1923, FO, 371/8469, A4371/592/26.
13 Evans, *Letters,* 222.
14 *Who Was Who in America* (Chicago: A. N. Marquis, 1943), 1:946, 1301–1302.
15 Evans, *Letters,* 227–230.
16 Cummins to Curzon, July 23, 1923, FO, 371/8469, A4995/592/26; Evans, *Letters,* 232.
17 Cummins to Curzon, July 23, 1923, FO, 371/8469, A4995/592/26.
18 Evans, *Letters,* 233.
19 Ibid., 239.
20 John W. F. Dulles, *Yesterday in Mexico: A Chronicle of the Revolution, 1919–1936* (Austin: University of Texas Press, 1961), 333.
21 Obregón to Serrano, Aug. 29, 1923, and Serrano to Obregón, Aug. 30, 1923, AGN-OC, 818-T-104.
22 Evans, *Letters,* 312.
23 "Informe sobre afectaciones ejidales a la Hacienda de 'San Pedro Coxtocán,' Estado de Puebla, propiedad de la extinta Sra. Rosalía Emma Caden vda. de Evans," oficio núm. 44724 of the CNA, Nov. 4, 1924, REP, box 4.
24 *Literary Digest,* Sept. 8, 1923.
25 John W. F. Dulles, *Yesterday in Mexico,* 167–170.
26 Evans, *Letters,* 240.
27 Ibid., 242; Interview with Paula Romero vda. de Montes, San Buenaventura Tecaltzingo, Feb. 22, 1992.
28 Gumaro García and Santiago García to Obregón, Sept. 14, 1923; Vecinos of Tepatlaxco to Obregón, Sept. 15, 1923; Obregón to Vecinos, Sept. 17, 1923; and Manjarrez to Obregón, Sept. 18, 1923, all in AGN-OC, 818-T-104. "Contra quienes resulten responsables del delito de invasión de tierras de la hacienda de San Damián de que se queja el Sr.

Honorato R. Mier, representante de los Sres. González Cosío Hermanos," Nov. 12, 1923, APJP, leg. 647, proceso núm. 17.

29 Evans, *Letters,* 244.

30 Ibid., 243–244; Evans to Cummins, Sept. 21, 1923, FO, 371/8467, A6661/187/26.

31 David Allen Brush, "The de la Huerta Rebellion in Mexico, 1923–1924," Ph.D. dissertation, Syracuse University, 1975, 98–107.

32 Montes to Calles, Oct. 3, 1923, and Calles to Montes, Oct. 4, 1923, both in Fideicomiso Archivo Plutarco Elías Calles, gaveta 46, núm. 5.

33 "Contra Adrián Solares, Domingo Solares y Juan Hernández por los delitos de injurias y golpes a un funcionario público," Oct. 23, 1923, APJP, leg. 652, proceso núm. 110. The contradictory agrarista version of these events is contained in "Criminal en contra del presidente de la Junta Auxiliar de Tianguisolco por los delitos de violación de garantías individuales y abuso de autoridad de que se queja el C. Catarino Alamedas," APJP, proceso núm. 652.

34 Monroy Durán, *El último caudillo* (Mexico City: J. S. Rodríguez, 1924), 377.

35 William Phillips to secretary of state, Nov. 23, 1923, SD, 812.00/26526.

36 "Instruido en averiguación de los delitos de asalto y robo de que se quejan los Sres. José Andrade y Jorge Straffen," Dec. 19, 1923, APJP, proceso núm. 27.

37 Phillips to secretary of state, Nov. 23, 1923, SD, 812.00/26526.

38 Ibid.

39 Paz to Calles, Dec. 11, 1923, in Carlos Macías, ed., *Plutarco Elías Calles: correspondencia personal (1919–1945)* (Mexico City: Fondo de Cultura Económica, 1991), 123.

40 *Memorandum sobre el amparo de José María Sánchez, ex-gobernador del Estado de Puebla* (Puebla: Imprenta de la Escuela de Artes y Oficios del Estado, 1923).

41 This charge was made by Luis Morones in the Chamber of Deputies, *Excélsior,* Sept. 27, 1924.

42 Fideicomiso Archivo Plutarco Elías Calles, exp. José María Sánchez, gaveta 61, núm. 79.

43 Evans, *Letters,* 247.

44 Cummins to Curzon, Dec. 12, 1923, FO, 371/8467, A7647/187/26.

45 Evans, *Letters,* 250.

46 Ibid., 262–263.

47 Brush, "De la Huerta Rebellion," 182–204.

48 Ibid., 162–170.

49 Ibid., 204.

50 Evans, *Letters,* 259.

CHAPTER EIGHT

1 Cummins to foreign office, Jan. 5, 1924, FO, 371/9564, A634/253/26.

2 Addendum to Cummins telegram, "Property and safety of Mrs. H.E.R. Evans," Dec. 19, 1923, FO, 371/9555, A 7472/592/26.

3 Rosalie Evans, *The Rosalie Evans Letters from Mexico* (Indianapolis: Bobbs-Merrill, 1926), 269–270.

4 *Chicago Tribune,* Jan. 6, 1924.

5 *Syracuse Herald,* July 14, 1924.

6 See, for example, Joseph Clayton, "The Rise of Ramsay MacDonald," *Current History,*

Apr. 1924, 7–14, which emphasizes the fact that MacDonald had married into money and learned to comport himself like a "gentleman." Also see, "Horny Hands on Britain's Helm," *Literary Digest,* Feb. 2, 1924, 10–11.

7   Memo, March 8, 1924, SD, 712.41/10; *Times,* Feb. 7, 1924.

8   *Parliamentary Debates,* House of Lords, Feb. 27, 1924, excerpted in SD, 712.41/11.

9   Ibid.

10 Evans to Pettus, Mar. 3, 1924, REP, box 2. This phrase was removed from the published letters.

11 David Allen Brush, "The de la Huerta Rebellion in Mexico, 1923–1924," Ph.D. dissertation, Syracuse University, 1975.

12 On the ideological underpinnings of this policy, see Michael H. Hunt, *Ideology and U.S. Foreign Policy* (New Haven, Conn.: Yale University Press, 1987), 137–138. The phrase "unwarrantable uprisings" was uttered by Charles Evans Hughes in an address on his Mexican policy to the Council on Foreign Relations in New York, Jan. 23, 1924. It is quoted in George Wheeler Hinman Jr., "The United States' Ban on Latin-American Rebels," *Current History,* April 1924, 69.

13 Hinman, "United States' Ban," 65.

14 For reasons that are not clear, Cummins is referred to as "Mr. Z——" in Evans's *Letters,* p. 293.

15 Evans, *Letters,* 298.

16 *Chicago Tribune,* Feb. 27, 29, 1924.

17 "Widow Assails U.S. for Helping Obregón Regime," *Chicago Tribune,* Feb. 26, 1928.

18 Obregón to Vicente Lombardo Toledano, Dec. 27, 1923, AGN-OC, 101-R2-E-98.

19 Evans to Pettus, March 3, 1924, REP, box 2.

20 *Chicago Tribune,* Feb. 23, 1924.

21 Mexía to Obregón, Feb. 26, 1923, AGN-OC, 101-R2-E-98.

22 Evans, *Letters,* 284.

23 E.g., Katherine Gleadell to Rosalie Evans, Dec. 24, 1923, REP, box 2. Katherine Gleadell had no ideological disagreement with Mrs. Evans. In fact, she owned several large haciendas in the state of Yucatán and was no admirer of the agrarian reform movement.

24 Evans to Pettus, Mar. 3, 1924, REP, box 2. This sentence was edited from the published letters.

25 On Obregón's propaganda efforts, see John A. Britton, "Propaganda, Property, and the Image of Stability: The Mexican Government and the U.S. Print Media, 1921–1929," *SECOLAS Annal* 19 (Mar. 1988): 5–29. Britton notes that E. J. Dillon, with whom Mrs. Evans was acquainted, was probably a sincere and unremunerated admirer of Obregón. Lorenzo Meyer, *Su Majestad Británica, contra la Revolución Mexicana, 1900–1950: el fin de un imperio informal* (Mexico City: El Colegio de México, 1991), pp. 333, 338, suggests otherwise.

26 Meyer, *Su Majestad,* 342.

27 Ibid., p. 350.

28 Cummins to Curzon, Jan. 19, 1924, "British White Paper, Mexico—no. 1," reprinted in Evans, *Letters,* 430.

29 *Times,* July 17, 1924.

30 Boston *News Bureau,* Aug. 5, 1924.

31 Sáenz's statement on the Cummins affair can be found in AHSRE, 6-10-227 (IV).

32 This order was given by Sáenz on Jan. 9 and acknowledged by War Minister Serrano on Jan. 12, 1924. AHSRE, 17-12-200, exp. 243.12.

33 *Chicago Tribune,* Mar. 3, 1924.

34 Friedrich Katz, *The Secret War in Mexico: Europe, the United States, and the Mexican Revolution* (Chicago: University of Chicago Press, 1981), 469–481.

35 Sáenz to FO, Apr. 25, 1924, British "White Paper," in Evans, *Letters,* 435.

36 Brush, "De la Huerta Rebellion," 261–262.

37 *Parliamentary Debates,* House of Lords, Feb. 27, 1924.

38 Quote in Summerlin to Department of State, June 21, 1923, SD, 812.00/26398; see also Brush, "De la Huerta Rebellion," 80.

39 See Enrique Krauze, *Caudillos culturales en la Revolución Mexicana* (Mexico City: Siglo Veintiuno, 1976), 172–177.

40 Evans, *Letters,* 287–288, 308.

41 On the federal army's intervention in the agrarian reform, see Summerlin to Department of State, June 21, 1923, SD, 812.00/26398, and Hans-Werner Tobler, "Las paradojas del ejército revolucionario: su papel social en la reforma agraria mexicana, 1920–1935," *Historia Mexicana* 21.1 (July–Sept. 1971): 38–79.

42 Evans, *Letters,* 291.

43 Ibid., 285.

44 Ibid., 316.

45 Ibid., 317–320.

46 Quoted in Ross Parmenter, "Zelia Nuttall and the Recovery of Mexico's Past," manuscript, 83.

47 "Statement by Mr. Camp," Aug. 7, 1924, FO, 371/9566, A5208/253/26.

48 Interview with Andrés Robles, San Jerónimo Tianguismanalco, March 8, 1992 (T. Henderson, R. Bell, and M. Escobedo).

49 On the regionales, see chapter 5 in this book, pp. 102, 108–112.

50 Vecinos of Tecaltzingo to jefe del Sector de la Plaza de Texmelucan, Apr. 2, 1924, APJP, "Correspondencia Oficial — Varios — Consignaciones Pendientes."

51 Probably the most sweeping charges of this kind came from the villagers of San Baltasar Temaxcalá in a letter to Calles, June 15, 1925, AGN-OC, 818-P-5, anexo 1.

52 "En averiguación del delito de abuso de autoridad de que se quejó el Ing. Manuel M. Hernández en contra de Antonio García, presidente del Comité Administrativo de San Gregorio Aztotoacán," Sept. 12, 1924, APJP, proceso núm. 50; "Diligencias varias, #6," Nov. 13, 1924, APJP; correspondencia del produrador general del estado, presidente auxiliar de San Gregorio Aztotoacán to procurador general del estado, June 29, 1924, APJP.

53 On the complex phenomenon of Mexican agrarian caciquismo, see Paul Freidrich, *The Princes of Naranja: An Essay in Anthrohistorical Method* (Austin: University of Texas Press, 1986); and Guillermo de la Peña, "Poder agrario y ambigüedad revolucionaria: bandidos, caudillos y facciones," in *Las formas y las políticas del dominio agrario: homenaje a François Chevalier,* ed. Ricardo Avila Palafox, Carlos Martínez Assad, and Jean Meyer (Guadalajara: Editorial de la Universidad de Guadalajara, 1992), 232–259, and his "Populism, Regional Power, and Political Mediation: Southern Jalisco, 1900–1980," in *Mexican Regions: Comparative and Historical Development,* ed. Eric Van Young (San Diego: Center for U.S.-Mexican Studies, University of California, San Diego, 1992).

54 Vecinos of Tianguismanalco to delegado of the Comisión Local Agraria de Puebla,

Apr. 22, 1924, "Correspondencia del C. procurador general del estado," Aug. 21, 1924, APJP, exp. núm. 22.

55 Gral. Benigno Serrato, jefe temporal de operaciones militares, to officer in charge of the destacamento of San Pedro Coxtocán, n.d., Archivo de Relaciones Exteriores, 17-12-200.

56 Evans, *Letters,* 326–327.

57 Evans, *Letters,* 332; Cummins to MacDonald, May 21, 1924, "White Paper," in ibid., *Letters,* 451.

58 Camp statement, Sept. 3, 1924, "Legal Documents, 1925 *et passim,*" REP, box 6.

59 Cummins to MacDonald, May 21, 1924, in Evans, *Letters,* 453.

60 Evans, *Letters,* 331–335; Cummins to MacDonald, June 4, 1924, "White Paper," in ibid., 466–470.

61 "Diligencias previas demandadas por los vecinos del pueblo de San Jerónimo Tianguismanalco contra la Sra. Rosalía Caden vda. de Evans," May 19, 1924, APJP, proceso núm. 13; Delegado Ingeniero de la Comisión Nacional Agraria to presidente municipal de San Martín Texmelucan, May 8, 1924, and presidente municipal de Tepeyecac to presidente municipal de San Martín Texmelucan, May 14, 1924, both in AMSMT, caja "Justicia."

CHAPTER NINE

1 Cummins to Sáenz, May 3, 1924, "White Paper," in Rosalie Evans, *The Rosalie Evans Letters from Mexico* (Indianapolis: Bobbs-Merrill, 1926), 461–462.

2 MacDonald to Cummins, May 20, 1924, "White Paper," in ibid., 442.

3 Evans, *Letters,* 362–363.

4 Lorenzo Meyer, *Su Majestad Británica contra la Revolución Mexicana, 1900–1950: el fin de un imperio informal* (Mexico City: El Colegio de México, 1991), 361–362.

5 *La Prensa,* June 16, 1924.

6 *Times,* June 20, 1924.

7 *El Paso Times,* June 24, 1924.

8 *Daily Telegraph,* July 12, 1924; *Times,* July 12, 1924; *Evening News,* July 12, 1924.

9 *San Francisco Journal,* June 8, 1924; Gerald Campbell to British Consulate-General, June 9, 1924, FO, 371/9565, A3967.

10 "Great Britain's Break with Mexico," *Literary Digest,* July 5, 1924, 19.

11 R. D. Peck of Bush House, Aldwych, to A. P. Carrillo, June 30, 1924, Archivo de Relaciones Exteriores, 6-10-227(I).

12 See N. Stephen Kanes, "Bankers and Diplomats: The Diplomacy of the Dollar in Mexico, 1921–1924," *Business History Review* 47.3 (autumn 1973): 335–352.

13 Evans, *Letters,* 349.

14 Ibid., 371.

15 Cummins to MacDonald, May 21, 1924, "White Paper," in ibid., 457.

16 Leone B. Moats, *Thunder in Their Veins: A Memoir of Mexico* (New York: Century, 1932).

17 Evans, *Letters,* 348–349.

18 Ibid., 339.

19 Eduardo Cordero, Arturo Perdomo, and Martín R. Toscano to Obregón, June 25, 1924, AGN-OC, 428-P-22-I; *Excélsior,* June 24, 1924.

20 Warren was quoted by H.A.C. Cummins in his June 4, 1924, dispatch to MacDonald, FO, 371/9565 A3994/253/26.

21 Montes and Solís to Obregón, May 22, 1924; Obregón to Montes and Solís, May 23, 1924, AGN-OC, 818-T-104.

22 Obregón to Ruperto Becerra, June 21, 1924; Obregón to Guerrero, June 23, 1924; "Memorandum de Cargos que el Gobierno del Estado hace el ejército regular e irregular," n.d.; each in AGN-OC, 428-P-22-I.

23 Report of visitador de la administración, Hermelindo Martínez, June 23, 1924, AGN-OC, 428-P-22-I.

24 Gregorio Meneses and Genaro Solís to Obregón, June 30, 1924, AGN-OC, 818-N-1; Adrián Flores to Obregón, July 2, 1924, AGN-OC, 428-P-22-I; "Correspondencia del C. procurador general del estado—regidor de gobernación, Gregorio Meneses to Guerrero," Aug. 21, 1924, APJP, proceso núm. 22.

25 Cruz Rivera et al. to Obregón, June 23, 1924, and Confederación Social Campesina "Domingo Arenas" to Obregón, July 8, 1924, both in AGN-OC, 428-P-22-I.

26 Santibañez to Obregón, July 8, 1924, AGN-OC, 428-P-22-I.

27 *Excélsior,* July 10, 1924.

28 H. legislatura del Estado de Puebla to Obregón, n.d., AGN-OC, 428-P-22-I.

29 David G. LaFrance, *Mexican Revolution in Puebla, 1908–1913: The Maderista Movement and the Failure of Liberal Reform* (Wilmington, Del.: Scholarly Resources, 1989), 71–72, 114.

30 Obregón to Almazán, July 10, 1924, AGN-OC, 428-P-22-I.

31 Evans, *Letters,* 347.

32 Camp statement, Sept. 3, 1924, REP, box 6.

33 Evans, *Letters,* 340.

34 Camp statement, REP, box 6.

35 R. Hollocombe to Consul-General King, July 2, 1924, FO, 371/9565.

36 Evans, *Letters,* 346.

37 [Francis Price?] to James Sheffield, n.d., REP, box 6.

38 "Jack" (Camp) to his mother, Feb. 2, 1925, REP, box 4.

39 Evans, *Letters,* 356.

40 Ibid., 362. Mrs. Evans admitted to Charles Warren that Camp hoped to kill Montes. She related the information in her letter of July 15, 1924, though it was edited from the published letters. See REP, box 2.

41 Cummins to MacDonald, June 4, 1924, "White Paper," *Letters,* 469.

42 At this time, Mrs. Evans still controlled about 70 percent of the hacienda's original 1,085 hectares. About 785 hectares had been definitively expropriated, although only about 150 of those hectares had been seized in actual fact.

43 Interview with Andrés Robles, San Jerónimo Tianguismanalco, Mar. 8, 1992. (T. Henderson, R. Bell, and M. Escobedo).

44 Evans, *Letters,* 369.

45 Hollocombe to Consul-General King, July 2, 1924, FO, 371/9565.

46 "Statement by Mr. Camp," Aug. 7, 1924, FO, 371/9566, A5208/253/26.

47 Letters of July 14, 15, 1924, REP, box 2. This nickname was excised from the published letters.

48 Evans, *Letters,* 390–394.

49 Ibid., 404.

50 The cases can be found, dated July 23 and July 26, in the AMSMT, caja "Justicia," núm. 135.

51 Pedro Romero to Juez menor y correccional, Huejotzingo, AMSMT, caja "Justicia," núm. 134.

52 Claude Philippe Dussaud, "Agrarian Politics, Violence, and the Struggle for Social Control in Puebla from 1918 to 1927: The Case of Rosalie Evans," M.A. thesis, University of Virginia, 1990, 78, n. 1.

53 Evans to Pettus, Aug. 2, 1924, REP, box 2, folder "1924, June–Oct."

54 This detail was supplied by George Camp, who reached his conclusion based on the positions of the bullet holes. Statement of George Camp, Sept. 3, 1924, REP, box 6.

55 This account of the murder is based on the following sources: "The Murder of Mrs. Evans and Further Particulars Regarding the Same," typescript, REP, box 6, folder "1911 et passim"; Statement of George Dashiel Camp, REP, box 6, folder "1925 et passim"; Daisy C. Pettus to Mary Adams, Aug. 17, 1924, REP, box 2, folder "1924, June–Oct."; and affidavits by Strathaus and Modesta, in Evans, *Letters,* 413–418.

CHAPTER TEN

1 Daisy Caden Pettus, REP, box 2.

2 *San Francisco Examiner,* Aug. 6, 1924.

3 *Excélsior,* Aug. 4, 1924.

4 Undated newspaper clipping, *La Acción,* Archivo de Relaciones Exteriores 6-10-227 (I): Obregón, quoted in *New York Tribune,* Aug. 10, 1924.

5 *Excélsior,* Aug. 10, 1924.

6 These episodes and opinions were reported in the *New York Times,* Aug. 5, 1924.

7 *New York Tribune,* Aug. 7, 1924.

8 Strathaus statement, Santa Barbara, California, Sept. 18, 1925, REP, box 6.

9 Oficial mayor of Puebla to Lic. Miguel Márquez Gamboa, Aug. 21, 1924, reprinted in Servando Ortoll, "Rosalie Evans y los informantes de Alvaro Obregón," *Estudios del Hombre,* no. 1 (Nov. 1994): 107.

10 Zafra to Obregón, Aug. 10, 1924, AGN-OC, 104-E-35.

11 Obregón to Zafra, Aug. 11, 1924, AGN-OC, 104-E-35.

12 Strathaus statement, Sept. 18, 1925, REP, box 6.

13 Camp to Pettus, Sept. 25, 1924, REP, box 6.

14 This practice is a convention in Mexican politics aimed at establishing whether a member's election was legitimate. It often devolved into merely another forum for venting partisan passions.

15 *Excélsior,* Aug. 26, 1924.

16 Barry Carr, *El movimiento obrero y la política en México, 1910–1929* (Mexico City: SepSetentas, 1976), 1:127–128.

17 *Excélsior,* Aug. 26–27, 1924.

18 *Gil Blas,* Oct. 20, 1924.

19 *Gil Blas,* Oct. 21, Oct. 23, 1924; *Excélsior,* Oct. 22, Oct. 25, Nov. 2, 1924; *New York Times,* Oct. 29, 1924.

20 "Memorandum" from "el abogando consultor" (name illegible), Oct. 28, 1924, AGN-OC, 428-P-22 (II).

21 *Excélsior,* Nov. 3, 1924.

22 Gustavo Abel Hernández Enríquez, *Historia moderna de Puebla,* vol. 2: *el periodo de la anarquía constitucional,* (Puebla: n.p., 1988), 144.

23 *Excélsior,* Nov. 5, 1924.

24 Casasola, *Historia gráfica de la Revolución Mexicana, 1900–1970,* 2nd. ed. (Mexico City: Editorial Trillas, 1973), 5:1696–1697; *Excélsior,* Aug. 13, 1924.

25 *Excélsior,* Nov. 15, Nov. 16, Nov. 17, 1924.

26 *Excélsior,* Dec. 26, 1924.

27 German chargé to Norman King, British legation, Nov. 13, 1924, REP, box 4. U.S. consul general Alexander Weddell to Pettus, Feb. 4, 1925, REP, box 6.

28 Strathaus to Francis Price, n.d., REP, box 7.

29 Strathaus statement, Sept. 18, 1925, REP, box 6.

30 Camp to Francis Price, Apr. 24, 1925, REP, box 4; various statements by Strathaus and Francis Price, REP, box 6.

31 Strathaus statement, n.d., and Strathaus statement, Sept. 18, 1925, both in REP, box 6.

32 Robert Freeman Smith, *The United States and Revolutionary Nationalism in Mexico, 1916–1932* (Chicago: University of Chicago Press, 1972), 232–237.

33 "Statement of Rosalie Evans Case in Mexico," REP, box 6, "Legal docs., 1925 *et passim*" folder; Price to Sheffield, n.d., REP, box 6. Price to Pettus, May 18, 1925, REP, box 6.

34 Smith, *United States and Revolutionary Nationalism,* 150–151, 234; the quotation is from George Agnew Chamberlain, *Is Mexico Worth Saving?* (Indianapolis: Bobbs-Merrill, 1920).

35 Smith, *United States and Revolutionary Nationalism,* 234.

36 For example, "Other Nations Defied in Mexican Congress," *The New York Times,* Sept. 5, 1925, 4, quoted Antonio Díaz Soto y Gama as saying "What do we care if the United States is annoyed and England becomes angry. Let another Kellogg note come. This Congress will not be so servile as to forget the dignity of Mexico through fear of England and the United States."

37 Carleton Beals, "Who Wants War with Mexico? The Operation of the Great Artichoke Theory in International Relations," *New Republic,* Apr. 27, 1927, 266–269.

38 On Zelia Nuttall's biography, see Ross Parmenter, *Explorer, Linguist and Ethnologist: A Descriptive Bibliography of the Published Works of Alphonse Louis Pinart, with Notes on his Life* (Los Angeles: Southwest Museum, 1966), 22, 32; on her home and importance in Mexico City society, see Charlotte Cameron, *Mexico in Revolution* (London: Seeley, Service, 1925), 119–123.

39 Evans, *Letters,* 222.

40 Zelia Nuttall to Daisy Pettus, July 5, 1925, REP, box 7.

41 Daisy Pettus to Sen. William E. Borah, July 24, 1925, REP, box 7.

42 Gayou to Calles, Sept. 5, 1925, AGN-OC, 104-E-35.

43 Max Weber, steward of International Geneve Association of Hotel and Restaurant Employees, to Price, Oct. 28, 1925, REP, box 7.

44 Daisy Pettus, note, Oct. 15, 1925, REP, box 7.

45 Zelia Nuttall to Daisy Pettus, Oct. 3, 1925, REP, box 7.

46 Francis Price to McKenney and Flannery, Oct. 22, 1925, REP, box 7.

47 Strathaus to Zelia Nothel [*sic*], Dec. 25, 1925, REP, box 7.

48 R. P. de Negri to Obregón, Nov. 18, 1924, AGN-OC, 818-S-66.

49 Camp to Sheffield, May 9, 1925; Camp to Sheffield, May 19, 1925; Camp to Arthur Schoenfeld, May 25, 1925; all in REP, box 6.

50 "Contra el administrador de la Hacienda de San Pedro Coxtocán por el delito de robo de que se queja el Sr. Darío Méndez, vecino de San Jerónimo Tianguismanalco," July 29, 1925, and "Contra Jorge de Campe [sic], admor. [administrador] de la Hacienda San Pedro Coxtocán por su desobediencia a un mandato legítimo de autoridad competente," Aug. 22, 1925, APJP, núm. 1 and núm. 57.

51 Sheffield to Camp, Dec. 16, 1924, REP, box 6.

52 "Es un hombre bastante nervioso por no decir otra cosa." Sáenz to Sheffield, Dec. 18, 1925, REP, box 7.

53 Price to McKenney and Flannery, Apr. 22, 1925, REP, box 6.

54 Murray compiled and translated a book of Calles's speeches, which was intended as a reply to the offensive Kellogg statement. Murray, *Mexico before the World* (New York: Academy Press, 1927).

55 Schofield to Price, Apr. 5, 1925; Price memo, n.d.; Price to McKenney and Flannery, Apr. 22, 1925; Price to McKenney and Flannery, May 18, 1925; all in REP, box 6.

56 The villagers of Santa María Moyotzingo had been granted land in 1920. The grant had been made definitive, and amparo was denied in late 1923. Even so, owing to opposition from Mrs. Evans and Camp, by late 1925 Moyotzingo had still not taken active possession of the land.

57 Price to Pettus, June 9, 1925, REP, box 6.

58 Pettus to Price, n.d. [probably Sept. 1925], REP, box 7.

59 Camp to Price, July 6, 1925, REP, box 7.

60 There is, in fact, some circumstantial evidence to support this claim. References in Mrs. Evans's letter of May 17, 1924, point to an urgent telegram, supposedly sent by Camp's partner in Mexico City, requesting that he return at once. Camp's partner later denied sending such a telegram, and Mrs. Evans suspected it was a ruse by Warren to get Camp away from the hacienda. Such an interpretation seems to point to somewhat more sinister goings-on in view of the fact that references to this telegram were edited from the published letters. This theory is undercut by several considerations, however, not the least of which is common sense. According to Camp's reasoning, as expressed to Ross Parmenter in an interview of June 9, 1963, Warren hoped to have Mrs. Evans killed so she would not interfere with the cordial relations he was trying to maintain between the United States and Mexico. Camp did not explain, however, how the murder of Mrs. Evans was supposed to enhance those relations. Moreover, other passages deleted from the letters suggest another story. In her letter of July 15, 1924, Mrs. Evans admitted to Warren that Camp wished to kill Manuel Montes. Warren, then, may have had very good reasons to want to remove Camp from the region that had nothing to do with killing Mrs. Evans because the murder of Montes by an American would obviously be damaging to the United States. There is also evidence of a serious falling-out between Camp and Mrs. Evans that was expurgated from the July 31, 1924, letter. Daisy Pettus, writing in the immediate aftermath of her sister's murder, when she was still fairly sympathetic to Camp, notes that Mrs. Evans "was so anxious about Camp that she intended to persuade him to return to the city. She did so. Is it not a pity?" Pettus to [?], Aug. 17, 1924, REP, box 2.

61 Notes of interview with Ross Parmenter, Harvard Club [Cambridge, Mass.?], June 9, 1963. My thanks go to Mr. Parmenter for generously lending me this material.

62 Gertrude Atherton, "How Rosalie Evans Died Fighting in Mexico," *Literary Digest International Book Review,* May 1926, 352–354.

63 Howlin to Pettus, Apr. 6, 1925, REP, box 2.

64 The particular phrase comes from the review of *The Rosalie Evans Letters* in the *New York Evening Post Literary Review,* Apr. 10, 1926.

65 Bobbs to Pettus, Sept. 29, 1925, REP, box 2.

66 Correspondence between Pettus and Price in REP, box 2.

67 Evans, *Letters,* "Foreword."

68 Ibid., 71.

69 Price to Sheffield, n.d., REP, box 6.

70 Pettus to Price, May 13, 1926.

71 D. C. Chambers to Pettus, Mar. 7, 1927, REP, box 2.

72 "Confidential Memo for Mr. Chambers," n.d. (1925), REP, box 2.

73 Carleton Beals, "Mrs. Evans," *Nation,* June 16, 1926.

74 The phrase is from the review by Ernest Gruening, *Saturday Review of Literature,* May 29, 1926.

75 *New Yorker,* Apr. 24, 1926.

76 Atherton, "How Rosalie Evans Died Fighting in Mexico."

77 Warren was sixty-five years old at his death. See obituary, *New York Times,* Feb. 4, 1936.

78 *Catholic World* 123.85 (Sept. 1926): 849–850.

79 Charles Beard, "Americans in Mexico," *New Republic,* Oct. 13, 1926), 225–226.

80 Evans, *Letters,* 296–297.

81 *The New York Times Book Review,* March 21, 1926.

82 U.S. consul general Alexander Weddell, for instance, charged that Beals has pursued the "apparently profitable game of befouling the country of his birth for the edification of Mexicans and Nicaraguans." Weddell to Andrew J. McConnico, June 7, 1928, Alexander Weddell papers, Virginia Historical Society, MSS1, W41266 FA2, box 30.

83 Beals, "Mrs. Evans."

84 Quoted in *The Borzoi Book of Short Fiction,* ed. David H. Richter (New York: Random House, 1983), 1254.

85 Katherine Anne Porter, "La Conquistadora," in *The Collected Essays and Occasional Writings of Katherine Anne Porter* (New York: Delacorte, 1970), 416–420.

86 Ovier to Pettus, Oct. 11, 1926, REP, box 2.

87 Temple Bodley to Pettus, Aug. 5, 1926, and Ovier to Pettus, Oct. 11, 1926, both in REP, box 2.

88 Rosalind Buel Thayer to Pettus, Mar. 31, 1926, REP, box 2.

89 Julio Cuadros Caldas, *Mexico-Soviet* (Puebla: Santiago Loyo, 1926), 284.

90 Parmenter interview with Camp, June 9, 1963.

91 Although I have varied the metaphor, this description of the post-1924 political structure is similar to that advanced by Juan Felipe Leal, *Agrupaciones y burocracias sindicales en México, 1906/1938* (Mexico City: Terra Nova, 1985), 162.

92 Raymond Th. J. Buve, "Tlaxcala: Consolidating a Cacicazgo," in *Provinces of the Revolution: Essays on Regional Mexican History, 1910–1929,* ed. Thomas Benjamin and Mark Wasserman (Albuquerque: University of New Mexico Press, 1990), 250, 259.

93 *Excélsior,* Jan. 13, 1927.

94 July 4, 1927. Another anti-Montes editorial can be found in the edition of Jan. 25, 1927.

95 *Excélsior,* Jan. 12, 1927.

96 Homero Sánchez y Sánchez, "Sindicalismo en San Martín Texmelucan (1922–1928)," *Boletín-Cambio,* Feb. 1990.

97 Vecinos of Acatlán to Calles, Jan. 25, 1927; Manuel Ruiz to Calles, Jan. 31, 1927; Sindicato de Campesinos Progresistas de San Salvador el Seco, Feb. 1, 1927; all in AGN-P-20, leg. 4.

98 *Excélsior,* Feb. 19, 1927.

99 *Excélsior,* June 30, 1927.

100 *Excélsior,* July 13, 1927.

101 Alfonso León de Garay, *Veinte meses de gobierno. Bravo Izquierdo: su obra, su régimen, su herencia* (Puebla: n.p., 1929), 30–32.

102 *Excélsior,* July 5, July 7, 1927.

103 *Excélsior,* July 1, 1927.

104 This account of the killing is based on *Excélsior,* Aug. 31, Sept. 1, 2, 3, 1927; and "Instruido en contra del que o los que resulten responsables del delito de homicidio del quien en vida respondió al nombre de Manuel P. Montes, hecho que tuvo lugar en el pueblo de San Martín Texmelucan, el 30 de agosto próximo pasado," Sept. 29, 1927, APJP, leg. 637, núm. 78.

EPILOGUE

1 *Excélsior,* Sept. 2, 1927.

2 Interview with Diputado Antonio Montes, El Moral, Mar. 21, 1992 (T. Henderson).

3 *Excélsior,* Sept. 2, 1927.

4 *Excélsior,* Sept. 4, 1927.

5 Donato Bravo Izquierdo, *Un Soldado del Pueblo* (Puebla: n.p., 1964), 290. I'd like to thank Leticia Gamboa Ojeda for bringing this to my attention.

6 *El Machete,* no. 78 (Sept. 3, 1927), reprinted in Favio Barbosa Cano, *La CROM, de Luis N. Morones a Antonio J. Hernández* (Puebla: ICUAP, 1980), 395–397.

7 Interview with Juana Montes García, San Martín Texmelucan, July 9, 1990 (T. Henderson).

8 Quoted in Enrique Krauze, *Plutarco E. Calles: reformar desde el origen* (Mexico City: Fondo de Cultura Económica, 1987), 89.

9 Sánchez to Calles, May 23, 1929, Fideicomiso Archivo Plutarco Elías Calles, exp. José María Sánchez, gaveta 61, núm. 79.

10 Sánchez to CNA, Oct. 25, 1933, DAACP, dotación núm. 103, Santa Ana Xalmimilulco; interview with Domingo Romero Téllez, Santa Ana Xalmimilulco, April 8, 1992 (T. Henderson and J. César R.).

11 W. O. Jenkins to Alexander W. Weddell, Apr. 29, 1926, REP, box 7.

12 Interview with Andrés Robles, San Jerónimo Tianguismanalco, March 8, 1992 (T. Henderson, R. Bell, and M. Escobedo). Corroborating this information was Ignacio Téllez Escalona, Santa Ana Xalmimilulco, Mar. 30, 1992 (T. Henderson, R. Bell, and M. Escobedo).

13 *Excélsior,* Sept. 7, 1927.

14 "Entrevista con el Sr. Bonifacio Reyes Sebastián, realizada for María Alba Pastor, el día 8 de junio de 1974, en San Jerónimo Tianguismanalco, Edo. de Puebla," Archivo de la Palabra, Instituto de Investigaciones, Dr. José María Luis Mora, Mexico City, PHO/1/138.

15 Rodolfo Stavenhagen, "Marginalidad y participación en la reforma agraria mexicana," *Revista Latinoamericana de Sociología* 5.2 (1969): 249–274.

16 Jeffery M. Paige, "Land Reform and Agrarian Revolution in El Salvador: Comments on Seligson and Diskin," *Latin American Research Review* 31.2 (1996): 127.

17 Alan Knight, "Land and Society in Revolutionary Mexico: The Destruction of the Great Haciendas," *Mexican Studies/Estudios Mexicanos* 7.1 (winter 1991): 73–104.

18 A good case in point is recounted by Daniel Nugent and Ana María Alonso for Namiquipa, Chihuahua. See "Multiple Selective Traditions in Agrarian Reform and Agrarian Struggle: Popular Culture and State Formation in the Ejido of Namiquipa, Chichuaha," in *Everyday Forms of State Formation: Revolution and the Negotiation of Rule in Modern Mexico,* ed. Gilbert M. Joseph and Daniel Nugent (Durham, N.C.: Duke University Press, 1994), 209–246. Many other examples of recalcitrance toward agrarian reform could be cited. In Michoacán, for example, suspicion of the federal government was compounded by the religious issue. See especially Luis González y González, *San José de Gracia: Mexican Village in Transition,* trans. John Upton (Austin: University of Texas Press, 1974).

19 See Manuel L. Carlos, "Peasant Leadership Hierarchies: Leadership Behavior, Power Blocs, and Conflict in Mexican Regions," in *Mexican Regions: Comparative and Historical Development,* ed. Eric Van Young (San Diego: Center for U.S.-Mexican Studies, University of California, San Diego, 1992), 91–114, and Guillermo de la Peña, "Populism, Regional Power, and Political Mediation: Southern Jalisco, 1900–1980," in ibid., 191–223.

20 T. J. Byres, "The Agrarian Question and Differentiation of the Peasantry," foreword to *Peasants and Classes: A Study of Differentiation in Bangladesh,* ed. Atiur Rahman (London and New Jersey: Zed Books, 1986), ix.

21 See Patrice Melé Credal, "Poder local y urbanización en la ciudad de Puebla," in *Poder local, poder regional,* ed. Jorge Padua and Alain Vanneph (Mexico City: El Colegio de México, 1986), 222–245, esp. 235–237.

22 This account is based on various correspondence in DAACP, especially from the expedientes for Santa María Moyotzingo (núm. 87) and Santa Ana Xalmimilulco (núm. 103).

23 See "Debate sobre el ejido," *La Jornada,* Nov. 26, 1991.

24 Interview with Ignacio Téllez Escalona, Santa Ana Xalmimilulco, Mar. 30, 1992 (T. Henderson, Josué César Romero, and Moisés Zamora Peregrina).

25 Leonardo Arce Téllez, *El campesino en acción,* Nov. 12, 1971, DAACP, "Dotación de Santa Ana Xalmimilulco," exp. 103; interview with Leonardo Arce Téllez, Santa Ana Xalmimilulco, Apr. 28, 1992 (T. Henderson and Josué César Romero).

26 Pettus to Price, July 29, 1929, REP, box 8.

27 Pettus to Huger Sinkler, attorney, of Blowing Rock, N.C., July 6, 1939, REP, box 5.

28 Ernesto Von Raesfeld to Huger Sinkler, Mar. 20, 1947, REP, box 10. U.S.-Mexican Claims Commission to Jerdone Pettus, Dec. 17, 1945, REP, box 10.

29 Interview with Carlos R. Fernández, San Pedro Coxtocán, c. July 1990.

30 "Introduction," manuscript, REP, box 2.

31 *The Proud Tower* (New York: Bantam, 1962), 544.

32 Carleton Beals, "Mrs. Evans," *Nation,* June 16, 1926.

33 Rosalie Evans, *The Rosalie Evans Letters from Mexico* (Indianapolis: Bobbs-Merrill, 1926), 352.

Bibliography

ARCHIVES

AGET   Archivo General del Estado de Tlaxcala, Fondo Revolución Obregonista
AGM-BN   Archivo Gildardo Magaña, Biblioteca Nacional de México
AGN   Archivo General de la Nación
            CNA (Comisión Nacional Agraria, Resoluciones Presidenciales)
            Tierras
            Fondo Presidentes
                FZ (Fondo Zapata)
                    Francisco I. Madero
                OC (Obregón-Calles)
AHEE   Archivo Histórico de la Embajada de España
AHSRE   Archivo Histórico Genaro Estrada–Secretaría de Relaciones Exteriores
AMSMT   Archivo Municipal de San Martín Texmelucan
APJP   Archivo del Poder Judicial del Estado de Puebla
DAACP   Departamento de Asuntos Agrarios y de Colonización de Puebla
FO   Great Britain, Public Records Office, Foreign Office
ORAP   Oficina de la Reforma Agraria de Puebla
REP   Rosalie Evans Papers (#2895), Special Collections Department, University of
            Virginia Library
SD   U.S. State Department Archives, Record Group 59
USMIR   U.S. Military Intelligence Reports
Fairfax Harrison Papers, Virginia Historical Society
Fideicomiso Archivo Plutarco Elías Calles y Fernando Torreblanca

"Entrevista con el Sr. Luis Sánchez Pontón, realizada por Daniel Cazes, en abril de 1961 en la Ciudad de México." Archivo de la Palabra/Instituto de Investigaciones Dr. José María Luis Mora, Mexico City, PHO/1/20.

"Entrevista con el Gral. Brigadier Tiburcio Cuellar Montalvo, realizada por Eugenia Meyer, el día 8 de mayo de 1973, en la Ciudad de México." Archivo de la Palabra/Instituto de Investigaciones Dr. José María Luis Mora, Mexico City. Proyecto de Historia Oral (PHO)/1/45.

"Entrevista con el Sr. Pedro L. Romero Cortés, realizada por María Alba Pastor el día 8 de junio de 1974 en San Martín Texmelucan." Archivo de la Palabra/Instituto de Investigaciones Dr. José María Luis Mora, Mexico City. PHO/1/139.

"Entrevista con el Sr. Bonifacio Reyes Sebastián, realizada por María Alba Pastor, el día 8 de junio de 1974, en San Jerónimo Tianguismanalco, Edo. de Puebla." Archivo de la Palabra/Instituto de Investigaciones Dr. José María Luis Mora, Mexico City. PHO/1/138.

"Entrevista al Sr. Máximo Flores, realizada por María Alba Pastor, el día 14 de junio de 1974, en San Martín Texmelucan, Estado de Puebla," Archivo de la Palabra/Instituto de Investigaciones Dr. José María Luis Mora, Mexico City. PHO/1/140.

George Camp, Harvard Club, June 9, 1963, by Ross Parmenter.

C. Edmonds Allan, New York City, June 12, 1963, by Ross Parmenter.

Juana Montes García, San Martín Texmelucan, July 9, 1990 (T. Henderson).

Paula Romero vda. de Montes, San Buenaventura Tecaltzingo, Feb. 22, 1992 (T. Henderson and Robert Bell).

Francisco Alvarado and Isaura Escobedo Montes, San Buenaventura Tecaltzingo, Mar. 3, 1992 (T. Henderson and R. Bell).

Antonio García Ramírez, Santa Ana Xalmimilulco, Mar. 3, 1992 (T. Henderson and J. César R.).

Andrés Robles, San Jerónimo Tianguismanalco, Mar. 8, 1992 (T. Henderson, R. Bell, and M. Escobedo).

Nina Avila de Manjarrez, Rancho de San Carlos, San Buenaventura Tecaltzingo, Mar. 14, 1992 (T. Henderson, R. Bell, and Marcela Escobedo).

Primitivo Martínez, San Buenaventura Tecaltzingo, Mar. 14, 1992 (T. Henderson and R. Bell).

Antonio Montes, El Moral, Mar. 21, 1992 (T. Henderson).

Martín García, San Francisco Tepeyecac, Mar. 28, 1992 (T. Henderson, R. Bell, and M. Escobedo).

Ignacio Téllez Escalona, Santa Ana Xalmimilulco, Mar. 30, 1992 (T. Henderson, Josué César Romero, and Moisés Zamora Peregrina).

Miguel Juárez César and Hermelinda Espinosa Maro, Santa Ana Xalmimilulco, Apr. 2, 1992 (T. Henderson, J. César R., and M. Zamora P.).

Saturnino Memetla Ramírez, Santa Ana Xalmimilulco, Apr. 2, 1992 (T. Henderson, J. César R., and M. Zamora P.).

Domingo Romero Téllez, Santa Ana Xalmimilulco, Apr. 8, 1992 (T. Henderson and J. César R.).

Jesús Pérez Ramírez, Santa Ana Xalmimilulco, Apr. 10, 1992 (T. Henderson, J. César R., M. Zamora P.).

Nazalio Pérez Bravo, Santa María Moyotzingo, Apr. 13, 1992 (T. Henderson, J. César R.,
M. Zamora P., and Ascensión Rosas Rivera).

Juan Sansón Pérez, Santa María Moyotzingo, Apr. 13, 1992 (T. Henderson, J. César R.,
M. Zamora P., and Ascensión Rosas Rivera).

Vidal Solís Rivas, Santa María Moyotzingo, Apr. 13, 1992 (T. Henderson, J. César R.,
M. Zamora P., and Ascensión Rosas Rivera).

Leonardo Arce Téllez, Santa Ana Xalmimilulco, Apr. 28, 1992 (T. Henderson and Josué César
Romero).

BULLETINS, MEMORIAS, AND OFFICIAL DOCUMENTS

Boletín de la Sociedad Agrícola Mexicana (BSAM).

Censo general de la República Mexicana, Estado de Puebla. Mexico City: Secretaría de Fomento,
1902.

Ferrocarril de México á Veracruz: contestación al comunicado del licenciado.

Informe de la Secretaría de Fomento.

Investigation of Mexican Affairs. Doc. no. 285. Pursuant to S. Res. 106. Washington: GPO, 1920.

Memoria de la Secretaría de Fomento, Industria y Comercio de la República Mexicana. Mexico
City: Oficina Tipográfica de la Secretaría de Fomento, 1885.

Periódico Oficial del Estado de Puebla.

*Puebla Memoria instructiva y documentada del Departamento Ejecutivo del Estado, presenta al XX
Congreso Constitucional*. Puebla: n.p., 1909.

Mexican Financier.

Texas Journal of Commerce.

BOOKS

Aubertin. J. J. *A Flight to Mexico*. London: Kegan Paul, Trench, and Co., 1882.

Banco de Londres y México, S.A. *Cien años de banca de México, 1864–1964*. Mexico City: n.p.,
1964.

Barbosa Cano, Favio. *LA CROM, de Luis N. Morones á Antonio J. Hernández*. Puebla: ICUAP,
1980.

Bartra, Armando. *Los herederos de Zapata: movimientos campesinos posrevolucionarios en México,
1920–1980*. México: Ediciones Era, 1985.

Bowring, Edgar A. *The Poems of Schiller*. London: George Bell and Sons, 1874.

Bravo Izquierdo, Donato. *Un soldado del pueblo*. Puebla: n.p., 1964.

Bremauntz, Alberto. *Setenta años de mi vida: memorias y anécdotas*. Mexico City: Ediciones
Jurídico Sociales, 1968.

Calderón de la Barca, Fanny. *Life in Mexico during a Residence of Two Years in That Country*.
Mexico: Ediciones Tolteca, 1952.

Calles, Plutarco Elias. *Mexico before the World*. Translated and edited by Robert Hammond
Murray. New York: Academy Press, 1927.

Calvert, Peter. *The Mexican Revolution, 1910–1914: The Diplomacy of Anglo-American Conflict*.
Cambridge: Cambridge University Press, 1968.

Cameron, Charlotte. *Mexico in Revolution*. London: Seeley, Service, 1925.

Carr, Barry. *El movimiento obrero y la política en México, 1910–1929*. 2 vols. Mexico City: SepSetentas, 1976.

Cartwright, Gary. *Galveston: A History of the Island*. New York: Atheneum, 1991.

Casasola, Gustavo. *Historia gráfica de la Revolución Mexicana, 1900–1970*. 2nd. ed. 10 vols. Mexico City: Editorial Trillas, 1973.

Castillo, Porfirio del. *Puebla y Tlaxcala en los días de la Revolución*. Mexico City: n.p., 1953.

Chávez Orozco, Luis. *Documentos para la historia económica de México*. Vol. 10: *Orígenes del agrarismo en México*. Mexico City: Secretaría de la Economía Nacional, 1936.

Chevalier, François. *Land and Society in Colonial Mexico: The Great Hacienda*. Berkeley and Los Angeles: University of California Press, 1970.

Cline, Howard. *The United States and Mexico*. New York: Atheneum, 1963.

Contreras Hernández, Jesús. *Texmelucan: Identidad Olvidada*. Puebla: Granrica, 1991.

Craig, Ann L. *The First Agraristas: An Oral History of a Mexican Agrarian Reform Movement*. Berkeley and Los Angeles: University of California Press, 1983.

Creelman, James. *Díaz, Master of Mexico*. New York: D. Appleton, 1912.

Cuadros Caldas, Julio. *Mexico-Soviet*. Puebla: Santiago Loyo, 1926.

Cumberland, Charles C. *Mexican Revolution: Genesis under Madero*. Austin: University of Texas Press, 1952.

——. *Mexican Revolution: The Constitutionalist Years*. Austin: University of Texas Press, 1972.

de Beer, Gabriella. *Luis Cabrera: un intelectual de la Revolución Mexicana,* translated by Ismael Pizarro y Mercedes Pizarro. Mexico City: Fondo de Cultura Económica, 1984.

de la Peña, Guillermo. *A Legacy of Promises: Agriculture, Politics, and Ritual in the Morelos Highlands of Mexico*. Austin: University of Texas Press, 1981.

Díaz Soto y Gama, Antonio. *La Revolución agraria del sur y Emiliano Zapata, su caudillo*. Mexico City: El Caballito, 1976.

Dulles, John W. F. *Yesterday in Mexico: A Chronicle of the Revolution, 1919–1936*. Austin: University of Texas Press, 1961.

Esteva, Gustavo. *The Struggle for Rural Mexico*. South Hadley, Mass.: Bergin and Garvey, 1983.

Evans, Rosalie. *The Rosalie Evans Letters from Mexico*. Indianapolis: Bobbs-Merrill, 1926.

Fábila, Manuel. *Cinco siglos de legislación agraria en México, 1493–1940*. Mexico City: Secretaría de la Reforma Agraria and CEHAM, 1981.

Florescano, Enrique. *Origen y desarrollo del problema agraria en México, 1500–1821*. Mexico City: Era, 1971.

Frías Olvera, Manuel. *Historia de la Revolución Mexicana en el Estado de Puebla*. Mexico City: Instituto Nacional de Estudios Históricos de la Revolución Mexicana, 1980.

Friedrich, Paul. *Agrarian Revolt in a Mexican Village*. Chicago: University of Chicago Press, 1977.

——. *The Princes of Naranja: An Essay in Anthrohistorical Method*. Austin: University of Texas Press, 1986.

Gardner, Lloyd C. *Safe for Democracy: The Anglo-American Response to Revolution, 1913–1923*. New York: Oxford University Press, 1984.

Gillow, Eulogio. *Reminiscencias del Ilmo. y Rmo. Sr. Dr. D. Eulogio Gillow y Zavalza, arzobispo de Antequera*. Edited by José A. Rivera G. Los Angeles: El Heraldo de México, 1920.

Gledhill, John. *Casi Nada: A Study of Agrarian Reform in the Heartland of Cardenismo*. Albany: Institute for Mesoamerican Studies, 1991.

González Navarro, Moisés, ed. *Estadísticas económicas del Porfiriato: fuerza de trabajo y actividad económica por sectores.* Mexico City: El Colegio de México, 1965.

González Roa, Fernando. *El aspecto agrario de la Revolución Mexicana.* Mexico City: Liga de Economistas Revolucionarios, 1975. Originally published 1919.

González y González, Luis. *San José de Gracia: Mexican Village in Transition,* translated by John Upton. Austin: University of Texas Press, 1974.

Graves, Robert, and Hodge, Alan. *The Long Week-End: A Social History of Great Britain, 1918–1939.* New York: W. W. Norton, 1940.

Gruening, Ernest. *Mexico and Its Heritage.* New York: Century, 1928.

Guzmán, Martín Luis. *El liberalismo mexicano en pensamiento y en acción.* Vol. 5: *Leyes de Reforma, Gobiernos de Ignacio Comonfort y Benito Juárez (1856–1863).* Mexico City: Empresas Editoriales, 1947.

Hanrahan, Gene Z., ed. *Documents on the Mexican Revolution.* Vol. 8: *The Rebellion of Félix Díaz.* Salisbury, N.C.: Documentary Publications, 1983.

Hart, John M. *Anarchism and the Mexican Working Class, 1860–1931.* Austin: University of Texas Press, 1978.

Havighurst, Alfred F. *Britain in Transition: The Twentieth Century.* Chicago: University of Chicago Press, 1962.

Hernández Enríquez, Gustavo Abel. *Historia moderna de Puebla.* Vol. 1: *1917–1920. Gobierno del Doctor Alfonso Cabrera Lobato.* Puebla: n.p., 1986.

———. Gustavo Abel. *Historia moderna de Puebla.* Vol. 2: *1920–1924. El período de la anarquía constitucional.* Puebla: n.p., 1988.

———. Gustavo Abel. *Historia moderna de Puebla.* Vol. 3: *1925–1926. La contrarrevolución en Puebla.* Puebla: n.p., 1988.

Hewitt de Alcántara, Cynthia. *Anthropological Perspectives on Rural Mexico.* London: Routledge and Kegan Paul, 1984.

Hunt, Michael H. *Ideology and U.S. Foreign Policy.* New Haven, Conn.: Yale University Press, 1987.

Irving, Washington. *Life and Voyages of Christopher Columbus.* New York: Lovell Coryell, n.d.

Joseph, Gilbert M. *Revolution from Without: Yucatán, Mexico, and the United States, 1880–1924.* Durham, N.C.: Duke University Press, 1988. Originally published 1982 by Cambridge University Press.

Joseph, Gilbert M., and Nugent, Daniel. *Everyday Forms of State Formation: Revolution and the Negotiation of Rule in Modern Mexico.* Durham, N.C.: Duke University Press, 1994.

Kaerger, Karl. *Agricultura y colonización en México en 1900.* Translated by Pedro Lewin and Gudrun Dohrman from the German edition of 1907. Mexico City: Universidad Autónoma Chapingo, 1986.

Katz, Friedrich. *The Secret War in Mexico: Europe, the United States, and the Mexican Revolution.* Chicago: University of Chicago Press, 1981.

Knight, Alan. *The Mexican Revolution.* 2 vols. Cambridge: Cambridge University Press, 1986.

Krauze, Enrique. *Caudillos culturales en la Revolución Mexicana.* Mexico City: Siglo Veintiuno, 1976.

———. *Plutarco E. Calles: reformar desde el origen.* Mexico City: Fondo de Cultura Económica, 1987.

LaFrance, David G. *The Mexican Revolution in Puebla, 1908–1913: The Maderista Movement and the Failure of Liberal Reform.* Wilmington, Del.: Scholarly Resources, 1989.

Leduc, Alberto, Lara y Parod, Luis, and Roumagnac, Carlos. *Diccionario de geografía y biografía mexicana*. Paris and Mexico City: Librería de la Vda. de C. Bouret, 1910.

León de Garay, Alfonso. *Veinte meses de gobierno. Bravo Izquierdo: su obra, su régimen, su herencia*. Puebla: n.p., 1929.

Lewis, Oscar. *Life in a Mexican Village: Tepoztlán Restudied*. Urbana: University of Illinois, 1951.

———. *Pedro Martínez: A Mexican Peasant and His Family*. New York: Random House, 1964.

Lira, Miguel N. *Corrido de Domingo Arenas y México — Pregón*. 3d ed. Mexico City: Ediciones Botas, 1938.

Lomnitz-Adler, Claudio. *Exits from the Labyrinth: Culture and Ideology in the Mexican National Space*. Berkeley and Los Angeles: University of California Press, 1992.

Luman, Enrique. *Almazán: vida de un caudillo y metabolismo de una revolución*. México: Editorial "Claridad," 1940.

Macías, Carlos, ed. *Plutarco Elías Calles: correspondencia personal (1919–1945)*. Mexico City: Fondo de Cultura Económica y Archivo P. E. Calles, 1991.

Manuel P. Montes: su vida revolucionaria, su actuación política. Puebla: n.p., 1927; reissue 1976.

Martin, Percy F. *Mexico of the Twentieth Century*. 2 vols. New York: Dodd, Mead, 1908.

McBride, George M. *The Land Systems of Mexico*. New York: American Geographical Society, 1923.

McCaleb, Walter Flavius. *Present and Past Banking in Mexico*. New York: Harper and Bros., 1920.

Medina Rubio, Arístedes. *La iglesia y la producción en Puebla, 1540–1795*. Mexico City: El Colegio de México, 1983.

Memorandum sobre el amparo de José María Sánchez, ex-gobernador del Estado de Puebla. Puebla: Imprenta de la Escuela de Artes y Oficios del Estado, 1923.

Mexico, Instituto Nacional de Estádistica, Geografía e Informática. *Estádisticas históricas de México*. Vol. 1. Mexico City: SEP, 1988.

Meyer, Eugenia. *Luis Cabrera: teórico y crítico de la Revolución*. Mexico City: SepSetentas, 1972.

Meyer, Lorenzo. *Su Majestad Británica contra la Revolución Mexicana, 1900–1950: el fin de un imperio informal*. Mexico City: El Colegio de México, 1991.

Moats, Leone B. *Thunder in Their Veins: A Memoir of Mexico*. New York: Century, 1932.

Monroy Durán, Luis. *El último caudillo*. Mexico City: J. S. Rodríguez, 1924.

Montmarquet, James A. *The Idea of Agrarianism: From Hunter-Gatherer to Agrarian Radical in Western Culture*. Moscow: University of Idaho Press, 1989.

Nickel, Herbert J. *Morfología social de la hacienda mexicana*. Mexico City: Fondo de Cultura Económica, 1988.

Obregón, Alvaro. *The Agrarian Problem: Short-Hand Notes of the Impressions Exchanged between the President Elect and a Numerous Group of Congressmen, October 1920*. Mexico City: Imprenta de la Secretaría de Relaciones Exteriores, 1924.

———. *Discursos del General Alvaro Obregón*. Mexico City: Biblioteca de la Dirección General de Educación Militar, 1932.

Obregón, Arturo. *Alberto Santa Fé y la Ley del Pueblo, 1878–1879*. Mexico City: Centro de Estudios Históricos del Movimiento Obrero Mexicano, 1980.

Ocampo, Javier. *Las ideas de un día: el pueblo mexicano ante la consumación de su independencia*. Mexico City: El Colegio de México, 1969.

Palacios, Juan Enrique. *Puebla: su territorio y sus habitantes.* 2 vols. Puebla: Junta de Mejoramiento Moral, Cívico y Material del Municipio de Puebla, 1982. Originally published 1917.

Patterson, Orlando. *Slavery and Social Death: A Comparative Study.* Cambridge, Mass.: Harvard University Press, 1982.

Pletcher, David. *Rails, Mines, and Progress: Seven American Promoters in Mexico, 1867–1911.* Ithaca, N.Y.: Cornell University Press, 1958.

Pombo, Luis. *México: 1876–1892.* Mexico City: Imprenta de "El Siglo Diez y Nueve," 1893.

Powell, John Duncan. *Political Mobilization of the Venezuelan Peasant.* Cambridge, Mass.: Harvard University Press, 1971, 2.

Prem, Hanns J. *Milpa y hacienda: tenencia de la tierra indígena y española en la cuenca del Alto Atoyac, Puebla, México (1520–1650).* Mexico City: Fondo de Cultura Económica, 1988.

Quirk, Robert E. *The Mexican Revolution, 1914–1915: The Convention of Aguascalientes.* Bloomington: Indiana University Press, 1960.

Ramírez Rancaño, Mario. *Domingo y Cirilo Arenas en la Revolución Mexicana.* Mexico City: Centro de Estudios Históricos del Agrarismo en México, 1991.

———. *La Revolución en los volcanes: Domingo y Cirilo Arenas.* Mexico City: Instituto de Investigaciones Sociales, UNAM, 1995.

Rees, Peter. *Transportes y comercio entre México y Veracruz, 1519–1910.* Mexico City: SepSetentas, 1976.

Reina, Leticia. *Las rebeliones campesinas en México (1819–1906).* Mexico City: Siglo XXI, 1980.

Ronfeldt, David. *Atencingo: The Politics of Agrarian Struggle in a Mexican Ejido.* Stanford, Calif.: Stanford University Press, 1973.

Ruiz, Ramón Eduardo. *The Great Rebellion: Mexico, 1905–1924.* New York: W. W. Norton, 1980.

Salamini, Heather Fowler. *Agrarian Radicalism in Veracruz, 1920–38.* Lincoln: University of Nebraska Press, 1971.

Sánchez, José María. *La reivindicación del obrero.* Mexico City: n.p., 1923.

Sanderson, Susan Walsh. *Land Reform in Mexico: 1910–1980.* Orlando, Fla.: Academic Press, 1984.

Schmidt, Arthur. *The Social and Economic Effects of the Railroad in Puebla and Veracruz, Mexico, 1867–1911.* New York: Garland, 1987.

Scott, James. *Weapons of the Weak: Everyday Forms of Peasant Resistance.* New Haven, Conn.: Yale University Press, 1985.

———. *Domination and the Arts of Resistance: Hidden Transcripts.* New Haven, Conn.: Yale University Press, 1990.

Silva Herzog, Jesús. *El agrarismo mexicano y la reforma agraria: exposición y crítica.* Mexico City: Fondo de Cultura Económica, 1959.

Simpson, Eyler N. *The Ejido: Mexico's Way Out.* Chapel Hill: University of North Carolina Press, 1937.

Sinkin, Richard. *The Mexican Reform, 1855–1876: A Study in Liberal Nation-Building.* Austin: Institute of Latin American Studies, University of Texas, 1979.

Smith, Robert Freeman. *The United States and Revolutionary Nationalism in Mexico, 1916–1932.* Chicago: University of Chicago Press, 1972.

Southworth, J. R. *El Estado de Puebla.* Puebla: n.p., 1901.

Tannenbaum, Frank. *The Mexican Agrarian Revolution.* New York: Macmillan, 1929.

Terry, Philip. *Terry's Guide to Mexico.* Boston: Houghton Mifflin, 1927.

Thomson, Guy P. C. *Puebla de los Angeles: Industry and Society in a Mexican City, 1700–1850.* Boulder, Colo.: Westview, 1989.

Thorpe, D. R. *The Uncrowned Prime Ministers.* London: Darkhorse Publishing, 1980.

Tischendorf, Alfred. *Great Britain and Mexico in the Era of Porfirio Díaz.* Durham, N.C.: Duke University Press, 1961.

Tuchman, Barbara. *The Proud Tower: A Portrait of the World Before the War: 1890–1914.* New York: Bantam, 1962.

Ungar, Frederick, ed. *Friedrich Schiller: An Anthology for Our Time.* New York: Frederick Ungar, 1959.

Vanderwood, Paul. *Disorder and Progress: Bandits, Police, and Mexican Development.* Lincoln: University of Nebraska Press, 1981.

Velasco, Francisco de. *Autobiografía.* Puebla: n.p., 1946.

——. *Puebla y su transformación: mis proyectos y mi gestión en el Ayuntamiento de Puebla de 1907 á 1910.* Puebla: Imprenta "El Escritorio," 1912.

Warman, Arturo, *Y venimos a contradecir: los campesinos de Morelos y el estado nacional.* Mexico City: Ediciones de la Casa Chata, 1976.

Wells, Allen. *Yucatán's Gilded Age: Haciendas, Henequen, and International Harvester, 1860–1915.* Albuquerque: University of New Mexico Press, 1985.

Wells, Allen, and Joseph, Gilbert M. *Summer of Discontent, Seasons of Upheaval: Elite Politics and Rural Insurgency in Yucatán, 1876–1915.* Stanford, Calif.: Stanford University Press, 1996.

Womack, John. *Zapata and the Mexican Revolution.* New York: Vintage, 1968.

ARTICLES

Arias González, Facundo. "Historia de las relaciones del movimiento obrero con el campesino. El caso de la CROM y la Confederación Social Campesina Domingo Arenas, 1921–1929." In *Historia y sociedad en Tlaxcala: memorias del Primer Simposio Internacional de Investigaciones Socio-históricas sobre Tlaxcala.* Tlaxcala, Tlax.: Universidad Autónoma de Tlaxcala, 1985, Mexico City: Universidad Iberoamericana, 1986.

Britton, John A. "Propaganda, Property, and the Image of Stability: The Mexican Government and the U.S. Print Media, 1921–1929." *SECOLAS Annal* 19 (Mar. 1988): 5–29.

Buve, Raymond Th. J. "Agricultores, dominación política y estructura agraria en la Revolución Mexicana: el caso de Tlaxcala (1910–1918)." In *Haciendas in Central Mexico from Latin Colonial Times to the Revolution.* Amsterdam: Centre for Latin American Research and Documentation, 1984.

——. "Movilización campesina y reforma agraria en los valles de Nativitas, Tlaxcala (1917–1928): estudio de un caso de lucha por recuperar tierras habidas durante la revolución armada." In *El trabajo y los trabajadores en la historia de México,* edited by Elsa Cecilia Frost, Michael C. Meyer, and Josefina Zoraida Vázquez. Mexico City: El Colegio de México and University of Arizona Press, 1979.

——. " 'Neither Carranza nor Zapata!': The Rise and Fall of a Peasant Movement That Tried to Challenge Both, Tlaxcala, 1910–19." In *Riot, Rebellion, and Revolution: Rural Social Conflict in Mexico,* edited by Friedrich Katz. Princeton, N.J.: Princeton University Press, 1988.

———. "Patronaje en las zonas rurales de México." *Boletín de Estudios Latinoamericanos y del Caribe* 16 (June 1974): 3–15.

———. "Peasant Movements, Caudillos and Landreform during the Revolution (1910–1917) in Tlaxcala, Mexico." *Boletín de Estudios Latinoamericanos y del Caribe* 18 (June 1975): 112–152.

———. "State Governors and Peasant Mobilisation in Tlaxcala." In *Caudillo and Peasant in the Mexican Revolution,* edited by D. A Brading. Cambridge: Cambridge University Press, 1980.

———. "Tlaxcala: Consolidating a Cacicazgo." In *Provinces of the Revolution: Essays on Regional Mexican History, 1910–1929,* edited by Thomas Benjamin and Mark Wasserman. Albuquerque: University of New Mexico Press, 1990.

Byres, T. J. "The Agrarian Question and the Differentiation of the Peasantry." Foreword to *Peasants and Classes: A Study of Differentiation in Bangladesh,* edited by Atiur Rahman. London and New Jersey: Zed Books, 1986.

Cabrera, Luis. "La reconstitución de los ejidos." In *Problemas Agrícolas e Industriales de México* 4.2 (Apr.–June 1952): 192–203.

Cardoso, Ciro F. S. "La agricultura en la economía mexicana del siglo XIX." *Boletín de Estudios Latinoamericanos y del Caribe* 58 (June 1981): 49–86.

Carlos, Manuel L. "Peasant Leadership Hierarchies: Leadership Behavior, Power Blocs, and Conflict in Mexican Regions." In *Mexican Regions: Comparative and Historical Development,* edited by Eric Van Young. San Diego: Center for U.S.-Mexican Studies, University of California, San Diego, 1992.

Chasteen, John Charles. "Violence for Show: Knife Dueling on a Nineteenth-Century Cattle Frontier." In *The Problem of Order in Changing Societies: Essays on Crime and Policy in Argentina and Uruguay,* edited by Lyman L. Johnson. Albuquerque: University of New Mexico Press, 1990.

Chiu, Aquiles, "Peones y campesinos zapatistas." In *Emiliano Zapata y el movimiento zapatista.* Mexico City: INAH, 1980.

Coatsworth, John. "Anotaciones sobre la producción de alimentos durante el porfiriato." *Historia Mexicana* 26.2 (Oct.–Dec. 1976): 167–187.

Cumberland, Charles C. "The Jenkins Case and Mexican-American Relations." *Hispanic American Historical Review (HAHR)* 31.4 (Nov. 1951): 586–607.

de la Peña, Guillermo. "Podor agrario y ambigüedad revolucionaria: bandidos, caudillos y facciones." In *Las formas y las políticas del dominio agrario: homenaje a Françoise Chevalier,* edited by Ricardo Avila Palafox, Carlos Martínez Assad, and Jean Meyer (Guadalajara: Editorial Universidad de Guadalajara, 1992), 232–259.

———. "Poder local, poder regional: perspectivas socioantropológicas." In *Poder local, poder regional,* edited by Jorge Padua and Alain Vanneph. Mexico City: El Colegio de México, 1986.

———. "Populism, Regional Power, and Political Mediation: Southern Jalisco, 1900–1980." In *Mexican Regions: Comparative and Historical Development,* edited by Eric Van Young. San Diego: Center for U.S.-Mexican Studies, University of California, San Diego, 1992.

Di Tella, Torcuato S. "The Dangerous Classes in Early Nineteenth Century Mexico." *Journal of Latin American Studies* 5.1 (1973): 79–105.

Dillon, E. J. "Mexico and Great Britain." *Fortnightly Review* 96 (Aug. 1924): 189–200.

Diskin, Martin. "Distilled Conclusions: The Disappearance of the Agrarian Question in El Salvador." *Latin American Research Review* 31.2 (1996): 111–125.

Dumond, D. E. "An Outline of the Demographic History of Tlaxcala." In *The Tlaxcaltecans: Prehistory, Demography, Morphology and Genetics,* edited by Michael H. Crawford. Lawrence: University of Kansas Publications in Anthropology, no. 7, 1976.

Dyckerhoff, Ursula. "La región del alto Atoyac en la historia." In Hanns J. Prem, *Milpa y hacienda: tenencia de la tierra indígena y española en la cuenca del Alto Atoyac, Puebla, México (1520–1650),* Mexico City: Fondo de Cultura Económica, 1988.

Falcón, Romana. "Force and the Search for Consent: The Role of the Jefaturas Políticas of Coahuila in National State Formation." In *Everyday Forms of State Formation: Revolution and the Negotiation of Rule in Modern Mexico,* edited by Gilbert M. Joseph and Daniel Nugent. Durham, N.C.: Duke University Press, 1994.

Foster, George M. "Interpersonal Relations in Peasant Society." *Human Organization* 19.4 (winter 1960–1961): 174–180.

———. "Peasant Society and the Image of the Limited Good." *American Anthropologist* 67.2 (Apr. 1964): 293–315.

Fraser, Donald J. "La política de desamortización en las comunidades indígenas, 1856–1872." *Historia Mexicana* 21.4 (Apr.–June 1972): 615–652.

García de León, Antonio. "Los contornos regionales del problema de la tierra en la revolución mexicana." *Revista Mexicana de Sociología* 49.3 (July–Sept. 1987): 83–103.

Garciadiego, Javier. "Higinio Aguilar: milicia rebelión y corrupción como modus vivendi." *Historia Mexicana* 41.3 (Jan.–Mar. 1992): 446–449.

González y González, Luis. "El agrarismo liberal." *Historia Mexicana* 7 (July 1957–June 1958): 482.

Hall, Linda B. "Alvaro Obregón and the Agrarian Movement, 1912–1920." In *Caudillo and Peasant in the Mexican Revolution,* edited by D. A. Brading. Cambridge: Cambridge University Press, 1980.

———. "Alvaro Obregón and the Politics of Mexican Land Reform, 1920–1924." *Hispanic American Historical Review* 60.1 (May 1980): 214.

———. "Banks, Oil, and the Reinstitutionalization of the Mexican State, 1920–1924." In *The Revolutionary Process in Mexico: Essays on Political and Social Change, 1880–1940,* edited by Jaime E. Rodríguez O. Los Angeles: University of California, Los Angeles, Latin American Center Publications, 1990.

———. "Obregón y de la Huerta." *Boletín 8 del Fideicomiso Archivos Plutarco Elías Calles y Fernando Torreblanca.* Mexico City, 1991.

Hansis, Randall. "The Political Strategy of Military Reform: Alvaro Obregón and Revolutionary Mexico, 1920–1924." *Americas* 36 (Oct. 1979): 199–233.

Hinman, George Wheeler, Jr. "The United States' Ban on Latin-American Rebels." *Current History,* April 1924, 69.

Hirschberg, Julia. "Social Experiment in New Spain: A Prosopographical Study of the Early Settlement at Puebla de los Angeles, 1531–1534." *Hispanic American Historical Review* 59.1 (1979): 1–33.

Hoekstra, Rik. "Profit from the Wastelands: Social Change and the Formation of Haciendas in the Valley of Puebla, 1570–1640." *European Review of Latin American and Caribbean Studies* 52 (June 1992): 91–123.

Joseph, Gilbert M. "On the Trail of Latin American Bandits." *Latin American Research Review* 25.3 (1990): 7–53.

Kane, N. Stephen. "Bankers and Diplomats: The Diplomacy of the Dollar in Mexico, 1921–1924." *Business History Review* 47.3 (autumn 1973): 335–352.

Knight, Alan. "Land and Society in Revolutionary Mexico: The Destruction of the Great Haciendas." *Mexican Studies/Estudios Mexicanos* 7.1 (winter 1991): 73–104.

———. "Mexican Peonage: What Was It and Why Was It?" *Journal of Latin American Studies* 18 (May 1986): 41–74.

LaFrance, David G. "Carrancismo and the State Governorship in Puebla, 1917–1920." Paper presented at the Rocky Mountain Council for Latin American Studies, El Paso, Texas, Feb. 1992.

———. "Puebla: Breakdown of the Old Order." In *Other Mexicos: Essays on Regional Mexican History, 1876–1911*, edited by Thomas Benjamin and William McNellie. Albuquerque: University of New Mexico Press, 1984.

Lipsett-Rivera, Sonya. "Indigenous Communities and Water Rights in Colonial Puebla: Patterns of Resistance." *Americas* 47.4 (Apr. 1992): 463–483.

Macías, Anna. "The Mexican Revolution Was no Revolution for Women." In *History of Latin American Civilization: Sources and Interpretations*, vol. 2. Edited by Lewis Hanke. Boston: Little, Brown, 1973.

Melé Credal, Patrice. "Poder local y urbanización en la ciudad de Puebla." In *Poder local, poder regional*, edited by Jorge Padua and Alain Vanneph. Mexico City: El Colegio de México, 1986.

Meyer, Eugenia. "Estudio Introductorio." In Rosalie Evans, *Cartas desde México*, translated by Thelma E. de Santamaría. Mexico City: Editorial Offset, 1986.

———. "Haciendas y ranchos, peones y campesinos en el porfiriato. Algunas falacias estadísticas." *Historia Mexicana* 35.3 (1986): 477–509.

Miller, Simon. "Mexican Junkers and Capitalist Haciendas, 1810–1910: The Arable Estate and the Transition to Capitalism between the Insurgency and the Revolution." *Journal of Latin American Studies* 22 (May 1990): 229–263.

Mintz, Sidney. "The Rural Proletariat and the Problem of Rural Proletarian Consciousness." *Journal of Peasant Studies* 1.3 (Apr. 1974): 293.

Nickel, Herbert J. "Agricultural Laborers in the Mexican Revolution (1910–40): Some Hypotheses and Facts about Participation and Restraint in the Highlands of Puebla-Tlaxcala." In *Riot, Rebellion, and Revolution: Rural Social Conflict in Mexico*, edited by Friedrich Katz. Princeton, N.J.: Princeton University Press, 1988.

———. "The Food Supply of Hacienda Labourers of Puebla-Tlaxcala during the Porfiriato: a First Approximation." In *Haciendas in Central Mexico from Late Colonial Times to the Revolution*, edited by Raymond Buve. Amsterdam: Centre for Latin American Research and Documentation, 1984.

Nugent, Daniel, and Alonso, Ana María. "Multiple Selective Traditions in Agrarian Reform and Agrarian Struggle: Popular Culture and State Formation in the Ejido of Namiquipa, Chichuaha." In *Everyday Forms of State Formation: Revolution and the Negotiation of Rule in Modern Mexico*, edited by Gilbert M. Joseph and Daniel Nugent. Durham, N.C.: Duke University Press, 1994.

Oñate, Abdiel. "Banca y agricultura en México: la crisis de 1907–1908 y la fundación del primer banco agrícola." In *Banca y poder en México, 1800–1925,* edited by Leonor Ludlow and Carlos Marchal. México: enlace/historia grijalbo, 1986.

Paige, Jeffery M. "Land Reform and Agrarian Revolution in El Salvador: Comment on Seligson and Diskin." *Latin American Research Review* 31.2 (1996): 127–139.

Pletcher, David M. "The Building of the Mexican Railway." *Hispanic American Historical Review* 30 (Feb. 1950): 26–62.

Porter, Katherine Anne. "La Conquistadora." In *The Collected Essays and Occasional Writings of Katherine Anne Porter.* New York: Delacorte, 1970.

Powell, T. G. "Los Liberales, el campesinado indígena y los problemas agrarios durante la Reforma." *Historia Mexicana* 21.4 (Apr.–June 1972): 653–675.

Prem, Hanns J. "Cambios estructurales de la propiedad rural en la provincia de Huejotzingo durante el primer centenario después de la conquista." *Comunicaciones* 7 (1973): 99–100.

———. "Early Spanish Colonization and Indians in the Valley of Atlixco, Puebla." In *Explorations in Ethnohistory: Indians of Central Mexico in the Sixteenth Century,* edited by H. R. Harvey and Hanns J. Prem. Albuquerque: University of New Mexico Press, 1984.

———. "El Río Cotzala: estudio histórico de un sistema de riego." *Comunicaciones* 11 (1974): 53–76.

———. "Los afluentes del Río Xopanac: estudio histórico de un sistema de riego." *Comunicaciones* 12 (1975): 27–46.

Ramírez Rancaño, Mario. "Un frente patronal a principios del siglo XX: El Central Industrial Mexicano de Puebla." In *Clases dominantes y estado en México,* edited by Salvador Cordero H. and Ricardo Tirado. Mexico City: UNAM, 1984.

Riguzzi, Paulo. "México, Estados Unidos y Gran Bretaña, 1867–1910: una difícil relación triangular." *Historia Mexicana* 41.3 (1992): 365–436.

Roseberry, William. "Peasants as Proletarians." *Critique of Anthropology* 11 (1978): 3.

Rosenberg, Emily. "Economic Pressures in Anglo-American Diplomacy in Mexico, 1917–1918." *Journal of Interamerican Studies and World Affairs* 17.2 (May 1975): 123–152.

Sánchez y Sánchez, Homero. "Sindicalismo en San Martín Texmelucan (1922–1928)." *Boletín-Cambio* (Feb. 1990): 1–5.

Scott, James. "Everyday Forms of Peasant Resistance." *Journal of Peasant Studies* 13.2 (Jan. 1986): 5–35.

Seligson, Mitchell A. "Agrarian Inequality and the Theory of Peasant Rebellion." *Latin American Research Review* 31.2 (1996): 140–157.

Skocpol, Theda. "What Makes Peasants Revolutionary?" *Comparative Politics* 14.3 (1982): 351–375.

Stavenhagen, Rodolfo. "Marginalidad y participación en la Reforma agraria mexicana." *Revista Latinoamericana de Sociología* 5.2 (1969): 249–274.

———. "Social Aspects of Agrarian Structure in Mexico." In *Agrarian Problems and Peasant Movements in Latin America,* edited by Rodolf Stavenhagen. New York: Doubleday, 1970.

Thomson, Guy P. C. "Montaña and Llanura in the Politics of Central Mexico: The Case of Puebla, 1820–1920." In *Region, State and Capitalism,* edited by Mario Cerutti. Amsterdam: CEDLA, 1989.

Tobler, Hans-Werner. "Las paradojas del ejército revolucionario: su papel social en la Reforma agraria mexicana, 1920–1935." *Historia Mexicana* 21.1 (July–Sept. 1971): 38–79.

Trautmann, Wolfgang. "Examen del proceso de despoblamiento en Tlaxcala durante la época colonial." *Comunicaciones* 7 (1973): 101–103.

———. "Métodos y resultados preliminares de investigaciones históricos sobre las poblaciones indígenas de Tlaxcala en los siglos XVI y XVII." *Comunicaciones* 2 (1970): 1–5.

Tuma, Elias. "Agrarian Reform in Historical Perpective Revisited." *Comparative Studies in Society and History* 21.1 (Jan. 1979): 8.

Vollmer, Günter. "El perfil demográfico de Huejotzingo: realidades de la base documental e imponderables de la reconstrucción." *Comunicaciones* 16 (1979): 191–198.

Wyatt-Brown, Bertram. "The Mask of Obedience: Male Slave Psychology in the Old South." *American Historical Review* 93.5 (1988): 1228–1252.

THESES AND DISSERTATIONS

Brush, David Allen. "The de la Huerta Rebellion in Mexico, 1923–1924." Ph.D. dissertation, Syracuse University, 1975.

Chapman, John Gresham. "Steam, Enterprise and Politics. The Building of the Veracruz-Mexico City Railway: 1837–1880." Ph.D. dissertation, University of Texas, Austin, 1971.

Dussaud, Claude Philippe. "Agrarian Politics, Violence, and the Struggle for Social Control in Puebla from 1918 to 1927: The Case of Rosalie Evans." M.A. thesis, University of Virginia, 1990.

Flores Flores, Alvaro. "Movimientos campesinos y reparto agrario en Puebla, 1923–1926." Tésis de licenciatura, Universidad Autónoma de Puebla, 1989.

Index